RUSSIA AND THE ARABS

RUSSIA
— AND THE —
ARABS

Behind the Scenes in
the Middle East
from the Cold War
to the Present

YEVGENY PRIMAKOV

Translated from the Russian by Paul Gould

A Member of the Perseus Books Group
New York

Designed by Brent Wilcox

Library of Congress Cataloging-in-Publication Data
Primakov, E. M. (Evgenii Maksimovich)
  [Konfidentsial'no. English]
  Russia and the Arabs : behind the scenes in the Middle East from the Cold War to the present / Yevgeny Primakov ; translated from the Russian by Paul Gould.
      p.   cm.
  Includes bibliographical references and index.
  ISBN 978-0-465-00475-1 (alk. paper)
  1. Middle East—Politics and government—1945-   2. Middle East—Foreign relations—Soviet Union.   3. Soviet Union—Foreign relations—Middle East.   4. Middle East—Foreign relations—Russia (Federation)
5. Russia (Federation)—Foreign relations—Middle East.   I. Title.
  DS63.1.P772513 2009
  327.47056—dc22
                                                      2009014923

327.47056
P952

Dedicated to my grandson Yevgeny Primakov Jr.
(Yevgeny Sandro), who has embarked on his own
"Middle Eastern journey."

CONTENTS

PREFACE

As you get older, you find yourself looking increasingly not to the future, but to the past. You become less and less concerned with the world of work. And as your children—then your grandchildren—start to lead their own lives, your part in their future ever more noticeably starts to diminish. What is more, your memory of the distant past comes into sharper focus. You start to see things that you did not see before; the hindsight of the years you've put behind you allows you to make sense of what you once failed to understand or mistook for something else. Nothing makes me more aware of this than looking through the dozens of notebooks that I kept for many years and have not gotten around to sorting out.[1]

For a long time I have been nursing the idea of writing a book about the Middle East.[2] It is a region I have followed for half a century as a journalist, academic, and politician—as a correspondent for *Pravda*; as deputy director (and later director) of the Institute of World Economy and International Relations at the USSR Academy of Sciences; at the Academy's Institute of Oriental Studies; as head of the SVR (Russia's foreign intelligence service); as Russian foreign minister, as Russian prime minister, and as a deputy in the Duma, Russia's parliament.

There are events in the Middle East—many of them subject to false rumors—that have unfolded before my very own eyes. Some of these events either are not known about or have been forgotten. Meanwhile they have played a huge role in making the region what it is today—

diverse, multihued and complex; a region that is dangerously obstinate, naïve at times, and all too often betrayed. It is far too easy to get the wrong idea of a region so crucial to world politics and the global economy today—worse still, we can come to associate the Middle East with the Islamic extremist threat hanging over the "civilized" world. Unless, that is, we unravel the peculiarities of Arab nationalism and get to the essence of the main players on the Middle Eastern political stage: Gamal Abdel Nasser, Yasser Arafat, Anwar Sadat, Saddam Hussein, Hafez Assad, Muammar Gaddafi, King Hussein of Jordan, and others; unless we examine the root causes of the evolution that Arab regimes underwent in the second half of the twentieth century; and unless we thoroughly analyze the policies of other states towards the Middle East, along with the impact of the Arab-Israeli conflict and that of the cold war.

This book is not a chronological account of events in the Arab world, nor is it a systematic description of their history in the latter half of the last century. Rather it focuses on the basic processes that emerged in the Arab world after the end of colonialism, and describes individual episodes from history that I not only had the chance to observe but in some cases even participated in.

I am truly grateful to my friends and colleagues who took the trouble to read my manuscript and made a series of comments—which I have of course taken into account—Yuri Stepanovich Gryadunov, Irina Donovna Zvyagelskaya, Yuri Vasilyevich Kotov, Namik Hamidovich Yakubov, and to numerous SVR and foreign ministry staff, both past and present. And without the painstaking technical work of my loyal assistants Maria Yuryevna Osipova and Yelena Vyacheslavovna Popova, this book could never have seen the light of day.

— 1 —

THE NATIONALIST
REVOLUTIONARIES

IN THE MIDDLE of the twentieth century, colonial rule disinte-
grated, leaving new nation-states to appear on the map of the
world. The collapse of imperial power also meant that regimes in
supposedly sovereign Middle Eastern states found their days were
numbered. In many newly independent countries, such as Egypt, it
was abundantly clear that the leaders who had just gained power
would not last long.

Of all these leaders, the one who stayed in power longer than the
rest was Gamal Abdel Nasser of Egypt. More than any other newly
independent Arab country, Egypt had all the characteristics of Arab
revolutionary nationalism: a concerted push to eradicate the colonial
powers' residual military and economic presence; the absence of
strong links between the state apparatus and Islam or terrorism; and
an adherence to a progressive socialist agenda. Domestic policy was
anticommunist in tone while foreign policy was pragmatic, as shown
by Egypt's qualified cooperation with the Soviet Union and the twists
and turns of its relations with the United States; and there was a vis-
cerally hostile attitude to Israel.

In the Arab world today, the global ambition of revolutionary nationalism has waned, even vanished. Yet it makes up an entire chapter of Arab history, and without a grasp of its specifics we cannot
make head or tail of the Middle East as it is now.

A NEW BREED OF LEADERS COMES TO POWER

Despite all they have in common, there are differences both among Arab countries and among the ways their new leaders won power after the end of colonial rule.

In Iraq, Prime Minister Nuri al-Said was savagely murdered and his corpse dragged for hours through the streets of Baghdad; one officer from the Iraqi army, which had rebelled against its government, cut off a finger from Said's corpse and took it to Egypt, thinking it would make the best present to give to Lieutenant Colonel Nasser. Nasser, leader of the Free Officers who came to power in Egypt following the deposal of King Farouk, was shocked by the offering. In 1952, Farouk had been driven out of Egypt by the Free Officers but was allowed to sail off on his yacht to Italy, where he spent his remaining years in debauched parties and casinos. A very different fate befell not only Nuri al-Said but also the young King Faisal of Iraq: he was killed by rebels who cared nothing that the king belonged to the Hashemite dynasty, direct descendants of the prophet Muhammad.

In Algeria and Tunisia, the colonial powers withdrew in the face of armed struggle by their peoples; in Libya and Yemen, monarchies were deposed; in Syria and Sudan, pro-Western rulers were ousted. None of this happened all at once. But the point is that it *did* happen, and that sovereignty came to the Arab world as a whole. The West retained influence over the politics of individual Arab countries, but the ways it exerted influence changed so much that its actual impact was a patchy, uneven affair.

For all their differences, the upheavals across the Arab world in the mid-twentieth century had something in common: colonial and semicolonial regimes fell because it had become untenable for their former leaders to cling to power. Of course, the situation in the rest of the world had a huge impact, too. The balance of power had shifted after Hitler's Germany, Fascist Italy, and a militaristic Japan were crushed in the Second World War; the Soviet Union took its place alongside the United States as a superpower; nationalist liberation movements triumphed in China and elsewhere; and colonial rule had run aground everywhere you turned. But the events at the heart of the radical changes in the Arab countries happened closer to home.

It is widely speculated that Moscow lent a hand in bringing anti-colonial forces to power, but this does not remotely stand up to scrutiny. This conjecture was fueled most of all by the coup in Iraq, where the monarchy was deposed and a republic proclaimed on July 14, 1958. The Western media persistently spread rumors of Soviet involvement, as did a succession of sadly mistaken politicians. Yet the diplomats based in Iraq tended to get it right about the cause and nature of events there: ten days after the monarchy fell, Sir Michael Wright, the British ambassador to Baghdad, reported to the Foreign Office that, as in Egypt six years earlier, the coup in Iraq was triggered by rising dissatisfaction with the policies and actions of King Faisal and his sidekick, Prime Minister al-Said. In 1954 another British ambassador to Iraq, Sir John Troutbeck, had warned London in a diplomatic telegram that there was growing "indignation at the corruption and greed of the ruling classes, the tough living conditions of the poor, the lack of career opportunities for young people leaving education, and an ideological vacuum that grows wider each year as the influence of Islam diminishes."[1] Ambassador Wright pointed out that to the Iraqis, the policies that had provoked the upheaval against al-Said and the ruling dynasty were identified with Britain.

Waldemar Gallman, the U.S. ambassador in Baghdad, told his superiors that "Moscow was not behind the coup."

The Soviet Union did not stay at the sidelines of events in Egypt, Iraq, or Syria. It built links with their new leaders—or rather *the new leaders* built links—but this was after their revolutions. These leaders seized power not because of any plots orchestrated by Moscow but because of the collapse of the policies of Britain and France, imposed either directly or by their corrupt Arab representatives.

RELIANCE ON MILITARY FORCE

In most Arab countries, armies played a pivotal role in overthrowing colonial and quasi-colonial governments. This was because, in the absence of political parties capable of opposition, armies were the most disciplined force. One of Egypt's political groups during Farouk's reign was al-Wafd (the Delegation party). No political party in any colonial-era Arab country could compare with it in size and influence. Al-Wafd would sometimes take a stand against Farouk's court, but its leadership was mired in intrigue and locked in collusion with the interests of big landowners and some of the feudal lords.

At first, the army only toppled a hated regime; it had neither the will nor the experience to govern the country. The officers who led the coup against the old order were middle-class intellectuals. It is no coincidence that some time before they launched the coup, on the night of July 23, 1952, they wanted to restore al-Wafd to power. Colonel Ahmed Anwar was sent to meet Fouad Sirag al-Din, the party's general secretary, and it was proposed that al-Wafd impose its authority on the king by force. Al-Wafd refused, not wishing to enter into any alliance with the Free Officers. Its leaders feared a popular revolt at a time when armed conflict was brewing in the Suez Canal zone. In fact, they did not want to see Farouk deposed, and they were anxious to avoid confrontation with Britain. But it fell to the army to take charge of the country.

Britain had formally granted Egypt independence years earlier, in 1922, although this sovereignty was watered down with stipulations that made it nearly worthless. Britain retained the right to protect its "routes of empire" on Egyptian soil, which meant primarily the Suez Canal, but also the safeguarding of its foreign interests.

Things changed a little in 1936, when Britain signed the Anglo-Egyptian Treaty, which softened these restrictions but stopped short of granting Egypt genuine political independence. Britain retained a military presence there, and its ambassador continued to meddle in the country's domestic affairs. But as the British sought to free up more of their soldiers to be redeployed in Europe, they ordered Egypt to increase its army from 11,500 men to 60,000. Before that, the officer corps of Egypt's small army had traditionally been made up of the sons of rich families. A clause in the pact forced King Farouk to increase troop strength by recruiting officers from the middle class. Egypt's military academy began to accept and train the sons of middle-income families, who would become the backbone of the under-ground group known as the Free Officers.

But I do not think this class uniformity is any part of the reason that the Egyptian regime established in 1952 turned out as stable as it did, despite upheavals like the joint British-French-Israeli invasion of 1956 or the Six-Day War of 1967, or even the internal economic measures affecting the interests of major foreign and Egyptian property owners. The chief factor that guaranteed Egypt's government such a long life was popular support for Nasser's leadership. This did not come overnight. The 1952 coup was led by a small group of people. But as its reforms bore fruit and it built up an overseas policy seen by many as patriotic, Nasser's regime gained widespread support that allowed it to weather its mistakes.

The constant turnover of those in power—not always through violent revolutions—came largely because Middle Eastern countries lacked an evolved party political system, and the army filled the vacuum. Military coups came one after another in Syria, Iraq, and North Africa. Salah Jadid, who had led the Syrian coup of February 23, 1966, that brought down the right-wing Ba'ath Party administration, died after years in prison. A similar fate awaited Yusuf Zuaiyin, prime minister in Syria's post-coup government. Both men had been cast out by another left-wing Ba'athist group, led by Hafez Assad. In Iraq, Abdul Karim Qassem was gunned down in a Baghdad television studio by his former brothers-in-arms; in Algeria, Ben Bella, leader of the revolution against French colonial power, was sentenced to long years in prison by his own revolutionary comrades.

After Nasser's death in 1970, the tide of change reached Egypt too. One of Nasser's close cohorts, Anwar Sadat—whom the Russians wrongly thought of as an interim figure—took advantage of the laxity of those loyal to the deceased leader; these people held practically all the power in the land, and Sadat ordered his guards to arrest them all. For years he was the unchallenged master of Egypt. Although he started out with Nasser in the first phase of the Free Officers, Sadat managed to steer Egypt away from a Nasserite path in both domestic and foreign policy. He too met a sorry end: he was assassinated by Islamic extremists.

A DIFFICULT COEXISTENCE WITH ISLAMIC EXTREMISTS

The struggle for power is the likeliest explanation for most of the coups in the newly independent Arab countries. Differences existed, of course, between those who were ousted and those who seized power, yet all professed a common ideology: nationalism. But there was more to the nature of the forces supplanting one another, and nationalism varied from one Arab state to the next. Regardless of who was overthrown by whom, some adherents got no further than advocating a purely nationalist worldview; others introduced aspects of social reform. Nasser was of the latter camp, as were Syria's Hafez Assad and Algeria's Houari Boumédienne.

Above all, it is important to note that the nationalism espoused by the new postcolonial Arab leaders had no ideological ties to Islam. None of the Arab states went through a revolution under the banner of religion, even though the populations of these republics had always consisted of practicing Muslims, some of them fanatics. Moreover, leaders in many countries came into conflict with Islamic groups seeking to fill what they saw as a power vacuum left by the colonial rulers' departure. Besides, confronting Islamists was no easy matter. In Egypt, for example, the Muslim Brotherhood, a mass Islamic organization founded in 1928 and one that had opposed British rule, could count up to 2 million members at its peak. In its early days, the Free Officers had to reckon with the popularity of the Brotherhood, especially after its "supreme guru," Hassan al-Banna, was killed on the king's orders in 1949, crowning the Brotherhood with the halo of martyrdom.[2]

After Farouk was deposed, the Free Officers banned all political parties and organizations, except the Brotherhood. But its new supreme guru, Hassan Ismail al-Hudaibi, published a statement calling for a referendum in Egypt on creating an Islamic republic governed by Sharia law. It was then that the Free Officers' crucial battle with the Brotherhood was joined. In 1954, two Brotherhood leaders who had organized an attempt on Nasser's life, deputy supreme guru Abdul Qader 'Udda and Ibrahim al-Taib, a commander of armed terrorist groups, were publicly hanged in front of reporters; al-Hudaibi was sentenced to life in prison.

The Brotherhood enjoyed considerable popularity; the students protesting at Cairo University in early 1954, for example, had voiced their support for it. This did nothing to stop Nasser and his disciples, nor did the Brotherhood's close ties to General Muhammad Naguib, who at that time officially chaired the Revolutionary Command Council and held the post of President of Egypt. A popular figure in Egypt, Naguib was asked by the Free Officers to join them in order to boost the prestige of their organization. The Brotherhood's support was one of the reasons Naguib was later removed from his position.

Far from being an obstacle, Nasser's fight with the Islamic extremists can be seen as helping him secure his place not only as the sole ruler of Egypt but also, crucially, as a leader recognized across the Arab world. Some scholars of this period of Egypt's history have concluded that Nasser's undisguised and bitter confrontation with the Muslim Brotherhood was provoked by its attempt to assassinate him. I do not agree. It was perhaps the final straw, but the rift itself was the logical outcome of the Free Officers' rise to power.

After the king was ousted it took only a year for the Free Officers and the Muslim Brotherhood to descend from consensus into out-and-out conflict. The Brotherhood pinned its hopes on winning over a wide cross section of the population in the countryside, where the young officers' support was weak. Brotherhood leaders decided to exploit the fact that theirs was the only legal organization, and made a calculated gamble that the Officers would be forced to deal with them so as not to end up completely isolated in Egyptian politics. At first the Brotherhood demanded a place in the government; when this was refused, it declared that it would seek to set up a committee with the power to ratify all laws passed in Egypt to ensure their compatibility with Islam. So the founders of a similar committee in Iran after the Iranian revolution get no prize for originality. But events unfolded quite differently in Egypt: Nasser's Free Officers categorically refused the Brotherhood's requests and launched an agrarian reform program that made inroads into the countryside.

Nasser was not merely hostile but a ruthless adversary of the Brotherhood. This could be seen in his attitude toward its spiritual leader, Sayyid Qutb, who was jailed more than once. Finally, when it became evident that Qutb would not give up on his condemnation of Nasser's "secularism"—he compared the state of the country under Nasser with *jahiliya* ("the dark ages" that Arabs see as the period before Islam)—he was arrested once more, sentenced to death, and executed in 1966.

More than mere rivalry divided Nasser from the Islamists. This was not a confrontation between two uniform forces competing for power: Nasser consciously ruled out using Islam as an instrument of authority. He was not alone in being at odds with those seeking to impose an Islamic state or society by force. In the late 1970s and early 1980s, two Syrian factions of the Brotherhood, operating in Aleppo and Hama, joined forces to fight Hafez Assad's regime. Brotherhood militants, who happened to be followers of Qutb, mounted an attack on Aleppo's artillery school, killing thirty-four students. Reprisals were swift: Assad sent in army divisions that wiped out thousands of Islamic extremists. Troops were also used to crush advocates of an Islamic state in Algeria and Tunisia.

It is clearly wrong to depict the nationalist revolutionaries who seized power in many Arab countries as having rejected Islam or even Islamic fundamentalism; nor were they oblivious to how religious their populations were. Yet they waged open war against Islamic extremists and against "politicized Islam." In his 1973 biography of the Egyptian leader, Jean Lacouture examines the ideas and motives behind Nasser's falling-out with the Muslim Brotherhood and other Islamic groups. He writes that although Nasser was himself a Muslim, he was convinced it was impossible to run a modern nation on the basis of the Koran. This conviction was shared by the revolutionaries who came to power in Syria, Iraq, South Yemen, Algeria, Tunisia, and Libya.

BEHIND THE RALLYING CRY OF ARAB SOCIALISM

In a succession of Arab countries throughout the 1950s and 1960s, new postcolonial powers announced they had chosen a socialist path. Islamic organizations, meanwhile, were hardly untouched by the widespread enthusiasm for socialist ideals. Many Muslim clerics declared kinship between the roots of Islam and socialism, and even preached "Islamic socialism," which attracted a fair number of disciples from the intelligentsia in Arab countries. But acute ideological differences between Islamic extremism and Arab nationalism worked to prevent the two forces from merging into one. "Arab socialism" was not "Islamic socialism" in either origin or spirit, although these two socialisms did have some superficial features in common.

With all the strife between the revolutionaries and radical Islamic organizations, Islam left its mark—and its influence—on Arab socialism. There was a tangible basis for this: no Arab leader could ignore the deep-rooted devoutness of his subjects. But this did not make Arab socialism, especially as interpreted by Nasser or the Algerian leaders, identical to Islamic socialism. The former largely confined Islam's sphere of influence to spiritual life and left social and economic matters to be developed on a secular basis. Islamic socialism inferred that there was a socialist philosophy in Islam and called for it to permeate all aspects of life as taught by scriptures in the Koran. In none of the Arab countries that had pinned its flag to the socialist mast did Islamic ways of structuring society take root, nor did they come to control the state apparatus, the economy, or the judiciary.

Failing to see this and failing to dig any deeper into its history, Eastern bloc critics condemned the relationship between Arab leaders and Islamic extremists, while Western critics objected to Arab leaders' "compliance with Islamic practice." In the West, this kind of criticism was bound up with an attempt to show that the rift between nationalist revolutionaries and Islamists was narrowing, if it still existed at all. Blinkered by dogma, ideological advisers from the Soviet Union insisted—albeit only in closed meetings—that Arab declarations of socialist principles were hardly compatible with speeches that began, "In the name of Allah, the beneficent and the merciful!" These ill-starred ideologues excommunicated from "true socialism" not only Muslims but anyone who was not an atheist.

There were several reasons why a string of Arab countries chose the socialist route. First, Arab nationalism in the latter half of the twentieth century had at its core the struggle for independence against overseas rule—and yet the movement lacked any actual program for national reconstruction. Second, this absence of a program grew all the more palpable when the center of gravity shifted to social and economic matters after independence had been won. Third, the call to build socialism was one of the most widely heard in the world—at the time, socialism reigned in many countries—and this could not fail to influence the countries, including the Arab states, where colonial rule had ended.

Arab socialist ideas thrived amid the disillusionment that a sizeable cross section of the Arab intelligentsia felt about Western prescriptions for "targeted economic development," which ensured that postcolonial states remained adjuncts to their former rulers. The drive for equality and social justice overseas as well as at home clashed directly with prescriptions of this sort.

But devotees of Arab socialism regarded society as one big united family, without divisions into class and social groups, and this set their ideas firmly apart from Soviet scientific socialism, bringing them closer to Islamic socialism. It was in the interests of this united family that reforms in the socialist Arab countries were drafted and carried out. These countries still introduced a range of measures to improve the lot of the poorest in society, but they were not, as a rule, presented as a "redistribution of wealth." For Nasser, class struggle, the dictatorship of the proletariat, and rejection of religion had no place in Arab socialism. Other Arab socialist leaders thought similarly, except perhaps those in South Yemen, whose interpretation of socialism more closely resembled that of the Soviet Union and other socialist bloc countries.

This specific interpretation arose because Arab socialism was seen as a category of Arab nationalism. Because socioeconomic affairs fell within the remit of Arab socialism, it set itself the task of nationalizing foreign-owned assets. This was a direct policy decision. In itself, the creation of a state-owned sector began life as a move against overseas influence, against attempts by foreign powers to maintain their control over the newly independent states in a new guise. Among the Free Officers' first acts in Egypt was the state takeover of the foreign-owned Suez Canal Company; in Iraq the same happened with the Iraq Petroleum Company.

Another platform on which Arab socialism stood was agrarian reform—vitally important in all Arab countries, where the vast majority of people depended on the land and the inequality of land distribution was keenly felt.

Nasser Invites Yevsei Liberman to Cairo

Egypt, like several of its neighbors, went further and strengthened the state sector of its economy by nationalizing large-scale business assets, Egyptian as well as foreign owned. Banks, insurance firms, and big manufacturing industries were all nationalized, and in 1958 the amount of land that could be owned was sharply curbed in a second round of agrarian reform. Up to 80 percent of industry and manufacturing was in state hands, as were the entire banking system, all of the transport network, and overseas trade. With the exception of prospecting for oil, the whole mining sector was declared out of bounds to foreign capital. There were some joint ventures, albeit with the Egyptian government as the majority shareholder.

Nationalization on this scale was a radical move influenced by the example of socialist countries. At the start of the 1960s, the Soviet leadership supported Nasser in his efforts at large-scale nationalization and put Soviet ideological advisers at Nasser's disposal. But the Egyptian leader appears to have been too pragmatic to stick to an all-out program of nationalization. He did not turn his back on market forces and gave substantial attention to the development of small-scale enterprise, especially in the service sector. This was not to everyone's liking in Moscow. At the time, dogmatic ideas of what socialism should be were on the wane in the Soviet Union, and even the party-controlled newspaper *Pravda* had published articles by Kharkov economist Yevsei Liberman about how important it was for the economy that industries make a profit. Even so, many in Moscow were unhappy when Nasser invited Liberman to Egypt.

Nasser talked one-on-one with Liberman for several hours, in English, without an interpreter. As the *Pravda* correspondent in Cairo at the time, I met Liberman, who told me Nasser had been keen to know whether socialism could coexist alongside private enterprise. It was this pragmatism that steered Nasser's thinking, not any inclination toward Islamic socialism.

Nasser gave Liberman an exceptionally warm welcome, inviting him to spend a few days' vacation in Alexandria. During the trip, the presidential car in which Liberman was traveling (along with Sergei Tarasenko, his interpreter and future aide to Eduard Shevardnadze) skidded off the road and overturned. Fortunately, no one was hurt, but Nasser insisted that Liberman go to a hospital for checkups and sent one of his officials to visit him with an enormous bouquet of flowers.

Like the socialist project all over the world, Arab socialism turned out to be short-lived. By the end of the twentieth century, it survived only in Libya—and there only in an experimental form. Nevertheless, the efforts by Arab countries to embrace it and make it a reality add up to a noteworthy chapter in their history.

THE GENESIS OF MIDDLE EASTERN TERRORISM

So what is the connection between Arab nationalism and terrorism? This is a key question if we are to get to the heart of the nationalism espoused by those who took the place of colonial authority in the Middle East.

Middle Eastern terrorism has gained worldwide infamy, but there are no grounds to believe it originated in Arab nationalism or was ever a part of it. Consider the example of Egypt's Free Officers. In theory, they never ruled out terrorism as a means of seizing power, especially against those in the service of the British. In their early stages, driven by a raw feeling of downtrodden national pride and unable to accept the yoke of foreign rule, the Officers even had a "terrorism committee." But as they prepared to actually seize power, they rejected the use of terror tactics. They resorted to terror only once, when they tried to assassinate the reviled Sirri Amer, an army general mired in corruption and with close links to colonial authorities. Here is how Nasser describes his response to the assassination attempt in his book, *The Philosophy of the Revolution*:

During a sleepless night in a smoke-filled room, I asked myself: can we genuinely alter the country's destiny by removing this person or that person, or is it a much deeper, more complex problem? . . . It was with the utmost conviction that the answer came to me: we have to take a different path . . . the roots are deeper, the problem is somewhat more serious.[3]

At issue were terrorist strikes against individual figures, mainly Arabs, who had collaborated with the foreign occupation. That Nasser opposed even this kind of attack is shown by the farewell ceremony for the deposed King Farouk, who sailed away to Italy on his yacht *Al-Mahrousa*. General Naguib and the entire Free Officers leadership turned out to see the king off from Alexandria—all except Gamal Salem. Nasser barred him from taking part in the ceremony because he knew Salem had been an advocate of assassinating Farouk.

After a cease-fire in the first Palestine conflict in 1948, Nasser met with two Israeli officers in Falluja; one of them, Yigal Allon, would later become Israel's military chief of staff. Nasser took great interest in asking about tactics they had used to coordinate their fight against the British. Apart from anything else, the Israelis could have shared their knowledge of terrorist activity. But the Egyptian leader never put this knowledge to use in planning and executing the 1952 coup. Nor did terror become one of Nasser's tactics afterward.

Islamic terrorist groups raised their heads in Egypt only after Arab revolutionary nationalism had begun to fade from the political scene. Groups such as al-Jihad, al-Gamaa al-Islamiya, and al-Takfir wal-Hijra sprang up in the late 1970s. In their efforts to overthrow Egypt's secular regime, they unleashed a wave of terrorist activity across the country. One of their victims was Anwar Sadat; they also planned several attempts on the life of President Hosni Mubarak and carried out terrorist attacks on Egyptian ministers and foreign tourists. Rejecting even the Muslim Brotherhood as "too moderate" and "irrelevant to current circumstances," groups from this "new Islamic wave" instead established links with al-Qaeda.

It could be said that the ancestor of Middle East terrorism was Lehi, the group formed in Palestine during the Second World War and led by Abraham Stern (killed by British police in February 1942). Lehi's reins were later taken by a triumvirate, one of them future Israeli prime minister Yitzhak Shamir. In 1943 the group led an attempt on the life of the high commissioner to Palestine; some months later it assassinated former Colonial Secretary Lord Moyne in Egypt. When the 1948 war ended, Lehi assassinated the United Nations (UN) representative Count Bernadotte, the Swedish diplomat assigned to supervise the cease-fire.

Individual terror acts were not the whole story. Alongside Lehi there was another terrorist group, Etzel, whose leader in 1944 was also a future Israeli premier, Menachem Begin. On June 22, 1946, Etzel planted two milk churns packed with explosives in the kitchen of the King David Hotel, where British administrators were housed. The blast left ninety-one dead and forty-five wounded—Britons, Arabs, and Jews.

It is hardly surprising that the Israelis would use similar tactics to force the Arabs out of Palestine. In his memoirs, the British general John Bagot Glubb, founder of the Arab legion in Trans-Jordan, recalls a conversation between a British officer and an officer of the Zionist militant group Haganah that took place before the creation of Israel. When the British officer remarked that Israel's population might be split down the middle between Jews and Arabs and that this would cause difficulties, the Haganah officer replied: "Difficulties can be overcome—a little bloodshed and we'll be rid of them." The events that followed echoed those words. In January 1948, an explosion in a square in Jaffa, a town then populated by Arabs, killed twenty-two people and left many more wounded. A far worse atrocity was the massacre on the night of April 10, 1948, when extremists from Lehi and Etzel slaughtered 254 inhabitants of this Arab village of Deir Yassin, on the outskirts of Jerusalem.

Bloody reprisals against the Arab population continued after the creation of Israel; it took a long time before there was any focus on integrating the Palestinian Arabs into Israeli society. Some of these acts triggered such an outcry abroad, and even in Israel itself, that criminal proceedings were brought against those who were killing Arabs. In October 1956, on the eve of the Anglo-French-Israeli invasion of Egypt, an Israeli patrol opened fire on inhabitants of Kafr Qasim, an Arab village on Israeli territory, supposedly for breaching a curfew that had been imposed without warning. A court found Major Shmuel Malinki and Lieutenant Gabriel Dahan guilty of slaughtering forty-three Kafr Qasim residents and sentenced them to seventeen and fifteen years in prison respectively; Sergeant Offer got fifteen years for killing forty-one Arabs. Other perpetrators were also tried and sentenced. But early in 1960, a little over three years after the massacre, all were out free. Meanwhile, Brigadier Issachar Shadmi, who gave the command to "show no mercy," was tried separately and fined the equivalent of one cent—an insult to the memory of the dead. (Among the first terrorist acts against Egypt carried out by Israeli agents was the so-called Lavon affair [also known as Operation Susannah]. See chapter 2.)

After the state of Israel was founded, terror was widely used by Palestinian groups based in neighboring Arab countries. Their victims were not only residents of Jewish settlements on Arab land but also civilians in Israel proper. Frequent bombings claimed dozens of lives in crowded spots such as hotels, shops, and discotheques. Hizbollah rockets, fired from the group's base in Lebanon, rained down on Israeli towns and villages in Northern Galilee.

Terrorist attacks, some of them carried out by suicide bombers, grew more and more frequent, especially during the second intifada, which was sparked by Prime Minister Ariel Sharon's visit to Jerusalem's Temple Mount, the site of the Al-Aqsa Mosque, one of Islam's holiest shrines. These violent terror attacks hampered the quest for a political settlement and proved counterproductive for the Palestinians by serving to isolate them in the world. They also provoked large-scale reprisals from the Israeli army, which claimed the lives of many Palestinians.

The Palestine Liberation Organization (PLO) was undergoing a painful evolution (for more on this see chapter 14). After the PLO agreed to recognize UN resolutions and entered into negotiations with Israel, it renounced terrorism in its battle for the rights of the Palestinian people. But other militias and groups still carry out attacks on Israeli civilians. The Palestinian Authority has condemned these acts, and under the chairmanship of Mahmoud Abbas (also known as Abu Mazen) antiterrorist operations have been intensified.

There is no great mystery to this. In my own nation of Russia, as in the Soviet Union, many people divided terrorists into those fighting for "just" causes and those who employed terror for "unjust" causes. Now our eyes have been opened by the terrorist acts of Chechen separatists. But even well before the bloodbath in Chechnya, both Russia and the former Soviet Union took a firm stance against the Palestinians' using terrorism to fight for their rights. This subject was always raised—I repeat, *always*—whenever Russian officials held talks with Fatah, the Popular Front for the Liberation of Palestine (PFLP), the Democratic Front for the Liberation of Palestine (DFLP), Hamas, or any other Palestinian groups. It still is.

At the end of 1970, for example, the Central Committee of the Soviet communist party (which was in charge of such matters at the time) sent me to Beirut with our future ambassador to Jordan, Yuri Gryadunov, who then headed the party's international section (Arab affairs fell within its remit). Our mission was to persuade the leaders of the PFLP to call off the hijacking of planes. The talks were long and hard, and involved the entire PFLP leadership. George Habash and others told us that the reason they carried out the hijackings was to force the Israelis—their own government—to find accommodation with the Palestinians. We answered that terrorist activity was not only unacceptable but also counterproductive, as it had the effect of rallying Israelis around their government. The PFLP leaders subsequently confirmed that their moratorium on hijackings came about thanks to Soviet influence.

Another example: as director of Russia's foreign intelligence agency, I flew to Tripoli at the behest of the Russian government and held productive talks with the Libyan leadership, including Colonel Muammar Gaddafi; my European colleagues were making similar efforts. In the mid- to late 1990s, the training camps in Libya used by the extremist Palestine Liberation Front and Islamic Jihad were razed to the ground. Gaddafi broke off all relations with them and expelled the terrorist group led by Abu Nidal.

In May 2005 I accompanied President Vladimir Putin on his Middle East tour, during which he bluntly told Palestinian and Israeli leaders alike that they had to call off both terrorist acts *and* the equally dangerous reprisals, which also made victims of innocent civilians.

But the terror inflicted by both sides in this Middle East conflict was not the breeding ground for the international terrorism seen at the end of the twentieth century and the beginning of the twenty-first. For starters, Middle Eastern terrorism was by its nature political, not religious. It has seldom, as a rule, spread beyond the region, although both sides have carried out "overseas" terrorist attacks on representatives of the other side: the attempt by Abu Nidal's group to assassinate Israel's ambassador to London, for example, or the gunshots fired at PLO activists in Europe. There have also been terrorist acts by individual Palestinian groups against others on their own side with whom they disagree. The group headed by Sabri al-Banna, best known as Abu Nidal, was distinct in this regard. Having branded as traitors the leaders of Arafat's Fatah, the Abu Nidal Organization (ANO) set out to annihilate them. Often it did so on direct orders from Iraq's secret services; then, when it had relocated to Syria, it was linked with the Syrian secret services, and in Libya with the Libyan services. On his return to Iraq in 2002, not long before the U.S. invasion, Abu Nidal was either killed or committed suicide.

The network known as al-Qaeda did not arise from the Palestinian movement. Al-Qaeda was a religious-extremist catalyst used by the United States during the cold war—with, as it turns out, no thought to the consequences. It came into being with the aid of the Central Intelligence Agency (CIA) for the purposes of fighting the Soviet army in Afghanistan. Osama bin Laden was given a green light to seek al-Qaeda recruits, even on American soil, and his bandits were secretly armed with Stinger missiles for use against Soviet military aircraft.

History had the last, bitter laugh on anyone who thought al-Qaeda would continue to do as it was told. After the Soviet pullout from Afghanistan, al-Qaeda turned its sights on the United States.

RISING ANTI-WESTERN SENTIMENT, BUT CLOSER TIES WITH WASHINGTON

Let's go back to what was distinctive about these revolutionary nationalist Arab regimes. Anti-imperialism emerged from a sense of

wounded national pride; it was not a stance adopted by Arab nationalists. Politicians often overlook this heightened, even bombastic feeling of patriotism—characteristic of all Eastern leaders, not just
Arabs—and thus pass up realistic chances to solve a whole range of
problems, not least of which is the resolution of conflicts.

Even King Farouk, before he was deposed, felt a growing resentment
at Egypt's humiliation at the hands of foreign officials. The Egyptian
people had no great love for Farouk, and while Nasser shared their feelings, he still regarded the king, whatever his standing, as Egypt's head of
state. So Nasser and his fellow officers were outraged to learn that
British ambassador Sir Miles Lampson had gone to Abdin Palace on
February 4, 1942, and demanded that the prime minister be replaced
with someone more pro-British. Throughout Egypt there were rumors
that Lampson would address the king not as "your Majesty" but as
"my boy"—and this, remember, was a full twenty years after Egypt was
granted independence from Britain. In a letter to a friend written at the
time, Nasser said: "I am ashamed that the army did not react to this af-
front." These were the words of a man who fully understood the hopelessness of an armed confrontation with the British forces based in the
Suez Canal zone, let alone a wider conflict with Britain, whose military
capabilities were in a different league from those of Egypt. But the sense
of insult to Egypt's national pride overcame other considerations.

Nasser raised this episode with the king during his first and only
meeting with the then British foreign secretary, Sir Anthony Eden, at
the British Embassy in Cairo in February 1955. Eden listened as the
young Egyptian president gave his downbeat assessment of the Treaty
of Baghdad. But Eden made it clear that he thought Nasser was out
of his depth in world politics, and brushed aside the concerns he had
raised; instead, he started asking about the Koran and Arabic literature. It made Nasser see how condescending the British government
was towards the new Egypt.

American contempt was no less withering. At an official luncheon
in 1955 the U.S. ambassador, Henry A. Byroade, protested that the
Egyptians had beaten up an American in the Suez Canal zone, having
taken him for a spy. At one point during his outburst, Byroade splut-
tered, "I thought I was in a civilized country."

Nasser stood up and left the meeting, and did not come back even when the tactless American diplomat apologized.

But if the nationalist revolutionaries' anti-imperialist stance was originally shaped by raw emotion, this was quickly superseded by politics, and their decisions came to be based on studying and comparing the options before them. Pragmatism began to take precedence over anti-imperialism. After these new leaders came to power in Egypt, Syria, and Iraq, it was some time before they hardened their stance against the former colonial powers or the Western European states that retained custody over their officially independent countries. It was on Nasser's orders that Britain was warned two days before the coup in Egypt. The U.S. assistant military attaché, David Evans, was also informed via Ali Sabri, one of the Free Officers. Evans's reaction was unequivocal: as long as they were not communists, he said, they could go ahead. He said the United States would seek to build an alliance with the Middle East in order to halt the growth of local communist parties and stop the Soviet Union from getting a foothold in the region.

But I think U.S. officials, and British ones even more, were kept in the dark about how far the Free Officers would go to depose King Farouk in 1952—and especially when they would take action. They may even have suggested to the British that they would do nothing more than pressure the monarchy to agree to greater democracy. But Miles Copeland, the CIA resident in Cairo, said the Americans not only knew that a coup was being planned but that Nasser had consulted them about it and had been given the green light. Meanwhile, as soon as the Free Officers seized power, they were contacted by another CIA official, Kermit "Kim" Roosevelt, grandson of former President Theodore Roosevelt.

One way or another, the very existence of this kind of contact shows that the Free Officers did not want to jeopardize relations with Britain, and still less with Washington. And the American response, passed on via Ali Sabri, actually inspired the young officers and raised their hopes of building ties with the United States.

It is further evidence of the Officers' reluctance to jeopardize relations with London that they allowed the monarchy to continue for some time after King Farouk was ousted. Having forced Farouk to abdicate, the Free Officers agreed to let the throne pass to his son Ahmad Fuad, who was less than one year old. They also agreed that the deposed king's relatives would head the government as well as the regency council that ruled in Ahmad Fuad's place. Not until June 1953, almost a year after the coup, was Egypt declared a republic.

Nasser made a series of compromises with Britain. On February 12, 1953, Cairo signed an agreement with London that would lead to the withdrawal of all troops, British and Egyptian, from Sudan. There was in Sudan a powerful movement advocating unification with Egypt, and similar sentiment was widespread in Egypt. However, Cairo made it a priority to recognize Sudan's independence—in effect abandoning anti-British activity there. Immediately after taking power, Nasser and his inner circle began negotiations with the British government with the aim of securing a pullout of British troops from the Suez Canal. The young officers stressed the need to reach a peaceful political agreement that would end Britain's seventy-four-year-old occupation of Egypt. And they succeeded: a treaty mandating the withdrawal of all British troops from Egypt was signed in Cairo in October 1954.

At about this time, the idea of cooperation with the United States was gaining favor among the Free Officers. It was an idea that sometimes bore fruit: the United States was trying to squeeze a weakened Britain out of the Middle East and reckoned that it would be able to use the new regime in Egypt for its own ends. The United States was not regarded in the Arab world as a colonial power, and great hopes rested on it being a counterweight to Britain and France.

The American secretary of state, John Foster Dulles, visited Cairo in May 1953, when U.S. diplomats were offering to act as intermediaries in the decommissioning of Britain's Suez base. The Free Officers, in their quest to end Britain's military presence in Egypt, were grateful for America's patronage. A package of U.S. aid to Egypt worth $50 million was put in place, and a wave of U.S. officials, political aides, and businessmen flocked to Cairo.

Many people—including many in Cairo—understood that Dulles's goal was to encircle the Soviet Union with U.S. military and political alliances. In the words of the prominent Egyptian commentator Mohamed Hassanein Heikal, Dulles approached this mission with a "religious fervor." After his Cairo trip, the Americans put forward a plan to build a military bloc composed solely of Muslim states—the Arab countries, plus Turkey and Pakistan—which the United States thought would be more attractive to Egypt and its Arab neighbors. This would have served American interests well in a standoff with the Soviet Union.

The fact that an Egyptian military delegation headed by Ali Sabri went to the United States at the end of 1953 seems to counter any notion that this plan was derailed by the Egyptians. They did, however, insist that their position was linked to being able to buy American weaponry. Sabri had a meeting with General George Olmsted, head of the Pentagon's overseas military aid program, but Olmsted preferred to stick to abstract discussions about the usefulness of an Islamic bloc. What caught the attention of the Egyptian delegates was Olmstead's frank account of the goals of such a bloc: "It could wield crucial influence over the Muslims of the Soviet Union and China." The general was convinced that a Muslim "fifth column" had to be created in these countries. The Egyptians, of course, had had other expectations of their meeting.

It goes without saying that recommendations of this kind turned out to be vital even after the end of the cold war and the demise of the Soviet Union.

A Failed Chance for
Arab-Israeli Relations

Contrary to widespread belief, the rise of revolutionary nationalist regimes across the Arab world was not in itself to blame for escalating the Arab-Israeli conflict. The main player behind the scenes in the first Palestinian war, the one that followed the creation of the state of Israel in 1948, was in fact Britain, which was trying its best to hold on to its monopoly of power in the Middle East. At that time there was practically no armed Palestinian resistance; the losers in that war were the Arab countries that were, in effect, client states of Britain.

How It All Began

Defeat in that war had, of course, helped shape the outlook of patriotic army officers—many of whom subsequently came to power. But their wrath was largely aimed not at Israel, which had won the war, but at the corrupt Arab regimes associated with colonial powers that had lost it. In that post-cease-fire meeting in Falluja (see chapter 1) with two Israeli army officers, Yigal Allon and Mordechai Cohen, Nasser picked their brains about the Israelis' tactics in their successful campaign against the British authorities.

The way this episode unfolded demonstrated the attitudes then held by Nasser and his inner circle. After the truce, Cohen had been made a member of the joint Egyptian-Israeli commission; when he learned from his Egyptian counterparts that Nasser had had a baby boy, he congratulated him and sent him a present. In return, Nasser sent Cohen a box of candy from Cairo's renowned Groppi Café, and also invited him to Cairo to meet with him. Cohen asked Israel's foreign ministry for permission to travel, but was refused.

After the Free Officers came to power in Egypt, they took steps to keep their border with Israel trouble free; increased tension with Israel was not in the new leaders' interests. There were rumors—not far from the truth—that Egyptian intelligence officers had been tipped off about planned cross-border raids by Palestinians and had arrested a number of fedayeen. One Palestinian who ended up in an Egyptian jail in 1954 was a little-known guerrilla named Yasser Arafat.

The Palestinian leadership, represented back then by the High Council headed by the Mufti of Jerusalem, focused on carrying out sporadic raids from across the border in Jordan. The people who carried out these raids were largely Palestinian refugees who had been herded into camps on Jordanian territory. For every raid there were Israeli reprisals; the specially formed Unit 101, commanded by Ariel Sharon, was particularly brutal, as evidenced by the October 1953 Israeli army operation that followed the killing of an Israeli family on a kibbutz near the border. The Jordanians used a meeting of the joint commission to condemn the killing and vowed to find its perpetrators, but this did not stop sweeping retaliation in the Arab village of Qibiya, in which Unit 101 killed dozens of civilians and blew up several houses. The UN Security Council condemned the Israeli action, but Prime Minister David Ben-Gurion tried to deflect criticism from the Israeli army by describing the attackers as "enraged landowners."

Yet on the Egyptian-Israeli border all was quiet. The new Egyptian leadership was preoccupied with domestic political and economic worries: consolidating their hold on power, eradicating the Muslim Brotherhood's opposition, introducing land reform, and of course making sure British troops left Suez. The Arab-Israeli conflict took second or even third place. What better proof could there be of this than that the new Egyptian leaders—army officers, no less—cut the country's military spending in 1953, 1954, and 1955? The money saved was used to support small and medium-sized farms.

It was then that secret contacts with Israel were established in a bid to reach a set of agreements. In his memoirs, published after Nasser's death, his fellow officer Khalid "Red Major" Mohiedin wrote: "Nasser never closed the door on peace. He always kept it wide open." Nasser's first contact was with the Paris-based Israeli Peace Committee; when he got a positive reaction from Tel Aviv, he decided to move this contact onto a permanent basis, and the man he put in charge of this was Abdul Rahman Sabiq, an attaché in the Egyptian embassy in Paris. When Anthony Nutting, a British Foreign Office minister, arrived in Tel Aviv after a visit to Cairo, he told Prime Minister David Ben-Gurion he had brought him "good news": Nasser was so preoccupied with raising Egyptians' standard of living that it was a higher priority than conspiring to wage war against Israel. The Israeli replied: "You call that good news?" Behind Ben-Gurion's question was his anxiety that Egypt's new policy could win the Free Officers even more favor from the United States, which had already shown its willingness to back the Egyptian leadership.

The contact that Egypt and Israel had established was being derailed. Ben-Gurion demanded a summit meeting with Nasser, who declined. Equally damaging were the endless leaks: Israel promptly informed the United States of the contacts that had been made. This could not have come at a worse time for Nasser, who was anxious for Washington to be sure that Egypt was doing nothing behind its back.

NASSER'S SECRET CONTACT WITH SHARETT

Nutting's exchange with Ben-Gurion took place shortly before Moshe Sharett became prime minister of Israel. (Ben-Gurion had taken a five-month break, telling his colleagues he needed to "recharge his brain's batteries," but by December 1953 he had resigned.) Sharett was a very different figure from his predecessor: he did not enjoy the same popular support as Ben-Gurion, nor was he as hawkish. Sharett emphasized Israel's integration into the Middle East region; he spoke

Arabic and had a reputation as an Arab culture expert. The Arab world saw him as probably the most realistic of Israeli politicians. A number of positive statements by Nasser himself, as well as those who had spoken to him, gave reason to believe that the Egyptian president was personally well disposed toward Sharett.

A correspondence began between the two leaders. Their messages were aloof but courteous, and usually unsigned—although both knew from whom they had come. Sharett wanted Nasser to lift the blockade on Israeli ships passing through the Suez Canal and the Gulf of Aqaba. Nasser, significantly, was concerned with the problem of the Palestinian refugees, and he did not rule out a compromise on the number of refugees who had to be repatriated.

Three factors attest to the importance of their exchange. First, the United States was involved in these contacts, which were arranged with help from the CIA and State Department, and it was in U.S. interests to pull the strings of the new Egyptian regime. After Sharett took office, the Egyptians and the Israelis held face-to-face talks in Washington. The Israeli side was represented by future president Chaim Herzog and the diplomat Gideon Rafael, the Egyptian side by Colonel Abdul Hamid Galeb. Second, there were no serious border incidents while the talks were going on: Nasser kept the fedayeen in check, while Sharett avoided any so-called revenge attacks. Third, Nasser's relations soured with the Mufti of Jerusalem, Hussam Al-din Jarallah. As head of the high Arab council, the Mufti took a very tough line against Israel and did not hide his opposition to contacts between Cairo and Tel Aviv. There was reason to believe that he began to collaborate with the Muslim Brotherhood in order to form a substantial opposition to Nasser in Egypt.

A succession of intermediaries attempted to arrange a personal meeting between Nasser and Sharett. One was India's ambassador in Cairo, the historian K. M. Panikkar, well known for his connections with Jawaharlal Nehru, independent India's first prime minister. Until spring 1955, when the Israeli army entered Gaza, Panikkar had chaired negotiations on a Nasser-Sharett meeting. Another failed would-be mediator was the future Maltese prime minister Dom Mintoff.

Yet another mediation attempt involved Ira Hirschman, a former Roosevelt envoy who had negotiated a ransom to get a thousand Jews out of Nazi prison camps during the Second World War. Hirschman had close ties with the Zionist movement, and it is hard to imagine him finding common cause with the Free Officers. But after meeting with Nasser, he would write that the new Egyptian leader's constructive attitude had greatly impressed him. That same day, Hirschman flew to Tel Aviv for a talk with Sharett and Ben-Gurion. When he suggested there should be contact between Israeli leaders and Nasser, Ben-Gurion replied, "Nasser won't be in the saddle for long."

By now no one had any doubt about who was in the driver's seat in Israel. Before leaving office, Ben-Gurion had appointed Pinhas Lavon minister of defense and Moshe Dayan chief of military staff. Through them, he effectively continued running the country from his kibbutz in the Negev desert. Israelis said that as Sharett read the newspapers each morning, his hands would tremble in fear of what Dayan and Lavon might have done overnight. Perhaps this exaggerates how far removed Sharett was from anti-Arab activity, but many experts have written that the two Israeli military chiefs—who secretly hated each other—had free rein to conduct anti-Arab operations and did not even supply the prime minister with military or strategic intelligence.

Not without reason, alarm bells began ringing. On May 15, 1954, the *Times* of London reported that Israel was planning to attack Egypt; on June 7, the *New York Times* reported the same story. On June 12 the United States threatened to cut off military aid to any country that did not abide by the Middle East peace agreements. signed after the first Arab-Israeli war. This warning may have served to cool the ardor of the Israeli hawks.

OPERATION SUSANNAH

It was about this time, on June 30, 1954, that Israeli special agents in Egypt launched a covert operation code named "Susannah." The Lavon affair—possibly the biggest political scandal in Israel's history—erupted after Operation Susannah was foiled.

A network of Egypt-based agents assembled by Israeli spymaster Abraham Dar (who passed himself off in Egypt as "John Darling," a representative of a British electronics company) was given the mission of setting off bombs at British and American establishments in Cairo and Alexandria. The operation was carried out by Unit 131 (in charge of diversionary tactics) of Aman, Israel's military intelligence directorate. The aim was to create tension between Egypt on one side, and Britain and the United States on the other, in order to give the "Suez lobby" in the British Parliament a pretext for revoking the agreement mandating the withdrawal of British troops from Egypt. Susannah could also serve the emerging "Israel lobby" in the United States, which was fighting Washington's tendency toward flirtation with the new regime in Cairo.

There followed a series of bombings of American information centers in Cairo and Alexandria. Two Israeli agents were arrested during an attempt to take a bomb into a Cairo movie theater in December 1954. After they confessed to the crime, other members of the network were arrested as well. In the ensuing trial it was proved that Tel Aviv was behind the provocation. Two agents were given the death sentence, another committed suicide in prison and the rest were exchanged for Egyptian POWs after the Six-Day War of 1967.

In Israel, the entire trial was dismissed as "stage-managed." Nevertheless, the unmasking of Operation Susannah resulted in Pinhas Lavon's resignation as Israeli defense minister in 1955. He was made the scapegoat for the decision to order the anti-American bombings in Cairo. Lavon denied giving the order but was unable to prove that his signature had been forged, so he resigned, giving way to David Ben-Gurion as defense minister. Ben-Gurion's return to this key cabinet post foreshadowed his de facto takeover as prime minister, which later became official.[1]

The Lavon affair sparked a debate that raged at all levels of Israeli society for years: who gave the order? Who was responsible for the operation? Was the director of military intelligence lying when he maintained that in mid-July Defense Minister Lavon had used a tête-à-tête meeting (with no witnesses present) to give him similar instructions? Was the defense minister lying when he insisted that no such meeting had taken place? Were the relevant documents forged? And what of Moshe Dayan, who for some reason had summoned one of the main witnesses for a confidential meeting before he was officially interrogated? Was Dayan a party to the forgery? And so on and so forth. This public debate distracted attention from the crucial point that the operation had been designed to stoke up tension.

It did not take long for events to confirm what course the Israeli leadership had taken. Once he was back in government, Ben-Gurion and Dayan started to plot an operation against the Egyptian army contingent in Gaza, which had been placed under Egyptian control as a condition of the 1949 truce. Just one week after Ben-Gurion returned from his kibbutz, a massive assault on Gaza was launched. Egypt's military headquarters were destroyed in the attack, which left thirty-eight soldiers and officers dead and thirty wounded. Convinced that he could no longer exert any real influence on events, Sharett resigned.

Some commentators on the Middle East conflict have identified the Gaza offensive as an open declaration of war against Nasser and his brand of nationalism. This was of course clear to Nasser too.

Still, it would be wrong to suggest that the new Egyptian regime had been single-mindedly bent on making peace with Israel until the assault on Gaza. Even as he moved to ease the tension between Cairo and Tel Aviv, Nasser stepped up the blockade of the Straits of Tiran, blocking access to the Gulf of Aqaba and the Israeli port of Eilat. At the time, however, he felt there was no support for Sharett's policy within Israel; only a minority advocated peace with the Arabs; and only a minority tried to back away from Israel's policy of expanding its territory at the expense of the surrounding countries. Nasser, meanwhile, having taken on the mantle of pan-Arab leader, did not want a separate treaty with Israel. Nevertheless, he sought to set a course that would lead to a settlement.

There is no doubt that Israel's isolation and the widespread support for the hawkish figures of Ben-Gurion, Dayan, Lavon, and others, were reactions to threats to wipe the new Jewish state off the face of the earth. This threat had been made openly by Ahmad Shukeiri, then leader of the Palestine Liberation Organization. It was a rallying cry used unthinkingly—to their own detriment—by Arafat and his followers in the 1960s. In March 1977, however, a meeting of the National Council of Palestine in Cairo decided on a new official resolution setting out its goal: to create a Palestinian state, not in Israel's place but alongside Israel, on the West Bank of the River Jordan and in the Gaza Strip. Arafat had spoken to me of this idea six years before this resolution. But we shall return to that later.

The calls of the extremists caused great damage to the Arabs. But I would venture to say that even during the 1973 war started by Egypt and Syria, leaders of the frontline Arab states did not aspire to the goal of destroying Israel. This is a conclusion I was able to draw after a round of frank talks with Anwar Sadat of Egypt, Hafez Assad of Syria, and King Hussein of Jordan.

– 3 –

THE INEVITABLE CONFRONTATION WITH THE WEST

FRANCE AND BRITAIN HAD their differences with the United States over the Middle East. They were not bitter disputes, just differences. The old colonial powers had begun to realize that nothing could restore their traditional position in the world, nor could they block the rise of American influence in the region. The French, who tried to use military force to maintain their dominance in North Africa, maybe took a little longer to grasp this than the British.

But for all their differences, the overall policy of the United States, Britain, and France was based on a common effort to draw sovereign Arab states into military blocs controlled by the West. This policy was fueled by the fear that several newly independent Arab states would gravitate toward the Soviet camp at a time when the cold war was gathering strength.

MILITARY ALLIANCES FAN THE FLAMES

Washington, bent on drawing Egypt into a military alliance, dangled the prospect of an arms deal but kept delaying any actual agreement. The "Islamic Union" having failed to materialize, the United States

instigated a two-way axis of Turkey and Pakistan, intent on turning it
into the hub of a wider military bloc that the Arab states would be required to join. But Egypt remained on the sidelines; Nasser was not
inclined to join any military coalition after the United States rejected
an early effort to get Israel to sign up.

On February 24, 1955, Washington and London succeeded in
bringing Iraq and Turkey together in a military alliance under the
Baghdad Pact (subsequently known as METO, the Middle East
Treaty Organization). Britain officially signed on, later joined by Pakistan and Iran. The United States, officially, stayed out.

Egypt opposed the Baghdad Pact and made its opposition known
throughout the Arab world. But its inability to buy modern armaments from the United States was no longer the main reason for its
hostility. Cairo could not have failed to notice that Iraq had acquired
U.S. military assistance once it joined the pact. But Iraq, ruled as it
was by the pro-British King Faisal and Prime Minister Nuri al-Said,
could never serve as an example for Nasser's Egypt. Indeed, Cairo's
hostility to the Baghdad Pact arose mainly because the bloc was being
used to try to isolate Egypt from other Arab countries.

After Adib al-Shishakli's pro-American regime was overthrown in
Syria and replaced with a government headed by National party
leader Sabry Asali, the United States became particularly anxious to
stop Egypt and Syria from forming a counterweight to the Baghdad
Pact. On February 26, 1955, the U.S. ambassador in Damascus
handed the Syrian government a memorandum suggesting that Syria
should refrain from signing a military pact with Egypt. When Syria
rejected this suggestion, it began to experience a sharp deterioration
of its relations with Turkey and Iraq. There were also attacks by Israel, and Adnan Malki, Syria's patriotic deputy chief of military staff,
was murdered. None of this was independent of U.S. influence.

Britain played the same game. Shortly before he became prime
minister in April 1955, Anthony Eden offered Nasser a "carrot": in a
secret message, he promised Nasser he would not let any more Arab
countries into the Baghdad Pact if Nasser would call off his campaign
against the pact. The proposal suggested how effective Egyptian propaganda was becoming, especially after Voice of the Arabs radio,

which was heard across the Arab world, began broadcasting from Cairo. But pressure didn't work, and neither did manipulation: on October 20, 1955, Egypt and Syria signed a defense alliance.

It evidently came as a great surprise to the Americans that Saudi Arabia also joined the new alliance—especially as the Saudi family had traditionally been enemies of Iraq's Hashemite dynasty. At this point, Saudi Arabia suffered a downhill slide in its relations not only with Iraq but also with the Sultan of Muscat, a pawn of the British who had laid claim to the Buraimi oasis.

This tripartite alliance was not confined to defense. By the mid-1950s, it was clear that Egypt found itself on the opposing side from the British as well as the French. In April 1955, Nasser addressed the conference of twenty-nine Afro-Asiatic states in Bandung, Indonesia, a conference that played a considerable part in shaping his anticolonial views. "Why must we consider it natural that the countries of North Africa, which for centuries had been independent centers of learning and ancient civilization, should be reduced to the status of peripheral districts, deprived of freedom and independence?" he said.

Egypt started backing the Algerian rebels against French occupation. The Cairo-based leaders of Algeria's National Liberation Front (FLN), who had been kept under scrutiny by Egyptian intelligence and not allowed to conduct any anti-French activity on Egyptian soil, began secretly receiving financial aid, and Egypt stepped up its propaganda campaign in support of the FLN, especially through the Voice of the Arabs radio station.

All this time, Nasser and his associates persisted in believing that America's position in relation to the Arab countries was markedly different from that of Britain or France.

ARMS AND THE DAM

Nasser's most pressing problems at the time were buying weapons and securing assistance with construction of the Aswan High Dam. The Free Officers regime regarded both as vitally important. The arms question had largely arisen because of the conflict with Israel.

The High Dam, meanwhile, was considered by Cairo to be essential not only to solve Egypt's grave economic problems but also to stop the catastrophic flooding of the Nile and boost the amount of land put to agricultural use by one-third. The Aswan dam was also central to the Free Officers' effort to consolidate their power, which was not yet fully stable. After raising Egypt's hopes on both issues, the United States ultimately refused to help with either one.

Eventually, Nasser and his cohorts realized the ever-shifting talks were going nowhere, as the United States was clearly stringing out its decision on supplying arms to Cairo. Washington, they concluded, was trying to keep Egypt weak, with the aim of "taming" the country.

I believe it was only after the West slammed the doors in its face that Egypt turned for help to the Soviet Union. At first it asked Moscow for arms supplies, and later for help with construction at Aswan. I could be mistaken: in May 1955, just back from Bandung, Nasser authorized that contact be made with Leonid Nemchenko, military attaché of the Soviet Embassy in Cairo. Maybe he wanted to test the reliability of the recommendations made to him in Bandung by Chinese premier Chou En-lai. But Egypt's government was at the time still counting on American arms supplies; it was not yet 100 percent disillusioned with U.S. policy. It was no accident that Nasser decided to inform Henry Byroade, the U.S. ambassador to Cairo, of his contact with Nemchenko. Perhaps there was a reason why Byroade told CIA resident Miles Copeland that Nasser was bluffing. Nasser kept hoping, while Washington kept stalling.

Nemchenko later worked for the Institute of World Economy and International Relations in Moscow when I was its deputy director. The two of us met on many occasions and spoke of that time when he had been a key figure in talks over Egypt's purchase of Soviet arms via Czechoslovakia. Nemchenko had no doubt that the first time Nasser approached him to sound out the possibility of an arms deal, his intent was to put pressure on the Americans. But even a conversation was a very serious matter, especially in light of what Nasser had told *Pravda* editor in chief Dmitry Shepilov, and Moscow decided to go ahead with the deal. The Soviets were, if anything, more doubtful even than Cairo about the Americans' willingness to supply an unknown quantity like

Nasser with up-to-date weaponry. The U.S., moreover, was bound by all sorts of obligations to its allies in Western Europe and Israel. In the end, things turned out just as the Soviets had supposed they would.

In September 1955, Nasser made a public announcement about the supply of arms to the Egyptian military—not merely that there had been dealings with the Soviet Union and Czechoslovakia but that an agreement was already in place. He simply could not afford to wait any longer, now that Israel had said it would use force to try to re-open the Gulf of Aqaba to shipping. In a bid to persuade Nasser to renege on his deal with the Soviets, Robert Anderson, a personal friend of U.S. president Eisenhower, flew to Cairo. In order to give greater weight to his mission and perhaps in a genuine attempt to ease the tension with Israel, he engaged in shuttle diplomacy between countries. He returned to Egypt from Israel amid "active operations" by the CIA, which had sent Nasser a verbal proposal via "Kim" Roosevelt offering him a secret, unwritten deal to buy American arms. Nasser was not swayed.

After the failure of the arms talks with the Americans, Egypt's relations with the West suffered yet another breakdown that hit the new regime exceptionally hard: the collapse of negotiations to secure Western credit for construction of the Aswan High Dam. Cairo had refused to agree to a series of demands that, according to Nasser, would impose de facto outside control over Egypt's finances, budget, and economy. This refusal had led the U.S. and British governments and the World Bank to withdraw their respective offers to lend $55 million, $15 million, and $200 million for the project.

These refusals came as a surprise to Egypt's government, which to a certain extent had been blinded by American gestures intended to sink its arms deal with the Soviets. In December 1955, Washington had declared that the United States and Britain were willing to finance not just the first phase of construction at Aswan but all subsequent phases too. The young Free Officers had also been inspired by President Eisenhower telling the United States Congress in the second half of 1955 that building the Aswan High Dam was "the key to Egypt's future ability to safeguard its growing population." All these statements, which came after Cairo said it was buying Soviet arms, raised Egypt's hopes. The sudden, coordinated rebuff was a stunning disappointment.

Egypt initially decided to keep knocking on the door after it had been closed. It first heard of the U.S. refusal to finance the dam from John Foster Dulles in July 1956. Britain's announcement came the day after. Perhaps not quite realizing that Washington ruled the roost in the World Bank and that the U.S. refusal would be the factor that determined the bank's decision, Nasser turned to the president of the bank. He asked him to take on 100 percent of the financing—the bank's share had in any case eclipsed the loans on offer from Britain and the United States. But Nasser's request was denied.

What made the United States turn so strongly against Egypt? Was it the decision to buy arms from the Soviet Union? Not quite. The CIA operation in Cairo had reported back that Egypt's purchase of Soviet weaponry should not be taken as "an act of hostility against the U.S." So was it Egypt's recognition of the People's Republic of China in May 1956? Again, not quite. The Egyptians could feasibly have explained this decision to the CIA's Kermit "Kim" Roosevelt, pointing out that it was also not directed against the United States. Egypt had wanted other arms suppliers to fall back on because it feared that once the Soviet Union had tested the ground, it could reach a deal with the United States, Britain, and France to impose an arms embargo on the Middle East.[1] Nor was U.S. policy necessarily affected by Egypt's talks with Dmitry Shepilov, now the Soviet foreign minister; his visit to Cairo came at the same time as meetings with top officials from many Western countries.

In truth, the United States was already unhappy with Cairo's policy of nonalignment—its balancing act, intended to preserve its independence, between the "free world" and the socialist camp in the cold war. It was a policy seen in Washington as Nasser's unwillingness to put himself under Western control.

This shows that when the Free Officers took power, anti-imperialism was not their primary motive: it evolved gradually, with a few stops and starts, and gained momentum as Nasser's Egypt came up against Britain's real policy toward it. Growing tensions with the United States later turned into outright enmity.

THE START OF OPEN CONFLICT

Five days after the United States refused Egypt a loan for the Aswan project, Nasser addressed a rally celebrating the completion of a gas pipeline from Suez to Cairo. "The high dam will be built," he declared, and then, intoxicated by the frenzied support of his crowd, he added: "May the West choke on its own anger!" This was his warning shot to the West.

On July 26, 1956, in a speech broadcast across the Arab world, Nasser addressed a rally marking the fourth anniversary of King Farouk's abdication. The Egyptian president spoke on Mohammed Ali Square in Alexandria—an act laden with symbolism, this being the exact spot where the Muslim Brotherhood had tried to assassinate him. In the course of his speech, he uttered a code word several times in succession, which was a cue for groups that had been on standby to take control of all offices belonging to the Suez Canal Company, located in Port Said, Suez, and Ismailiya. "At this moment, as I speak to you," Nasser announced, "the Suez Canal Company has been nationalized in the name of the Egyptian people."

Britain and France immediately rejected the nationalization. Within twenty-four hours, British prime minister Anthony Eden had secured his cabinet's approval to use military force against Nasser. President Eisenhower, who reckoned that such action could destabilize the entire Middle East, telephoned Eden on July 31 to ask that he "exercise restraint." France, which took a stand similar to the British, entered secret talks with the Israelis.

From a legal perspective, Egypt's nationalization of the company was beyond reproach. This is why Eden did not act on Eisenhower's recommendation that he refer the matter to the International Court of Justice. Eden instead declared that it was a question of "Egypt not being fit to control this canal, which is so important to the whole world." To begin with, it was a propaganda war: millions of people across the Arab world listened to Voice of the Arabs for every speech of Nasser's. Not one Arab radio station spoke out against him even in countries whose regimes had close ties to the British. The only exception was the Muslim Brotherhood radio station in Cyprus, which had been set up with British help and which regularly accused the Egyptian president of "dragging his country into chaos." One of Nasser's closest colleagues told me he feared the British were using the radio station to organize a plot against him in Egypt. Instead, events began to unfold along very different lines.

The canal operated normally, even though its former owners had severed the contracts of canal pilots from Western European countries and sent them home (their place was taken by Greek, East German, and Russian pilots); it seemed as if a peaceful solution could be found. The U.S. administration made its position clear to Nasser: Washington would not openly condemn its allies' military preparations but would do so behind closed doors. In the UN Security Council, there was stalemate as the Soviet Union blocked an Anglo-French resolution that was blatantly anti-Egyptian. Britain and France, meanwhile, vetoed a resolution seeking a peaceful solution while allowing Egypt to retain control over the canal.

British and French plans to attack Egypt had already entered the practical phase. On October 14 and 16 there was an exchange of visits, with French envoys coming for talks in London and Eden traveling to Paris with British foreign secretary John Selwyn Lloyd. Israel, which had so far stayed in the background and had dealt only with the French, emerged as the frontline force in the armed assault on Egypt. Israeli prime minister David Ben-Gurion had been given a guarantee by the British that they would destroy the Egyptian air force on the ground; he asked UN observers to leave their base in Al-Awja.

October 29, 1956, was set as the invasion date. It had evidently been chosen with two factors in mind: the United States was in the middle of presidential elections, while the Soviet Union was caught up in the Hungarian uprising against the Communist regime. That day, an Israeli parachute battalion landed near the Mitla Pass in Sinai. On October 30, Britain and France issued an ultimatum demanding that the two sides withdraw their troops to a line ten miles from the Suez Canal. This meant that Egypt, which had sent its army into Sinai against the Israelis, had to retreat thirty miles within its own territory, while the Israelis could advance sixty miles toward the canal. In line with their prior arrangement, the Israelis agreed to the demand while the Egyptians rejected it. It was then that Britain and France stepped in, launching bombing raids against Egyptian targets; on November 5 British paratroopers landed in Port Said, and French ones in Port Fouad.

There followed a demand from President Eisenhower that all nations halt military action and pull their troops out of Sinai. Meanwhile, Soviet premier Nikolai Bulganin issued an unprecedented statement, threatening to launch missiles against the countries that had attacked Egypt unless their troops left Egyptian soil. (I do not think this threat could have been carried out.) Even before the three-pronged assault on Egypt, Nikita Khrushchev had intimated to Nasser that Moscow would not let Suez escalate into a world war; it would appear that Nasser fully understood that message.

Soviet foreign minister Dmitry Shepilov offers some fascinating recollections of those events in an interview with my old *Pravda* colleague Aleksei Vasilyev, who later became director of the Africa Institute at the Russian Academy of Sciences. Vasilyev's book on Russia's place in the Middle East quotes Shepilov as saying that the Soviet government had "firmly decided not to let it turn into all-out war. But I did come up with some psychological tactics, which I then applied, and summoned the ambassadors of Britain, France and Israel at night." Moscow's move was also helped by Khrushchev's eccentricity: "God only knows what trick he might play." Additionally, it was announced via the Soviet news agency TASS on November 10 that "unless the aggressors withdraw their troops from Egyptian soil, the government will not stand in the way of Soviet citizens volunteering to travel to Egypt to do their bit in the Egyptian people's armed struggle for independence." This could not fail to be noted by those behind the invasion.

In the end, external pressure forced the British, French, and Israelis to pull out of Egyptian territory. As for Egypt's army, its weakness—now made all too apparent—stood in sharp contrast with the upsurge of patriotism of Egyptians wanting to fight for their country.

Egypt had taken delivery of Soviet arms only at the beginning of 1956; its army had very little time to master their use. It was imperative,

therefore, to have specialists who could quickly train Egyptian soldiers to use those arms—but it was only significantly later that Soviet
military specialists were invited to Egypt. It is hard to criticize the
Egyptian leadership for this; perhaps it was only after the three-
pronged assault on Egypt that Nasser truly realized how much his
country needed an army that was fit for combat. From 1948 until
then, all the armed confrontations between Egypt and Israel had been
no more than localized clashes. Nasser had not really considered the
prospect of a wider war.

During the Anglo-French-Israeli invasion, Nasser had even spoken
with his confidants about transforming the army into small partisan
groups that would fight inside Egypt should it succumb to occupation. Even just before the invasion—at a point when Nasser knew it
was unavoidable—he had phoned Syrian president Shukri al-Kuwatli
and King Hussein of Jordan, asking them not to enter the war. He
told Hussein he wanted "to spare Jordan's army from defeat." This
demonstrates two of Nasser's concerns: he wanted to avoid a wider
war against Israel, especially when it was backed by Britain and
France; and he had made a sobering assessment not only of the Egyptian army's combat readiness but of the armies of other Arab countries
too. Furthermore, even after taking delivery of Soviet arms, Nasser
clearly did not want to push things too far with Washington. Eyewit-
nesses close to Nasser quote him as saying, during the invasion, that
"now it is clear to all that our main hope is the United States."

The October 1956 invasion of Egypt did teach the Egyptian government one particularly tough lesson: Israel's war machine had
started to pose a direct threat not only to the Palestinian fedayeen,
and not only to Jordan and Syria, from whose territories anti-Israeli
attacks were launched, but also to Egypt. As Nasser's stature in the
Arab world grew, this threat only intensified.

Egypt had domestic achievements to its credit; it had resisted Western efforts to corral it into a military alliance and to stop Egypt getting arms supplies from the Soviet Union; it had managed to gain
sufficient financing to begin the desperately needed Aswan dam even
after the West denied it a loan; and ultimately, it had gained the support of much of the international community when it was invaded.

All of this served to bring Arabs closer together. During the invasion of Egypt, Syrian workers blew up three pumping stations on an Iraq Petroleum Company pipeline carrying gasoline to the Mediterranean; under pressure from its people, the Saudi government imposed an embargo on the supply of oil to Britain and France; and all Arab countries took diplomatic action against these countries.

Like the Free Officers in Egypt, the leaders of the 1958 coup in Iraq were not primarily motivated by anticolonialism, nor were they at all anti-Western. They assured British officials that relations with Britain would remain a major priority, and General Abdul Karim Qassem told the U.S. ambassador that "we, the Iraqis, want good relations with the United States." Importantly for the West, these assurances were backed up by indications that the Iraq Petroleum Company would continue to honor its contracts.

But these assurances had no effect on the way either Britain or the United States reacted to events in Iraq. Entry to the Baghdad Pact now became harder and harder. Washington and London may have been afraid that the overthrow of the monarchy in Iraq would trigger a chain reaction across the Arab world. That Iraq and Egypt might build closer relations and perhaps even join forces may have been another source of unease in the West, especially after this prospect was openly raised by Abdul Salam Arif, number two in the new Iraqi regime.

. On July 15, 1958, United States Marines began landing in Lebanon; their numbers quickly climbed to twenty thousand. Six thousand British troops were deployed in Jordan. The level of equipment and sheer size of these military contingents left little doubt that their mission was not to defend Lebanon and Jordan from any theoretical Iraqi threat; what was in prospect was the danger of United States and British troops invading Iraq. Turkey, Iran, and Pakistan also appeared willing to preserve the disintegrating Baghdad Pact by force and crush the new Iraqi regime.

That no such invasion took place is partly a result of the Soviet Union's taking military steps to pacify Turkey and Iran. Nor was Eisenhower inclined toward a military assault on the new regime in Baghdad—the CIA had briefed him on General Qassem's anti-Nasser sentiments, and the United States president reckoned that the Iraqi leader might someday be useful. But as soon as Qassem pulled Iraq out of the Baghdad Pact, started buying arms from the Soviet Union, and even included a few communists early on in his government, Washington's attitude changed. Allan Dulles, then director of the CIA, publicly called Iraq "one of the most dangerous corners of the world."

— 4 —

NATIONAL INTERESTS
TAKE PRECEDENCE OVER
ARAB UNITY

THE NATIONALIST REVOLUTIONARIES in power in the Arab nations were far from alike in their thinking on pan-Arab unity. In
Egypt and elsewhere, national interests took priority over "pan-Arab
nationalism." Disagreements between the Arab countries that had recently shaken off colonial rule grew wider and wider, despite their
leaders' mutual assurances of willingness to stand up for the unity of
the Arab world, even to make it their overriding goal.

SLOGANS AND REALITY

One of Nasser's rallying cries was "We are all Arabs" (*Nakhnul arab*
in Arabic). But this appeal to Arab unity did not mitigate the urgent
tasks the Free Officers faced within Egypt: consolidating their own
power; preventing any resurgence of the corrupt old British-influenced
parliamentary party apparatus, in the form of King Farouk or anyone
else; carrying out land reform, thereby making inroads in the countryside and curbing the influence of the Islamists; ending Britain's
occupation of the Suez Canal zone. These were the tasks that determined Nasser's initial policies, not only toward the United States but

also toward Israel. The rallying cry of Arab unity, while still heard, had begun to part ways with political reality.

It may have been significant that Nasser had yet to become a pan-Arab leader; in fact, it was Syria's Ba'ath Party (or Party of Arab Socialist Renaissance) that was seen as giving birth to the idea of Arab unity. Formed by a group of Syrian intellectuals in the 1940s, the party's ranks were swollen in 1953 by the absorption of another Syrian-born organization, the Arab Socialist Party. Since then the group has been known in Syria by its current name, the Ba'ath Party. To this day, support for the unity of the Arab nation, the Arab world, is written into all its policies. A separate Ba'athist pan-Arab authority existed in Iraq until the overthrow of Saddam Hussein's regime.[1]

The unifying tendency in the Arab world—present in its shared written language, culture, religion, and traditions—was reinforced by Egypt's distinct cultural influence. Egyptian radio, television, and cinema fought to win the hearts and minds of Arabs everywhere; the seductive voice of the Egyptian singer Umm Kulthum reached every corner of the Arab world; and students from many lands studied at Cairo University. Even in 1957, when tension between Egypt and Iraq was at its height, four hundred Egyptian teachers arrived in Iraq to work in Iraqi schools. At the same time, the rise of pan-Arab nationalism was also driven by the solidarity that Arabs had developed in the context of the independence movement and the Arab-Israeli conflict. This is why many felt that the postcolonial Arab world would move toward forming an Arab community or even a unified territory, much of which had been artificially carved up by Britain and France. Nasser's Egypt became a magnet for people from other Arab countries, including not only admirers of Nasser but also political parties and other groups that declared themselves "Nasserite." The Egyptian president was holding himself up as the leader of pan-Arabism.

In this environment it was no surprise that steps were taken toward an actual merger of states. In 1958, Egypt and Syria created the United Arab Republic (UAR)—possibly the boldest attempt in history to create a union of Arab states that could act as a nucleus capable of attracting other Arab countries. Indeed, this Egyptian-Syrian state was later joined by Yemen. Libya would try several times—without success—to unite with Egypt.

BEHIND THE CREATION OF THE UAR

The creation of the UAR was a difficult and complex affair, despite the Arabs' yearning for their countries to be joined.

The first Syrian leader to come from the ranks of the military was Colonel Husni Zaim, who took power in Damascus with the aid of the CIA in 1949. Within eight months he was deposed and killed by another colonel, Sami al-Hinnawi, who was suspected—not without reason—of being involved in a pro-British operation. Three months later, again with the aid of the CIA, another coup was orchestrated, and Colonel Adib al-Shishakli came to power in Damascus. His regime lasted four years. But in 1954, when Shukri al-Kuwatli became Syria's president, Syria started to shift rapidly to the left. The well-organized Syrian Communist Party was gathering strength, and General Afif Bizri, the Syrian army's chief of staff, was viewed as being close to the Communists.

The direction of events in Syria was not lost on Nasser. The Egyptian leader warned President al-Kuwatli and Colonel Hamid Sarraj, head of Syria's intelligence corps, that there was a danger of the nationalist movement slipping into the lap of the Communists. There was more to this warning than Nasser's real fear that the red flag would be raised above Syria, the "heart of the Arab world." Nasser apparently also feared Syria would divert some of the Soviet support and aid upon which Cairo had become more and more dependent.

The authorities in Damascus too were becoming alarmed at the Syrian Communists' growing influence. It was clearly this, and not a drive for Arab unity, that brought a Syrian delegation headed by President al-Kuwatli and Prime Minister Khalid al-Azm to Cairo. They told Nasser that political union with Egypt was the only thing that would save Syria from chaos and "the danger of Communism." Nasser, a more pragmatic politician, at first rejected the Syrians' proposal for immediate union. To make their plan a reality, he said, would require at least five years of preparation.

Before long a second Syrian delegation visited Cairo with the same mission: to seek the unification of the two states. This time Nasser took a more flexible position, but he was inclined to favor a federal structure. The Syrians insisted on a single, merged state, and eventually Nasser came around to their idea. What most likely prompted his change was his fear that the Communists really would come to power in Syria. Tellingly, right after the UAR was formed, on February 1, 1958, Nasser removed Bizri from his top military post and launched an open attack on the Syrian Communist Party. The same period also saw Egyptian leftists come under harsh persecution.

The United States was undoubtedly reluctant to see this unifying tendency in the Arab world succeed, especially under Nasser's leadership, and it adopted a very relaxed attitude toward the creation of the UAR. On January 23, just a week before the UAR was founded, the U.S. ambassador in Cairo, acting on instructions from Washington, informed Nasser that the union of Egypt and Syria was an internal affair for Arabs and that the U.S. government would adopt a passive stance on the matter. After Nasser's meeting with Lebanese president Fuad Chehab at Shtora, on the Lebanese-Syrian border, when he ordered an end to the supply of arms and cash to pro-Syrian forces in Lebanon, the United States produced a timetable for withdrawal of the Marines it had deployed in Lebanon immediately following the coup in Iraq. The United States also resumed supplying wheat to the Egyptian-Syrian state as part of its humanitarian aid program. Such was the reaction of the United States and Britain to the founding of the United Arab Republic; when it came to the coup in Iraq in July 1958, the two powers would react far differently.

The peoples of the two merged Arab states—and of other Arab countries too—greeted the founding of the UAR with great joy. On the streets of Arab cities, there was unparalleled glee at the appearance of a shared UAR flag and joint leadership. Many expected that Iraq would join the union after the 1958 coup. But that is not how things turned out.

Nasser was not behind the events of the revolution in Baghdad, nor did he see any connection between them and the prospects for Arab unification. Soon after the creation of the UAR, Syrian intel-

ligence chief Hamid Sarraj went to Daraa to meet two Iraqi officers, who told him that a secret organization had been formed
within the Iraqi army with the aim of deposing the monarchy. Their
main question for Sarraj was: could they count on the UAR in the
event of a coup? Naturally, Sarraj informed Nasser of this meeting
with the Iraqis, who were none other than Abdul Karim Qassem
and Abdul Salam Arif, the future leaders of the coup. I think if
Nasser had been set on creating an Arab state on a wider scale than
the UAR, he would have given them the guarantee they wanted—
though only verbally. But he ordered Sarraj to break off contact
with them.

After the coup in Baghdad, Arif directly raised the question of
Iraq's joining the UAR, but Nasser was not in favor. This was reflected in Nasser's conversation with Nikita Khrushchev during a secret trip to Moscow immediately after the Iraqi coup. When
Khrushchev asked about the possibility of union with Iraq, Nasser's
answer was clear-cut: "Iraq will be facing a multitude of difficult
problems, and joining [the UAR] should not bring additional compli-
cations on top of these. Iraq is very different from Syria, and there are
quite enough problems between Egypt and Syria as it is. I think there
will be some ties between the UAR and Iraq, but what kind exactly
will depend on many different circumstances."

It would be wrong to think of Nasser as opposing Arab unity,
Arab solidarity, or pan-Arab interests. There was, however, a pragmatism to his way of thinking that led him to discard the idea of creating a pan-Arab state. His support of General Jaafar Nimeiri, who
led the coup in Sudan, was not a step toward establishing such a
state, nor was it the reason that Egypt's seventy-thousand-man army
was sent to aid Yemeni tribes that had rebelled against their monarchy. Nor was there any motive of founding a unified Arab state behind Cairo's support of the Algerian pro-independence rebels or of
Muammar Gaddafi, leader of the Libyan officers who deposed King
Idris. Nasser was indeed crowned the unofficial leader of the Arab
world, its guiding light; yet he himself—especially after the sorry
demise of the Egyptian-Syrian republic—did not see any link between
this role and the amalgamation of Arab states.

The Egyptian-Syrian republic fell apart in 1961 because of opposition by Syrian officers in Damascus. Sheer differences between
one Arab country and another was one deciding factor in its
demise, but again it was nationalism—local nationalism this time—
that took the upper hand. Incidentally, the Syrian Communists
were not the driving force behind the collapse of the UAR; far from
it. This was a victory for the Syrian nationalists, who reckoned that
Nasser's regime was turning Syria into nothing more than an extension of Egypt.

The demise of the UAR had serious implications for the Arab
world. Nasser himself called off an order, given on impulse, to deploy
Egyptian troops in the Syrian port of Latakia in a bid to keep the
Egyptian-Syrian state intact. This was undoubtedly the moment when
he grasped the sheer impossibility of using military force to corral
Arab countries together.

Within two years Nasser had clearly turned his back on the idea of
a unified Arab state. In March 1963, two Ba'athist delegations arrived in Cairo, one Syrian and one Iraqi, at a time when the party
held power in both countries and before the two national parties split
from one another. For two and a half weeks, they held talks with
Nasser and the Egyptian government. The delegations were impres-
sive: Syria's was headed by the Ba'ath party founders Michel Aflaq
and Salah Bitar, and Iraq's by Ali Saleh Saadi, leader of the party's
Iraqi wing. By prior arrangement, both delegations traveled to Cairo
at the same time, reckoning that a joint appeal would make Nasser
better disposed toward the idea of a three-way merger of the Egyptian, Syrian, and Iraqi states. And how did Nasser respond? According
to witnesses, he was blunt and noncommittal with the Syrians, who
had pulled out of the UAR just two years earlier—an action, moreover, that he knew both Aflaq and Bitar had favored. Then he talked
about the theoretical possibility of a tripartite federation many years
in the future. This, he felt, had to begin with the merging of the three
countries' defenses and overseas policies, while preserving their sovereignty for a prolonged period. One other condition he insisted on
was that there should first be a step-by-step renewal of the Egypt-
Syria federation, to which Iraq would sign up later.

Although Nasser put forward this proposal, it is unlikely that he truly took on the task of a merger between the three states. Why else did he not confine himself to a retrospective criticism of the reasons behind the UAR's collapse? Instead he went further, accusing the Iraqi regime of having links with the CIA, which was supplying Baghdad with light artillery for its war against the Kurds. Nasser specifically named William Lakeland, an American spy with links to the Iraqi leadership, whom he had known when Lakeland was an attaché at the U.S. Embassy in Cairo. While he was not opposed to any Arab country having good relations with the United States, he insisted that they had to rule out any activity that could lead to an Arab country— in this case Iraq—surrendering its position to the CIA. Nor was Nasser opposed to the suggested federation's new three-starred flag, but he said the federation should take shape systematically and very, very slowly.

It seemed that there would be a follow-up to these negotiations, but none occurred. Evidently, all parties had concluded that there was no real chance of preventing a schism in the Arab world. Given the collapse of the UAR in 1961, creating another unified Arab state afresh was impossible in the short term; this judgment was reinforced by the equally fair conclusion that it would be very hard—if it was possible at all—to get a run of peaceful years in which to reach phased agreements between three Arab regimes that differed so much.

The only viable unified state in the Arab Middle East was the United Arab Emirates. But the UAE was made up of territories that had not been fully formed states before, so it did not provide grounds for local nationalism to arise.

This form of nationalism soon overtook the pan-Arab variety and undermined a succession of attempted state mergers across the Arab world, even when conditions seemed conducive to their success. In 1958, Iraq and Jordan—both then ruled by the same Hashemite dynasty—set up a joint federal government under Nuri al-Said, but it turned out to be a sham. Nor was there union between Iraq and Syria after the Ba'athists came to power in Baghdad and Damascus in February and March 1963—before the party split in two. Attempts to form such a union failed even despite the June 1979 meeting in

Baghdad of a specially convened Higher Political Committee, chaired by presidents Ahmed Hassan al-Bakr and Hafez Assad; not only was a decision taken that the two countries would become one, they also set up a bilateral commission to draft a single constitution and another committee to coordinate the merger of the two ruling parties. Even this, a unification that seemed to be well underway, did not work out in the end.

To be fair, differences with the local nationalists were this time compounded by disputes between two factions in the Iraqi leadership—those of al-Bakr and those of Saddam Hussein. Saddam claimed to have "uncovered a plot" against him in Baghdad and had the "Syrian agents" close to al-Bakr arrested.

On August 22, Assad phoned Saddam during the night and asked, "What's going on?" Saddam replied: "Nothing in particular." Assad suggested that someone should come to him and explain; Saddam rejected this request. But on August 25, Syrian foreign minister Abdul Halim Khaddam and Syria's chief of military staff went to Baghdad, where they were shown a "plotter who had confessed." Once back in Damascus, Khaddam strongly denied any Syrian link to the events. In response, Saddam decided he would break off contact with the Syrian government. When the Iraqi and Syrian leaders met in Havana, there were offers of mediation from the president of Algeria as well as from Yasser Arafat and King Hussein of Jordan. But Saddam snubbed all attempts to mend fences between himself and Assad. Iraq's Revolutionary Command Council called off the unification process. By August the "plotters" had been shot and relations between the two Ba'athist regimes had again slipped into open confrontation.

Toward the end of the twentieth century, the Arab world had definitively taken the route to multiple statehood rather than a merger into one or several unified states. Will this situation change in light of the growing trend toward integration that has done much to shape the world today? It is certainly true that integration has gained momentum in Latin America and Southeast Asia, not to mention Europe, of course. In the Arab world, however, this shift can be seen only in the countries of the Arabian peninsula, and even they are a long way from creating any national, or supra-national, structures.

Globalization brings a degree of interpenetration between economies. Even nations whose languages and histories are vastly different can feel the shift toward integration. It will eventually reach even the Arab world, or at least parts of it. But not in the near future.

A FAILED MECHANISM FOR UNIFICATION

The Arab League, founded in 1945, failed not only in its mission to create a unified Arab state but even in the secondary mission of establishing an integrated structure under which each country would retain its sovereignty. The idea of setting up a pan-Arab organization originated in London, as part of Britain's plans to maintain its dominance in the Middle East. It is unlikely that the Arab community was aware of these plans; indeed many thought the League represented a serious step toward pan-Arab unity or maybe toward putting a single Arab state on the map of the world, even in the form of a confederation. This was not to be.

Arab League summits often served as forums for letting off steam or ironing out differences. At times the way this took place was the stuff of caricature. A typical example was the summit in Cairo after the Black September of 1970, so-called after the bloody clashes between Jordan and the Palestinians. Libya's Colonel Gaddafi first protested that he would not sit at the same table as a "murderer," by which he meant King Hussein of Jordan. Both reached for their guns, the Saudi king had to restrain them, and then, thanks to intervention by Nasser, everybody hugged one another. But these events had no impact on relations between Arab countries.

Having adopted a pan-Arab position on the Arab-Israeli conflict in 2000, the league showed itself in a positive light when the leaders of Arab nations collectively renounced their longstanding objection to the existence of Israel; they even went as far as to recognize it, not just within the borders drawn up by the UN General Assembly in 1947 but within those to which Israel had expanded during the first Arab-Israeli war in 1948. A meeting of the Arab League approved the principle of "peace for land" put forward by Crown Prince Abdullah of

Saudi Arabia (who was then the country's de facto ruler while King Fahd was ill, and who became king of Saudi Arabia following Fahd's death in 2005). The peace-for-land formula was interpreted as the establishment of peace and diplomatic relations between the Arab countries and Israel, in return for Israel agreeing to return the Arab territories it occupied in the 1967 Six-Day War.

But while it has often played a constructive role, the Arab League has never risen to the task of creating a unified Arab state or any joint umbrella structures between Arab states. Amr Moussa, the League's general secretary, is someone I have known well for a long time, and I value him as an extraordinary professional and a man erudite in many ways. His efforts to bring the Arab world together have been considerable—and that, he told me, is his main objective. But achieving this task is much harder than recognizing the necessity of a union like the Arab League.

In his book, *Nasser: The Last Arab*, Said K. Aburish, one of the Egyptian leader's biographers, writes:

> The pull toward Arab unification was on a collision course with reality, and its romantic appeal to the average Arab was fading from one day to the next. The Lebanese Christians feared they would drown in a sea of Islam that would deprive them of their identity. The Jordanians, whose history was only a short one, did not want to be reduced to the status of a small tribe. The Iraqis were in need of something that could sort out their country's ethnic and religious divide. It would be far worse for the Kurds, for example, to find themselves in one large Arab state than in Iraq. The Syrians rejected anything that detracted from their taking a leading role, because they considered themselves to be truer Arabs than the others. And in Saudi Arabia's case, the fear arose that it would have to share its oil wealth with the poorer Arabs from Egypt, Syria and Jordan.[2]

The gradual snuffing out of the shift toward Arab unification also left its mark on the Arab-Israeli conflict.

Occasionally, support for the Palestinians is diluted by those Arab countries that have diplomatic relations with Israel. There are other criteria, too, as reflected in the conduct of several states. After the conflict between Shiites and Sunnis in U.S.-occupied Iraq, some Arab states occasionally show a pro-Sunni bias in their attitude to Shiite Hizbollah. That is what happened, for example, when Arab League foreign ministers failed to agree to a common position on the events in Lebanon in 2006.

Gone is the time when many people in America, Europe, and elsewhere felt that they had to support any action whatsoever by the Israelis; they, after all, would say it ultimately served to ensure the survival of a state surrounded by one vast Arab world hostile to Israel. Two trends that have also left their mark on Arab-Israeli relations are the emergence of multiple statehood and the fact that each state's interests have taken precedence over Arab unity—ruling out any apocalyptic scenario for Israel. To be sure, Israel's security is still a problem—one crying out for a solution—but it is not the same thing now that the state is no longer identified solely with the problem of its survival.

HOW AZIZ AND KHADDAM CAME TO MOSCOW

America and Russia have taken quite divergent approaches to Arab unity. It seems that both understood the hopelessness of trying to establish large-scale mergers of Arab states. Soviet propaganda often voiced support for Arab unity, but what was envisaged was a coalition of Arabs in a pro-independence struggle against Western attempts to unseat the new revolutionary regimes. At times the Americans too wanted the Arabs to pull closer together, but only at a local level and only on an anti-Nasser or anti-Syrian basis; in other words, they sought to create conditions for attacking nationalist regimes with backing from the conservative, pro-U.S. Arab states.

The Soviet Union never sought to undermine these conservative regimes from within, nor did it try to turn Egypt, Syria, or Iraq against them. On the contrary, Moscow tried on many occasions to overcome disputes between Arab countries—even disputes *within* countries—regardless of where they stood, and not only on issues related to its own Middle East policy. Moscow's refusal to play games with disputes in the Arab world can be illustrated in a number of examples. They include its efforts to prevent a flaring up of differences between Iraq and Syria; its tactics during the Iraqi invasion of Kuwait in 1990; its efforts to end the civil war in Lebanon; and its determination to settle disputes between the Palestinians, Jordanians, and Syrians. It would be wrong to suggest that all these Soviet initiatives were carried out without an eye on Moscow's interests. Of course Moscow had its interests in the Middle East, but they were protected without exploiting the ongoing disputes between Arabs.

I would like to highlight one example that few people know. At the beginning of the 1980s, Moscow's relations with Iraq took a turn for the worse, especially with regard to the Iran-Iraq war; at the same time, the Soviet Union was building better relations with Syria. This came against the backdrop of rapidly escalating tension between Iraq and Syria. Rather than exploit this tension, the Politburo decided to organize a meeting of top-level officials from Iraq and Syria in Moscow, in the hope that it would facilitate a rapprochement between the two countries. Holding such a meeting would enhance the Soviet Union's authority in the Middle East. But the main motivation was to stabilize the situation between Iraq and Syria.

In those days I was director of the Institute of Eastern Studies at the USSR Academy of Sciences. In this capacity I was given the task of organizing the meeting in Moscow, along with talking through all the issues with both Saddam Hussein and Hafez Assad. First I flew to Baghdad. There, on July 6, 1983, I met with Saddam, who agreed straight away to our proposal. That same day, Tariq Aziz, the Iraqi foreign minister, confirmed that there was agreement and told me Saddam had entrusted him with the mission to Moscow, which "had to be strictly confidential."

This was the package I took to Damascus, where I met President Assad on July 10. Assad too gave our proposal the thumbs-up. He was visibly pleased when I told him about Saddam's positive response, but nevertheless asked for four or five days to reach a final decision. He kindly invited me to spend this short break in Latakia, an invitation I was pleased to accept. It gave even greater pleasure to the many people who accompanied me on the trip—members, I was told, of the Syrian president's personal bodyguard.

On July 15 I met again with Assad, who informed me that his envoy to the talks would be Syria's vice premier and foreign minister Abdul Halim Khaddam. We had a long talk, during which Assad shared some thoughts with me. He said Moscow suited him particularly well as a place to hold the talks. Officials from other Arab countries had approached him several times, offering to mediate between Syria and Iraq, but he realized their main concern was to work toward ending the Iran-Iraq war. He asked me if we had let Saddam Hussein know that our talks were not about simply normalizing relations but about improving them. He also asked: "What do you think Iraq expected from these talks when it agreed to them?" I replied—truthfully—that my conversation with Tariq Aziz led me to believe that Iraq was interested in the same thing.

On July 25, 1983, Aziz and Khaddam arrived in Moscow. Their talks were held in one of the government mansions in the Lenin Hills. We deliberately left them alone, but in the evening I stopped in to find them enjoying a game of billiards. It seemed like a good sign. They also talked throughout the next day, and then both Aziz and Khaddam asked if a meeting could be arranged with someone from the top level of the Soviet government. The best person would have been Foreign Minister Andrei Gromyko, but unfortunately he was on vacation in Crimea. It transpired that there was "nowhere to accommodate" the Iraqi and Syrian representatives in Crimea, so they did not make it there either.

This prosaic stumbling block proved fatal for the talks. I was sure that had Gromyko met Aziz and Khaddam, it would have been possible to work toward a solution—if not a definitive one, at least a half-baked one—but a solution nonetheless. But this did not happen. Both sides reported that they had failed to reach agreement on a range of fundamental issues. Yet, at the same time, both Khaddam and Aziz pointed out that their talks had not been without value. Their meeting was kept top secret.

With the end of this last gesture toward unity, two brands of nationalism sank into terminal decline and have since disappeared from

the political scene. There was the failed ideology of pan-Arab nationalism, which collapsed under pressure from individual nations' interests, as well as the secular nationalism of the revolutionary but
noncommunist Arab regimes that had shaken off the yoke of Western
dominance. The end of the twentieth century and the beginning of the
twenty-first have seen a marked mobilization of forces with links to
Islam. The long failure to solve the Arab-Israeli conflict has been instrumental in bringing about this situation, as have the deployment of
Soviet troops in Afghanistan and the U.S.-led invasion of Iraq.

At the same time, a different sort of nationalist is gaining strength
in the Arab world—this one lacking the social orientation of Nasser's
generation of revolutionaries.

The Soviet Union and the Arab World

A Difficult Path to Closer Ties

T HE POLICIES OF THE FORMER colonial powers, and later those of the United States, had the effect of driving a number of Arab countries into partnership with the Soviet Union. So too did the Arab-Israeli conflict. Moscow's stance during critical points of this standoff meant that even the Arab monarchies, with their close ties to the West, came to be favorably disposed toward the Soviet Union. It was, however, the countries led by the nationalist revolutionaries, as well as the Palestinian opposition movement, that entered most fully into partnership with Moscow.

Support for the anticolonial pro-independence movements was one of the ideological pillars of Soviet foreign policy. But the ideology that then ruled the Soviet Union meant that Moscow's relations with the authoritarian regimes of the Arab world, which were not ideologically socialist, developed slowly and were far from easy to maintain.

THE HURDLE OF ANTICOMMUNIST SENTIMENT

In the early days, the overriding factor that determined the Soviet Union's line on any new Arab regime was its relationship with local communist parties. Although this criterion applied for some time, its importance gradually diminished.

Anticommunist sentiment appeared in various forms and to quite differing degrees in Egypt, Syria, and Sudan; but it was especially violent in Iraq. In Yemen too, the procommunist elements were barely tolerated. After the unification in 1990 of Northern and Southern Yemen (the Arab Republic and People's Democratic Republic respectively), the left, which had been in power in the south, was sidelined once and for all. Similarly, the intolerance shown by the Arab countries' new leaders toward local communists never really abated, although it tended to lessen when they were cultivating relations with the Soviet Union.

The communist groups that had evolved in the Arab countries, even under colonial rule, were directly associated with the Soviet Union via Comintern (the Communist International). The Soviet Communist Party's Central Committee had an international department in charge of contacts with all overseas communist parties, and within that department was a section that handled Arab communist parties. The Party greatly valued its status as the center of the world communist movement and attached particular importance to the number of communist parties in the world, even those with few members or little influence.

The Party followed a dogmatic line. It stressed that the independence struggle against the colonial powers would flourish only if led by communists—or at the very least if communists helped lead it. Political systems that dismissed or persecuted their local communist parties were seen as reactionary, regardless of the communists' relationship with the authorities; sometimes they were even dubbed fascist. Not until the latter half of the 1960s did Soviet leaders start to distance themselves from this view, and even then they did it slowly and not very decisively.

While the attitude of Arab regimes toward local communists may have been a prime factor in shaping Soviet policy, Moscow was not guided solely by ideological considerations. Soviet leaders reasoned that anticommunist sentiment weakened the authority of the petit bourgeois (lower middle class) forces, which had alienated a large cross section of the intelligentsia that did not even have any structural association with communist parties. Yet there was no hardening of the Soviet line against all these anticommunist Arab leaders; Moscow had already forced Egypt, Syria, and at times Iraq to back down in their campaigns against communists and other left-wingers.

What also changed the situation was an innovation in the theory of communism put forward in Moscow. A theory was developed under which a country that had liberated itself from colonial rule could in the initial stages set its own course toward communism instead of taking the "traditional" route of the proletarian dictatorship. This is how the "socialist orientation" theory came about. For countries on the road to developing a noncapitalist system, the key criteria became wide-scale nationalization of the means of production—in other words, putting the economy in state hands—and also the setting up of political parties or unions under the banner of socialism. But the theory was not the same thing as "Arab socialism"; while recognizing that Arab countries could develop along noncapitalist lines, it did not remove the question of class struggle. Rostislav Ulyanovsky,[1] deputy head of the international department of the Central Committee of the Soviet Communist Party, played a major role in developing this theory. Several Soviet experts, myself included, also took part in this exercise. The goal of the new theory was to bolster radical regimes in the Middle East and stop local communist parties from attacking them. It was reasoned that these regimes were the ones with the real power: ideology was once again shown to be applied as the "servant" of politics.

Starting in the mid-1960s, a new, more pragmatic party line began to gain momentum in the Soviet Union, in which events in the Middle East were viewed less from the perspective of disputes between the nationalist regimes and communist parties. The Central Committee made clear to these parties' representatives that they had to find accommodation with certain Arab leaders, and advised them to accept that the revolutionary nationalist leaders, not they, were the leading force in the Arab world's pro-independence movement. The communists were essentially invited to work in partnership with Arab nationalists—

whom the Soviets understandably saw as being capable of becoming an even more serious force for revolution.

Apart from the anticommunist sentiment of the Arab nationalist regimes, Soviet relations in the 1950s and early 1960s with these Arab countries were hampered by the cold war. The Soviet Union sought to get the pro-independence movement to side with it in its standoff with the United States. At the same time, as the escalation of the arms race brought the two powers dangerously close to nuclear war, the Soviet Union had a vested interest in the easing of international tensions. But Arab countries, including Egypt, saw the Soviets' interest in détente as hampering their own capacity to benefit from the standoff between the two superpowers.

There were more particular reasons why the sun did not always shine on the Soviet Union's relations with Egypt. Thousands of Soviet consultants—civilian and military—worked there and had brought their families with them. The same was true, though on a smaller scale, in Iraq and Syria. On the whole, Soviet citizens had good relations with the locals, and many kept up lasting friendships. But it wasn't always like that at an official level. There was discontent at Arab dependency on Soviet aid, at experts being "trained by foreigners," and at unwarranted efforts to get results as quickly as possible. Nasser and the other Arab leaders tried to stifle such sentiments.

Some Soviet officials were guilty of arrogant and tactless behavior. One example, during Nikolai Podgorny's January 1971 visit to Cairo, was the Supreme Soviet chairman's "instruction" to President Anwar Sadat: "The time has come for you to get rid of [political commentator Mohamed] Heikal." This was no way to talk about a man who still played a major role in the formation of Egyptian policy. He was, moreover, a friend of Sadat and a figure whose views were far from anti-Soviet.

The attitudes of several of the Arab communist leaders were also unhelpful. Although they had no grounds to do so, they claimed to be the dominant force in any Arab country that had a radical regime. This put some party leaders at odds with the theory of "socialist orientation." Khaled Bakdash, head of the Syrian Communist Party, once told me the theory was "retreat bordering on revisionism." He also criticized the theory publicly, if obliquely. In many cases, the region's communist parties argued that the Soviet Union should go through them to apply its policy in the Middle East, since they and no one else were the allies of the Soviet Communist Party. Because they apparently considered themselves "indispensable" custodians of Soviet policy in the Middle East, some Arab party leaders did not always bother to keep the Soviet leadership informed of their plans, reckoning that on ideological grounds they would always get Moscow's backing.

Of course, it took time for much of this to become clear. But none of it in any way detracts from the selflessness, heroism, and patriotism of thousands of Arab communist party members.

SHEPILOV AND MOSCOW'S U-TURN TOWARD NASSER

When the Free Officers first came to power in Egypt, Moscow's attitude to them could charitably be described as skeptical. Back then, the main consideration in evaluating any new regime was the gap that separated it from the local communists. In Egypt's case that gap was considerable.

The communist movement in Egypt was weak and fragmented. At best, groups had maybe a few hundred members, drawn largely from the liberal intelligentsia. In 1922, after the Egyptian Socialist Party was allowed to join Comintern, it began calling itself the Egyptian Communist Party (ECP) and published its manifesto in the party newspaper *Al-Hisab* (meaning "account") as well as in the Cairo newspaper *Al-Ahram*. Unlike Egypt's mainstream parties, its manifesto set out many policies that were later promoted by the Free Officers regime. Among them was the transfer of the Suez Canal to national ownership.[2]

The ECP did not last long: all its members fell victim to persecution in 1924 after a major strike by textile workers in Alexandria, and its first general secretary, Anton Maroun, died in prison. Egypt's communist movement continued in the form of small groups, and it was not until 1947 that these groups joined forces to create the Movement for National Liberation (Hadetu) with a total membership of about 2 million. Its manifesto talked of fighting for the interests of the working class and said it had chosen the "Marxist-Leninist theory of class struggle as its guiding star." This document, published just one year before the forced abdication of King Farouk, did nothing to endear the Egyptian communists to the Free Officers.

Many Egyptian communists and their sympathizers were honest, well-educated patriots devoted to their country—which became evident in later years when many of these individuals started to work with Nasser's regime. But in the immediate aftermath of Farouk's abdication, relations between the Free Officers and the communists were tense—even though many of Egypt's political prisoners had been released after the coup.

Not all Egyptian communists were in favor of the Free Officers' reforms. Many were too uncompromising to appreciate the merits of the new leadership's first steps. Anwar Malek, a Hadetu activist, dismissed the first phase of land reform as merely restricting private ownership of land instead of abolishing it outright; that, he wrote, was why "the American ambassador was happy with it."

Similarly abstract criticisms, out of touch with the reality in Egypt and often greatly exaggerated, were reported back to Moscow by the Soviet Embassy in Cairo. They chimed in with criticisms from the Syrian, Iraqi, and Lebanese communists. What developed, based on bogus ideological concerns, was a distinctly hostile attitude to the new Egyptian regime. Until the 20th Congress of the Soviet Communist Party in 1956, when Khrushchev made his sensational speech condemning Stalin, the cult of Stalin was sustained even after his death. His ideological legacy was the guiding principle for anyone who had anything to do with the formulation or conduct of Soviet foreign policy. And the thrust of Stalin's short speech at the end of the 19th Party Congress in October 1952 was that the nation's bourgeoisie had "abandoned" the independence struggle; it was a cause that the communists had to pick up.

The Kremlin's change of tack toward Nasser's regime had much to do with Dimitry Trofimovich Shepilov. This educated, decent, strikingly handsome man led a hard life. In 1926, he graduated in law from Moscow State University, and then from the "Red Professors" Institute—one of the most important Bolshevik party educational institutions of the 1920s. During the Second World War, he went to the front to fight as a volunteer, and by the end of the war had been made a major general. For ten years, he worked for *Pravda*, including a spell as the newspaper's editor in chief. He became an associate member of the USSR Academy of Sciences, Secretary of the Central Committee of the Soviet Communist Party, and Soviet Foreign Minister. But at a plenary session of the Central Committee on June 22, 1957, he was accused of belonging to the "anti-party group" of Malenkov, Kaganovich, and Molotov, which had spoken out against Khrushchev. Fired from all the posts he held, Shepilov was expelled from the party and not readmitted for fifteen years.

To get an idea of just how humiliating government service could be for an educated man like Shepilov, one need only consider a diplomatic telegram he received as foreign minister during one of his trips abroad. Signed by Khrushchev and Bulganin, the telegram said: "Before you leave, give those imperialists a smack in the face."

I am quite sure this message was conveyed in a way that avoided such coarse language—without being flattering, either—as Shepilov prepared to head for Cairo in 1955 to attend the celebrations of the third anniversary of the Egyptian revolution. It was the first time a Soviet official had been invited from Moscow to attend an Egyptian event of this kind. Shepilov had been editor of *Pravda* in 1955 but was presented to the Egyptian leadership as chairman of the Supreme Soviet's Foreign Affairs Committee (he had indeed done this job, which was a very important one at the time). The very fact that Shepilov was sent on this trip, and that he flew to Cairo on a scheduled flight with a change of planes in Rome, showed that the Kremlin was reluctant to "upgrade" its relations with Egypt. Shepilov had probably intended to look at the lay of the land and then report back on what he saw. It was a good thing that this task was entrusted to him.

Shepilov's visit to Cairo was closely watched by Valentin Alexandrov, a colleague of mine who was then the Egypt correspondent for the Soviet news agency Tass. Alexandrov's observations are interesting enough to merit dwelling on them in some detail. He tells how Nasser was addressing a rally of thousands to mark the anniversary of the July 22, 1952, revolution. Shepilov was seated in one of the front rows ahead of the rostrum. To his right was Soviet ambassador Daniil Solod; to his left was the Soviet Embassy's minister-counselor Arkady Sobolyev, an excellent Arabic speaker who had taken it upon himself to act as interpreter. In line with Moscow's official policy, the only independence struggle these Soviet diplomats could conceive of was one that involved the local communist party and partnership with the Soviet Union. Since Egypt was pursuing neither of these, there could be no question of recognizing the progressive aspects of Nasser's agenda. Moreover, because power had been seized by the military, which had disbanded parliament and banned political parties, their regime was regarded as bordering on fascist. The Soviet Embassy's assessments of all Nasser's statements had been predominantly skeptical or negative. His calls to arms against foreign dominance were interpreted as the words of a demagogue. These were the attitudes of both Shepilov and the ambassador as they arrived at Takhrir Square.

It was the first time Shepilov had experienced the bewitching effect of Eastern oratory. But the political content of Nasser's speech caught his attention even more. Meanwhile, Ambassador Solod, who did not speak Arabic and was listening to the speech being translated into Russian, kept interjecting with comments to the effect that Nasser was not to be trusted: "Typical demagogue . . . independence—*what* independence? They're running hat-in-hand to the Americans."

Shepilov listened to the ambassador at first, according to Alexandrov, but soon seemed to lose interest in what he was saying; instead, he keenly joined the applause of the audience and before long was applauding virtually every passage of Nasser's speech, which covered Egypt's land reform, its economy, training of its own specialists, and improving education, health care, and the supply of drinking water to remote villages.

When Shepilov first started to applaud, the ambassador stopped making comments, evidently unsure what to make of his behavior—was it just a visiting minister's personal desire to curry favor with the Nasserites? Or was it a sign of a new policy direction in Moscow? Either way, he dropped his expression of disdainful indifference, started to look interested, and joined Shepilov in applauding Nasser's speech, albeit with more restraint.

After the rally Shepilov asked if a personal meeting with the Egyptian president could be arranged. He gave a report on the content of his cordial encounter once he was back in Moscow; that report was not made public. However, it speaks volumes that on leaving Cairo, Shepilov took with him numerous photographs of an Egyptian military parade, which featured a few outdated armored vehicles, and soldiers equipped with rifles that dated back to the First World War.

MIKOYAN'S MISSION:
QASSEM AS AN ALTERNATIVE TO NASSER?

When it came to Iraq, everything was different. The Soviet Union was quick to welcome the 1958 Iraqi revolution, largely because it pulled the rug out from under the Baghdad Pact. The Soviets also benefited from the experience they had gained with Egypt's revolutionary nationalists. In response to the deployment of U.S. Marines in Lebanon and British troops in Jordan, the Soviet defense ministry announced maneuvers by the Black Sea Fleet as well as in the Turkmen and Caucasus regions (which border Iran and the Caspian Sea). These operations were also joined by Bulgaria. The Soviet Union and all other members of the Warsaw Pact immediately recognized the new government under Abdul Karim Qassem—something that the West was in no hurry to do. Britain took an especially hard line, but the U.S. State Department saw things differently, fearing that failure to recognize Qassem would drive Iraq into Nasser's embrace. The Americans' concerns were conveyed to the Foreign Office in London via Lord Hood, the British minister-counselor in Washington. By the start of August 1958 the new Iraqi regime was recognized by Turkey, Iran, Pakistan, and then by Britain and the United States.

On August 4, at a meeting of the Presidium of the Soviet Communist Party (which at that time had replaced the Politburo), Khrushchev said the recognition of Qassem's regime by the Western powers signaled that "they were not minded to launch an attack on the Iraqi Republic nor on any other Arab countries in the Middle East." He continued: "This was our main objective, and since it has been achieved, the order has been given to halt military exercises." Field Marshal Andrei Grechko, who had led the maneuvers, was recalled to Moscow. Later, in 1963, Khrushchev described the Kremlin's tactics to Egypt's Field Marshal Abdel Hakim Amer: "The Soviet Union decided back then to show its support, to stand up for the revolution in Iraq. In order to deter Turkey, Pakistan and Iraq, which could have thwarted the revolution, we conducted military exercises on our borders with Turkey and Iran, as well as on the Bulgarian-Turkish border."

Moscow was supportive of Qassem even when he launched his war against the Kurds. But I think the Soviets were less happy that their rescue of the government in 1959, during the anti-Qassem Ba'athist revolt in Mosul, was accompanied by the bloody persecution of Iraqi communists. The revolt had the support of Nasser, who suddenly took a much harsher line against the communists, many of whom were arrested in both the Egyptian and Syrian parts of the UAR. This started to affect Nasser's relationship with the Soviet Union. The Egyptian leader was pointedly showing that he could overcome the rift that had opened between Egypt and the United States just before the foundation of the UAR. It could not have gone down too well when Nasser refused Moscow's request to let Soviet officials examine all the documents that had been transferred to Cairo from the headquarters of the Baghdad Pact after the coup in Iraq. The Egyptian government said it was willing to hand over only a few extracts. I would not be surprised if Egypt also let the Americans know it had done this. Whatever the truth, Mohamed Heikal comments that the refusal was prompted by a desire to not let the United States think that Egypt had become a "Soviet puppet"—and that this would sour Egypt's future relations with Washington.

We can imagine the reaction in Moscow too when it transpired that Nasser had ordered the distribution of an Arabic-language pamphlet, published in the United States, about the Soviet Union's "bloody actions" in Hungary in 1956.

Soviet-Egyptian relations deteriorated into a bitter public row that went right to the top of government. It was against this backdrop that the Soviet leadership started to think it ought to give precedence to General Qassem. Even the Soviet deputy premier, Anastas Mikoyan, a man of great intelligence and an experienced diplomat, had this to say to Qassem when he was in Baghdad on April 14, 1960: "We support and always have supported the independent Republic of Iraq and highly value its policy of positive neutrality." This assessment was correct, but Mikoyan went on to elaborate his thinking:

> We hope this policy will serve as an example to other countries. It gives your authority an even greater boost among the other Arab nations. Nasser wanted to unite the Arab countries—he managed to lure Syria, but has treated it very badly, and now there are no others wanting to join him. He has totally lost his way and has decided to declare war on communism; he has launched an anti-communism campaign—but this will undermine his authority even more. Nasser wanted to do the same with the Iraqi Republic as he did with Syria.[3]

"If you handle matters well and handle them correctly on a democratic basis," Mikoyan told Qassem, "it will be of great significance for the entire Middle East. Its peoples will compare you to Nasser, but it won't be a comparison that casts Nasser in a favorable light."

In the end, both sides saw a need for restoring and building on Soviet-Egyptian relations. Nasser made gestures of reconciliation by releasing the communists who had been jailed and by implementing a series of economic measures that favored the masses. He was also convinced that the West, including the United States, could never be allies with an independent Egypt. On Moscow's part, it was increasingly reckoned that Nasser was destined for a political future as the leader of Egypt and as a leader acknowledged across the Arab world. What also helped the Soviet Union return to a policy of building bridges with Egypt was a rejection of dogmatic notions about the "ideological purity" of a leader like Nasser.

It could be said that from the collapse of the unified Egyptian-Syrian state until Nasser's death, the Soviet Union never sought any alternative bases of support among the radical Arab regimes. This policy remained constant, despite some clashes and downturns in Soviet-Egyptian relations. Although it did build multilateral relations with Syria and Iraq, Moscow did not do so in a way that interfered with building a partnership with Egypt.

In Iraq, meanwhile, Qassem quickly established a dictatorship, causing a crisis to begin brewing in the country. Anti-Qassem sentiment grew rapidly in the army, which he had seen as one of his power bases. He also clashed increasingly with his former comrade Colonel Arif, who now headed the opposition. Arif was fired from all his posts and sentenced to death; he went into exile. Qassem pardoned him, but Arif secretly returned to Iraq and led a plot to depose him. The domestic crisis allowed the Iraqi Communist Party to regroup, strengthen its position and turn into a serious political force bolstered by increasing popular support. It was this, not Qassem's dictatorial behavior, that had caused alarm in Washington and London.

In spring 1959 the United States and Britain came to the conclusion that Qassem was "sliding toward the extreme left." Yet by this time the Iraqi leader had already changed tactics—communists were being arrested, and a bloody war was launched against the Kurds in the north of Iraq. Still, the new Qassem was no more to Washington's or London's liking than the old one.

It was then that the young Saddam Hussein joined the plot to assassinate Qassem. Speaking to reporters in the mid-1980s, CIA veteran Miles Copeland said that after Qassem seized power, the CIA had maintained "very close contact" with the Ba'ath Party. Saddam was housed in an apartment on Baghdad's Al-Rashid Street, next door to the Iraqi Defense Ministry. Adel Darwish, author of *Unholy Babylon: The Secret History of Saddam's War*, is satisfied that the CIA was fully briefed on all aspects involved in the planning of the assassination attempt, and that Saddam's CIA contact was an Iraqi dentist, who also worked for Egyptian intelligence.

The actual assassination attempt failed: General Qassem's chauffeur was killed while Qassem himself, who threw himself onto the floor of his car, was only wounded in the hand. Saddam, who suffered a bullet wound in the leg when he was accidentally shot by another of the would-be assassins, managed to escape with the help of the CIA and Egyptian intelligence. He fled first to his hometown of Tikrit, then to Syria, where Egyptian agents helped him to reach Beirut. There the local CIA station took him under its wing, paying for his apartment and other everyday expenses. Some time later, the CIA helped transfer Saddam to Cairo. In 1963, he returned to Iraq, where he headed the Ba'ath Party's intelligence operations.

In February 1963, Qassem was taken prisoner and executed after a coup that CIA agents working under the cover of the U.S. Embassy had helped to plan. He was soon officially replaced by Colonel Arif.

The Ba'athist takeover in Iraq was marked by a wave of bloody reprisals in which thousands of Communist Party members and their sympathizers were slaughtered. National Guard troops would burst into people's homes and kill them there or on the street. Lists of communists and their addresses had been painstakingly drawn up by the CIA.

With the Ba'athists' orgy of violence against the communists, the Soviet Union's relations with Iraq became practically nonexistent. My late friend Oleg Kovtunovich once told me an anecdote that illustrates the unconcealed hostility of the Soviet leadership to Abdul Salam Arif, whose first weeks in power had been marked by this anticommunist bloodbath. Kovtunovich, who was minister-counselor at the Soviet Embassy in Egypt, was interpreting a conversation between Khrushchev and Nasser in 1964. It took place after ceremonies at Aswan to mark the damming of the Nile, and both leaders had decided to relax by taking a trip on the yacht *Houria* to do some fishing; they were in high spirits. Nasser decided to introduce Khrushchev to Iraq's President Arif, who was also on board.

Nasser described Arif as a "patriot" who was trying to "mend fences with the Soviet Union" and who wished to "rebuild relations afresh by turning the page on this terrible episode."

Khrushchev, never one to mince words, replied: "Why I wouldn't even piss in the same field as him!" When Oleg faltered in his translation of this expression, Khrushchev yelled at him: "Translate it word for word!" Nasser later managed somehow to smooth over the situation.

THE BREAKTHROUGH WITH THE SYRIAN BA'ATH PARTY

Whether the Soviet Union would have warmer relations with Syria depended on how the Soviet leadership perceived the Syrian Ba'athists—the Party of Arab Socialist Renaissance (PASR)—in Damascus. Its early reaction was shaped by the impression that the Syrian Ba'athists supported their Iraqi counterparts' policy of violent persecution of communists. Nor did it help that the Syrian PASR was viewed at the time as a single entity with no dissenting factions.

In October 1965, just a few months after I had taken up my post as *Pravda* correspondent in Cairo, the newspaper sent me to Damascus. My trip yielded an article in *Pravda* under the headline "Multi-Story Damascus." The piece opened by describing how the height of buildings in the Syrian capital was restricted to that of the minarets of local mosques, so instead they extended underground by a few floors, but not just in the form of cellars. There would be spaces around these floors allotted to growing flowers or shrubs—distinctive little gardens set well below the ground floor. From a distance, it was hard to make out how many floors there were in buildings like these—you could see it only by coming right up close. In my mind I came to associate this utterly eccentric architecture with the Syrian Ba'ath Party. In those days *Pravda* set the tone for the entire Soviet press, and "Multi-Story Damascus" was the paper's first article on diversity and progressive elements within the Syrian Ba'ath Party.

The article was based on my conversations with several Ba'athists in Damascus. One of them was Khalid al-Jundi, chairman of the General Federation of Trade Unions. He told me that as a Ba'athist he openly contrasted his point of view on the future development of Syria with the platform of his party's founders, Salah Bitar and Michel Aflaq. I later met his brother Abdel Karim al-Jundi. He too stressed the need for a break with stagnation, the need to transform agriculture in the interests of the peasants—he was adamant that land had to be taken away from landowners and that peasants' cooperatives be set up. Both brothers and many others were firmly opposed to the anti-communism at the top of the PASR. I later found out that after my article came out, many in the party had wanted to expel Khalid al-Jundi, but they did not succeed in doing so before the coup took place on February 23, 1966; Bitar's government was toppled and the left wing of the party, to which both brothers belonged, took over in Damascus.

Vasily Kuznetsov, the Soviet Union's deputy foreign minister, went to see Colonel Nasser just as the Egyptian intelligence services informed their president of the coup. The information genuinely alarmed Nasser, and he shared his news with Kuznetsov. After his audience with the Egyptian president, the minister passed the news on to the heads of the Soviet Embassy in the presence of a certain *Pravda* correspondent in Cairo. According to the information received, he said, there had been a violent takeover of power in Damascus by those who were unhappy with Bitar's recent efforts to improve relations with Cairo, and that Bitar had been ousted. Using Nasser's words, Kuznetsov described the new regime as right-wingers and "opponents of Nasserite Egypt."

That day the deputy editor of *Pravda* phoned me with instructions to fly to Damascus. This was no easy matter. There were no scheduled flights to Damascus, so I flew to Beirut, where I joined some Czech and Polish journalists to journey to the Syrian border by car. The border turned out to be closed: the authorities would admit only Syrian citizens who were returning home. So we went back to Beirut empty-handed. Then I decided to take a flight from Beirut to Baghdad on a Czech airplane that had to make a routine stop in Damascus. I was warned that I would not be able to stay in Syria, and that is almost how it turned out—at the Damascus airport a Syrian officer notified me that I would be sent straight back to Beirut. The officer nevertheless allowed me to phone the man I had met on my previous trip to Damascus, Abdel Karim al-Jundi. It turned out that al-Jundi was now in charge of the Syrian Special Forces. The astonished officer obligingly put me in the car that al-Jundi sent, and there I was in Damascus.

My "Multi-Story Damascus" article had helped open doors to the people who were now in power. So I was the first foreigner to be invited to talk to Prime Minister Yusuf Zuaiyin; let us stop to consider my meeting with him on March 3. Even before this, my talks with the al-Jundi brothers, with the leaders of the Syrian Communist Party and with Ibrahim Makhus, the country's foreign minister, had allowed me to see that the people now in power in Syria were neither right-wingers nor anti-Nasserites. On the contrary, they were opponents of the Ba'ath Party's right-wing leadership and were trying to instill good relations with Egypt. For this reason, after hearing Zuaiyin's account of his government's progressive intent, I said to him: "Tomorrow, as far as I know, you will be calling a press conference. I have accurate information to suggest that Cairo sees you as an enemy of Nasser's Egypt. I think it would be helpful to refute this speculation, to refute it categorically." The next day, Zuaiyin did just that. I was glad to have done even a little bit to prevent disagreement between Egypt and Syria.

But the Kremlin's view of Syria was evidently still influenced by Nasser's initial judgments. *Pravda* did not publish two of my early reports that cast events in Syria in a markedly positive light. Publication of my interview with Zuaiyin was held up. The Soviet ambassador to Damascus at the time, Anatoly Barkovsky, was also fretting about the reaction of the Soviet Foreign Ministry to the impartial reports he was sending. After he and I had had a long discussion about developments in Syria, he cabled Moscow with a proposal to have me report to the ministry. On March 11, at *Pravda*'s behest, I flew to Moscow and on the following day appeared before the Communist Party Central Committee to report back on the discussions and impressions I had had in Syria. Barkovsky and I were naturally pleased with the initiative he had taken; he was sent confirmation from the ministry that his reports on Syria were accurate, and my articles made it into *Pravda*. On March 24 I flew back to Damascus.

Of course there were still clouds looming over Syria, but it had become clear that the forces now in power there were willing to develop close relations with the Soviet Union. However, relations between the two countries did not really take off until 1970, with the ascent of an even more radical regime under Hafez Assad.

My first meeting with Assad had been in March 1966. After the February 23 coup and my meeting with Prime Minister Zuaiyin, I was invited to a rally marking the anniversary of the Ba'ath Party's founding. There on the stage were the new leaders. I was introduced to Assad, then commander of the Syrian air force, who arrived during the event and climbed up onto the platform. With him were a group of men wielding machine guns and keeping a sharp eye on the people passing in front of the stage—things had still not settled down after the February coup, the bloodiest Syria had ever seen.

President Assad was genuinely surprised when I interviewed him in the 1970s and reminded him of how we first met: "Are you really that same correspondent from *Pravda* whom I met back then at the rally?" he asked.

– 6 –

THE LOST CAUSE OF
COMMUNISM

ALTHOUGH THE SOVIET LEADERSHIP of the 1950s and 1960s was inclined to support the Arab countries' local communist parties, nothing could mask the reality that communism was a lost cause in the Middle East. As I have mentioned, it took a while for this to be understood in Moscow, and the Kremlin was slow to show support for the Arab revolutionary nationalists. Nevertheless that support did materialize, and those who believed there was even the slightest chance of keeping communists or procommunist forces in power in the Arab world may have had their doubts erased once and for all by events in Sudan and Southern Yemen.

COMMUNIST OPPOSITION TO NIMEIRI IN SUDAN

I first visited Sudan in January 1966, some time after General Ibrahim Abboud's military dictatorship had been toppled. Power was now in the hands of the National Unionist Party (NUP) and the more reactionary Umma party. After the military regime was disbanded, the Sudanese Communist Party (SCP) was a legal entity for several months; but shortly before my visit a law had been passed banning the party. It had gone underground again while managing to retain substantial influence in the country. The ruling parties totally denied the SCP any place in Sudan's political life.

Nevertheless, hostility toward local communists did not affect efforts to build relations with the Soviet Union by those at the top of the NUP and among Umma's more reform-minded members (such people did exist). I heard this from NUP chairman Ismail al-Azkhari as well as from the thirty-year-old Umma leader Siddiq al-Mahdi—both focal figures for the "reformists" in their parties. Meanwhile, when I visited Sudan's minister of information—a member of the Umma faction—I saw on his desk a photo of his son, a history student at Leningrad University. "I sent him to study in London," the minister said, "but he wanted to study in the Soviet Union." I was also told that in November 1965, crowds of demonstrators had gathered in the Sudanese capital chanting anticommunist slogans. Yet a few days later, at the opening of the Soviet Cultural Center in Khartoum, Umma chairman Siddiq al-Mahdi delivered a speech full of warm praise for the Soviet Union.

On May 25, 1969, a group of army officers led by Jaafar Nimeiri seized power in a military coup. Right away, *Pravda* sent me to interview the victorious new leaders as well as those of the Sudanese Communist Party. So I flew to Khartoum from Cairo, and on May 29 I met the SCP secretary Abdelkhalid Mahjoub. This is what he told me (I quote from my own notes):

The new regime is a progressive one. The coup was planned and executed with the involvement of a group of communists in the army. But the communists do not intend to get swallowed up in the revolutionary council set up by Nimeiri. And while several communists have been allowed to join the government, it is in a personal capacity—based on what the prime minister said were their personal merits. The comrades they chose are not bad, but they were appointed without consulting the central committee of the SCP. We will continue to fight for there to be a link between those in power and the revolutionary people they govern; for that to happen, there needs to be equal partnership with the Communist Party, which is at the moment the only real force capable of working with the popular masses.

The phrase "equal partnership" grated somewhat, and my doubts grew stronger after I talked with General Nimeiri himself.

We met the next day, May 30, at the general military staff headquarters. The person who helped me become the first foreigner to meet the leader of the revolution was my colleague Shota Kurdgelashvili, an outstanding Eastern affairs expert and head of the Soviet Cultural Center in Khartoum. He had excellent relations with many Sudanese who were close to the new regime. It was only the fifth day after the old order had been overthrown, and the new one had not yet fully stabilized. It faced active opposition from both Umma and from the Popular Democratic Party, which led Sudan's two biggest religious groups.

A tired-looking figure in a khaki shirt, his eyes red from lack of sleep, came out toward me on a balcony inside the general staff building. It was General Nimeiri. We introduced ourselves and he agreed to let me ask a few questions, the answers to which would be published in *Pravda*. My interview with him had to be sent via a secure telegram system through a contact at the Soviet Embassy. There was no other way as the telephones were not working in Khartoum. It was probably the only time that a diplomatic telegram—with my questions and Nimeiri's answers—got stamped "for publication in *Pravda*" by the Soviet Communist Party's all-powerful ideology chief and party secretary, Mikhail Suslov.

The interview reflects the ideas that Nimeiri's regime brought with it when it took power—this is a judgment shared by my close colleague Ahmed Hamroush, who had flown with me from Cairo to hold talks with Nimeiri and bring him a message from Colonel Nasser. I present the interview word for word:

YEVGENY PRIMAKOV: Could you outline the basics of the current situation in Sudan?

JAAFAR NIMEIRI: The new regime is stabilizing. We have managed to take the running of the country into our hands. The regime we ousted was rotten to its core. We have the support of the overwhelming majority of the people. We are full of resolve to crush all forces that act against the people. The revolution must be defended.

We must not allow the south of Sudan[1] to be turned into a base for counter-revolution. We have spent hours meeting the government to discuss this subject. The problem in the south is a complicated one—one that cannot be solved in a day or two. But we have set ourselves the goal of settling the situation, and we will do that. We will grant national rights within the framework of a united Sudanese state to the tribes of the south, who are all ethnically, religiously and linguistically different. They will be offered a form of autonomy. We can draw on the example of many countries and how they have settled their nationalities question, including the Soviet Union.

YP: What form could Sudan's domestic development take in the near future?

JN: After we came to power on May 25, we banned rallies and protests so that the reaction could not be used to cause trouble or rioting. But we do not think we can govern the country by purely administrative methods. We do not envisage a future without widespread participation by the people or without a united front being shown by all progressive forces, including the Sudanese Communist Party. That will involve taking all of Sudan's nationality and religious differences into account.

YP: What steps does your government plan for building Sudan's economy?

JN: The Revolutionary Council was set up to ensure that the country develops along progressive lines. Practical measures, including those to do with the economy, will be handled by the civilian government. The main objective is to overhaul an extremely backward national economy, and in order to do so, Sudan has enormous natural resources at its disposal. Economic development must serve the people; the government's very first step— lowering prices on essential goods such as salt, tea and coffee—showed that we care about the people.

We plan to reorganize the existing body that oversees cotton production. The new administrative structure will have a sound economic basis that meets the needs of the state and of tenant farmers. The government has decided to write off the debts previously owed by peasants who rent land to grow cotton.

In their bid to undermine our revolution, reactionary elements are trying to sow seeds of doubt among the masses, spreading rumors to the effect that the government is planning to nationalize private property. These rumors are false. The revolutionary government is conscious of the role of Sudanese and foreign capital in the economy, and realizes that our country will have multi-layered economy in which the state sector must, over time, take the dominant position.

This is how the general answered my question on Sudan's foreign policy:

We will stand side-by-side with all forces that are fighting colonialism. One of our new leadership's first diplomatic moves was to recognize the German Democratic Republic [the former East Germany]. The Sudanese people feel very grateful to the Soviet Union for its enormous support in the pro-independence struggle, in the Arabs' battle for their rights against the forces of imperialism. We see our future as one of multilateral partnership with all friendly countries, including the Soviet Union.

I remember well my sense of satisfaction at hearing this. I stayed behind with Nimeiri a few minutes longer, while a hot dark night seemed suddenly to fall upon Khartoum and they started putting out folding beds on the balcony. Members of the Revolutionary Council were staying here both day and night, taking only a few short hours for sleep. Outside, at the barrier blocking the gate, armored cars took up their positions.

Unfortunately, many of the ideas Nimeiri expressed in the interview never became a reality, not least because of a sectarian line taken by the leadership of the SCP. Alongside that policy, there were acts of genuine heroism from Sudanese communists who were willing to make sacrifices, even to sacrifice themselves, for the sake of the nation's people.

Nimeiri finally abandoned the ideas he had originally advocated after he managed—not without great difficulty—to crush the plot against him in 1971. The conspirators included leaders of the SCP.

The Soviet Union had gone to great lengths to take Arab communist parties under its wing. But these parties did not always let the Soviets know what their plans were—especially if those plans included overthrowing regimes that had close ties with Moscow. When the leaders of the Sudanese party took part in the 1971 plot to oust Nimeiri, whose government had built a close partnership with the Soviet Union, they kept their intentions hidden. There were many Soviet advisers in Sudan, including in the army, which was equipped with modern Soviet weaponry.

For the Sudanese party to have taken part in the plot to oust Nimeiri strikes me as adventurist. After being arrested by the conspirators, Nimeiri was set free by his supporters, and the ringleaders of the plot against him were given the death sentence. Boris Ponomarev, who headed the International Department of the Soviet Communist Party and was in Cairo at the time, went to see President Sadat accompanied by the ambassador. Ponomarev saw his mission as urgent enough to merit calling on Sadat late at night. He asked the Egyptian president to get in touch with Nimeiri so as to prevent the death sentence being carried out on Abdelkhalik Mahjoub, secretary of the Sudanese Communist Party, and a number of other party leaders. But Nimeiri answered, "Too late, they've already been executed."

After his dramatic return to power, Nimeiri's policies took a sharp turn to the right in both domestic and foreign arenas. Sudan's chances of developing along democratic lines were over. He turned his back on the progressive economic reforms that had been launched not much earlier. There was also an intensification of moves to Islamicize the country; Nimeiri declared that from then on, Sudan's legislation would be related to Sharia law. But with a battered economy, the resurgence of war in the south and growing sociopolitical instability, he was forced out of office by a bloodless coup in April 1985 and emigrated to Cairo. His exit was followed by a string of leadership changes in Sudan, and religious leaders asserted their influence on all spheres of life. The National Islamic Front was founded, headed by Sheik Hassan al-Tourabi, who was simultaneously chairman of parliament and general secretary of the ruling National Congress Party.

Al-Tourabi's decade of de facto rule, from 1989 to 1999, saw Sudan turn into a haven for Islamic extremists. The country was blacklisted by the United States as a sponsor of terrorism. And after he was stripped of Saudi citizenship, the al-Qaeda chief Osama bin Laden spent several years in Sudan—as, it is suspected, did the terrorist Carlos "the Jackal." In December 1999, Sudan's military command, led by President/General Omar al-Bashir, forced al-Tourabi to relinquish all positions of authority in an effort to bring the battered country out of international isolation and to end the war in the south. The country gradually started to recover.

SOUTHERN YEMEN: A DESTRUCTIVE LURCH TO THE HARD LEFT

The political theory to which the Soviet Union gave birth envisaged two stages in the development of a noncapitalist or socialist-oriented society: first national-democratic and then popular-democratic— rather closer to socialism. The People's Democratic Republic of Yemen was one of the "second generation of socialist-oriented countries" insofar as it had won independence under the leadership of a revolutionary group whose aim from the outset had been the creation of a socialist society. Both during its fight for independence and in its plans to build a new state, the leading force that emerged was committed to (scientific) socialism.

This could not fail to kindle hopes within the Soviet Union that an Arab country would join the socialist camp, and that that country would be the People's Democratic Republic of Yemen. These hopes were not to be realized. The methods used to build socialism and put it into practice in the Soviet Union and elsewhere could not survive

Yemeni society's demands and vested interests. I do not wish to dissect the pluses and minuses of those methods. Besides, it is worth pointing out that the example of Southern Yemen showed the perils of making a "leap" to socialism without taking account of the country's socioeconomic and political situation.

On October 14, 1963, an anticolonial uprising began in Southern Yemen. It was led by the National Front (NF), which declared the building of socialism to be its ultimate goal. Years of armed conflict followed, and on November 30, 1967, Southern Yemen proclaimed its independence from the British protectorate. The new government, made up of NF members, was backed by the country's peasants, its small working class, its middle class, the intelligentsia, and the Popular Democratic Union, an international group founded in the early 1960s by Abdul Baazib. The left-wingers, who dominated the leadership at the time, were based in Southern Yemen itself, while general secretary Qahtan Muhammad al-Shaabi and his associates were based in Cairo.

Even before independence was won, serious disagreements started to appear. That the first government was made up of moderates only worsened these disagreements. With backing from Egypt, al-Shaabi became prime minister. At the NF's fourth congress, early in March 1968, the front's left wing, headed by culture minister Abdel Fattah Ismail, made a series of demands: the immediate introduction of land reform, the creation of state-run industries, the disbanding of the old police force and army, and the formation of a people's revolutionary army. Many of these demands were adopted by the congress; they were not, however, put into practice because of pressure from high-ranking military officers on the right, who attempted to stage a coup d'état.

Early in 1968 I went to Aden, where I met Baazib, Fattah Ismail, President al-Shaabi, and Muhammad Avlaqi, general secretary of the Aden Congress of Trade Unions. I came away with the strong impression that the leftists were trying to force reforms in all spheres of the nation's life, even though there were no real grounds for such a radical approach. Under British rule the tribal system in the south of Yemen had eroded far more than in the north, but the sultans, or feudal chieftains, still wielded considerable power. The closure of the Suez Canal after it was nationalized had left tens of thousands out of work in Aden, and before they pulled out, the British had given officers and soldiers a threefold pay rise. Officers received more than £200, and regular soldiers £60 to £80—huge amounts for Aden at the time. The result was an army caste that naturally tried to block any activity that could undermine it. Local residents were subjected to radio propaganda from Saudi Arabia warning that social reforms "could lead to the rejection of Islam."

Fattah Ismail ignored all this and told me, "Since we have chosen the path of scientific socialism, the Soviet Union owes us a helping hand. That way it would also be helping itself, while we devote ourselves to socialist reform. It is essential for the defense of the revolution too. Now that the front enjoys widespread popular support, we must set up a political party. It is our duty to put the republican regime in the north [the Yemen Arab Republic] on the right path too. They must give the people greater opportunities for republican revolutionary ideas to be made flesh."

President al-Shaabi was a great deal more cautious, both about the reforms planned in the south and about relations with the north. He spoke of the need for a step-by-step approach to solving problems, of the need for experiment. Stressing how "terribly backward" the country was, he said: "We want to take a chance on offering concessions to foreign companies, including those from friendly countries, but not on unequal terms as it was in the past . . . The state will govern overseas trade but only in the future. What we must do first of all is devote our attention to social development in the country—some villages don't even have wells of drinking water. We are counting on aid from the Soviet Union, but our main concern is that that aid should not affect our freedom or sovereignty." What al-Shaabi was talking about was neither socialism nor Marxism-Leninism.

As I leaf through the yellowed pages of my notebooks from this era, it occurs to me time and again that there was absolutely no basis for al-Shaabi to be categorized as a "right-wing opportunist." This is how many leftist elements in Southern Yemen labeled him, as did some in the Soviet Union. Al-Shaabi had a better feeling for the lay of the land than many others, and he was less prone to being swayed by dogma. The position of the NLF's left wing did not change even after Fattah Ismail, its leader, dissociated himself from the hard-line extremist faction following a fierce political battle. The extremists had tried to seize power by force in their bid to bring about immediate socialist reforms across the board. After their mutiny was crushed, many hard-liners fled abroad.

During the first two years of independence, Ismail and his associates managed to strengthen their position. On June 22, 1969, they seized power, accusing al-Shaabi of having breached the principle of collective leadership. The former president was arrested, and in summer 1970 he was killed "during an attempt to escape." There was then a purge of the officer corps and the state apparatus.

The Yemen Socialist Party (YSP) was founded in 1968. The announcement of the new party was postponed—again, it must be noted, by substantial disagreements between the groups of which the party was composed. Moreover, relations within the party were increasingly affected by tribal affiliations. One prominent faction was led by Salem Ali Rubayi (Salmeen), a figure backed by tribes from three provinces. With their support, Salmeen resolved to remove Ismail from the presidential council and take power into his own hands. But his plot was discovered, and Salmeen was executed. In the party press, Salmeen's faction was simultaneously accused of "leftist deviations" and "coalescence with right-wing opportunism."

After the failure of Salmeen's plot, there was a power struggle between Ismail and Ali Nasser Muhammad. Muhammad emerged the victor, and Ismail was forced to make a written request to be allowed to step down "for health reasons." The party's central committee dismissed Ismail from all his high-ranking party and state posts, and he emigrated to Moscow. Ali Nasser Muhammad became general secretary of the YSP while also remaining chairman of the Council of Ministers (prime minister). Before long he was also elected chairman of the Supreme People's Council. As often happens, the one removed from power was blamed for everything from attempts to unite the south and north of Yemen by military force to economic blunders. Meanwhile, it was clear that the main reason for the schism that divided the left was not a few differences between its leaders of the left but a simple quest for power.

In January 1983, Fattah Ismail arrived in Aden, having received an invitation to return to his homeland and join the party leadership. The decision to invite him had been taken by Nasser Muhammad, ostensibly in the interests of party unity—but the true reason for the invitation soon became all too clear. At the very first session of the Politburo of the Yemen Socialist Party, Fattah Ismail and his followers were shot dead. The drama did not end there: bloody fighting broke out across Aden, killing ten thousand people. Nasser Muhammad's followers were defeated, while he himself managed to flee north—to the Yemen Arab Republic.

In December 2005, after an absence of many years, I had the chance to pay a visit to Yemen, to both Sana'a and Aden. I had a meeting with Ali-Abdullah Saleh, president of the Republic of Yemen, and with prime minister Abdel Qader Badjamal. One of the subjects that cropped up in conversation with the prime minister was the country's past. Badjamal had been elected to the central committee of the Yemen Socialist Party in 1980 and had later become minister for industry and chairman of the petroleum and mineral resources committee. But in January 1986 he was accused of fraternizing with Nasser Muhammad and jailed for three years. This relatively mild sentence, when dozens were being executed, suggests that Badjamal did not take direct part in any "factional activity"—but he did spend three years in prison. Badjamal told me that the leftist ways of the government at the time had reached the point where prisoners were indiscriminately banned from reading the Koran or any books containing religious subject matter, and were forced to study Marxist literature instead.

After unification in 1990, Badjamal was elected to the Republic of Yemen parliament, and became a member of the permanent committee of the ruling General People's Congress Party. This educated economist spoke of the utterly unjustified sacrifices caused by the leftist deviations of Southern Yemen's leaders. "The real revolution," he said, "began with unification between north and south."

Yemen, of course, is still an underdeveloped country with a largely tribal social structure. But big changes have taken place over the past fifteen years: widespread construction in towns and cities, a visible increase in the number of cars on the roads. Many of its professional class studied in the Soviet Union, and some members of the government completed their higher education in Eastern Europe. I was told that five government ministers speak Russian.

It was very bad that the Soviet press typically avoided any criticism of Arab communist parties. The only harsh judgments to be heard were aimed at groups that chose the Chinese as their guiding stars in the ideological battle raging between the Soviet Union and China. But among the Arab communists, these were very few. Maybe the ideological standoff between the Soviet and Chinese parties was what impeded even oblique criticism of the Arabs' "own" pro-Soviet parties.

The communist movement in the Arab world disappeared from the political scene even before the Soviet Communist Party ceased to function, before the demise of the Soviet Union. But it would be wrong to conclude that the communist movement of the Arab world has played no part in its history. Despite all its mistakes and difficulties, it paved the way for moderate forces to evolve across all Arab nations.

AMERICA STEPS FORWARD

AFTER THE SECOND WORLD WAR, America's chief objective in the Middle East was to maintain control of the region's vast petroleum resources. But its continuing standoff with the Soviet Union gave rise to an additional strategic objective: to establish a U.S. military foothold close to the borders of the USSR. The two goals were not always complementary. The U.S. gamble was to build stronger ties with the Arab monarchies, since it was on their territories that the major oil deposits were to be found. But this tactic required some deft maneuvering. For example, although it not only supported the Baghdad Pact but had helped create it using Britain as a conduit, the United States found that it could not itself join the alliance without unduly complicating its relationship with Saudi Arabia, which had a far from untroubled relationship with Iraq's Hashemites. Efforts to build bridges with Nasser's Egypt had also constrained the United States from having a direct military presence in the Middle East. But by the end of 1956, this would change. In the aftermath of the Suez conflict, there was a rising tide of sympathy for Egypt and the Arab nationalist cause throughout the so-called Third World; the influence that Nasser's Egypt exerted in the Arab world was growing stronger—dangerously so, from an American perspective. It was against this backdrop that the Eisenhower Doctrine was declared in January 1957.

THE EISENHOWER DOCTRINE:
AN END TO THE COURTING OF ARAB NATIONALISM

The Eisenhower Doctrine stated the United States's determination to protect the countries of the Middle East against communism and its agents. To this end, it was willing to use all means—even direct interference in the affairs of sovereign countries. I do not believe that Washington had simply failed to understand that there was no real threat of communism taking hold in the Middle East at the time. The Eisenhower Doctrine was designed to win the support of America's allies in the anticommunist Arab kingdoms—who at the same time would not look kindly on the doctrine if it were seen to be targeted at any one Arab country. Yet judging by its content, the circumstances in which it appeared, and the events that followed its proclamation, the doctrine was very much aimed at neutralizing the influence of Nasser's Egypt, "a Soviet ally in the Middle East." At the same time, it provided a means for the United States to project power in the Middle East directly, without having to use Britain or France as a go-between.

On March 31, 1957, three months after the doctrine was declared, the Soviet ambassador visited the Egyptian president at his country residence in Barraj. Nasser told him about his latest exchanges with the United States. The American ambassador had just returned from Washington, where he had evidently received new instructions. When Nasser told him that he was "striving to improve relations with the U.S.," the ambassador, speaking "in the name of President Eisenhower," replied, "While you, the Egyptian government, remain close to the Soviet Union, we can neither offer you aid nor seek to improve our relations." To which Nasser replied, "The U.S. wants to drive us to suicide—first to reject friendly relations with the Soviet Union, then to go hat-in-hand to Eisenhower so the U.S. can get us in a stranglehold and dictate its conditions to us."

With America thus ending its flirtation with Nasser's nationalist regime, U.S. foreign policy became increasingly focused on Israel. Israel had grown in importance for the United States, and not just because steadfast support for its government was one of the cornerstones of Washington's official Middle East policy. Israel had become a direct ally in the cold war as well. The Arab-Israeli wars provided American manufacturers with opportunities to see the latest U.S. weaponry tried and tested on the battlefield. After each of these conflicts, Israel promptly provided the United States with any Soviet military hardware it had captured. Israel used other means to obtain Soviet weapons for the United States as well—in 1965, an Iraqi pilot recruited by Israeli intelligence defected with a Soviet MIG-21 aircraft, which was handed over to the United States in return for a million dollars and political asylum for the pilot's family. Meir Amit, the head of Mossad, told CIA director Richard Helms that the Americans could now form a realistic picture of the military capabilities of the Soviet MIGs and fine-tune their own aircraft accordingly. Another plane, a MIG-23, was delivered by a Syrian pilot in the pay of Mossad in 1989. Israel also "shared" information with the CIA and U.S. Air Force Intelligence about new radar equipment that it had seized from Egyptian positions along the Suez Canal during a paratrooper operation.

Not to be underestimated in the formulation of U.S. policy in the Middle East was the influence of American public opinion, which was carefully cultivated by the pro-Israeli lobby, especially in Congress and the U.S. media. To get an idea of the critical role Israel occupied in American thinking about foreign policy, we need look no further than a speech delivered at a congressional hearing in 1970 (well before the critical events of Black September in Jordan). Voicing an opinion shared by many of those who took part in the hearings, the American political scientist I. Kennan (not to be confused with George F. Kennan, whose views were of quite a different order) said that without Israel, "Jordan would long ago have been swallowed up by either Egypt or Syria, and Lebanon would be next in line." A similar fate, he said, would have befallen Northern Yemen, Saudi Arabia, and the Emirates of the Persian Gulf. Kennan went even further: if, he said, Israel did not exist, "the Russians would rush to fill the vacuum left by the British in Aden."[1] His thinking was shared by many in America at the time.

From the moment the Eisenhower Doctrine was declared, U.S. foreign policy entered an aggressive phase; its aim was to create an anti-Nasser camp in the Arab world. Three months before the doctrine was unveiled, pro-Nasser forces had won the elections in Jordan, with Suleyman Nabulsi becoming prime minister. By April 1957, the CIA was helping to orchestrate the toppling of Nabulsi's government. Once Nabulsi was safely out of power, the United States offered Jordan an annual grant of $50 million.

Even as Nabulsi was being overthrown, Israel was threatening to occupy the West Bank if Nasser tried to interfere with events in Jordan. Saudi Arabia had sent several thousand troops into Jordan (Iraq had wanted to do the same but Israel blocked this through U.S. channels). Yet there is no reason to believe that Nasser had tried to take control of the Jordanian regime during Nabulsi's brief premiership, even though he had had plenty of supporters in the country at the time.

The Eisenhower Doctrine was immediately adopted by Israel, as well as by President Camille Chamoun of Lebanon, followed by King Saud, King Hussein of Jordan, and Iraqi prime minister Nuri al-Said.

THE UNITED STATES AND ISLAMIC EXTREMISM

Paradoxical as it sounds, particularly after September 11, 2001, with President George W. Bush declaring a war on global terrorism that particularly targets Islamic extremists, the United States has a long history of using Islamic extremist organizations to further its own interests.

In the 1970s and 1980s, the United States supported and supplied arms to the Mujahideen—whose forces fought under the banner of Islam—to force the Soviet Union out of Afghanistan. In a 1998 interview published in the French journal *Le Nouvel Observateur*, no less a figure than former U.S. national security adviser Zbigniew Brzezinski admitted that even *before* Soviet military forces entered Afghanistan, he had sent President Jimmy Carter a note in which he proposed supplying arms to the Mujahideen. As he put it, this kind of "covert operation was an excellent idea" because it increased the likelihood that the Soviet Union would intervene to support the Afghan regime and thus "would get its own Vietnam War." At the time, many Americans believed that using Islam as a weapon against the Soviet Union was trading a lesser evil for a greater good, but they were clearly in the throes of self-delusion. This reckless—I repeat, reckless—policy paved the way to the tragedy of September 11, 2001. All along, the Mujahideen had planned to turn against the United States once they'd rid Afghanistan of the Russians. And even back in those days, calls to restore the Islamic caliphate were spreading among the Afghan Mujahideen—a call that Osama bin Laden would pay particular heed to. Incidentally, the Soviet Union could not be accused of similarly relying on or exploiting Islamic extremist groups during its cold war confrontation with the United States. Its operations may not have always been whiter than white, but Moscow fully understood how dangerous it was to promote the strength of Islamic extremism.

Equally delusional is the claim that this was the first time that the United States had ever made use of Islamic extremists. As far back as the 1950s, the United States decided that its main pillars of support in the Arab world were those who not only stood up for Muslim values but were willing to resort to terrorist methods to do so. With the help of Aramco, the Saudi oil company, the CIA set up a network of small Islamic groups in eastern Saudi Arabia in the 1950s. It is not clear exactly what use it intended to put them to, but the fact that the CIA set them up is beyond dispute. When it transpired that Egypt had not been driven into a corner by the defeat of the Nasserites in Jordan, the CIA helped establish the Muslim Brotherhood's Islamic Center in Geneva, where a number of assassination attempts against Nasser were orchestrated—all of which either ended in failure or were abandoned for one reason or another.

During Lyndon Johnson's presidency, from 1963 to 1969, U.S. exploitation of Islamic groups as proxies in the battle against Arab nationalism intensified. Johnson's administration took a much harder line everywhere, not just in the Middle East—it escalated the Vietnam War and intervened militarily in the Dominican Republic. During John F. Kennedy's presidency, there had been a thaw in U.S.–Egyptian relations. Although the two presidents never met, they did write to each other. After Kennedy's assassination, U.S.–Egyptian relations deteriorated once again: to begin with, there was a propaganda campaign against Nasser; then Johnson's advisers decided to throw their weight behind the King of Saudi Arabia as the leader of the Islamic anti-Nasser opposition. Anybody in the U.S. establishment who so much as hinted that this might be a shortsighted policy was swiftly reined in.

YEMEN: A FAILED ATTEMPT TO FIGHT BACK

Sensing that the United States was helping to turn Saudi Arabia into the center of gravity for anti-Egyptian forces, Nasser began to play them at their own game. When the Imam Ahmad died in Yemen—the "soft underbelly" of Saudi Arabia—in 1962, his son and heir Muhammed al-Badr was ousted in just one week. Al-Badr managed to go into hiding: one midday, when all the men guarding him went to lunch, he slipped out unnoticed through the back gate, riding on a donkey, dressed in women's clothing. There is no direct evidence that al-Badr's ouster was orchestrated by Cairo, but events both before and after the coup suggest that Egyptian special agents were more than just passive observers.

Either way, Egypt did not inform the Soviet Union of a planned coup in Yemen. That is not to say, of course, that Soviet intelligence had no other sources of information about the situation brewing in that country, but Colonel Abdullah Sallal, who came to power in Sana'a after the toppling of the monarchy, was in no way linked to the Soviet Union. Moreover, the Kremlin had enjoyed good relations with Imam Ahmad, who was treated by Soviet doctors, as well as with his would-be heir al-Badr, who had paid a visit to the Soviet Union at the end of the 1950s. Undergraduates and others from Yemen studied in the Soviet Union, and many returned home after the declaration of the republic.

The Soviet Union never conspired to bring down an Arab monarchy; Moscow always respected the Arab kingdoms. The Soviet Union understood that it was impossible to bring about sociopolitical change in another country via an imported revolution; it had to happen from within, when the time was ripe. And the time would be ripe only when the people could no longer live the way they used to—and when it was no longer possible to govern them the old way. Logic rather than ideology dictated their relations. The one time that the Soviet Union deviated from this principle was when it sent troops into Afghanistan. Needless to say, it was an exception that proved a rule.

Nasser's Egypt had increasingly turned to Moscow after the collapse of its union with Syria. When Egypt threw its support behind the coup in Yemen, the Soviet Union did not stay on the sidelines but actively and openly backed Egypt, not only politically but with military and logistical supplies. Along with its obligations to Egypt, the Kremlin could not ignore the fact that progressive reforms in Yemen were under threat from outside forces. The revolution in Yemen had been started by a group of young officers whose duties had taken them to Cairo on more than one occasion and who could not conceal their enthusiasm for the changes that Nasser had introduced to his country. It was only natural that they felt about Nasser's Egypt as they did, given that Yemen was still stuck in the Middle Ages. Yemen's tribal system had survived in an almost primordial form, with powerful sheiks and with autocratic, unquestioned authority vested in the most important figure of all, the imam, who was also the spiritual leader of the Zaydis, Yemen's most powerful Muslim sect. Incidentally, Colonel Sallal, who led the uprising against the monarchy, was at the time the chief of al-Badr's personal guard—but before that, on Imam Ahmad's orders, he had spent five years literally chained up in a pit. The food he ate was thrown to him.

But, as backwards as Yemen was, it was not completely cut off from the rest of the world. Hundreds of thousands of Yemenis took to the streets of Aden in angry protest against Britain's actions in the neighboring sultanates of southern Arabia. Ideas that sprang from the unstoppable stream of technological and cultural developments halfway across the world would reach Al-Hudayda, Sana'a, and Taizz as a faint trickle, but nonetheless lay the groundwork for the republic that it would become. When Yemen finally entered the twentieth century, it would find itself entangled in an astonishing mass of contradictions.

Nothing illustrated life in monarchical Yemen more clearly than Imam Ahmad's palace in Taizz, where he spent the last years of his life. Shortly after the imam's rule was overthrown, *Pravda* sent me to Yemen, where I had the chance to spend some time in the imam's quarters, which were still filled with his possessions. Ahmad was evidently a great lover of clocks, for the walls were covered with them. But for all the sound of ticking and striking clocks, the imam was deaf to the changing times: beside his bed lay the leather whip he used to lash his servants and concubines. On his desk, a framed photograph showed the imam at the arch of the city gates of Sana'a, which were ornately inscribed with proverbs from the Koran; there he stood, complacently observing a public execution. The number of blows it took for the saber-wielding executioner to sever the unfortunate prisoner's head from his neck had been predetermined by the court that had passed the death sentence.

I was puzzled to see a pair of shackles in the room. My Yemeni guide explained to me that if anyone incurred the wrath of the imam, he would order his guards to shackle them on the spot. On the wall, along with the clocks, was a photograph of Yuri Gagarin that the imam had carefully cut out of a newspaper. On a small writing desk there were two starter's pistols loaded with blanks. The imam would pretend to shoot himself with them in front of his guards to demonstrate that no bullets could harm him. On a three-legged stand in the middle of the room was a portable screen and, in front of it, a small projector. Every day, a film would be screened for the imam's private viewing pleasure, but this was the only "cinema" in the whole of Yemen, for Ahmad strictly forbade ordinary people from watching movies.

And one final "exhibit": on Imam Ahmad's bedside table was a little box that contained a lethal poison, just in case he ever needed to take it—and he never did. Yet just seven days after his death, this despotic regime was overthrown.

The United Arab Republic and Saudi Arabia soon found themselves dragged into the events in Yemen, the UAR on the side of the republicans, and the Saudis on the side of the monarchists. There was long-standing enmity between the royal households of Riyadh and Taizz; the Saudis were not motivated by brotherly love for al-Badr or his late father Ahmad. But the Saudis did fear that the events in Yemen might spill across its borders. Meanwhile, the UAR, which formed a counterweight to the Saudis' anti-Nasser policy, was eager to underpin its standing in Yemen. Both the United States and Britain also chose sides. It served no use for Washington to have a pro-Egypt Yemen on the doorstep of its petroleum empire on the Arabian peninsula. In London, the worry was not just about oil but also over the future of the British military base in Aden.

Republican forces found themselves struggling after Saudi Arabia began to provide extensive support and armaments to those Yemeni tribes who remained loyal to the monarchy; at the republicans' request, Nasser sent thousands of troops into Yemen. But as the conflict descended into a quagmire, Saudi Arabia and the UAR agreed to negotiate. In the Saudi city of Jeddah, on August 24, 1965, an accord was signed between President Nasser and King Faisal that provided for a referendum on Yemen's future to be held no later than November 23, 1966. The agreement mandated a period of transition under a provisional government, an end to Saudi interference, and the gradual withdrawal of Egyptian troops from Yemen.

King Faisal, who had replaced his brother Saud since the conflict began (Saud would die in exile in Egypt in 1969) had apparently begun to feel that his country's anti-Nasser policy was becoming burdensome. Nasser, for his part, began to see the danger of becoming bogged down in Yemen, which would tie his hands in Egypt and beyond. Above all, it would seriously weaken Egypt's capacity for resistance in the event of an armed conflict with Israel.

The UAR-Saudi agreement seemed to establish conditions that would help the Yemeni people decide their future without outside interference. And so a conference of all of Yemen's political groups was convened in Harad at the end of November 1965. Allow me to go into some detail that might give a better picture of the situation: I flew to Sana'a from Cairo on an Antonov-12 Soviet military transport plane with a group of Egyptian soldiers. The soldiers had to wear oxygen masks during the flight as the cockpit was the only pressurized part of the aircraft. I was lucky though: Commander Major Zabiyaka allowed me to come into the cockpit, where I slept for the duration of the five-hour flight on the floor, at the feet of the Soviet pilots—and for that I was very grateful. On a few occasions we were approached by Saudi fighter jets, but we reached our destination without incident. Major Zabiyaka told me that he had made that same flight more than 200 times. Indeed, the duties being undertaken by Soviet military pilots at the time amounted to hard labor: they would fly the five hours from Cairo to Sana'a, then back from Sana'a twenty minutes later and do the same again two days later, living in hotels far from their families.

My flight from Sana'a to Harad, however, was on an official aircraft, a small Ilyushin-14 piloted by an Egyptian. Also aboard the flight were some Egyptian officers, three Soviet news correspondents, and an East German television crew. One of the officers happened to know the pilot, who decided to show off his flying skills by dropping the aircraft to a low altitude, skimming barely thirty to fifty meters above the desert. It was a far from pleasant experience for any of us, but the first to protest were our East German colleagues. "What are you worried about?" the Egyptian pilot said in a bid to reassure them. "I've been flying for two years." This kind of reckless self-confidence would prove to be the undoing of many an Egyptian pilot in the not-too-distant future.

In Harad, a small settlement near the Saudi Arabian border, the republican flag was flying. The nearby hills, however, were controlled by promonarchy forces. David Smiley, then the military affairs correspondent of the British newspaper the *Daily Telegraph*, told us that the deposed Imam al-Badr had his headquarters in those very hills. He knew what he was talking about. As Colonel Smiley, he had been Britain's military attaché in Stockholm. He had also spent more than two years as an adviser to al-Badr.

The big multicolored marquee where the meetings were held was fenced off with barbed wire, and an armored car equipped with machine guns was stationed at its entrance. The conference encampment as a whole was guarded by Saudi as well as Egyptian soldiers. Saudi Arabia's key representatives were Emir Abdullah al-Sadr and Rashad Faraon, head of its special forces. Thinking that the East Germans were West Germans, Faraon's son told them a tale that they passed on to me and two other Soviet correspondents, *Izvestiya*'s Leonid Koryavin and Aleksandr Timoshkin of Moscow Radio. The story went that he was afraid to go to sleep at night because there were two cases of gold in his tent. He used them for "serious talks" with tribal leaders.

I clearly recall the first day of the conference, when the representatives of the prorepublic tribes came face-to-face with their opposite numbers from the promonarchy tribes. They hugged each other like old friends, kissed each others' hands, and, once the initial greetings were over, spent a good while strolling around the enclosure hand in hand, as is the local custom. But on the third day, the monarchists' tents and belongings were hurriedly loaded onto military trucks, at which many of them protested. Their tents were unpacked and set up again, but this time some distance away from the republicans'. From that moment on, all personal contact between delegates ceased. According to the Egyptian journalists, the monarchist delegation had been removed at the Saudis' insistence.

The conference then went badly off track. It took four days just to confirm the agenda. It was unbearably hot, a situation made worse by the humidity typical of the Tihama coastal plain, with torrential rains at night. We Soviet journalists had no way to contact our editors in Moscow, and when we asked when we would be able to leave we were told that no information must be allowed to leak out in case it jeopardized the conference. They had been fighting for three years; the conference could go on for at least three weeks. Nevertheless, thanks to pressure from the Egyptians, we managed to get out of Harad a week later. With nothing settled, the conference wrapped up in December when the Muslims started to observe Ramadan.

One story well illustrates the Yemenis' attitude to Russians and other people from the Soviet Union: A group of Soviet geologists working a few kilometers from Sana'a ran into a band of armed pro-Badr tribesmen. When the tribesmen realized they were Russians, they not only let them go in peace but also had mercy on their bodyguards—who were republicans—warning them: you'll have us to deal with if you so much as lay a finger on the Russians.

Yemen's monarchist forces, who enjoyed foreign backing, were loath to lay down their arms. Under the tribal system, whose hold on society was undiminished since the overthrow of the imam, the sheiks ruled the roost, deeming themselves the supreme masters of their ancestral lands. So when the republican government showed its determination to create a strong, centralized administrative system, the effect was to turn many tribal sheiks against the regime. Nor could it be ignored that some tribes' leaders had been subjected to intensive antirepublican propaganda; not to mention the monthly payments of gold from the republic's overseas enemies that many sheiks were receiving. The new regime in Yemen thus found itself in a standoff with Islam that was not of its own making.

More than any other factor, it was the resistance of the tribal sheiks that accounted for the republican government's failure to form an effective army in the early years of revolution. There were numerous drives to call up recruits, military schools were established, and a succession of Yemeni officers received military training overseas. But the country remained without a regular army as such. The republic's armed forces, such as they were, were formations of various tribes. Their sheiks would decide whether to send them into action or not. Some, including some of the most important tribal sheiks, did choose to throw their weight behind the republic. But more often than not this was a result of the deep-seated enmity that some sheiks felt toward the dynasty of Hamid ed-Dinov, to which the deposed al-Badr belonged. And loyalties were fluid. Even major tribal alliances, not to mention individual tribes, changed their allegiances several times depending on the circumstances. The republic found a more organic and therefore more dependable source of support among traders, craftsmen, and other town and city dwellers.

The regime faced a very real threat at the end of 1967 and the beginning of 1968, when promonarchy forces stepped up their activities after Egypt called its troops home from Yemen. Cairo was in desperate need of well-trained armed units to rebuild its military capacity after the disaster of the Six-Day War. On the political front, Egypt had redoubled its efforts to bring about unity across the Arab world. The way to do this, of course, was to ease tensions with Saudi Arabia. That was another factor behind Egypt's withdrawal from Yemen.

In September 1967 I was in Khartoum for the first Arab summit meeting since the Six-Day War in June. One of the most important problems for the conference to tackle was that of Yemen. A compromise was tabled under which Egypt promised to complete its troop withdrawal that same year in return for Saudi Arabia undertaking that it would no longer interfere in Yemen's internal affairs. Following talks between President Nasser and King Faisal, it was announced that three of the oil-producing kingdoms would make payments to the UAR that were roughly equivalent to the losses it had incurred due to the forced closure of the Suez Canal.

The same summit meeting saw the formation of a committee to help solve the Yemen question, a body that included representatives from Sudan, Iraq, and Morocco. President Sallal was still in power in Yemen at the time; his foreign minister read out an intransigent, harshly worded statement declaring that his government would not recognize any decisions that flowed from the Nasser-Faisal talks. The minister also said that members of the "committee of three" would not receive visas to enter Yemen. After a two-hour meeting with Nasser, Sallal issued a more conciliatory statement. Many observers believed that Sallal's government was on its last legs—he had made too many enemies even within the republican camp. Some of them spoke out against him for personal reasons, while others accused him of lacking political flexibility.

As expected, Yemen underwent a change of government when Egypt's military units left the country. Sallal was replaced by a Republican Council headed by former prime minister Abdul Rahman al-Iryani, who had spent about a year in exile in Cairo. Shortly after this, in December 1967, promonarchy forces laid siege to Sana'a. Al-Iryani turned for help to the Soviet Union, which organized an airlift of medical supplies, foodstuffs, and ammunition. The civil war that ensued came to an end in April 1970 when an accord was signed giving monarchists places in the republican government. But this formal end to hostilities did not bring internal stability to Yemen: one group after another seized power; often after assassinating the previous head of state.

Events in Yemen were increasingly shaped by the state of affairs in the south, where revolutionary forces had secured control of the former British protectorate of Aden. On November 30, 1967, British troops finally withdrew from the territory of the newly declared People's Republic of South Yemen, which was renamed the People's Democratic Republic of Yemen in accordance with the constitution of

November 30, 1970. This too came about only after bloody internecine fighting.

Eventually, the north and south of Yemen would merge to form a unified state, but not without suffering armed clashes, much meddling in each others' affairs, and war. On May 22, 1990, more than two and a half decades after the overthrow of the hated Hamid ed-Dinov dynasty, the united Republic of Yemen was finally declared. Egypt did not remain on the sidelines throughout these turbulent changes, but neither did it actively intervene.

Is it possible that Egypt's initial intervention in Yemen during the overthrow of the monarchy was not justified? I raise this question because many historians have, with hindsight, condemned Nasser for this intervention, which cost Egypt dearly. I do not agree with them. Suppose there had *not* been a coup in Yemen with Egypt's involvement: Who's to say that Saudi Arabia wouldn't have forged ahead with its plans to set up an anti-Nasser Islamic counterweight, a plan that stemmed from events following the unveiling of the Eisenhower Doctrine? Without Yemen's antimonarchist revolution, it is unlikely that Britain—especially after losing its Suez base—would have decided to pull out of Aden. Of course, shaking off its tribal system was (and still is) a very difficult process—even sheiks of a republican persuasion have shown themselves reluctant to work for democratization. But there is no denying that the Yemeni people—especially the emerging bourgeoisie in the cities, the merchant class, and then the lower-middle and industrial middle classes—are becoming more politically aware. Without Egyptian intervention, Yemen would have remained trapped in the Middle Ages for a very long time.

— 8 —

THE BEGINNING AND END OF
THE SIX-DAY WAR

THE WAR THAT BROKE OUT on June 5, 1967, between Israel, on one side, and Egypt, Syria, and Jordan on the other, can be seen as a turning point, not only in Egypt's history but for the entire Arab world. The magnitude of the Arab defeat seriously traumatized Arabs everywhere; in Egypt, it spelled the beginning of the end of socialism. The conflict, which became known as the Six-Day War, led to Israel's occupation of East Jerusalem, the West Bank of the Jordan River, the Gaza Strip, and the Golan Heights, and to an ever-proliferating number of Israeli settlements within those territories. In the aftermath of the war, the Palestinians were thrust into the front lines as an Arab people seeking to secure their own state. In subsequent efforts to broker a peace deal with Israel, the focus of Arab demands shifted to calls for a halt to settlements and for a withdrawal of Israeli troops from the occupied territories.

Israel's victory in the 1948 war could rightly be attributed to the corruption of its Arab adversaries. Most of those regimes were rotten to the core, easily bribed, and dependent on the colonial powers. But in 1967, Egypt, Syria, and Jordan were independent, nationalistic Arab states. What's more, they had been equipped with state-of-the-art Soviet weaponry and, in the case of the Egyptian and Syrian armies, they had Soviet military advisers at their disposal. Even so, they suffered crippling defeats within a matter of days.

OF NASSER'S ABORTED RESIGNATION

A few hours after Israel launched its military action, Mohamed Oda, Philippe Galyab, and a number of other Egyptian journalists and friends gathered at *Pravda*'s Cairo bureau, chattering gleefully about the dozens of Israeli aircraft that had been shot down in the first few hours of battle—reveling in the incredible Arab victory in the making. Judging by the astounding numbers of downed enemy planes that Radio Cairo was reporting in its half-hourly bulletins, one could easily imagine that almost the entire Israeli air force had been wiped out. Yet by the time I met up with them, Soviet military advisers had already told me what had really happened at the Cairo-West air base. Israel's first strike had badly damaged its runways. Although the advisers had urged the Egyptian pilots to take off from the taxiways and meet the second wave of Israeli planes in the sky, when the Israeli squadrons returned from refueling, the Egyptian fighters were still on the ground. Israeli bombs destroyed them all. The news, when they finally received it, left my colleagues feeling crushed and demoralized.

A couple of days later, by which time tidings of the Arab rout had spread far and wide, a rumor swept through Cairo that American planes with Israeli markings—flown by American pilots—had participated in the fighting. At 4:20 in the morning on June 6, Radio Cairo broadcast a statement from the Egyptian Supreme Command saying "there was irrefutable evidence to confirm that the U.S. and Britain had taken part in the air raids against Egypt." Many people believe that Muhammad Sidqi Mahmud, commander of the Egyptian air force, was responsible for this tale. Right from the early hours of June 5, he had been trying to convince everybody that the "sheer weight of numbers and efficiency of the enemy air force" pointed to U.S. and British involvement. He even maintained that an Egyptian pilot—a certain Hosni Mubarak—had reported seeing American planes during the raid on Luxor airbase. Marshal Amer immediately contacted the base at Luxor and spoke in person to Mubarak, who denied the story. The only aircraft he'd seen, said the future Egyptian president, had been Israeli.

But everybody listened to the radio, and once the rumors started, they were impossible to quell. All across Cairo the question could be heard: "So where are the Russians? They're supposed to be on our side. Why don't they fight off the American pilots?"

I will not go into detail about how the hostilities unfolded—much has already been written on this subject, some of it by military experts. As to the conflict's ending, here is what former Egyptian vice president Abdel Latif al-Bagdadi had to say: "We felt as though we were dreaming. It was mayhem, like a nightmare. How could our air force have been wiped out in the space of one day, and our ground troops decimated the next? How could they be so strong that we couldn't hold out for more than thirty-six hours?" His words echoed the dejection felt throughout Egypt.

Nasser realized how overwhelming a defeat Egypt had suffered, and since he held himself responsible for it, he went on national television on June 8 to announce his resignation. A succession of Egyptian politicians and journalists would later make it known how *they* interpreted the incredible events that followed. Many believed that they had been cleverly stage-managed—that all of those thousands of people marching in the streets, calling on Nasser to stay, were merely puppets. I do not subscribe to this view. I doubt that the Arab Socialist Union was capable of mobilizing a million defeat-weary people into mass demonstrations in such a limited time, let alone doing so in secret. The demonstrations were undoubtedly spontaneous. Significantly, Nasser phoned public information minister Mohammed Faik and asked him to cut the TV broadcasts about the floods of telegrams that were pouring into Cairo, calling on the president to stay.

Nasser was truly depressed and disheartened; I am certain that his decision to resign was heartfelt, as was his choice of Zakaria Mohieddin as his successor. But the masses felt differently. Instead of turning against the head of state who had brought them such unprecedented military humiliation, they demanded that he stay on as their leader, as Egypt's guiding light. Ultimately, the unprecedented public displays of support convinced Nasser. But during the interval between his resignation statement and its retraction—when Mohieddin had already started to appear on Egyptian TV screens—one more significant event occurred.

The day before Nasser's televised speech, a cipher communication arrived from Moscow for Dmitri Pozhidayev, the Soviet ambassador in Cairo, instructing him to inform Nasser that the Soviet Union would replace all the armaments Egypt had lost, including aircraft and tanks, free of charge. But Pozhidayev did not manage to get the message to Nasser before his resignation statement aired because the Egyptian president refused all visitors for three days. The ambassador's instructions were to inform the president and no one else, and only in person. Together with my colleague Vadim Sinelnikov, the Soviet embassy's adviser on relations with the Arab Socialist Union, we approached Pozhidayev and urged him to try to meet with Nasser again. This time they should tell him that the Soviet Union would hold to its offer only if he remained president. The ambassador later said that when he finally spoke to Nasser the Egyptian president was moved to tears. It is hard to be sure that this offer, of all things, was the main motivation behind Nasser's decision not to resign. But it could not have failed to influence him.

GRECHKO SUSPECTS NASSER OF BLUFFING

So how did the Six-Day War begin? This question has generated a lot of mudslinging, speculation, and falsehood. But a few distinct episodes, known only to a small number of people, throw light on the true course of events.

Several months before the war broke out, Marshal Andrei Grechko, commander of the Warsaw Pact's armed forces, paid a visit to Cairo. After meeting with Soviet military advisers, he sat down with President Nasser. Sergei Arakelyan, a counselor at the Soviet embassy and an expert Arab speaker, served as their interpreter. Later, he shared his impressions of the meeting with me. Nasser had asked Grechko for his opinion about the state of the Egyptian army, Arakelyan recalled. Grechko, evidently keen to boost the standing of Soviet military advisers, who had by then been in Egypt for some time, told him: "Your army is capable of carrying out any mission in the present theatre of war." This could hardly have failed to make Nasser sit up and listen. Of course, Grechko's assessment alone would not have influenced Nasser's decision to mount a show of strength, but it certainly encouraged him to believe that his armed forces were more formidable than they were and removed some of his hesitations about making use of them. This is not to say that Nasser took it upon himself to launch a full-blown military action either. In fact, I am certain that that was far from the case.

Were Nasser's prewar movements merely feints, a well thought out bluff? Not exactly. The phrase that most exactly captures Nasser's intentions, as I understand them, is the one just mentioned above—a "show of strength." Egypt had not planned to launch a preemptive strike; but at the same time, wrongly overestimating the capabilities of its armed forces, it reckoned that it could thwart Israel even if Israel struck the first blow. The Israelis surely realized this too: six months after the war, on December 22, 1967, the Israeli daily newspaper *Haaretz* published an interview with the then Israeli chief of staff Yitzhak Rabin, who admitted: "There's a difference between a build-up of troops where the aim is to start a war, and the kind of maneuver that could end up causing a war although it's not meant to—which is not the same thing. I think Nasser was thinking of the latter."

When Nasser ordered his troops into Sinai, they rode in a column of tanks, armored personnel carriers, and other military vehicles that were clearly visible from the windows of the American embassy in Cairo. The Egyptian president was looking to intimidate Israel and he trusted his message would reach them via the Americans. On May 16 Ambassador Pozhidayev, along with Soviet military attaché Fursov, held a meeting with Shamas Badran, the UAR's defense minister. According to the ambassador's report back to Moscow, Badran took the possibility of an Israeli attack on Syria very seriously. "If this happened, the UAR would immediately come to Syria's defense," Badran said. Pozhidayev knew that there had been constant skirmishes on the border with Syria, so he sought to clarify exactly what Badran meant by "attack." Badran replied that Egypt would consider any armed overland incursion whose aim was to seize territory to be an attack. He was eager to stress that the current low-level fighting, intermittent and desultory as it was, did not meet that definition—a view shared by the Syrians. Pozhidayev's dispatch served only to reinforce the Kremlin's belief that Nasser was not planning a preemptive strike.

On May 16, General Muhammad Fawzi, the Egyptian army's chief of staff, sent a message to General Indar Jit Rikhye, the Indian United Nations troop commander: "I have ordered the United Arab Republic's armed forces to be ready to take action, should Israel open hostilities against any Arab state. In order to carry out these orders, a detachment of our troops has been deployed on the eastern front in Sinai. To ensure the safety of the UN forces, I request that you withdraw them from the checkpoints where they are concentrated."

It was a move, perhaps an impromptu one, designed not as an actual attack against Israel but as an act of intimidation. It might well have been the doing of the Egyptian military rather than the high command. Many similar moves were to follow that were almost certainly carried out on impulse, without being carefully thought through; Nasser and Egypt's army were riding high on a tide of pan-Arab sentiment and their own overconfidence. Yet even so, and for all his overt saber rattling, Nasser remained cautious. According to Charles Yost, the former U.S. envoy to the United Nations, Nasser did not approve the wording of the Egyptian military command's request to UN Secretary General U Thant to withdraw UN emergency forces from Sharm el-Sheikh. Yost maintained that Nasser would have preferred the UN troops to stay where they were.

As was to be expected, the UN secretary-general could not agree to a partial pullout, abandoning only those areas where the Egyptian and Israeli armies were confronting each other head-on. But since Egypt was legally entitled to bar UN emergency forces from its own soil, U Thant offered to withdraw all of his forces instead. Here, Egypt fell into a trap of its own making: it had to agree to U Thant's proposal. Yet if Egyptian troops entered Sharm el-Sheikh, Egypt would have to show the Arab world that they did so for a reason. So Egypt announced that it was closing the Straits of Tiran (or Gulf of

Aqaba) to Israeli shipping and any other vessels that were carrying strategic cargo to Israel.

The straits had been opened ten years earlier, in 1957, in accordance with an agreement that allowed Israel to withdraw its troops from Sinai after the Anglo-Franco-Israeli assault on Egypt. The opening of the straits was of obvious significance for Israel: until then, the Red Sea had, to all intents and purposes, been an Arab "lake," off-limits to the Israelis; without access to the straits, the Israeli port of Eilat was essentially redundant. Nasser hoped to close the straits again—effectively turning the clock back to the way things were before Egypt was attacked in 1956—while still avoiding a military showdown with Israel. On two occasions, May 27 and May 29, he gave speeches in which he repeated: "We do not intend to be the first to fire; we do not intend to carry out any attack." If things had gone no further than the closing of the Straits of Tiran, that alone would have been seen in the Arab world as a stunning victory for Nasser, further cementing his place as the acknowledged pan-Arab leader. But that is clearly as far as Nasser wanted it to go. It was no coincidence then that when U Thant, backed by the United States, asked Egypt to forbear from inspecting ships passing through the Straits of Tiran, it didn't demur. At the same time, U Thant asked Israel to refrain from testing "Egypt's decision to close the straits"—in other words, to keep its ships out of the Gulf of Aqaba.

A wealth of information obtained by Soviet intelligence corroborates my interpretation of Nasser's intentions. He might have pushed matters right to the brink, but that was as far as he wanted to go. On May 26 he had a meeting with Yusuf Zuaiyin, during which the Syrian prime minister raised the subject of a preemptive strike against Israel. Nasser rejected the idea. And at a closed meeting of Egyptian ambassadors and the military command that took place on June 3, 1967, Nasser declared: "I will not be the one to start a war, because if I do, it will jeopardize my standing with our allies and other countries around the world." Citing UAR government sources, a report from the KGB station in Cairo said that at present Nasser's main goal was to secure as quickly as possible the advantage he had gained thanks to the UN troop withdrawal. Next he would call on Israel to carry out the resolutions on Palestine—but also to agree to the establishment of a demilitarized zone in the area where it had been before 1956.

Although the Soviet Union supported Egypt's actions during the runup to the conflict, it did so because it thought they lessened, rather than increased, the likelihood of an all-out war. In a telegram sent to the USSR's ambassador in Cairo on May 25, Soviet foreign minister Andrei Gromyko said that Egypt's demand for UN troops to withdraw from the Gaza Strip and the Sinai Peninsula was "justified" and called it a "determined move that had brought about the desired response." The Kremlin had done its utmost to ensure that this "determined move" would stop a crisis situation from getting even worse.

The United States was also anxious to prevent events from spiraling out of control. On June 1 a personal envoy of President Lyndon Johnson secretly traveled to Egypt to invite Egypt's General Amer to America for confidential talks with the president. Still thinking that he could achieve his strategic goals without having to go to war, Nasser instantly agreed to the Americans' request—though he wanted to send a different vice president, Zakaria Mohieddin. As he left, Johnson's envoy assured Nasser that Israel would not instigate any military action while diplomatic channels were still open. But Mohieddin's trip was not to be, because just four days later, the Six-Day War broke out.

Yet even before the war began, the U.S. position had shifted. This was in no small part due to a secret trip to America by Mossad chief Meir Amit, who met with CIA director Richard Helms and U.S. defense secretary Robert McNamara. U.S. intelligence and military officials removed any doubts that President Johnson might have had, and persuaded him that it would serve U.S. interests to exploit the situation by agreeing to an Israeli assault on the Arab forces; a speedy outcome was guaranteed as Israel could easily handle the Arab armies. On July 4, at a meeting in the premier's residence, Amit reported back to Israeli prime minister Levi Eshkol and several other senior Israeli ministers that the United States had essentially given them the green light; the next day a full meeting of the Israeli government voted in favor of a preemptive military strike. Israel launched its attack against the Arab armies that same day and won a swift victory.

Along with the assumption that Nasser had been planning a preemptive strike against Israel—a conclusion that was far from true but that nonetheless swiftly spread across the world—yet another myth emerged in the aftermath of the war. It was alleged that the Kremlin had encouraged Egypt's bellicosity in the months before the war and even urged it to make a preemptive strike.

Much is made of the fact that the Soviet government passed Nasser information about Israeli troops that were ready to attack Syria. According to Egyptian journalist Mohamed Heikal, Supreme Soviet chairman Nikolai Podgorny and deputy foreign minister Vladimir Semyonov tipped off Anwar Sadat when he met them in Moscow on his way back from North Korea in mid-May 1967. Their warning, given in strict confidence, was that Israeli troops were massing on the border with Syria and that an invasion was planned for May 18–22. Sadat immediately sent a diplomatic telegram to Cairo via the Egyptian embassy in Moscow.

Israel, of course, denied that it had any such plans. The Soviet ambassador in Tel Aviv was invited to travel to the Syrian border to see for himself that there were no troops gathering for an assault. The ambassador quite rightly turned down the invitation. He had no desire to participate in a cover-up of Israel's military intentions, and he was fully aware that he would be taken only to places where neither Israeli soldiers or military hardware were in evidence.

Meanwhile, the local Soviet foreign intelligence station had got hold of factual materials relating to the Israeli military buildup. By mid-May, the Israeli government had come to the conclusion that it needed to crack down on activity by the Palestinians—who enjoyed backing from the Syrians—and prevent any chance of their setting up camps along the Israeli-Syrian border. Several options were considered, including a massive overland assault against Syrian military bases. Eshkol wanted the air force to carry out the attack, whereas military chief of staff Yitzhak Rabin thought the operation should not be limited to air strikes.

Egypt too had its own intelligence. On May 22 Nasser told Soviet ambassador Pozhidayev that on May 12 in Tel Aviv a number of Israeli political and military leaders had made direct threats of war against Syria; they had even spoken of occupying Damascus. Nasser's reasoning behind his show of strength in the Sinai came across loud and clear: "Israel and its backers," he said to Pozhidayev, "clearly think the UAR is tied up in Yemen and can't give Syria any real help. The UAR had to show just how groundless it is to think like that."

It is difficult to understand Moscow's position objectively: not only because a lot of foreign political experts have been wide of the mark in their analyses, nor only because of persistent propaganda myths, but also because members of the Soviet military made throw-away comments that they had not thought through.

As Shamas Badran, the Egyptian defense minister, boarded his flight home after his trip to Moscow on the eve of the war, Marshal Grechko bade him farewell. According to Mohamed Heikal, these were his parting words: "Stand firm—don't give in to blackmail from the Americans or anyone else. Whatever happens, we will be at your side." After the plane had taken off, a smiling Grechko dismissed the significance of what he'd just seemed to promise, explaining to his entourage: "I just wanted to give him one for the road." This prompted Murad Galeb, the Egyptian ambassador in Moscow, to send a telegram to Cairo, saying that Grechko's words should not be taken at face value. But Badran, himself a military man like Grechko, may not have seen things that way. Galeb has assured me that this incident really did take place as Heikal described it.

Yet none of this provides any evidence whatsoever of the inclinations of the Soviet government, which categorically wanted to avoid a war. In fact, on May 26, when Badran was still in Moscow, he told Soviet prime minister Aleksei Kosygin that the Egyptians had indications that the Israelis would definitely strike and that it was necessary to outflank them—but Kosygin warned him against pursuing any such course. "You must not do that," he said, reflecting the view of the entire Soviet leadership. "It would make Egypt look like the aggressor."

On May 28, just days before the fighting broke out, the Politburo tried to ease the situation by arranging a meeting between Prime Minister Eshkol and President Nasser in Moscow. Via Marshal Amer, the Soviet ambassador in Cairo sought to find out how the president felt about this. Nasser's response was that he "fully shared" the Soviet

government's "wise proposals." "Since the UAR is not planning to attack Israel, it can't do Eshkol any harm to hold talks in Moscow," he
said. Moreover, he thought, "Israel's conduct would be calmer" after
Eshkol had been to Moscow.

In the early hours of June 2, Dmitri Chuvakhin, the Soviet ambassador in Tel Aviv, received a diplomatic telegram from the Soviet Foreign Ministry marked "priority." It instructed him to meet Israeli
prime minister Levi Eshkol without delay and to hand him an invitation from the Soviet government to travel to Moscow that same day
for a confidential meeting with President Nasser. At 3:00 a.m. Chuvakhin was received by Eshkol and Abba Eban in Jerusalem. After
briefly conferring with his foreign minister, Eshkol agreed to meet
Nasser in Moscow later that day. Given the Israeli government's declaration that Israel would not fire the first shot, it would have been
utterly at odds with the propaganda being spun by Tel Aviv to turn
down the Kremlin's proposal. Eshkol's willingness to meet reflected
his own ambivalent position too, as he was clearly still hesitating
about whether or not to launch a preemptive strike.

Chuvakhin immediately notified Moscow that Eshkol had agreed to
the meeting, but within the space of two hours another "priority"
telegram arrived from the Soviet Foreign Ministry, informing its ambassador that the meeting was off. Nasser had withheld his preliminary
consent to the meeting with Eshkol because of strong objections from
Syrian prime minister Yusuf Zuaiyin and President Nureddin Atassi,
who was in Moscow at the time. Nasser told the Soviet ambassador in
Cairo that although he did not share Damascus's overly hard line, the
meeting clearly could not take place without Syria's consent. The Syrians explained that their position was dictated by fears of an anti-Soviet
reaction across the Arab world, but I would not rule out the possibility
that the Syrian leadership believed a show of strength could still force
Israel to back down. If this were so, then Eshkol's agreement to meet
Nasser might well have reinforced the Syrians' belief that it was in the
Arabs' best interests to let the current situation drag on.

Ambassador Chuvakhin conveyed the news he had received from
Moscow to Eshkol. The Israeli premier did not seem disappointed; in
fact, his reaction was one of obvious relief, since his participation in

talks initiated by Moscow could have complicated matters for himself within the Israeli leadership. At the same time, it was not in Tel Aviv's interests to further delay a resolution to the crisis, as the Israeli economy was already buckling under the weight of full military mobilization.

Convinced that Egypt would not launch a military action on its own initiative, the Kremlin focused its efforts on preventing Israel from firing the first shots. On May 26, Soviet premier Aleksei Kosygin sent Eshkol a telegram via the ambassador in Tel Aviv urging the Israeli government to take all possible steps to avert a military conflict—and warning of dire consequences if they started one themselves. Similar letters were sent to U.S. President Lyndon Johnson and British Prime Minister Harold Wilson. A confidential letter addressed to France's President Charles de Gaulle spoke of the Soviet Union's willingness to maintain contact and to conduct bilateral consultations on the Israel-Egypt situation.

These were difficult times for Israel. Nasser's actions had spread alarm among much of the population; it was widely believed that a coordinated Arab assault on the country would begin in a matter of days. The feelings of the Israeli people could not have failed to influence its leadership, but it remained hesitant all the same. This hesitation was brought to an end at the end of May/beginning of June, when the Israeli opposition and military top brass demanded a pre-emptive strike against the Arab armies. From their point of view, it would be a serious mistake not to take advantage of the situation as it stood. Eshkol gave in to pressure, as did several other Israeli politicians—even those who realized that the Arabs were putting on a show of strength, not actually planning to use it. In fact there are grounds to believe that some in Israel's government did not even have serious fears that Nasser would close the Gulf of Aqaba, especially after U Thant's trip to Cairo.

MOSCOW AND WASHINGTON FEAR CONFRONTATION

Despite the obvious fact that the Soviet Union and the United States each backed a different side in the 1967 Six-Day War, both superpowers endeavored to stop the war from escalating into a global conflict.

Even before the bombs began to fall, the Soviet Union made overtures to the United States, as did the United States to the Soviet Union, each calling on the other to exert influence on their "client states." On May 27, Moscow sent President Johnson a warning that Israel was planning an attack on the Arab countries, and asked him to persuade them to call it off. President Johnson and Dean Rusk, the U.S. secretary of state, sent a message to Soviet prime minister Kosygin and foreign minister Gromyko in turn, urging them to tell Egypt to "cool things down."

Right at the outbreak of war on June 5, 1967, the two sides took steps to assure one another that they would not be drawn into the crisis militarily, and that each would endeavor to work out a resolution through the United Nations. As chairman of the Soviet government, Kosygin first used the Kremlin-White House "hotline" on June 5. In the ensuing six days of war, both the United States and the Soviet Union made repeated use of the hotline to clarify what was going on. Most of the exchanges that took place were concerned with reaching a cease-fire via the UN Security Council. However, when the USS *Liberty* was attacked by the Israelis on June 8, Johnson used the hotline to reassure Kosygin that the U.S. naval movements in the Mediterranean served no purpose other than to assist the crew of the *Liberty* and to conduct an investigation into the circumstances of the attack. Moscow was satisfied that the United States was not attempting to interfere in the course of the war.

Anatoly Dobrynin, the former Soviet ambassador to Washington, writes in his memoirs:

throughout these crucial events, President Johnson, along with Rusk, McNamara and other key officials were constantly to be found in the White House's Situation Room. At the Kremlin, the Politburo sat in continuous session. The hotline played an invaluable role in maintaining constant contact between Moscow and Washington; it allowed the White House and the Kremlin to keep their finger on the pulse of developments and prevent any danger

of either government not knowing about the intent and actions of
the other.[1]

Not that there was any need for U.S. interference: Israel's military
victory was all too obvious. The Soviet Union was in a quite different
position. On June 10, in the final hours of the war and in defiance of
the UN Security Council resolution calling for a cease-fire, Israeli
troops advanced on Damascus. The Soviet first deputy foreign minister Vasily Kuznetsov wasted no time in summoning Israel's ambassador in Moscow, Katriel Katz, and handed him a note that stated:
"If Israel does not cease military activities without delay, the Soviet
Union in conjunction with other peace-loving states [a reference to
the member states of the Warsaw Pact] will impose sanctions on Israel, with all the consequences that would entail." The note also declared: "The government of the Soviet Union has taken the decision
to break off its diplomatic relations with Israel."

As this was happening, President Johnson was notified via the
hotline that the Soviet Union felt impelled to declare itself ready "to
take a unilateral decision" and "to take necessary action" if Israel
failed to cease military activities in the next few hours. It was a very
stern warning, and it was taken seriously: within three hours of being
handed the Soviet diplomatic note, the Israeli government called off
military operations on all fronts. It was clear that the Soviet Union
would resort to military intervention to prevent Damascus—a close
ally to Moscow—from being taken. The U.S. administration realized
this was a "red line" that Israel must not cross—and Israel didn't
cross it.

Yet although the Soviet Union was prepared to resort to force for
the sake of certain Arab regimes, it did not exploit such situations to
build closer ties with them. Far from it. Speculation was rife about the
possibility that Egypt and Syria might join the Warsaw Pact after their
defeat in the Six-Day War. It was all smoke and no fire, because the
Soviet Union was not interested. In fact, the issue was raised by
Nasser on June 21 during a visit to Cairo by Supreme Soviet chairman Nikolai Podgorny. Initially Nasser had asked that Podgorny's
visit be kept confidential, but then he changed his mind. The question

of new forms of UAR-Soviet cooperation, including military cooperation, was put on the table for Podgorny's consideration. More specifically, Nasser said that what he had in mind was a formal departure from Egypt's policy of nonalignment with the Warsaw Pact. Podgorny answered as though he were thinking it over: "Suppose the UAR officially announces that it is going to abandon its policy of non-alignment; clearly that will prompt some Arab countries to abandon their partnerships with the UAR." He also stressed that in terms of military expediency, it would be necessary to analyze all aspects of the matter in depth and to consult with "countries of the socialist fraternity." In the course of the meeting, it emerged that Nasser had already felt out President al-Atassi of Syria and Abdelaziz Bouteflika, then Algeria's foreign minister, about his plan to join the Warsaw Pact. Al-Atassi fully supported him, saying that Syria must take the same path as Egypt. Bouteflika, however, "expressed surprise" at the UAR's intentions. In the end Nasser agreed that if the UAR abandoned its nonalignment policy, it could have a negative effect on the UAR's standing among third world Arab states as a whole, as well as causing difficulties on the domestic front.

ARAB FEELINGS RUN HIGH: KOSYGIN'S HANDS ARE TIED

On June 23 and 25, Soviet premier Aleksei Kosygin and foreign minister Andrei Gromyko met President Johnson in the small town of Glassboro, New Jersey. Most of the talks between Kosygin and Johnson were held one-on-one. They discussed the Vietnam conflict, with Johnson making a throwaway remark that U.S. bombing raids there could be brought to a halt if negotiations started immediately. Kosygin naturally mentioned the situation in the Middle East, where military operations had ended with large areas of Arab territory under occupation. Johnson agreed that Israeli troops must be pulled out of the occupied territories, with the caveat that Israel's right to exist had to be recognized. But Kosygin did not have the power to "put the deal on paper." This was the first Soviet–U.S. summit to take place without the presence of the party general secretary. But Leonid Brezhnev's absence did not mean that Kosygin had been granted extra latitude. Brezhnev regarded Kosygin's mission with jealous eyes: at the UN General Assembly session that Kosygin had attended as the head of the USSR delegation, the Glassboro meetings had been subtly denigrated, as merely an "interim" summit.

Because he lacked the necessary authority to make binding commitments, Kosygin was unable to act decisively. It seems to me that Johnson too wasted a real opportunity to deal with matters in the Middle East and Vietnam at one and the same time. Talks on Vietnam would have been very much in Johnson's interest, not least because the presidential elections were approaching. The Israeli link could not, of course, be made unless the Vietnamese were onboard, although there was reason to believe that it would be in their interests to have the Soviet Union act as mediators—which, to all intents and purposes, is what Johnson had proposed.

A few months later, at an emergency session of the UN General Assembly, the Arab states wasted another opportunity—possibly an even more significant one—to force Israel to pull out of the occupied territories, when they refused to adopt the Latin American resolution. The Arab delegates' intransigence was partly triggered by their dismay at a speech Kosygin made. Although he condemned Israel and demanded that its troops be withdrawn from the territories, the Soviet premier also declared that Israel had a right to an independent existence. Gromyko cabled the Central Committee of the Soviet Communist Party to report on the impasse in the UN General Assembly: "Right from the start, relations between the heads of individual Arab delegations have been verging on hostile . . . The unrealistic, extremist line taken by the Algerian and Syrian leaderships has put pressure on the UAR and Iraq, influencing their stance as well as that of other Arab states who keep one eye on the extremists for fear of being accused of making too many concessions toward recognition of Israel as a state."

The Latin American draft resolution had been circulated on July 13. Its main point was that "the annexation of territory as the result of war" should be inadmissible. It accordingly declared that "Israeli troops [must] be drawn back to their original positions." Acceptance of this resolution meant that the requirement for Israel's troops to pull out of all the territory annexed in the Six-Day War could be set out in an international agreement. The Arab countries, however, dug their heels in. By way of explanation, Syria's president Nureddin al-Atassi stated: "We discussed this matter during a conference of the heads of Arab states [a summit held in Cairo on July 18] and rejected this draft resolution along with all other drafts that make any assumption whatsoever that there is no longer a war going on."

Once the Arab states had rejected the Latin American draft resolution outright, the General Assembly's deliberations on the Middle East problem came to an end, and the matter passed to the UN Security Council. The Arab side, unable to rise above its emotionally driven response to events, had squandered an opportunity to find a solution at an international level that would have been to its benefit. The language about the necessity of withdrawing from the territories in the Latin American resolution was much less opaque—it offered Israel less wiggle room than the Security Council's resolution 242, which was adopted four months later.

Another quite significant factor was the situation inside Israel. At the time, there were grounds to hope that the Latin American resolution would not cause Israel's political elite to actively disengage from the process. There were serious differences of opinion with regard to the fate of the occupied territories within Israel, and not all key figures in the Israeli government were in favor of annexation.

But after the Arabs rejected the Latin Americans' draft UN resolution, a turn of events undoubtedly affected prospects of finding a peaceful settlement. In August, the Arab summit in Khartoum unanimously approved a threefold veto: against recognizing Israel, against talking with it, and against making peace with it. The United States also took a noticeably tougher line, distancing itself from proposals that it had supported during the emergency session of the UN General Assembly. Only the Soviet Union continued to seek a solution to the crisis that all parties could agree to. On instructions from Moscow, Soviet ambassador Anatoly Dobrynin met with Arthur Goldberg, the U.S. permanent representative to the United Nations, after the General Assembly had ended its session. Goldberg personally put in writing a compromise formula that was in keeping with the Latin American resolution. This was followed by a month of tough haggling with those Arab countries that had been dragged into the Six-Day War. Eventually the Soviet government persuaded them to accept the compromise. But when U.S. secretary of state Dean Rusk met Dobrynin on October 19, he refused to put the agreed-upon text before the UN Security Council. Kosygin sent a message to President Johnson on the matter, but that did not help.

Security Council resolution 242 was eventually adopted on November 22, 1967, with backing from both the United States and the Soviet Union. The gist of the resolution can be summarized in two main points:

1. The withdrawal of Israeli armed forces from the territories it occupied during the 1967 Six-Day War;
2. Recognition of the sovereignty, territorial integrity and political independence of every state in the region [especially Israel].

As time would tell, the resolution was a big step forward, but it nevertheless was significantly flawed. A series of difficult compromises had resulted in the omission (in English) of the definite article "the" before the word "territories," which allowed it to be interpreted in different ways. The Soviet Union insisted that it meant the withdrawal of Israeli troops from *all* occupied territories. The United States mostly agreed with this interpretation, but not in every respect. On November 2, for example, Rusk told the Egyptians that the United States would give its backing to a peace proposal that called for a complete pullout of Israeli troops from Sinai—implicitly not from the other occupied territories.

After Soviet foreign minister Andrei Gromyko's visit to Cairo at the beginning of December 1968, the Kremlin set out its position on finding a peace settlement. In Washington, meanwhile, the transfer of power to the new administration was already under way: Richard Nixon had become president, and it was to him that the Soviet proposals for a comprehensive settlement were passed. However, Nixon and Henry Kissinger, then the U.S. national security adviser, did not devote their personal attention to the Soviet proposals. Instead secretary of state William P. Rogers and his deputy Joseph Sisco were assigned the task of negotiating with Dobrynin. These negotiations continued against the backdrop of the War of Attrition that Egypt was waging against Israel. But after July 20, 1969, when the Israeli air force began to attack Egyptian positions—Egypt's antiaircraft defenses would be destroyed by October—the negotiations were deadlocked.

In October 1969, while attending a session of the UN General Assembly in New York, it was Gromyko's turn to be briefed on an American document known as the "Rogers Plan." But just a month earlier, in September, the United States had supplied Israel with its most up-to-date Phantom warplanes, blatantly upsetting the balance of Arab-Israeli military power. These were hardly the best circumstances in which to hold constructive U.S.-Soviet negotiations, especially since Israel began using those very aircraft in January 1970 to carry out sorties deep in Egyptian territory, posing a real threat to the Aswan High Dam, whose destruction could have put Egypt's very existence at stake. Minister Hassan Zaki, the eminent hydrological engineer who headed the authority in charge of the dam's construction, warned that in the event of its destruction by bombing, the ensuing catastrophe would not be confined to one area: the waters of the Nile could literally flood the whole of Egypt. This is how things stood when Nasser came to Moscow, at which time the Kremlin promised that it would swiftly install a modern antiaircraft defense system in Egypt.

Without consulting Moscow, on June 19, 1970, the United States called on both Egypt and Israel for a cease-fire. Even though the American demand was a unilateral initiative, the Soviet Union recommended that Egypt agree to it. The USSR was anxious to see a cease-fire too.

THE DEFEAT OF EGYPT'S MILITARY OPPOSITION

After the war ended, relations between President Nasser and Marshal Amer took a serious turn for the worse, putting Moscow in an awkward position. Throughout the postrevolution years, Amer had been in charge of Egypt's armed forces and had worked closely with the Soviet military. Both he and Nasser had been honored with the title "Hero of the Soviet Union." But Soviet intelligence reported that Amer was planning to head for the Suez Canal zone to take charge of units loyal to him. He would then issue Nasser with a series of ultimatums and remove him from power if he refused to comply with them. For the Soviet Union, neutrality was out of the question; all its energies were directed toward supporting the Egyptian president.

But Nasser and Amer were not on a level playing field. If Nasser had enormous popular support, Amer had an equally strong power base, thanks to his uncontested control of the army. As far back as 1962 he had thrown down the gauntlet to Nasser, threatening to resign if he was not given what amounted to unrestrained command over Egypt's armed forces. At that time, Nasser had given in. But after the war of 1967 exposed just how worthless Amer's military leadership was, Nasser was not about to give in to him again. Egypt's crushing defeat left no doubt that a reshuffle of the military command was called for. Amer was fired, along with several others. Although Amer was allowed to keep his post as vice president, he clearly was not happy with his reduced status.

The former air force command bore particular responsibility for the defeat in the Six-Day War, since it had known that Israel was planning to attack but had failed to take the necessary steps to prepare for it. However, several generals and senior air force commanders who ought to have accepted responsibility for the defeat managed to evade arrest for some time, taking refuge in Amer's home. Before long, Amer's central Cairo residence turned into an ad hoc center of opposition to Nasser's government. Weapons were illicitly delivered there, and the house was guarded by a special unit of men recruited from laborers who worked on an estate belonging to one of Amer's brothers.

Nasser met several times with Amer and tried to explain just how seriously he took the situation. Meanwhile, there were reliable reports that Amer and his group had begun to actively prepare for a coup. The action would begin on August 27, the day Amer was due to arrive at the eastern zone headquarters near the Suez Canal. He would be escorted by 150 armed cadets from the academy, whose commander had been roped into joining the plot. At the same time, former defense minister Shamas Badran would go to the headquarters of the fourth army division, assume control, and dispatch the division to Cairo. The former interior minister was responsible for ensuring that there would be adequate security in Cairo. Nasser's inner circle would be rounded up in a series of lightning arrests; then Amer himself would return to Cairo as the hero of the day. "Let Nasser see what is going on," he said.

All these facts came to light the day before Nasser set off for the Arab summit in Khartoum. From that point on, events unfolded as follows: Amer was summoned to see Nasser and, in the presence of vice presidents Zakaria Mohieddin and Hussein al-Shafia and National Assembly chairman Anwar Sadat, he was informed that he was being placed under house arrest. He was also informed that the ex-officers hiding in his house had been arrested and that the weapons stored there had been confiscated. A military tribunal was called, and Amer shot himself.

Immediately after the end of the 1967 war, *Pravda*'s Asia and Africa editor Igor Belyayev joined me in Cairo. Together we wrote a series of articles that appeared in *Pravda* and in the weekly *Za Rubyezhom*. Without any embellishment or exaggeration, the articles illustrated how difficult the socioeconomic situation had become in Egypt. We did not simply describe events but sought to analyze them too—and our analysis led us to the inescapable conclusion that the regime that Egypt had installed after the collapse of colonialism was in the throes of a whole range of systemic failures.

Before the July 1952 revolution, Egypt's ruling elite had very much been made up of members of the royal circles, along with major landowners, industrialists, and financiers. After the revolution, not only the ruling elite but also the country's bureaucracy, from top to bottom, were military officers. Many of them—both those who were still on active duty and those who had resigned their commissions—used their influential status to their own advantage or to that of people close to them. A dangerous imbalance had taken hold amid the new order: at one end of the scale, reforms were being carried out for the benefit of the masses, while at the other end an "officer class" was taking shape, a class that increasingly benefited from the fruits of these reforms.

The Six-Day War exposed a failure whose foundations had been laid some time earlier: both Egypt's armed services and its government bureaucracy had fallen into the hands of a reactionary "military bourgeoisie" who were opposed to the project of fundamental social reform, and were unprepared in practical terms to carry out their military roles or their patriotic duty. "It is difficult to imagine," we wrote, "that generals or senior officers whose families' interests were encroached upon by the reforms being implemented could show any enthusiasm for the said reforms or for President Nasser's domestic policies." These generals and officers would use their positions of privilege to further their own material well-being. When they retired from military service, they would leave the army and take up senior civilian posts that afforded them opportunities to get rich. An officer-dealer type emerged, who was more concerned with business than with training privates and sergeants to be ready for combat.

Belyayev and I opined that firing and replacing certain individuals, which is what happened in the army after its 1967 defeat, would not solve the problem, which infected the entire "officer class." The leaders of the UAR preferred to tackle the problem top-down, rather than from the roots—and that was its weakness. "It is possible to dismiss the military top brass without addressing other major challenges for the country's future," we wrote. "Almost everybody we have met believes that the most important battleground is domestic policy . . . Does that mean democracy? Of course it does. The people, and especially advocates of reform, expect its services to be put to work, from how the economy is managed in a small village, right up to planning on a nationwide scale." Regrettably, real-life events did not live up to these expectations, especially after Nasser's death.

Our analysis of Egypt's situation clashed with the prevailing views of the international section of the Soviet party's central committee, or rather with the views of the section's deputy head, Rostislav Ulyanovsky. He flatly denied the existence of the new officer class, insisting that Egypt's socialism couldn't possibly fall victim to domestic developments, of all things. Ulyanovsky censured us in a memo addressed to the central committee secretariat. Who knows how this memo might have affected our work at the time, had it not been for President Nasser. Our articles were translated for him, and at one of his routine meetings with the Soviet ambassador, Nasser told him that he had read them and agreed with their conclusions. The ambassador reported this to Moscow, and Ulyanovsky's memo to the secretariat of the party central committee never left his desk.

With hindsight, today we would be able to back up our analysis with even greater certainty than was possible then. As it turned out, it was precisely those inconsistencies and contradictions on the domestic front that we had discerned that showed the limits of how far Arab nationalism could progress in its original form. We in Moscow encouraged the Arab countries to opt for a socialist alternative, but it did not exist. The rallying cries of Arab socialism were losing their appeal, even as the noncapitalist model state that had been cobbled together since colonial days was starting to fall apart at the seams.

– 9 –

USA
Tactics in the New Middle East

T HE SIX-DAY WAR had created an utterly new set of circumstances in the Middle East, with Israel occupying not just Egyptian and Syrian territory but also a sizeable part of Jordan, a state with close ties to Washington. Now Egypt, Syria, and Jordan enjoyed the sympathy of all the Arab nations, even some of the conservative regimes whose support in its campaign against Egypt's President Nasser the United States had previously taken for granted. There was an unprecedented surge of anti-imperialist sentiment throughout the region as well. Many political observers argued—with good reason—that America's policies toward the Arabs were putting its oil supply at risk. Israel's undisputed victory could not compensate for the losses the United States had incurred in the region as a whole. And yet as the 1960s came to a close, America remained at loggerheads with itself, seemingly unable to formulate a single, coherent response to the changing circumstances in the Middle East.

DEBATE IN THE UNITED STATES OVER
MIDDLE EAST POLICY

Throughout the late 1960s and early 1970s there was much debate in Congress, the press, and at various academic conferences and symposiums about which direction the United States should take in its quest to resolve the situation in the Middle East. During a series of Congressional hearings[1] in 1970, John S. Badeau, the former U.S. ambassador to Egypt and the director of the Near and Middle East Institute at Columbia University, stated: "It is sometimes claimed that by backing an Israel that is armed to the teeth, the U.S. is somehow in a position to curb the growing strength of Soviet footholds in countries close to Israel's borders, or even to eliminate them. Such claims are quite without foundation." At the same hearings, Professor Marver H. Bernstein[2] of Princeton University stressed that the United States needed to avoid taking any steps in the Middle East that could "pose a threat to oil supplies and any other of the U.S.'s material interests."

The pressing question was not whether the United States should continue to support Israel and the conservative Arab regimes—there was an overall consensus for those policies. But many authoritative figures in U.S. political, academic, and business circles stressed that it would be both possible and desirable for the United States to enlarge its strategic foothold in the Middle East, even if that meant softening its outright opposition to nationalist regimes. Those regimes would almost certainly evolve over time, they argued. In fact, by the early 1970s, many of them were already evincing dissatisfaction with the "limited aid" they received from the Soviet Union.

The debate gained fresh impetus after Richard Nixon won the U.S. presidential elections in November 1968. At the core of the so-called Nixon Doctrine was the need to reconcile what America could do with the reality of what was happening on the international scene. Most of the internal discussions in the Nixon administration, as Harold (Hal) H. Saunders, who was assistant secretary of state in the 1970s, has documented, reflected one of two possible perspectives. One group argued that to safeguard American strength, it was necessary to prop up regimes that were already friendly to the United States, "to not let them fall." The most pressing task, they maintained, was to prepare the region to "fight off" the Soviet Union; priority should be given to building a "strategic consensus" with America's allies. A second bloc of officials argued that contacts should be established and support should be provided to the "forces of renewal"—in other words, to the same nationalist regimes that had been anathema in the past. The sooner a comprehensive peace was reached in the Middle East, this second group maintained, the easier it would be to preserve and reinforce America's foothold there.

The first group argued that the United States should support Israel unconditionally—no pressure to forge a compromise with the Palestinians should ever be brought to bear on its government, lest the strain on the relationship with such an important outpost of American influence prove too great to bear. The second group held that solving the Palestine problem was the only way to pull the rug out from under the anti-U.S. forces in the region and the only way to safeguard oil supplies. The first group contended that the United States should not allow itself "to be blackmailed by the oil-producing countries," "as happened in Western Europe," but that it should continue to pursue a hard line. The second group countered that since the "free world" was completely dependent on Middle Eastern oil, it had no choice but to seek "compromise solutions."[3]

Saunders, of course, belonged to the second group. He and I found much common ground during the Dartmouth meetings,[4] where we headed the U.S. and Soviet sides of a working panel on Middle East issues. This group was very active at a time when contacts between our two countries were still restricted at official levels. Though Hal was a deputy secretary of state, I was still in my post at Moscow's Institute of World Economy and International Relations. Even so, we understood that the authorities in both the Soviet Union and the United States would be briefed on the outcome of our talks, which went far to demonstrate how the two superpowers could work together to bring stability and peace to the Middle East.

In what he wrote about the Dartmouth meetings, Saunders said he highly valued the work we did there. I second his sentiments—and I would also like to add that he was not the only American whose ideas were so congenial; there were also Bill Polk, Bill Quandt, and Edward Jaredjan, to name but a few who were, at the time I met them, staff at the State Department or the U.S. National Defense Council. Many Americans—academics, experts, and journalists—had an excellent understanding of the Middle East situation. Unfortunately, there were also those whose anti-Soviet bias served as a poor substitute for their lack of knowledge and experience. But not everyone who shaped America's policy in that turbulent region, or tried to shape it, should be tarred with the same brush.

Writing in the *New York Times,* the U.S. diplomat George F. Kennan argued:

> We devote excessive attention to the Soviet military threat—the reality of which is unproven—and yet the greatest threats to our security remain the same as before: our self-created dependence on Arab oil, along with the way we have allowed ourselves to be sucked into a wholly unstable state of affairs between the Arabs and the Israelis. Do we forget that neither of these can be put right by military force or that the Soviet Union is not the major factor in either of these situations?

He was not the only one to ask this sort of question.

One prominent figure who publicly endorsed Kennan's view was Charles Yost, the former U.S. envoy to the UN, whom I have had the chance to meet on more than one occasion. Yost has always stood out, thanks to his independent mind and profound grasp of Middle East issues. An erudite, broad-minded diplomat and politician, he has never responded in a knee-jerk way but is unfailingly tactful, always seeking to grasp the points made by anyone he is talking with. He understood and made clear in no uncertain terms that there could never be a peaceful settlement in the Middle East unless there was a solution to the Palestinian issue, and that the only way to attain that was to create a Palestinian state.

A FOCUS ON ECONOMICS

Under Nixon, the United States began to steer a new course in the Middle East. There were no strategic U-turns or formal repudiations of previously stated goals, but there were subtle changes in relations with the more radical Arab regimes. Although these shifts provoked sharp differences of opinion in the U.S. administration, not to mention strong opposition from both Israel itself and from its U.S.-based lobbyists, it opened the door for the United States to develop a whole new approach to the Middle East. This was due, in no small part, to the quagmire in Southeast Asia. Having devoted most of his attention to Vietnam, Nixon was eager to do what he could to ease tensions in the Middle East. Moreover, as national security adviser Henry Kissinger would write in his 1979 book, *White House Years*, Nixon was prepared to use the Middle East as a bargaining chip in "some sort of deal with the Soviet Union" that would resolve the Vietnam crisis once and for all. There would be no such deal but, thanks mainly to Kissinger, the United States started Egypt down the road to drawing up its separate peace agreement with Israel.

As it became more and more obvious that economics played a role in America's Middle East policy, greater emphasis was placed on economic leverage as a means of effecting change. During one of our meetings in the early 1970s, Bill Quandt raised the example of Algeria: despite pinning its colors to the socialist mast and breaking off diplomatic relations in 1967, despite its leaders' stridently anti-imperialist speeches, the United States had nonetheless established good relations with Algeria, relations based solely on economic partnership.

Another example, in sharp contrast with its reaction to the Ba'athist regime in Iraq, was Washington's relaxed attitude to the coup in Libya that toppled the monarchy and installed Colonel Gaddafi as head of a new republican regime. Throughout the 1970s, America's economic ties with Libya expanded and flourished as they never had under the monarchy, particularly in the oil sector. And although Libya managed to secure the decommissioning of both U.S. and British military bases on its territory—including Willis Field, the biggest U.S. Air Force base in the Middle East—its foreign policy goals never interfered with trade.

The feat that America pulled off in the 1970s was to have maintained what looked like two diametrically opposed policies toward Libya at the same time. On the one hand, diplomatic relations were extremely strained, with U.S. war planes making constant incursions into Libyan airspace and the U.S. Navy conducting maneuvers provocatively close to the Libyan coast, including in the Gulf of Sidra, which Tripoli claims as territorial waters. On the other hand, Libya became the third biggest exporter of oil to the United States. By the end of the decade more than fifty different U.S. companies were active in Libya, most engaged in prospecting and drilling for oil; between 2,000 and 2,500 American citizens lived there. In the early 1970s, the United States also made overtures to Iraq and Syria. Although they did not ultimately result in improved relations, it is notable that the United States made the effort at all.

PROMISING CONTACTS WITH SADAT

For all this, Egypt continued to occupy a central place in America's strategic thinking. Almost as soon as Nasser died, U.S. officials began to seek ways to approach Egypt's new president, Anwar Sadat, hoping to bring him under their control. Sadat would lead a virtual coup d'état on May 13, 1971—the so-called Corrective Revolution—after which all of Nasser's former inner circle was removed from power. This would provide both sides with opportunities to make a fresh start.

But at this early date, in November 1970, just weeks after Nasser's death, the United States recognized that it would be counterproductive to make direct overtures to the new president, who was still trying to maintain the illusion that he was carrying on his predecessor's policies. Sadat was especially eager for the Soviet Union to continue to have faith in him. Though he had no need of Soviet arms at that moment, he had not yet entered the "game" with the United States and Israel that would enable him to dispense with Soviet support altogether—and that subsequently led to his signing the separate accord with Israel that the United States helped broker.

Saudi intelligence chief Kamel Adkham, a trusted aide of King Faisal, traveled to Cairo at the United States's request. Adkham told the Egyptian president that the Americans were alarmed by Russia's presence in Egypt. Sadat realized that what the United States was putting on the table were the first steps he would have to take to improve relations. He wasted little time in telling Adkham that he was willing to put an end to the "Soviet presence," but not before Israel completed an initial phase of withdrawing its troops from Sinai. For Egypt to take what it saw as a painful step toward meeting the Americans halfway, Sadat exacted a price, albeit a small one: all he asked for was an *initial* phase of Israeli troop withdrawal. He must have realized that a military pullout of this kind—without which it would be impossible to reopen the Suez Canal—posed no threat to the interests of the United States itself. When Adkham asked Sadat for his permission to convey his proposal to the Americans, Sadat gave him the go-ahead. Such was the first message the United States received from the new president of Egypt.[5]

Analysis of Sadat's public pronouncements gave the State Department and the U.S. National Security Council further encouragement. His speeches and interviews were sprinkled with references to "maintaining a Nasserite course" or to "our gratitude to the Soviet Union" or to "our duty to defend the interests of the entire Arab nation" and so on. Nevertheless, even these early statements hinted that he might be willing to "play ball" with the United States. It was evident in his interview with veteran CBS anchorman Walter Cronkite, broadcast on American TV on January 7 and 8, 1971, in which Sadat stressed that he was "totally in favor of a peaceful settlement" in the Middle East. He then added: "Nor am I dependent on any Soviet assurances" and "our policies are made in Cairo, made by us, and never made for us by other countries." Eventually, on February 4, 1971, delivering precisely the "message" the Americans had been hoping for, Sadat proposed reopening the Suez Canal, on condition that there be a "cessation of hostilities" and some withdrawal of Israeli troops to the east of the canal. His proposed resolution completely skirted the question of the other Arab territories annexed by Israel in 1967.

All of this—the Americans' appraisal of Sadat's character, their analysis of his first few speeches, and the intelligence they received from Saudi sources—helped shape the U.S. decision to test the waters openly, on an official, diplomatic level. Secretary of State William Rogers was tasked with meeting Egyptian foreign minister Mahmoud Riyad. Rogers deemed their meeting a success, so in early May 1971 he flew to Cairo for a meeting with Sadat himself.

It seems that neither Nixon nor Kissinger—nor the foreign affairs experts who worked for Rogers in the State Department—had expected this first meeting with the new Egyptian president to be quite as productive as it turned out to be. At one point in their discussion, Sadat abruptly changed the subject and, without beating about the bush, asked Rogers why he had not raised the issue of "the Soviet presence in Egypt." Kamel Adkham, the Saudi intelligence chief, had already told Rogers what Sadat had said about this issue. But now Rogers had the unique opportunity to hear corroboration of Adkham's report from Sadat himself—and without even having to dig around for it. Sadat confirmed that Soviet technicians would indeed leave Egypt after the first phase of Israeli troop withdrawal from the Suez Canal.

But the United States was still not quite ready to believe Sadat, especially after he granted Soviet warships the right to dock at several Egyptian ports. In fairness to Sadat, he had sent a confidential note to Nixon urging him not to object to this move, but American intelligence interpreted it as evidence that the Egyptian president was double-dealing—that he was still maintaining a pro-Soviet line, even as he made overtures to the United States.

Sadat was double-dealing, but not with the United States. On February 4, 1971, the same day that he announced his unilateral decision to open the Suez Canal, Sadat sent a message to the Soviet government in which he spoke of the need to stand firm against a "treacherous alliance of the enemies of peace, freedom and progress." He sent it via Sharavi Gomaa, a close ally of Nasser's who was well known in the Soviet Union. In order to lend further credence to his assurances that he was not backing down from Nasserite policy, Sadat allowed Gomaa to represent himself as his personal friend and colleague, one in whom he enjoyed complete trust. Within three months, Sadat would have this "friend and colleague" thrown in jail. Eventually Nasser's entire inner circle would be behind bars—but still Washington withheld its embrace. Struggling to find a way out of the Vietnam crisis, Nixon was in no hurry to sour U.S.-Soviet relations by openly cozying up to the "heir" of Nasser. Nixon's hesitation served only to entrench the Israelis. Sadat became anxious that the signals he had been sending to Washington were not getting through; after all, he had put a great deal at stake.

During the 24th Congress of the Soviet Communist Party, Sadat had sent a message to the Soviet leadership proposing an Egyptian-Soviet partnership treaty. Fearing that his American alternative was in tatters—and worried that his arrests of such pro-Soviet Nasser associates as Sabri, Gomaa, and Sharaf had damaged his standing with the USSR, Sadat signed the treaty, hoping it would safeguard his position in the Kremlin's eyes. At the same time, Sadat assured the Americans that the treaty with Moscow was not a snub; indeed, it could facilitate the forging of closer ties with the United States, by serving as a smokescreen. The United States remained noncommittal. It was against this backdrop that Sadat made another visit to Moscow in 1971. It was just like "the good old days." During one meeting Sadat lavishly praised his hosts: "I always tell my people that you stood shoulder-to-shoulder with us as true friends in our darkest hour. I believe that the imperialist powers are bent on driving a wedge between us and the Soviet Union. Only America and Zionism stand to gain from that."

It is deeply regrettable that the Kremlin took him at his word. Vadim Kirpichenko, head of the Soviet overseas intelligence station in Cairo, told me that he had been sending reports to Moscow on Sadat's two-faced efforts to change the direction of his foreign policy all along, but they weren't being heeded. Incidentally, General Kirpichenko—as he was called when I headed Russia's overseas intelligence service, a time when our friendship grew as he helped me come to grips with my new post—had been a friend of mine back when we were both students at Moscow's Institute of Oriental Studies. But no matter what arguments or facts we had at our disposal, it was hard, if not impossible, to break through the barriers raised by the then very powerful Soviet premier Nikolai Podgorny, Foreign Minister Andrei Gromyko, and Party Secretary Boris Ponomarev, all of whom traveled to Cairo for the treaty signing. Podgorny had made a point of getting the two men in charge of Soviet foreign policy "on board" for the treaty, which was presented to the Politburo as an achievement that would safeguard the legacy of Nasserism in Egypt. It was a line that the Soviet ambassador in Cairo, Vladimir Vinogradov, also maintained.

WHY SOME IN MOSCOW WERE UPSET BY MY REPORT

Other people in the Soviet leadership had their doubts about Sadat. In the first few days of June 1971, I was summoned to an urgent meeting with Leonid Zamyatin, who was then the director-general of the Soviet state news agency TASS. He told me he had attended a meeting of the secretariat of the Soviet central committee at which Party Secretary Pyotr Demichev had asked why there was no intelligence on Egypt from Primakov. (At that time I had already left *Pravda* to work for the Institute of World Economy and International Relations in Moscow.) "I've been asked to send you to the Middle East for a month as a special correspondent for TASS," Zamyatin informed me. "Is that OK with you?" It was a rhetorical question, of course.

Very soon afterward, I flew to Cairo. Once there, I had a lot of meetings with people I knew well from my five-year tour of duty as *Pravda's* Egypt correspondent. These included former prime minister Aziz Sidqi, who was then acting head of the not-yet-disbanded Arab Socialist Union. (While we were meeting, I took note of the fact that there were two portraits on the wall of his office: one of Nasser, one of Sadat. But in the public reception area outside his office there was only a picture of Sadat.) I also met minister of state Hasan al-Zayat, political figures such as Khaled Mohieddin, Ahmed Khamroush, and Fouad Moursi, and political commentators from leading Cairo newspapers such as Muhammed Oda, Philippe Galyab, Muhammed Said Ahmed, and Adil Hussein, as well as Tahsin Bashir, official representative of the government of the United Arab Republic (as Egypt still called itself at the time). From my conversations with all these figures, I was able to build a clear picture of the changes that had taken hold in Egypt after President Nasser's death.

I reported my findings to Moscow via encrypted telegrams, but sent them from Beirut, not from Cairo, the reasons for which will follow momentarily. First, though, let me turn to my June 12 meeting in

Cairo with Raymond H. Anderson, a correspondent for the *New York Times* and an American citizen. I knew the story of Anderson's stint in Moscow, where he had also represented the *New York Times:* he had fallen in love with a female student at the Moscow Institute of International Relations and braved the ensuing scandal to marry her. In those days, marriages to foreigners were not encouraged in the USSR, to put it mildly. Anderson was forced to leave the Soviet Union. I am not sure how long it took, but his wife was eventually allowed to join him—although she was given to understand that she would be barred from reentering the USSR. She had left behind elderly relatives in the central Russian city of Kuybyshev (now Samara); her husband clearly held out hope that the ban would be lifted some day. I mention these details because I believe our conversations were linked to his efforts to arrange a trip for his wife to visit her family.

Anderson invited me to lunch via my friend Viktor Kudryavtsev—sadly, now deceased—who was Cairo bureau chief for Soviet television and radio. The three of us headed out to a quiet little restaurant on the outskirts of Cairo. Anderson recounted an exchange that had taken place, literally days before, between Sadat and the U.S. provisional representative Donald C. Bergus, who was about to leave for Washington. (Bergus had headed the U.S. interests section in Cairo after Egypt broke off diplomatic relations with the United States during the Six-Day War.) Sadat had asked Bergus to assure President Nixon that all of his agreements with Secretary of State Rogers were still in effect with regard to ending the Russian presence in Egypt. "Pay no attention to some of those statements I've been making," Sadat said. "I was forced to say those things—my main decision has been made."

This was a crucial piece of information, so I immediately went to see Vladimir Vinogradov. Vadim Kirpichenko was present too as I told the Soviet ambassador of my conversation with Anderson and of the other impressions I had gained from my many meetings. Vinogradov could barely contain his anger.

"You think you can spend a few days here and come up with these ground-breaking revelations!" he snapped. "I meet Sadat five times a week, so believe me, I know the situation here better than you do."

"You have instructions from Moscow to allow me access to the embassy's secure telex line," I said, also starting to lose my temper. "I'll send my report to the Foreign Ministry and you're free to add that anything I write is a complete fabrication."

"I will not send your telegrams as I have no wish to misinform the Kremlin."

And that was the end of the conversation. So I decided to fly to Beirut, where I had been planning to go anyway, and file my reports from there. Apart from my conversation with Anderson, I reported on how I saw the situation in the UAR. The thrust of my reports was as follows:

1. Egypt is undergoing a shift to the right.

There is reason to believe, I said, that the impending trial of detainees from Nasser's inner circle will be used to discredit the entire legacy of the former Egyptian leader. "The Corrective Revolution" of mid-May was much more complex and far-reaching than a change of personnel in the Egyptian leadership. The group that was removed from power had represented a whole range of ideologies, as Nasser had brought the bourgeoisie under the same roof as socialism. The group that holds power under Sadat is much narrower, primarily representing the interests of the Egyptian bourgeoisie. This is not the "old" bourgeoisie, I added, whose property was expropriated or subject to restrictions when Nasser was in power, but a "new" bourgeoisie that had grown stronger even in Nasser's time due to the expansion of the state sector—only then they didn't have a clear route to power.

I also pointed out that here had been a marked increase in activity by reactionary Islamic groups. Talks on the new UAR draft constitution had been marked by ever-louder demands "for all that has been done, and all that will be done, to be done in accordance with Islam." Vice president Hussein Shafei said the changes afoot had been ordained in the Koran.

2. The political landscape has been transformed by the arrest or expulsion of leading figures from the Arab Socialist Union (ASU),

along with the dismissal of the secretary of the Socialist Vanguard group, which formed the core of the ASU.

The ASU had been practically inactive since 1967, but since it had
at its core a nerve center that managed to hold the six-million strong
ASU together, it was still one of the UAR's power bases. But under
Sadat the ASU's interim leadership were conservative figures from top
to bottom. Sadat had personally ordered the closure of any ASU organizations with two hundred members or less. For the most part,
those were workers' collectives.

3. The Egyptian army is unlikely to take action as a single entity,
   especially after the disbanding of Marshal Amer's unit, which
   had been the conduit through which the Egyptian military top
   brass had exerted influence over government policy. Still, I
   could not rule out the possibility of individual right-wing army
   units taking action—if not to actually seize power, then to position themselves so as to shift the balance of power in Egypt at a
   later date.
4. Sadat's June 11 speech, written by influential journalist Mohamed Heikal, assured the nation that he would continue to
   face down the reaction and steadfastly carry on with a program
   of social reform. If nothing else, it showed that those seeking
   to "steer" the new Egyptian president were trying to keep him
   on the political centerline. But Sadat was no Nasser, and he
   wasn't about to let himself be remade in his predecessor's
   image. The outlook for the UAR, I insisted, was one of
   change.

The three reports I wired from Beirut were distributed to the entire Politburo, both to full and candidate members, as well as to the
secretaries of the Party Central Committee. They also went to the Soviet Foreign Ministry, to Andrei Gromyko and first deputy foreign
minister Vasily Kuznetsov. On my return to Moscow, Zamyatin suggested that I write up my impressions for publication in the so-called
Special File, restricted information that TASS circulated only among

a select few senior figures in the Soviet establishment. I wrote a
lengthy article that argued that while the treaty that Moscow had
signed with Sadat was positive in many ways, it provided no panacea
against shifts in Egypt's domestic political landscape and changes to
its foreign policy outlook—changes that ran counter to the best interests of the Soviet Union. Though its circulation was restricted, the
file reached many more readers than the reports I had sent from
Beirut by wire.

Shortly after the Special File came out, I got a phone call from
Yevgeny Samoteykin, an adviser to Leonid Brezhnev, who told me
that the Soviet general secretary had shown an interest in its content
and had even taken it home to familiarize himself with it in greater
detail. Of course I was delighted to hear this. Two days later, however, there came another call from Samoteykin, whose abrupt message was : "I've just saved your skin." It turns out that Podgorny had
kicked up a scandal and ordered the Special File withdrawn from circulation. TASS had duly recalled it. But even that had not pacified
Podgorny: TASS director Zamyatin had to be punished too. When
Podgorny reviewed the pre-prepared lists of Central Committee
members who were up for selection at the next party congress, he
struck off Zamyatin.

Six months after my reports from Cairo had incurred Podgorny's
wrath, Sadat himself set out his position in a way that left no room
for doubt. In an interview with Arnaud de Borchgrave of *Newsweek*
on December 13, 1971, the Egyptian leader openly stated what he
had told Michael Sterner, head of the State Department's Egypt section, during his trip to Cairo the previous July: "Nixon wanted to
know if the treaty on Egyptian-Soviet friendship and cooperation had
in any way shifted our position away from that set out in my previous talks with [state secretary Bill] Rogers," Sadat told *Newsweek*. "I
told him it hadn't." Nixon's next question, Sadat said, "amounted to
whether I would stand by my promise to restore diplomatic relations
with the United States after the first phase of the Israeli troop withdrawal. Yes, I replied. The third question was whether I still intended
to send the Soviet military home [from Egypt] after the first phase of
the Israeli troop withdrawal. I told him I did."

KISSINGER ENTERS THE GAME

In his book *White House Years*, Kissinger wrote: "In December 1971, Nixon took a step that led to my having operational control over Middle East diplomacy." What was that step? Why was Rogers bypassed? Kissinger explained: In December Israeli prime minister Golda Meir paid a visit to President Nixon and "Both leaders came to a mutual understanding on the pivotal questions of [Middle East] tactics and strategy: that the search for a wider peace settlement would have to be suspended for the time being . . . Instead, fresh efforts should be made to seal a provisional accord with Egypt."

Mahmoud Riyad, Egypt's foreign minister, had long insisted that the reopening of the Suez Canal should be tied to concrete progress toward a comprehensive Middle East peace settlement. The U.S. secretary of state was also said to be an advocate of a comprehensive peace deal. As a result, both were excluded from the process of seeking a settlement, as were the Saudis, who were no longer used as a conduit to Cairo. Instead, direct channels were opened between the intelligence services of both countries, channels that the White House used to bypass the State Department, and Sadat to bypass the Egyptian foreign ministry. Sadat had told the Americans that he agreed to their interpretation of the so-called partial accord as early as the beginning of 1972, though he continued to pay lip service to the propaganda line of rejecting the principle of partial settlement—a theme he would enlarge upon at length on his visits to Moscow and in talks with Soviet officials in Cairo. But as Kissinger puts it in his memoirs: "It was so much clearer to us." It is possible, maybe even likely, that to begin with, Sadat believed that a partial accord could serve as a stepping stone toward an eventual set of agreements between Israel and other Arab countries and with the Palestinians. But there is no doubt that by late 1971/early 1972 he had rejected the idea of explicitly tying it to a comprehensive Middle East peace settlement.

Not long after secret channels were opened between Sadat and Kissinger, the Egyptian president decided to send the Soviet Union's military advisers home. He was so taken with this idea that he did not even engage in political horse trading with the Americans to squeeze whatever payback he could out of them. But judging by his memoirs, Kissinger nonetheless waited for Sadat to set out some concrete conditions before he began to bargain with him.

There was a certain logic behind Sadat's engagement with the United States. He probably reckoned that once he turned his back on the Soviet Union, the Americans would put their relations with Egypt on the same footing as their relations with Israel, given the fact that Egypt played such an important role in the Arab world. Sadat was genuinely incensed when he was confronted with the reality that the United States gave priority to its relations with Israel. Yet he did not abandon hope.

The Americans turned down Sadat's suggestion of a meeting with President Nixon, but it was agreed that Hafez Ismail, his national security adviser, would make an official trip to the United States. In February 1973, Ismail flew to Washington for a visit that would include a meeting with Nixon in the White House. Kissinger made only a brief token appearance at the White House meeting, so as not to create the impression that he—rather than the State Department— was orchestrating America's Middle East policies. But Kissinger saw Ismail on three other occasions in conditions of the utmost secrecy— including an intensive meeting at the home of Pepsi-Cola president Donald Kendall in Connecticut that lasted for several hours. Kendall was a personal friend of Nixon's, which strongly suggests that the president knew and approved of the fact that Kissinger was bypassing the State Department, which he had yet to take charge of.

Several years later, while attending a U.S.-Soviet Dartmouth meeting in the Latvian coastal resort of Jurmala, I found myself sitting next to Donald Kendall, who was also a participant in the conference, during a bus excursion. I asked him if it was true that he had hosted secret negotiations between the U.S. and Egyptian presidents' national security advisers.

"How do you know that?" Kendall asked, clearly alarmed. I decided to pull his leg for a while and didn't give him an answer straight away. But Kendall was looking at me so suspiciously I finally told him the truth. I'd read it in a newly published book by the well-known Egyptian journalist Mohamed Heikal, a copy of which the author had given me himself. Heikal was the first to publish revelations about the United States's secret relations with Egypt on the eve of the 1973 war—and the words Kendall used to describe him were, I think, some of the strongest in the English language.

Gerald Ford, who replaced Nixon as president in 1974, had hardly any experience in international affairs, so U.S. foreign policy remained firmly under Kissinger's control. Congress was unhappy that such important affairs of state were concentrated in the hands of one man. There was also a growing tide of public criticism, so at the end of 1975 President Ford appointed General Brent Scowcroft to the post of national security adviser. But, as Kissinger points out in his memoirs, the appointment did nothing to curb his sway over foreign policy. He had long enjoyed a good relationship with Scowcroft, and this had not changed. Scowcroft, quite apart from anything else, had been Kissinger's deputy when he was national security adviser. Kissinger continued to dominate U.S. policy on the Middle East, and most of his efforts were focused on Sadat, whom he was grooming to broker a separate treaty with Israel.

As we will see in the next chapter, the Yom Kippur War of October 1973 played a key role in Kissinger's game plan.

− 10 −

HIDDEN PRESSURES BEHIND THE YOM KIPPUR WAR OF 1973

FEW IN THE UNITED STATES imagined that the Arab countries would have the audacity to launch another all-out war against Israel, especially after the crushing defeat they had suffered in 1967. Yes, there might have been armed skirmishes from time to time; there were incidences, too, of tanks and artillery firing on Israeli positions across the Suez Canal. But a frontal assault on the "impregnable" Bar-Lev line that Israel had built along the east bank of the canal? Or, still less plausibly, coordinated operations by Egypt and Syria to retake the Suez Canal by force and march into the Golan Heights? That was a scenario that had never crossed anyone's mind.

When we were in New York in May 1973, the Soviet academician Vitaly Zhurkin and I were invited to speak at the Council on Foreign Relations, the prestigious think tank. Most of the people who attended were American experts on Middle East issues, and our talk all but turned into a dialogue with them. Among the scenarios we outlined was one in which the Arabs initiated a war against Israel and imposed an oil embargo. Of all of our hypotheticals, this one prompted the strongest criticism. One woman who introduced herself as a State Department staffer said that the Arab countries were all too aware of Israel's military supremacy, and moreover had nothing to gain from turning the whole Western world against them. Similar views were voiced by the rest of our interlocutors.

Needless to say, Zhurkin and I knew nothing about the military operation that Egypt and Syria were already planning. But we felt that it was illogical to categorically rule out the notion of an Arab attack, given the rising tide of resentment among ordinary Arabs at the lack of decisive action to liberate the territories occupied in 1967. When war did break out six months later—almost exactly along the lines envisioned by Zhurkin and myself—we began to experience problems with our visas that we'd never had before. In 1976, we were denied extensions to our stay in the United States that would have allowed us to attend a meeting of the UN Association of America. Only with the intervention of our colleague Marshall D. Shulman, the distinguished Soviet affairs scholar who was then working for the State Department, were we able to resolve our difficulties.

SADAT LETS THE CAT OUT OF THE BAG

Obviously, Egypt and Syria did not notify the Americans of their intention to launch a full-scale military action. In his memoirs, Henry Kissinger stresses that the scale of the Egyptian and Syrian mobilization and the coordination of their armed units came as a complete surprise to the U.S. administration. Did Egypt and Syria give the Soviet Union advance warning of the attack? When Nasser was still in power, Soviet military advisers had been closely involved in formulating a plan called Operation Granite, whose aim was to take the Suez Canal by force and liberate the occupied Egyptian territory on the Sinai peninsula. Under Sadat, there had been modified versions of the plan called Granite I and Granite II. During a meeting I had with Sadat that I will describe later, the Egyptian president told me that he had ordered that the military operations map be shown to the Soviet defense minister, Andrei Grechko, as early as February 1973. Sadat's words made it clear that on an operational level the military offensive had *not* been drawn up with the participation of Soviet officials. The map was merely *shown* to Marshal Grechko and, moreover, that was in February—the war did not begin until eight months later, in October. Intelligence from well-informed sources confirms that Sadat did not inform Moscow of when this full-scale offensive against Israel would begin. This version of events is corroborated by the fact that early reports coming out of Cairo and Damascus made out that it was Israel that had initiated the hostilities. (It later transpired that the content of these reports had been agreed upon in advance by the Egyptian and Syrian leaders.) Sadat clearly feared that the Soviet Union, which had nothing to gain from being dragged into a serious crisis in the Middle East, would try to block the operation. Syrian president Hafez Assad, meanwhile, stuck to the agreement he had made with Sadat about maintaining the "utmost secrecy" in regard to the planned operation.

Soviet intelligence reports of movement by Egyptian and Syrian army units caused great concern in Moscow. Even if the Kremlin did not expect the Arab attack, it could not rule out the possibility that Israel would launch a preemptive strike, as it had done at the outset of the 1967 Six-Day War. The order went out to evacuate families of Soviet diplomats and advisers from Egypt and Syria. Russia's greatest concern, of course, was for the safety of the women and children; but at the same time, once the evacuation began, it was as if an alarm bell were sounding. The Soviet Union's evacuation was inevitably interpreted by the Americans as a serious warning of impending conflict.

The Yom Kippur War can be divided into two parts. In the early part of the conflict, the Israelis were overwhelmed by the Egyptian and Syrian armies' vastly enhanced firepower. Later the Israelis regained the upper hand, bringing the Egyptian and Syrian armies to the verge of defeat. I was in Damascus during the war, and witnessed with my own eyes the massive initial losses suffered by the Israeli air force when its planes came under fire from Kvadrat antiaircraft missiles in the skies above the Syrian capital. Although the Kvadrat system was Soviet-produced, it was the Syrians who deployed it; there is no dispute about that. It was in Damascus, too, that I saw morale take a nosedive when locals found out that Syrian troops had retreated from Quneitra. Only a few days earlier, when the city had been briefly liberated from Israeli control, there had been outpourings of jubilation.

The scope of this book does not extend to unraveling the causes of this turning point in the war; I am happy to leave that to the objective scrutiny of military experts. Nor do I intend to recount what took place on the various battlefields. That subject has already been covered at great length in any number of articles and books. What concerns me are the underlying causes of the war, which, until now, have remained obscure. The following should shed some light on them.

It must have been easier for the Americans to make sense of Sadat's plans in relation to the Yom Kippur War than it was for us in the Soviet Union, at least at first. But allow me to skip two years ahead, and we will have a better understanding of Sadat's motives. In the fall of 1975 the prominent Soviet journalist and Middle East scholar Igor Belyaev and I were recipients of the International Nasser Prize for our book *Egypt: The Time of President Nasser*. When we arrived in Cairo for the award ceremony in which we were given medals, our friend Lutfi al-Kholi, the long-serving editor of *At-Taliya*—arguably Egypt's most respected monthly—forwarded us an invitation to meet Sadat. Obviously anxious to underline the unofficial nature of this meeting, Sadat arranged for it to take place at his country residence in Barraj. An offer of this sort was remarkable, since Sadat had stopped receiving Soviet officials, even diplomats. The meeting took place on November 25 and lasted for three hours: it consisted mainly of a rambling monologue on Sadat's part, in which he recounted the exploits of his army, interrupting himself only to criticize Moscow. Naturally, we challenged his accusations, prompting him to assure us that "just as in Nasser's day, he still felt connected heart and soul to the Soviet Union."

Belyaev and I had both met Sadat before, which clearly encouraged him to put on a show of openness and candor. He seemed especially anxious that we regard him as "the father of the nation" (his words), as a man shaping the course of history. We got the sense that Sadat had not yet been allowed to rest on Nasser's laurels; he was very keen to convince us that he had been guided by "higher concerns" during the war, and not just by the logic of the battlefield. From my notes I can reproduce almost word-for-word one of the things that Sadat told us:

My Third Army had been surrounded by the Israelis in Sinai. But General [Ariel] Sharon's tanks were surrounded by Egyptian forces that had broken through to the west bank of the Suez Canal. So even then, in the closing stages of the war, the situation was finely balanced. My generals were pressuring me to cut through the narrow corridor that connected Sharon's tanks with the rest of the [Israeli] forces and to strike at the bridgehead that we had captured. The whole point was to secure a double advantage—for our tanks as well as for our artillery. But Henry Kissinger sent me a message saying: "Mr. President, if Soviet weaponry inflicts another defeat on American weaponry, I will be in no position to defy the Pentagon, and that will deal a serious blow to our agreements."

"What agreements?" Belyaev and I asked in unison. Sadat abruptly changed the subject.

A conversation I had with Egypt's former defense minister, Muhammad Sadiq, sheds further light on Sadat's true motives. When I was the *Pravda* correspondent in Cairo I lived in the same apartment block as Sadiq, and we struck up a nodding acquaintance. I used to meet him in the street when he was out walking his dog early in the morning; when our paths crossed at night Sadiq would always greet me in Russian. While we were in Cairo, I asked if I could talk with him, and then and there he invited me to his home for what turned out to be a very friendly visit. "I'm retired now, and have been thinking a lot about what I've lived through," Sadiq told me. "Sadat recently gave a speech in which he stated that when he started the war in October 1973, he had enough ammunition for two days, while Syria had enough for twenty days. These were figures that he had to produce as part of his debate with Hafez Assad. But what it boils down to is that Sadat was the one who instigated hostilities. Which means that either he is a complete idiot [the word Sadiq used was a rather stronger one] or that by then he had already made an agreement—a firm agreement—that he would be stopped."

Sadiq knew what he was talking about. The Egyptian president and he had had serious differences of opinion over the planned military offensive. On October 24, 1972, a year before the war broke out, Sadat had called Egypt's top military brass to a meeting and explicitly called for a "limited war," arguing, unbelievably, that liberating as little as ten millimeters of territory on the east bank of the Suez Canal would strengthen his hand diplomatically. Sadiq and most of the generals were skeptical about the notion that a war could be so tightly contained. Two days later, Sadat's secretary called the minister at his home to tell him that the president would accept his resignation, even though he had not been asked for it.

On December 1, 1975, Belyaev and I flew out to Amman, Jordan. The next day we dined with King Hussein. There were only five of us at the table: the king, Prime Minister Zeid Rifai, Belyaev, myself, and R. V. Yushchuk, a Soviet intelligence officer who was later stationed in Britain. I had first met King Hussein at the end of the 1960s—and I had been late for our appointment. When he greeted me, he was wearing a colorful shirt and had his sleeves rolled up. "Your majesty, forgive me for being late," I said. "It's not my fault that Jordan is the only country in the Middle East where cars actually stop at red lights." The king had a good sense of humor; from that moment on, we enjoyed a close relationship that lasted for many years, right up until this wise, learned, and charming man passed away. One particular occasion speaks volumes about how true a friend he became. Somehow he found out that I was staying at the prime minister's house on the outskirts of Amman. He rushed out to see me—alone, and on his motorbike. You can hardly imagine the looks of fuming, silent anger I got from his bodyguards, who turned up a few minutes later, hot on the heels of their beloved monarch. Of course I did not agree with all of King Hussein's policies, but on a personal level I admired his courage and the perspicacity that he so often displayed. In the most difficult of times, it was these two qualities that helped him navigate his ship of state through treacherous waters.

Skilled at putting people at ease, the king often wore a rather shy smile on his face, even when discussing the most serious issues. This occasion was no different. Although Rifai kept his distance from the king in public, there was no sense of constraint or aloofness between them— after all, they were good friends who had been at college together.

It was quite evident that the Jordanian leadership had been sorely irritated by Sadat's recent conduct. As King Hussein put it: "We showed solidarity with the other Arab countries—especially Egypt—

by fighting in the 1948 war, the 1956 war, and the 1967 war. But when he opened hostilities in 1973, Sadat didn't even let us know. Nor did he consult anyone when he went and signed the agreement [for Israel to withdraw from part of the territory it had occupied in Sinai]. Sadat has squandered all of the advantages the Arab countries had. Instead of a comprehensive deal based on the post–October 1973 outlook, he made a separate deal to hand everything to the Americans."

"I think Sadat had a deal in place with Kissinger before the Yom Kippur War broke out," Rifai added. "A year and a half before the war, in an attempt to restore diplomatic relations between our countries, I went to Cairo for talks with Sadat. In a moment of candor, he told me that Kissinger was proposing 'some move that would give the secretary of state a free hand to take political action with a view to resolving the conflict.' Sadat made some connection between Kissinger's words and Egypt's plans to take the canal by force and secure a foothold on the east bank, even though this would cost the lives of 10,000 to 15,000 Egyptian soldiers and officers."

"Isn't that too high a price to pay?" Rifai had asked.

"The scale of the losses could be reduced by political means," was Sadat's cryptic reply.

For proof that the purpose of this "limited war" was not to liberate occupied territory but to secure a foothold that would revive the conflict with Israel, we need look no further than the minutes of the October 2 meeting of Egypt's National Security Council. It was here that Sadat reported that hostilities would be launched "in the next few days." When asked what form the forthcoming military operation would take, Sadat's unequivocal answer was: "a limited one."[1]

ASSAD DOTS THE I'S AND CROSSES THE T'S

Although Syria fought alongside Egypt in the Yom Kippur War, Sadat did not let President Hafez Assad in on his plans for this strictly "limited" offensive. For some interesting evidence of this we can turn to General Shazly, former chief of staff of the Egyptian army. Shazly wrote an account of a conversation he had in April 1973 with Ismail

Ali, who replaced Muhammad Sadiq as Egypt's defense minister. Ali had brought Shazly "instructions from President Sadat after he had been in contact with the Syrian government." In *The Crossing of the Suez: The October War*, Shazly writes:

> It was abundantly clear that if the Syrians realized that our plans were restricted to going no further than a 10-mile zone to the east of the canal, they would not join us in launching the attack . . . Ismail had a solution in mind: he instructed me to draw up another plan—a separate one from the plan to take the canal by force—detailing an Egyptian advance as far as the mountain passes. "The details of this other plan will serve the purpose of keeping the Syrians happy," he [Ali] said. But then he added that this plan was never to be put into action, except under the most favorable of circumstances . . . I was shocked by this duplicity, but I was obliged to comply and keep this a secret.[2]

It is of particular interest to know what Hafez Assad himself thought of all this. So when I met with the Syrian president in Damascus on June 2, 1983, I asked him. Once more, I can refer to my notes to reproduce what he said almost word-for-word. Assad told me:

> We had a preliminary arrangement with Sadat that we would be honest in our dealings. It goes without saying, though, that he didn't let us in on his true motive, which was that he cooked up this war just as a means of ending the stalemate and entering negotiations.
>
> We in Syria were aware that at the end of the war there had to be a political settlement built around UN Security Council resolutions. However, our plans were based on the assumption that by the time the UN intervened, we would have managed to liberate territory on both fronts that had been occupied by Israel in 1967. That was at the core of our plans for an incursion into the Golan Heights—the idea was that the Syrian army should advance across the entire Golan Heights.

"Did Sadat notify you of his plans to wage war on his front?" I asked Assad. "Was there any coordination of plans?"

He replied,

Sadat and I had an arrangement that Syrian and Egyptian troops would attack simultaneously. The plan was that the Egyptian forces would advance as far as the crossings into Sinai, and then have an "operational halt," while the Syrians would continue to advance into the Golan Heights. It was, actually, essential to have this kind of "halt" in the area of the Sinai crossings, since we envisaged the Egyptian army sustaining substantial losses and therefore needing troop reinforcements as well as fresh supplies of arms and ammunition. However, my arrangement with Sadat gave me to understand that after this "halt" the Egyptian army would continue to advance as far as the border with Israel.

"And how did things actually turn out?" I asked.

In reality they turned out very differently. Military action was launched on October 6, as set out in our joint plan, and Syria stuck to that plan. But it seemed that Sadat was acting in accordance with some scheme of his own, and after the Suez Canal was taken, the Egyptian forces took up positions and started to dig in. By October 8, [the Israeli commander Moshe] Dayan had announced that the position on the western front had stabilized, which allowed Israel to redeploy the bulk of its troops to the Syrian front. We would have been able to hold out against the onslaught—even at the expense of losing territory—if the Egyptian advance had been followed through, which would have forced the Israelis to redeploy their troops to the western front. But that is not what happened, and that is why Syrian troops bore the brunt of the Israeli offensive.

The Egyptians had reinforcements that were supposed to be mobilized within certain time limits. Two days went by, those time limits expired, and we sent Sadat telegram after telegram

admonishing him to honor this particular part of the agreement—
but he didn't reply.

Assad went on:

Nor did we did know about the political contacts Sadat had maintained throughout the war. Syria was taken unawares by a
telegram from him that said he had approached the UN Security
Council to request a cease-fire. Sadat sought to justify this, saying
that he had decided to bring the war to an end because, he said,
the United States had entered the conflict on Israel's side and he
could not fight against the Americans. I sent a telegram back, asking him not to call off military action, pointing out that Syria still
had a chance to close a breach in the area of the Golan Heights
and to launch a heavyweight counteroffensive. Sadat did not reply
to this telegram but went ahead and agreed to a cease-fire, while
the fighting continued on the Syrian front. When he found out that
Syria had not gone along with the cease-fire, Sadat phoned me and
tried to persuade me that this was a step we had to take. He insisted that the cease-fire agreement included U.S. guarantees that
the territory captured in 1967 would be liberated from Israeli occupation. This conversation took place on October 22.

KISSINGER'S CHALLENGES

In his memoirs, the former U.S. secretary of state denies the suggestion that "someone knew in advance what Sadat was thinking." But
it is hard to believe that that "someone" might not have been Henry
Kissinger—who, besides being a brilliant strategist, was also secretly
in contact with Sadat for several months before the outbreak of war.
As he writes in the *Years of Upheaval* volume of his memoirs:

Sadat knew, from two secret meetings in early 1973 between his
national security adviser Hafez Ismail and myself, that we intended to move toward a diplomatic settlement of the Middle East

conflict. But this could only lead him to two conclusions: first, that the entire Arab agenda for a wholesale pullout of Israeli troops was unattainable; and second, that Egypt could not take any immediate decision while appearing to do so from a position of weakness. It follows that Sadat's motive for declaring war was not to win back territory but to restore Egypt's sense of self-esteem and thus give it more room for maneuver diplomatically.[3]

Also very telling is Kissinger's reaction to worried reports of Egyptian troop movements in the run-up to the war. Straight away, he warned Israel not to launch any preemptive strikes—indeed, that would be the leitmotif of his many subsequent telephone conversations with Abba Eban, Israel's foreign minister, and Mordechai Shalev, its chargé d'affaires in Washington. I believe that apart from his desire to prevent a wider Arab-Israeli war from flaring up, Kissinger also feared that an Israeli strike would spoil the scheme that he and Sadat had secretly hatched together.

It becomes apparent that the U.S. response—or rather the lack of it in the first few days of the war, before events took a more threatening turn for the Israeli army—was based on the assumption that Kissinger's scheme would be put into effect. He was, after all, the leading player in U.S. foreign policy. Despite frenzied and insistent calls from the Israeli leadership, the United States took until October 12 to start an airlift to supply them with arms and spare parts. From that point on, U.S. policy was one of unconditional support for Israel, although Washington was careful to make the odd gesture toward Egypt, since it was not in America's interests for Sadat's standing to be diminished.

Further proof of the contention that Kissinger thought a "small military victory for Sadat" would help to solve the political and diplomatic challenge he was facing can be found in a telephone conversation he had with Anatoly Dobrynin, the Soviet ambassador to Washington, at noon on October 6. A meeting of the UN Security Council had been called, and the U.S. secretary of state sent out an urgent request for the Soviet Union's envoy to show restraint for the time being; not to rush into completely taking the side of "its client" as usual. "Kissinger assured us," Dobrynin reported, "that the U.S. would do the same. He said President Nixon wanted this to be conveyed urgently to the Soviet leadership."[4]

Avoiding the question of convening the Security Council, Leonid Brezhnev used secret channels to pass the following message to Richard Nixon on October 7: "It is of the utmost importance that there be a clear statement from Israel: a statement, with no strings attached, that it is prepared to pull out of the occupied Arab territories on the understanding that Israel's security would be guaranteed, as would that of the other countries in the region. What could be unacceptable to Israel about that?" His response made it clear that Moscow believed the Arabs' gains in the early days of the war should have paved the way for a multilateral Middle East peace settlement.

Nor did the Soviet Union's position change after the fighting turned in Israel's favor. Brezhnev called for a cease-fire, but in his message to President Nixon he again insisted that it was essential to reach an overall settlement.

Sadat, meanwhile, still believed he should "stay in the game" with Kissinger, even after the Arab forces' attack had backfired on them. It is hard to find any other explanation for the secret message that Sadat sent to Kissinger via Hafez Ismail during the secretary of state's visit to Moscow, which said that he was willing "to treat the cease-fire as an issue separate from that of a comprehensive settlement." Kissinger had not said anything on this matter to top Soviet officials. This is how Kissinger explains Sadat's initiative in *Years of Upheaval*:

> Along with its proposal for a cease-fire, Moscow sought to persuade Sadat that the Soviet Union's role at the conference [convened to seek an overall settlement] would be to exert pressure on the United States and Israel. But Egypt had already shifted the focus of its policy to the U.S. and accordingly switched from an all-encompassing approach to a step-by-step approach. This made it look less desirable, or even dangerous, for the Soviet Union to play a large part, since Moscow might call for radical solutions that worked against the outcome that Sadat had wanted to achieve.[5]

Sadat was obviously still hopeful that the United States would back him up. During the war, he had opened secret channels of communication with Washington. The U.S. authorities set great store by this: first, because the tone of his messages was friendly; and second, because it was a "risky matter" for Sadat, as the one waging the war, to have made secret contacts with the Americans via intelligence agents. Moreover, in his efforts to portray himself as "a player on the American side," Sadat assured Washington that he "had not given the Russians his agreement for a cease-fire." At the same time, being a short-sighted politician, he underestimated the extent to which the United States's strategic policy favored Israel. As soon as he received Sadat's message, Kissinger phoned Dobrynin to tell him that the United States would cease to make any further efforts via the Security Council and that the U.S. president was "forced" to reconsider its position on stopping the flow of American military supplies to Israel—in other words, the airlift would be resumed.

MOSCOW AND WASHINGTON IN THE GRIP OF THE ARAB-ISRAELI CRISIS

It is often said that the two sides in the Middle East conflict were caught in the vicelike grip of the two superpowers. It was, however, the other way round. Neither the United States nor the Soviet Union had any decisive means to control the course of events; both found themselves at the mercy of an escalating crisis in the region.

It should be remembered that the Yom Kippur War erupted just as the two superpowers were beginning to strive toward détente. The war threatened to undo their efforts. On October 14, 1973, after a ceremony to mark Gerald Ford's nomination as vice president of the United States, President Nixon took Ambassador Anatoly Dobrynin aside and asked him to tell Brezhnev that he, Nixon, "was being provoked in the U.S. into derailing detente." Yet even amid the current crisis, Nixon remained steadfast in his goals. When the White House disclosed that it was supplying $2.2 billion worth of American arms to Israel, it contacted Moscow with a proposal for both the United

States and the Soviet Union to halt weapons shipments after the cease-fire took effect. But Moscow's hands were tied, largely by its relations with Egypt—a clear case of the tail wagging the dog.

On October 20 Kissinger flew to Moscow, where it was agreed that the two superpowers would issue a joint draft Security Council resolution. It would call not only for an immediate cease-fire but also (at the insistence of the Soviet side) for full compliance with 1967's resolution 242. But much time had been wasted, and now that the course of the war had turned in its favor, Israel was in no hurry to implement a cease-fire. Nevertheless, on October 22 the UN Security Council adopted resolution 338, based on the agreement reached with the United States—but Israeli troops had by then reached the Suez Canal and encircled Egyptian troops.

Even as Israel was poised to crush Sadat's troops, Kissinger seemed to continue to play his "game," although in fairness, events had forced him to modify it somewhat. His emphasis now was on "saving Sadat." This meant convincing the Egyptian president that only the United States could stop the Israelis, so he applied pressure on Israel to spare the Egyptian forces.

Meanwhile, the domestic state of affairs in both the Soviet Union and America were exerting increasing pressure on the positions they were taking internationally. There was growing anger in the Kremlin that Israel was ignoring the Security Council resolution that both Moscow and Washington had agreed to. Brezhnev, a man who was usually calm and not given to drastic action, was compelled to call Nixon on the hotline on October 23. His message dispensed with diplomatic niceties, saying: "You can see better [than we can] why Israel gets away with this treachery. We see only one way to remedy this situation and to put our agreement into practice—and that is to force Israel to comply immediately with the Security Council decision." There was also a hint that the United States's inaction would lead to the collapse of détente: "There is too much at stake—not only in the Middle East, but also in our relations."

The Americans realized how grave matters had become. That same day, Nixon replied that the United States "took responsibility on itself to ensure there would be a complete cessation of hostilities by Israel."

In his message to Brezhnev, Nixon said: "Together we have reached a historic settlement, and we will not allow it to be blown apart."

Israel, however, continued to ignore the UN Security Council's demands that it cease hostilities and pull its troops back to the positions they'd held when resolution 338 was adopted. In Moscow, there was a stormy meeting of the Politburo; emotions were running high because a clearly panicked Sadat had phoned via the special hotline, imploring the Soviet Union to do everything possible to "save him and the Egyptian capital, which was surrounded by Israeli tanks." Little time was wasted in putting questions to the Soviet chief military adviser in Cairo, who told Brezhnev that Sadat was losing his mind. Several Israeli tanks had indeed crossed the Suez Canal, he said, but they posed no immediate threat to Cairo. His temperate report did not stop a number of Politburo members calling for tough military or political sanctions.

Many top Kremlin figures argued that Israel could not have thrown down the gauntlet to all and sundry as it was doing in defiance of the Security Council's cease-fire resolution unless it had received a go-ahead from the United States. Fighting words were spoken. Vasily Grubyakov, an aide to Andrei Gromyko who had accompanied the Soviet foreign minister to a Politburo meeting, told Dobrynin (who had been summoned back to Moscow) that defense minister Andrei Grechko had wanted "a show of force by Soviet troops in Egypt." Cooler heads prevailed. Aleksei Kosygin, the Soviet premier, strongly objected to any such measures and was backed by Gromyko. Brezhnev too was cautious, and warned against Soviet troops being drawn into the conflict. But he was nevertheless forced to agree to (1) sending Nixon a strongly worded communiqué hinting that Moscow might find itself drawn in militarily; and (2) to ordering Soviet air force maneuvers in the Caucasus.

In the end it was decided to expand this hint about military intervention into an unprecedented proposal, which was that Soviet and American troops be sent to Egypt on a joint mission whose goal was to force Israel to cease hostilities. The text that Brezhnev sent Nixon on October 24 went on to say: "I tell you bluntly that if you don't deem it possible to take joint action with us, then we would find ourselves forced to consider taking the necessary steps unilaterally . . . We have an agreement with you that we value very highly—and that is to take action together. Let us put our agreement into practice in this difficult situation and apply it to the case in point. It will serve as a good illustration of how we have agreed to act in the interests of peace."

I am pretty sure that the Soviet Union never really intended to pursue military intervention; rather, the communiqué was a feint aimed at "cooling" Israel's blood. At the same time, the move was dictated by developments on the domestic front: there was mounting anger in the Soviet Union at Israel's actions, and Brezhnev may have been afraid that his opponents in the Kremlin could exploit it.

The most powerful of these enemies was Aleksandr Shelepin, nicknamed "Iron Shurik." Shelepin had shown what he was made of in 1957 when he almost single-handedly saved Khrushchev from a plot by Malenkov, Molotov, and Kaganovich to remove him from power. Later, in 1964, Shelepin was a key figure behind Khrushchev's ouster. Because Shelepin held a string of senior posts in both the Party and in government, Brezhnev thought he might try to steal his crown as general secretary. With support from many of his closest associates, Brezhnev eventually decided to have Shelepin sidelined. By the time of the communiqué to Nixon, Shelepin had already been transferred to the lower-ranking post of chairman of the Central Council of Trade Unions. Nonetheless, right up until 1975 he retained his membership in the Soviet Politburo. And Brezhnev continued to be wary of him: he knew only too well that Shelepin enjoyed strong support, especially among former Communist Youth League officials who might accuse the general secretary of indecisiveness when faced with a defiant Israel backed by the United States.

America's reaction to Brezhnev's communiqué reflected its own domestic developments rather than any wish to intimidate the Soviet Union. As was to be expected, Nixon rejected the Kremlin's proposal for a joint military operation, adding that he was gravely concerned by the possibility of unilateral action by the Soviet Union, which "could trigger unforeseeable consequences." For greater effect, U.S. troops were put on a heightened level of combat readiness. Furious at this gesture, Dobrynin phoned Kissinger, who assured him that Moscow should not interpret the move as hostile, admitting that it was largely driven by domestic considerations. The same point was made by President Nixon himself, who told Dobrynin later: "Perhaps I was a little hasty in the heat of the crisis. I would point out—but not by way of justification—that right now I am under constant, relentless siege from the opposition and from many of my enemies who have joined forces over the Watergate affair."[6]

Some American commentators claim that the Soviet Union's true intention was to send its troops into the Middle East and that this was averted by the strong U.S. response. There is no truth to this theory. Indeed, after both superpowers had given each other a bit of a fright, they joined forces to prepare the ground for the Geneva conference.

TWO APPROACHES TO THE GENEVA CONFERENCE

As mentioned earlier, UN resolution 388 was adopted following talks in Moscow between Henry Kissinger and the leaders of the Soviet Union. The United States agreed that a cease-fire in the Middle East should at least be tied to movement toward an overall political settlement. The fact that the United States agreed to link the two issues was largely driven by its efforts to find a quick solution to the oil embargo.

The embargo was imposed by the Arab countries on October 19, 1973, thirteen days after the Yom Kippur War began. On October 16, Saudi Arabia, Iran, the United Arab Emirates, Kuwait, and Qatar unilaterally raised the price of their oil by 70 percent, taking it up to $3.65 a barrel—a price that looks laughably low as I write these words today. Then Saudi Arabia, Libya and other Arab states announced that because the United States had been providing Israel with arms, they would halt oil supplies to the United States altogether. On October 23 the embargo was extended to the Netherlands because it had allowed the Americans to use its air bases. On November 5, the Arab states announced that they would be cutting oil production by 25 percent. Eighteen days later, the embargo had been extended to Portugal, Rhodesia, and South Africa.

The oil embargo was lifted (except by Libya) on March 17, 1974. This was the result of U.S. efforts to be seen to be rebalancing its Middle East policy via diplomatic moves on troop disengagement. But by now a full-blown oil crisis had erupted. Up until this point, oil prices had scarcely risen since 1945. After the end of the Second World War, when the world economy was just getting back on its feet, a barrel of oil cost a mere $1 or thereabouts; before the 1973 oil embargo that price had risen to only $3 per barrel. But by the time the embargo was lifted, the average price per barrel had reached $12.

The 1973 oil embargo heralded a new era in which oil price movements were closely tied to events in the Middle East, a region that was—and still is—the main oil supplier to Europe, Japan, and the United States. In 1979, the year of Iran's so-called Islamic Revolution, the average annual price of oil was $30 a barrel. In 1980, when the Iran-Iraq War broke out, it reached $35.70. After that, prices declined. The average annual price of a barrel of North Sea Brent crude was $14.30 in 1986, setting a new benchmark. But in 1990, when Iraq invaded Kuwait, prices rose once more.

Understandably, many political leaders in the United States—and in the Soviet Union too—hoped oil prices would fall after tensions in the Middle East were eased. This is indeed what happened in 1998, after the Asian financial crisis had passed, when the price dropped back down to where it had been after the 1973 embargo was lifted. In 2002, however, prices rose sharply again and they kept going up without pausing for breath. At the beginning of 2006, the price of oil reached $70 per barrel. The oil embargo of 1973, sparked by the Yom Kippur War, marked the beginning of the end of cheap oil.

But let us now leave this "oil digression" and return to the Geneva conference. What appeared to pave the way to the success of the Geneva conference was Washington's agreement that any accord should be tied to an overall peace settlement. But in reality things were far more complicated; in fact the United States brought different terms of reference to the conference than what it had originally hammered out in partnership with the Soviet Union. Henry Kissinger later acknowledged this openly in *Years of Upheaval*, writing that the Geneva conference "was a means of gathering all interested parties together for one symbolic gesture that would allow each and every one to follow a separate course [of action], at least for a while. After organizing a gathering on this scale, it was difficult to make sure it didn't take action while the diplomatic machinery reverted to bilateral channels."[7] I couldn't put it better myself. But what was negotiated in Moscow during the visit of the U.S. secretary of state had been something quite different.

Fixated as he was with the idea of a separate Egyptian-Israeli accord, Kissinger applied his characteristic determination to make it happen. Nor did he stop at putting pressure on Israel, whose attempts to put obstacles in the way of troop disengagement might have hindered him. The following is a quote from *The Secret Conversations of Henry Kissinger,* a book by Israeli journalist Matti Golan, who obtained transcripts of Kissinger's talks in Israel and then made them public against the wishes of the Israeli government. (To do so, he obviously had to overcome very serious objections along the way.) Golan describes how Kissinger outlined his "general strategy" to the Israeli government on December 16, 1973, during his visit to Jerusalem:

> Kissinger explained that the point of negotiations on troop disengagement was to avoid having negotiations on borders and on a final peace settlement. If the talks [on disengagement] were successful, that would also accomplish one other thing—the lifting of the oil embargo. At the same time, this would bring an end to the international isolation of Israel and ease the pressure it was under, particularly from the Western European nations and Japan. No-one in Israel should have the slightest doubt, Kissinger warned, that if the disengagement talks failed, it would burst the dam holding back the pressure on Israel—this was no longer pressure for a partial withdrawal [of Israeli troops] but for a full withdrawal to the borders of 4 July 1967.[8]

Here Kissinger is seen leveling threats at Israel too, if it refuses to take the road he told it to follow. Although the Soviet Union and the United States disagreed over what they saw as the terms of reference of the Geneva Convention, they both had a shared interest—albeit for quite different reasons—in bringing about troop disengagement. The United States was largely motivated by its desire to break the Arabs' oil embargo, while the Kremlin feared that Syria was at risk of coming under attack from Israel once its troops had been pulled out of the Sinai. These fears were heightened by the unmistakably anti-Syrian mood in America.

After several trips to the Middle East by Soviet foreign minister Andrei Gromyko and several meetings with Kissinger, final accords were signed in Geneva on June 5, 1974. These set out a timetable for the disengagement of Syrian and Israeli troops, as well as for the withdrawal of Israeli forces from a total of 663 square kilometers of Syrian territory that Israel had seized in 1967. In a message to Leonid Brezhnev, President Assad stressed that Syria valued highly the support it had received from the Soviet Union.

On September 4, 1975, Egypt and Israel signed a second accord on the pullout of Israeli troops, the handover to Egypt of the strategic Mitla and Giddi passes in Sinai, and the extension of the UN buffer zone. But right up until Sadat signed the separate agreement with Prime Minister Menachem Begin of Israel, much of Sinai remained under Israeli occupation.

PARTIAL OR INTERIM MEASURES

The difference between the Soviet and American approaches to a Middle East peace settlement was not something that came out of nowhere at the Geneva conference; a divergence of strategy had surfaced long before the gathering was organized.

For a whole range of reasons the Middle East conflict is one of the most difficult in which to seek a peaceful settlement. The Palestinians who make up part of the Arab world were hit particularly hard—as any other people would have been—by the reemergence of a territorial claim going back many centuries that forced them to leave the land they had lived on for generations. It's easy to understand the other side too: it is not without good reason that the Israelis fear for the state they have created. Although this state is recognized by most of the international community, for decades it has been spurned and threatened with destruction by the Arab nations that surround it. Making it especially difficult to negotiate an end to this confrontation between competing nationalisms—whether anyone wishes to recognize it or not—are the wars Israel has fought, allowing it to expand its territory to the detriment of its neighboring Arab countries.

The situation was further complicated because both superpowers viewed it through the hostile prism that was typical of the cold war era. This is not to say that they incited their respective Middle East client states into fighting for them as proxies. On the contrary, the two superpowers (and I'm not talking about the attitude of individual political leaders, because they ultimately did not set the prevailing mood) expended great efforts to bring stability to the Middle East, which would have been impossible had they not sincerely sought solutions. Neither the Soviet Union nor the United States was willing to allow a situation to develop in which they might get drawn into a direct military confrontation with each other. Washington's policy on preventing an escalation of the Middle East conflict was also dictated by the fact that the White House understood that when the conflict spiraled into a crisis—as happened with the Yom Kippur War—a gulf opened between the United States and the Arab states, even those in its sphere of influence, such as the countries of the Arabian peninsula, the principal providers of oil for the United States and its cold war allies.

Yet Washington's objective interest in maintaining stability in the Middle East never impelled it to withdraw its support from Israel, let alone challenge or confront it, even at those times when the aggressiveness of its policies was clear for all to see. What the United States could and did do was try to persuade the Israeli regime not to do anything that might hurt American interests. Sometimes stern words passed between them. But that's about as far as it went.

U.S. foreign policy thus found itself with two, sometimes contradictory, foreign policy objectives: bringing stability to the Middle East and unconditionally backing Israel—a state that showed little sign of wanting to settle its conflict with the Arabs on the basis of the resolutions passed by the UN Security Council and General Assembly. In its bid to resolve this clear contradiction, Washington gambled on partial or, in other words, separate moves to settle the Arab-Israeli conflict.

A conflict as old and complex as the one in the Middle East cannot be ended in one fell swoop. The Kremlin too was aware of this. But the essential point on which the superpowers disagreed was that the United States was seeking separate, partial agreements—and indeed it got them by going it alone—while the Soviet Union felt that the quest for a peace settlement was so complex that any interim measures had to ultimately lead to the clearly defined goal that all had agreed to earlier, a comprehensive settlement. For the Soviets, a series of separate agreements raised the risk that as one Arab state after another dropped out of the peace process, Israel would be able to extort what it needed from each of them without having to give up anything substantial itself. Without balanced, compromise decisions that embraced all parties to the conflict, the prospect of lasting peace in the Middle East was doomed to remain chimerical.

For a while the Americans seriously considered dropping the idea of separate agreements, focusing instead on a step-by-step approach to a comprehensive peace settlement. In the summer of 1976, when Jimmy Carter's team was still campaigning for his election to the White House, I had the chance to meet one of its key figures—the man who would later become the president's national security adviser, Zbigniew Brzezinski. A couple of weeks later, we took part in a joint U.S.-Soviet symposium. Also participating was Cyrus Vance, who was working on the campaign at the time and would later become Carter's secretary of state. Brzezinski, and later Vance, had more or less the same things to say about the situation in the Middle East: that Kissinger and his policy of partial solutions had clearly run out of steam; that we needed to move toward a comprehensive political settlement; and that the Middle East process should involve a coordinated effort from the United States and the Soviet Union alike.

A report on the problems behind the search for a political settlement in the Middle East published by the Washington-based Brookings Institution made a deep impression in policy circles in the United

States. Its authors—among them Brzezinski and Bill Quandt, then head of the Middle East department at the Council for National Security—were the very people that were formulating the Carter administration's Middle East policy. Its main conclusion was that it was essential to reach a comprehensive settlement, which could not be achieved until a Palestinian homeland was created on the West Bank (of the River Jordan).

Two months after taking office, Carter announced that "the Palestinians must have a homeland." There were also a series of official statements indicating a wish to resume the work of the Geneva conference. The foundations were laid for a joint Soviet-American declaration on the region, which was published on October 2, 1977. The declaration referred directly to the necessity of achieving an all-encompassing settlement of the Middle East situation by solving such key issues as "the withdrawal of Israeli troops from territories occupied during the 1967conflict; the Palestinian question, which includes guaranteeing legal rights for the Palestinian people; bringing an end to the state of war and the establishment of normal, peaceful relations based on mutual recognition of the principles of sovereignty, territorial integrity and political independence." In other words, everything that appeared thirty-five years later (!) in the "road map to peace."

At the time, it seemed as if everything was well in hand: the Soviet Union and the United States had a mutual understanding, and there were like-minded people on both sides of the table who were committed to putting this understanding into action. But they had not reckoned with Israel's ability to exert pressure on U.S. Middle East policy when it came to the crunch. Once the Israeli government learned of the declaration, it set Washington's Israel lobby to work, especially in Congress. The declaration came under unprecedented attack. The White House faltered, and on October 4, just a couple of days after it was published, Israeli foreign minister Moshe Dayan, who was in New York for a session of the UN General Assembly, was invited to a meeting with President Carter. The Israelis had given advance notification that the meeting would be a short one—but it lasted the entire day. The so-called working document that Dayan and Carter emerged with in effect invalidated the American signature at the bottom of the joint U.S.-Soviet declaration. America had caved in completely. For several months after it signed the working document with Israel, the United States would raise the issue of the Geneva conference from time to time, but then it went unmentioned. From then on, U.S. Middle East policy shifted back to what it had been much earlier—a de facto refusal to cooperate with the Soviet Union, and an outright refusal to engage with or even consider an all-encompassing settlement.

There has been a fresh rapprochement between the United States and Russia—as the successor to the Soviet Union—on settling the conflict in the Middle East. But it has taken many years and has meant stepping up the process of mediation by the two powers, while failing to involve the European Union and the UN. The creation of the "quartet" of intermediaries was clearly due to Washington's belated realization that there was no future for a peace process monopolized by the United States. In 2003, the "road map" was published and adopted by the administration of George W. Bush, who called it the only route to peace. Events have meant that some of the timescales for carrying out the steps on this route have had to be modified. This is not ideal, but neither is it fatal. Most important is that the idea of a step-by-step move toward an overall settlement with a predetermined basic framework be preserved (the rest will be decided in talks between the parties most involved in the conflict).

– 11 –

THE MAKING OF THE
ISRAEL-EGYPT PEACE TREATY

WHEN MENACHEM BEGIN'S government came to power in 1977, former defense minister Moshe Dayan would be Israel's new foreign minister. Some time after he left office Cyrus Vance told me that Begin's victory had come as a surprise to the American "Arabists" (the label attached to those State Department and National Security Council officials who had advocated for a more balanced U.S. Middle East policy). Alfred Atherton, Hal Saunders, Bill Quandt, and others had been counting on Shimon Peres's Labor Party to prevail in the May elections that year. So had Egypt's Anwar Sadat. Which is why, two months later, Vance, along with a group of moderate American politicians, embarked on a round of shuttle diplomacy between Cairo and Tel Aviv. Vance understood the difficulties that Sadat was facing; even so, he was determined to persuade him to let down his guard and come to the table with Israel. He offered the Egyptian leader his personal assurances that any agreement he reached with Israel would not stand in isolation but would of necessity be accompanied by progress on other aspects of the peace process.

But Begin would adopt a stance that was diametrically opposed to Vance's. In his memoirs, *Hard Choices: Critical Years in America's Foreign Policy*, Vance later wrote: "Under prime minister Menachem Begin, it became crystal clear that his Likud-led coalition government intended to lay claim to sovereignty over the West Bank and possibly Gaza too, and not agree to pulling troops out of these territories."[1]

DAYAN AND HIS SECRET TRIPS

Hewing to this hard line, Israel would seize the initiative in the "game" with Sadat—and the United States did not stand in its way. It could well be that the Americans took this hands-off approach because of information they had pointing to differences of opinion between Begin and Dayan. The United States had reason to hope—at least initially—that Dayan would be able to exercise a moderating influence on his prime minister.

If Begin was eager to see Israeli settlers move into the West Bank and Gaza, Dayan realized that uncontrolled settlement of the occupied territories—in other words, establishing new Jewish settlements and expanding the existing ones—would put Israel on a collision course with the United States. Dayan basically shared the opinion of his Labor Party colleagues who wanted to see a "territorial compromise"—a division of the West Bank between Israel and Jordan. Where he disagreed with them, however, was in his sense of priorities.

And in this, he and his prime minister were in accord. Begin had invited Dayan to be foreign minister—and Dayan had accepted his invitation—because despite their other differences, both men believed that the most pressing issue facing Israel was the need to reach a separate agreement with Egypt. Dayan's feelings about Egypt had much to do with his personal misgivings over the Yom Kippur War. Though the Agranat Commission's investigation into the Israeli military's unpreparedness at the outset of the conflict had not found him personally culpable for the near catastrophe, as defense minister, he couldn't escape responsibility. Both he and Prime Minister Golda Meir had been forced to resign.

Of course, Begin had other reasons for inviting Dayan to join his government. He needed Dayan's political clout to boost his own personal standing within Israel. Also, Dayan had a reputation in America as an "accommodating figure"; his appointment as foreign minister could be interpreted as a sign that Begin's position on the West Bank had some give in it, that he did not want to leave Sadat cornered indefinitely. But most of all, Begin's decision followed from the two men's adherence to the same line: that they had to get Sadat to sign an agreement.

Sadat's faith in the possibility of reaching an agreement with Israel that was loosely tied to a resolution of the West Bank problem received a boost when Vance traveled to Cairo with a new U.S. plan of action. The Americans proposed that Israel's troops would remain in the West Bank as an interim measure while the territory was placed under UN control; later, within a few years, a referendum could be held to decide its future. Vance flew from Cairo to Israel, where he delivered the good news that Sadat was not displeased with the proposal. Thanks to Vance, the way had been paved for direct contacts between the Israelis and the Egyptians.

Right after meeting Vance, Dayan went on a series of secret trips: to Delhi, Tehran, London, and then to Fez. In Delhi, Dayan talked mainly about establishing diplomatic relations. In Tehran, Dayan not only discussed some economic cooperation schemes, he obtained assurances from the shah that he would back Israel in its opposition to the creation of an independent Palestinian state. All indications are that the "Egyptian matter" did not go unmentioned either—it was clearly no accident that two months later Sadat made sure that he informed the shah before anyone else of his plan to visit Jerusalem.

Cold water was poured on Dayan's plans in London, where he secretly met with King Hussein. Dayan had been nursing the hope that he could persuade the king to play at the very least a passive part in the Israeli "game" with Sadat. But the king's reply was that there would be no peace until Israel went back to the borders that were in place before June 5, 1967. Dayan pointedly remarked on the threat that a Palestinian state would pose to the Hashemite dynasty's throne, but Hussein was not easily frightened. Then Dayan asked him if he would convey a message to Sadat, but the wary king declined to act as a messenger boy.

Dayan's lingering frustration with King Hussein is evidenced in his memoir, *Breakthrough: A Personal Account of the Egypt-Israel Peace Negotiations*. Writing about their impasse, Dayan noted: "In two weeks' time, I would be faced with a far more fruitful experiment—a secret meeting with another Arab ruler; an experiment that boosted the prospect of reaching agreement with a neighboring country more important than Jordan."[2] On September 4, 1977, Dayan flew in secret to Paris. There he changed planes and headed for Fez, where his objective was to enlist Moroccan help in arranging a face-to-face meeting and conducting peace negotiations with Egyptian officials. On September 9, four days after he had returned to Israel, Dayan was informed by the Moroccans that the Egyptians had agreed to contact at the highest level, and that a meeting between him and Hassan Tuhami, Egypt's deputy prime minister, had been scheduled for September 16.

On September 15, Dayan flew to Brussels, where he had discussions not only with a gathering of Israeli ambassadors from the capitals of Europe, but with Alexander Haig, commander of NATO forces in Europe. Dayan and Haig were old friends; they'd met during Dayan's month-long visit to Vietnam in 1966, when Battalion Commander Haig had invited the Israeli general to join him in a punitive "jungle combing" operation.

Dayan's trip to Brussels was not a secret. But the scene that followed it was worthy of a spy novel. The Israeli foreign minister's entourage set off for the airport to catch a flight to New York, where a session of the United Nations General Assembly was getting underway. But the car carrying Dayan slipped away from the motorcade and into a side street, where it stopped at a private house belonging to the Israeli intelligence service. There, Dayan's trademark black eye patch (which he had worn since he'd lost his eye in the Second World War) was removed, his face was plastered with theatrical makeup, a dandyish false moustache was fastened above his lip, and he donned a pair of dark glasses. After a few changes of car and another change of plane in Paris, Dayan flew to Rabat, where Tuhami was waiting to meet him.

When he reported back to Begin on his negotiations with Tuhami,[3] Dayan drew attention to an argument made by the Egyptian deputy premier: that a solution to the Palestinian issue had to be included in any Egypt-Israel settlement. Otherwise, the Palestinians would "pave the way for the Soviets to rekindle their influence in our region." But Dayan was unswayed. The main impressions he took away from his meeting with Tuhami, he said, was that Sadat wanted to have a secret meeting with Begin; that he was trying to distance himself from the Geneva conference; and that he did not want the Russians to have any involvement in the peace process. Dayan told Begin that he didn't think the Egyptians were all that concerned about Palestinian independence;

he suspected that they would be satisfied with some kind of arrangement linking the West Bank with Jordan. What concerned the Egyptian government the most was that Sinai be returned to its control.

On the eve of Dayan's meeting with Tuhami, contact had been established—not via the CIA, but directly—between Mossad and Egypt's intelligence service. By using the vaunted Israeli intelligence corps, Begin wanted to show Sadat that he was not only protecting him from his opponents in Egypt but in the Arab world as a whole. Yitzhak Hofi, the director of Mossad, delivered on that promise almost immediately, when he passed intelligence on to his Egyptian counterpart that Libya was planning to assassinate Sadat. A few days later Sadat ordered a massive raid deep into Libyan territory. Meanwhile, with members of the Knesset left in the dark about his plans to meet with the Egyptian president, Begin told his surprised deputies that Israel should not be fighting Egypt in the Sinai peninsula.

SADAT, THE KNESSET, AND THE ENDS OF THE EARTH

Sadat was getting closer and closer to a meeting with Begin. He rejected his advisers' suggestion that he hold the meeting in secret, and was clearly right to do so: in Egypt, and for that matter in Israel too, secrets tended not to remain secret for very long. If Sadat's behind-the-scenes diplomacy were exposed, it could cost him dearly in Egypt and indeed across the whole Arab world.

As noted earlier, the first person outside Egypt to know of Sadat's plans for a visit to Jerusalem was the shah of Iran. Sadat had briefed the shah when he was in Tehran on his way home to Egypt from Europe, and he had strongly endorsed his plan. The next stop for the Egyptian president had been Saudi Arabia, but Sadat had decided not to let King Fahd in on his secret. But Sadat was impatient to sound out his own country, not to mention Israel and the world as a whole; to that end he addressed an open session of the Egyptian People's Assembly on November 9, 1977. In order to find a Middle East peace settlement, he declared, he was "ready to go to the ends of the earth if it will save one of my soldiers . . . I am ready to go to their house, to the Knesset." The Egyptian president's office assumed that Sadat was being hyperbolic and told the Cairo press corps not to pay too much attention to his rhetoric. When Sadat opened his newspapers the following morning, he was furious to see that his reference to "the ends of the Earth" had not made the headlines. By then, Sadat had put everything on the table. He needed to "come clean" to the Americans and the Israelis about what he intended to do.

Ten days later, at 8:30 p.m. on November 19, Sadat's plane touched down at Ben-Gurion Airport. Begin was waiting at the foot of the steps, along with a military guard of honor. A band played Egypt's and Israel's national anthems; a red carpet had been unrolled. Though the ostensible purpose of Sadat's visit was to attend prayers at the al-Aqsa Mosque in Jerusalem, the Israelis had done everything they could to underscore its official nature. There are grounds to believe that Sadat, in his vanity, welcomed all this pomp and ceremony, but in fairness, neither he nor his staff had stipulated anything like this sort of treatment in advance.

But for all the ceremony of his reception, Sadat would soon have cold water poured on his hopes. Even while they were still en route from the airport, an exchange between Dayan and the Egyptian minister of state Boutros Boutros-Ghali, who were traveling in the same car, made it clear that Israel had no intention of giving way or even compromising on the West Bank, just because Sadat had come to Jerusalem. Dayan described this exchange in his book *Breakthrough,* and Boutros-Ghali essentially confirmed his account during a conversation I had with him after he became UN secretary-general. Boutros-Ghali insisted to Dayan that Egypt could not sign a separate treaty. Israel could have no illusions about the attitude of the other Arab states to Sadat's Jerusalem trip—the Egyptian president was certain to be accused of destroying the united Arab front that was supposed to have been cemented at the Geneva conference. In Dayan's memoir, he recalls that the answer he gave was: "I am aware of the Arab world's opposition to Sadat. But I know for sure that there is no way of bringing the Palestinians and Jordan to the negotiating table. That's why Egypt must be prepared to sign a treaty with us even if the others don't sign up to it."[4]

Boutros-Ghali relayed his conversation with Dayan to Sadat, who had from the very outset been aware of the constraints the Israelis had imposed on their agreement. There is still no reliable record of the talks Sadat held in Jerusalem; it is possible that he had not yet backed down from the hope of a comprehensive peace altogether. On his return to Cairo, Sadat stated: "I will never sign a separate treaty." At the same time, he invited the Arab nations, Israel, the United States, the Soviet Union, and representatives of the UN to a peace conference in Cairo. The idea behind the conference seemed to be that it would cast Sadat's Jerusalem trip in a pan-Arab light—but events were already taking quite a different turn.

The United States quickly agreed to attend and the UN decided it would act as an observer. Israel accepted Egypt's invitation, but decided to use the conference to demonstrate that it was in charge. On the opening day of the Cairo "peace conference" (so-called despite its failure to attract many of its main participants), Benyamin Ben-Eliezar, the leader of the Israeli delegation and the prime minister's chief of staff, refused to enter the conference hall when he saw that a place had been set at the negotiating table for Palestine. Places had been set with the names of all the delegations invited to the conference, but even after the only ones allowed to remain on the table were those marked "Israel," "Egypt," "United States," and "United Nations," Ben-Eliezar was still not placated. This time, he objected to the flag of Gaza being flown outside the Hotel Mena House, where the conference was being held, even after it was explained to him that it was customary for the hotel to acknowledge guests from different countries or regions in this way. Ben-Eliezar got his way, however, and the poles outside the Hotel Mena House were stripped of their flags.

Reduced participation foredoomed the conference to failure, which is of course what happened. There followed another meeting between Dayan and Tuhami in Morocco, during which Sadat was shown Israel's handwritten draft of the peace treaty. Then Begin flew to Washington, where he got President Jimmy Carter's go-ahead for the treaty. Begin himself then came to Egypt; Carter meanwhile paid visits to Saudi Arabia and Iran, where King Hussein of Jordan had flown out to meet him. But Carter's efforts with the moderate Arab regimes did not secure their support for Sadat. In order to shore up the Egyptian president's standing, Carter met with him in Aswan.

But nothing did the trick. Having embarked on the path to a treaty that was framed solely in terms of Egypt's relations with Israel, Sadat had cut himself off from the rest of the Arab world. What dealt a particularly hard blow to his standing was Israel's decision to build twenty-three more Jewish settlements near the Rafa Salient in Sinai. General Ariel Sharon declared at the time that it was "important to get this done before the Israeli-Egyptian committees start meeting." Three other settlements were also built in the West Bank at this time.

PALESTINIANS THROWN OVERBOARD

Vance and his advisers were highly critical of these moves by Israel: in Vance's book *Hard Choices*, he says that they "dealt a blow to Sadat's initiative." But by this point, Vance and his circle of American "Arabists" were already taking a backseat to Carter's increasingly prominent national security adviser Zbigniew Brzezinski. On January 20, 1978, shortly after Jimmy Carter returned from his trip to the Middle East, Brzezinski pressed the president to take a direct personal role in the Israeli-Egypt negotiations. Brzezinski proposed that a summit be organized between Carter, Begin, and Sadat at Camp David. To get both sides to take part would require more than just persuasion, he said: they had to be "forced" into it, and Sadat would have to be given a "fig leaf" by supplementing the discrete Israel-Egypt treaty with a document titled *A Framework for Peace in the Middle East*. The expression "fig leaf" came from Brzezinski himself, who was aware right from the start that any such document would be designed to create the illusion—and nothing more—that the treaty transcended its very separate terms of reference.[5]

Bilateral and trilateral negotiations went on for the whole spring and summer of 1978. Now that Israel had gotten what it wanted, the bulk of the talks were devoted to producing a blueprint for the West Bank and Gaza that would not be too hard for Sadat to swallow. Yet close scrutiny of memoirs by Carter, Vance, Brzezinski, Dayan, and Israeli defense minister Ezer Weizman reveal that there was really only one issue on which the Americans sought to impose limits on Israel—the creation of new Jewish settlements in the occupied territories. But the American desire to influence Israel was not so strong that it was allowed to interfere with Israel's purchase of seventy-five F-15 and F-16 fighter aircraft (the United States also agreed to supply Egypt with fifty F-5 fighters at the same time—but they were not in the same league as the aircraft that were destined for Israel). It is no wonder that Israel felt it had been given free rein, even on the issue of the Jewish settlements.

The result, Vance wrote in *Hard Choices*, was that "despite the agreement that had been reached, there was in the end no exchange of letters between Carter and Begin on a moratorium stopping the Israelis from building new settlements on the West Bank and in Gaza." Simcha Dinitz, the Israeli ambassador in Washington, told Hal Saunders, then assistant secretary of state, that there was a delay because Begin was making some revisions to his letter. These "revisions" changed the permanent moratorium on settlements into one that applied only for the duration of the Israel-Egypt negotiations—a period of just three months or so. Vance does not conceal his anger at Begin's "complete overhaul" of the preliminary agreement. "That, however, was Begin's position and he would not budge from it," he writes.

Israel's "concession" of withdrawing troops from Sinai was closely linked to the "flexibility" Sadat had shown with regard to the question of the West Bank and Gaza—where Israeli troops would now remain with the Egyptian president's tacit blessing.

On September 17, 1978, Sadat, Begin, and Carter signed both the peace treaty and the "Framework for Peace" documents, the Camp David accords, at a grand ceremony in the East Wing of the White House. Two days earlier, Egyptian foreign minister Mohamed Ibrahim Kamel and chief legal adviser Nabil al-Arabi, who had been members of Egypt's delegation at Camp David, tendered their resignations, with Kamel declaring that he wanted no part of a deal that came at the expense of the Palestinians. Sadat accepted their resignations.

In the words of former Israeli defense minister Ezer Weizman, "as soon as the treaty [with Egypt] was signed, Begin rejected any further advance in the peace process." Weizman stresses in his book, *The Battle for Peace,* that Begin and his supporters regarded the Camp

David accords as "a way of perpetuating Israeli rule on the West Bank in some form or another."[6]

It is clear from this account of all these events who was the true winner in the "game" Sadat had started. The search for a solution to the Palestinian question would be delayed for decades; what is more, the Palestine Liberation Organization was in real danger of losing its influence in the Gaza Strip. During a meeting in Damascus on September 9, 1979, Abu Mazen (better known as Mamoud Abbas)[7] said "the gravest danger facing the PLO is the threat of a separate Israeli-Egyptian solution for the governance of Gaza." He stressed: "Even now there are some 60,000 blue- and white-collar workers from Gaza in Egypt; there are 10,000–12,000 studying in Egyptian educational establishments and in the region of 10,000 people actually *in* Gaza whose pay-packet is earned from Egyptian sources. The PLO's only foothold in the [Gaza] strip is the mayor, who is against Gaza becoming part of Egypt or the strip coming under Egyptian rule."

Zaid al-Rifai, the former prime minister of Jordan, made his views clearer still. When I met him at his home in Amman on March 30, 1981, he asked me: "Do you want to predict how events will unfold in 1982?" He went on: "Sadat has now solved his own territorial issues, so he'll turn back toward the Arabs, telling us, 'Now I can concentrate on other problems, so let us deal one by one with Gaza, or with the Golan Heights for example.' And the Arabs, often being inclined to forget everything, will end their policy of isolation toward Egypt."

But this was not to be, for on October 6, 1981, Sadat was assassinated.

I want readers to have the right idea about where I stand on this issue. In the final analysis, the Israel-Egypt Peace Treaty could have been a step in the right direction. But Sadat caved in on issues that could have made for an *unbroken* peace process—a fact that is hard to refute. Sadat's purely Egyptian nationalism and his willingness to give in to persuasion from Washington had the effect of seriously weakening the hands of both the Palestinians and the Syrians. Jordan was not affected since it had no territorial dispute with Israel, and its own treaty with Israel did not change the existing borders of the Arab kingdom.

— 12 —

LEBANON IN THE
EYE OF A STORM

IN THE MID-1970S, Lebanon assumed center stage in the Middle East, as events in that tragic, multilayered nation took a dramatic turn for the worse. This happened for a number of reasons, many of them interwoven with one another:

A critical mass of Palestinians: There had been Palestinian refugee camps in Lebanon ever since the first Arab-Israeli War, and their populations had swollen considerably when a second wave of refugees arrived after the Six-Day War. By the early 1970s, the number of Palestinians in Lebanon had reached critical mass: 600,000 in a country that had a relatively small population of its own. After the "Black September" of 1970, which ended with the expulsion of Palestinian organizations, and indeed the entire Palestine Resistance Movement, from Jordan, key Palestinian forces regrouped in Lebanon. Many Palestinian political groups—not just Fatah, but also al-Saiqa, the Popular Front for the Liberation of Palestine, the Democratic Front for the Liberation of Palestine, and others—were based there, as were their affiliated armed militias.

The Maronite elite: Lebanon is a multidenominational state—its population includes Maronite[1] Christians, Catholics, Orthodox Christians, Shiite and Sunni Muslims, and the Druze.[2] The Lebanese establishment has ensured that the most senior posts in government—such as those of the president, the commander-in-chief of the armed forces, and the chairman of the central bank—are always given to Maronites, fueling discontent among the Muslims and Druze, who currently make up the majority of the population.

Inter- and intrasectarian strife: The worst clashes were between the Maronites and Shiites, a state of affairs that was aggravated by the fact that the rest of the Lebanese Muslim population, as well as the Druze, supported the Palestine Liberation Organization. Lebanese Christians, especially Maronites, feared that the Palestinian presence in Lebanon threatened the multidenominational character of the state—or at least increased the likelihood that it might come to be led by Muslims.

If there was friction between Christians and Muslims, there were significant tensions within their communities too. There were constant shifts in the balance of power; confrontations between individual factions sometimes led to assassinations and armed clashes. What was peculiar to the situation in Lebanon was that most political parties—with the exception of a very few, such as the Lebanese Communist Party (LCP)—were built around clans. Lebanon's leading parties also had their own militias, which increased the likelihood that their differences would turn violent.

Border clashes: By the mid-1970s, the hundred-kilometer border between Lebanon and Israel had become a powder keg. Attacking from within Lebanon and from the sea, Palestinian militias fired across the border onto Israeli towns and villages in Northern Galilee; commandos infiltrated Israeli territory as well. Israel responded with harsh reprisals, conducting sorties deep within Lebanese territory. As the decade wore on, Israeli sentiment was clearly turning in favor of a "wider war" in order to wipe out the Palestinian Resistance Movement in Lebanon.

Lebanon's complex history with Syria: Another very important factor was the state of relations between Lebanon and Syria, which can best be appreciated by delving a little deeper into the history of the two countries. During the time of the Ottoman Empire, Lebanon had the status of an autonomous entity—its mountainous territory being largely populated by Maronite Christians—within Syria. After the victory of the Entente powers, Britain, and France, in the First World War, the territory that is now divided between Syria and

Lebanon went through a series of phases under French rule: (1) Once the war was over, the French conquered Damascus (Syria's central regions were at the time ruled by Emir Faisal, son of the sharif of Mecca Hussein al-Hashimi, who had declared himself king of Hejaz); (2) the French high commissioner in Beirut announced the creation of Greater Lebanon, consisting of Beirut and the coastal cities of Tripoli, Tyre, and the Bekaa Valley; (3) the League of Nations granted France the mandate to govern Syria as well as Lebanon. It wasn't until 1941 that Syria would become a separate sovereign state, followed by Lebanon in 1943. Sovereignty was at first a formal step, but it moved closer to reality after the French troops pulled out. The two countries have a closeness that is beyond doubt, but mixed in with it is a history of violent clashes.

THE CIVIL WAR BEGINS

While other Arab countries, primarily Iraq, Saudi Arabia, and Egypt, observed the unfolding events in Lebanon through the prism of their cynical desire to undermine Syria, it was in the best interests of both the Soviet Union and the United States to bring stability to Lebanon. But here too, the sympathies and objectives of one superpower were quite different from those of the other. While the Soviet Union did not want to weaken the Palestinian movement, this was exactly what the United States was trying to do. And while the Soviet Union wished to avoid undermining Syria, which by the mid-1970s was its main ally in the Middle East, the United States sought to keep Syria on a tight leash.

It was against this backdrop that the internecine violence in Lebanon began. In April 1975, bodyguards of Kataib Party leader Pierre Gemayel were assassinated. In response, Phalangist gunmen opened fire on a bus carrying Palestinians. This triggered the beginning of the civil war.

On one side were the right-wing Christian forces, which consisted of the Kataib Party, along with its military wing the Lebanese Phalange, the militia groups of the Franjiyeh clan, and the "Tiger" detachments set up by Camille Chamoun's National Liberal Party. Backed by small, right-wing pro-Christian armed factions from the other parties, together they joined forces to form the Lebanese Front.

The Muslim and left-wing forces were represented by Druze detachments from Kamal Jumblatt's Progressive Socialist Party, by the military wing of the Lebanese Communist Party, by armed groups from the Shiite Deprived Movement (renamed the Amal Movement in 1978), and militants from the Party of Arab Socialist Renaissance. They had the support of Nasserites from Tripoli and Sidon, and of the Sunni group al-Murabitun. They were all part of the National Patriotic Forces (NPF) bloc, whose de facto leader was the Druze chief Jumblatt. As a rule, detachments from the Palestine Resistance Movement fought on the side of the left-wing and Muslim forces in contravention of the 1969 Cairo agreement between the Lebanese government and the PLO, which stipulated that the Palestinians would not interfere in Lebanon's internal affairs.

Though bloody, the conflict was inconclusive at first. But the near collapse of Lebanon's army, which had been fighting on the side of the right-wing Christians, marked a critical turning point.

UNITED STATES BACKS SYRIAN TROOP DEPLOYMENT

The Syrians launched a conciliation mission, but it failed when the left-wing National Patriotic Forces bloc, which assumed it could achieve more by force than by negotiation, made demands that went beyond the scope of the compromise that Syria had suggested. This paved the way for overt Syrian military intervention. The first few Syrian army divisions were sent into Lebanon in April 1976, followed by a full-scale invasion on June 1. The Syrian troops fought on the side of the right-wing Christians, foreclosing what appeared to be an imminent NPF victory. As Jumblatt told me at the time, "If only Syria had remained neutral, we'd be in power within three months."

It wasn't until 2005—almost twenty years later, after the assassination of former Lebanese prime minister Rafik Hariri—that Damascus, under pressure primarily from the United States, was forced to withdraw its troops. At this late date it is important to remember how those troops came to be in Lebanon in the first place. They were re-quested by the Lebanese president. The Christian parties, who were in a very tight spot at the time, also called for Syrian troops to inter-vene. On the other side of the conflict, a number of NPF leaders also did not object to Syria's intervention—or at least never said they did. And what did the Soviet Union and the United States think about the intervention?

The Syrians did not give the Soviet Union advance notice of their intentions. Neither President Assad nor people close to him said any-thing to Soviet premier Aleksei Kosygin, who was visiting Syria at the time when the first troops crossed the border. The news was relayed to Kosygin by Oleg Grinevsky, deputy head of the Soviet foreign min-istry's Middle East department. It is worth noting his reaction, as re-ported in Grinevsky's *The Secrets of Soviet Diplomacy*:

> "This whole story of sending in the troops puts both the Soviet Union and me personally in a ridiculous position," Kosygin said. "Whatever I do, things will either be bad, or really bad. If we publicly state the whole truth—that our Syrian allies did not consult us—then firstly, no one will believe us, and secondly, they'll ask: Who's supposed to be the lead partner in this alliance—the Soviet Union or Syria? It would be a case of the tail wagging the dog. That's really bad.
>
> "It'll be even worse if I come out and condemn their action," Kosygin added. "That would pour oil on the flames of the Lebanese Civil War and might even provoke the Israelis and Amer-icans to send their own troops in. But no way can we come out in favor of the Syrian incursion. That would only encourage the hot-heads to widen the conflict and drag Israel into it. Then what would we do—intervene in their war?
>
> "The only option is the least bad one—to keep our mouths shut. But then they will say that their action was carried out with our [Soviet] tacit approval, and it was no coincidence that I'd been in Syria these past few days."[3]

Nuradin Mukhitdinov, the Soviet Union's ambassador in Damascus, struggled to contain his anger. As he put it: "The Syrians realized that

Moscow would not support this move—and that could have spoiled the mood of crucial talks between comrades Assad and Kosygin—talks that were of great value to the Syrian government." The fact that Syria had sent its troops into Lebanon at much the same time as the Soviet premier was in Damascus "just goes to prove that Syria is bent on showing the world how solid its relations with the Soviet Union are." Kosygin was sickened to see the Soviet Union cast in the role of the "driving force" behind its Middle Eastern allies, who were often confident that circumstances would compel Moscow to go along with actions that were entirely of their own making, and which they had never even discussed. That is how it was this time: the Soviet Union gave its support to the deployment of Syrian troops in Lebanon *post factum*, hoping that this would help to stabilize the situation there.

In fact, the United States not the USSR was behind Syria's decision to send its troops into Lebanon. According to DFLP leader Nayef Hawatmeh, during a meeting with Palestinian leaders Assad mentioned that he had discussed the possibility of sending troops into Lebanon with the U.S. ambassador in Damascus as early as October 16, 1975. The ambassador had assured him that Syria could count on American support. His only request, Assad told the Palestinians, was that regular troops not be deployed.

Yasser Abdrabo, who was on the PLO's executive committee, also told me about the part the Americans played in the invasion. He told me that "the Syrians had asked King Hussein of Jordan to persuade the Americans to support Syria's sending in its troops, or at least not to stand in its way." Abdrabo believed that when Damascus sent its armed forces into Lebanon, it "wanted a major trump card that would give it a significantly bigger role to play and therefore control over Lebanon and the Palestine Resistance Movement." Later, according to Jumblatt, some time after the Syrian army had entered Lebanon, U.S. special envoy Dean Brown offered to act as an intermediary between left-wing Lebanese forces and the Syrians, stressing that "a common policy had been agreed between Washington and Damascus."

By that time, however, differences had started to emerge between the United States and Syria. The Americans reckoned that, for numerous reasons rooted in Syria's historical relations with Lebanon, military intervention by the Syrians alone would not be very effective. So they proposed that there should be a pan-Arab military operation, the thinking being that 80 percent of the pan-Arab forces would be Syrians anyway. The American proposal won the backing of Egypt, Saudi Arabia, and Iraq, which saw it as a way to undermine Syria's foothold in Lebanon. But Jumblatt was against the idea of a pan-Arab force, insisting that a mixture of Lebanese and Palestinian detachments should be deployed to avert chaos in the country.

My conversations with Nayef Hawatmeh, Yasser Abdrabo, and Kamal Jumblatt took place in Beirut in April 1976. Each of them called for the Soviet Union to play a greater role in solving the crisis within Lebanon, a crisis that foreign powers were increasingly being drawn into. But there were so many unknowns: How did the Maronites regard the USSR? What was the extent of their hostility toward the Palestinian groups? How close was one side to Syria and the other to Israel? We considered and discarded the idea of meeting with Lebanon's legitimate president, Suleiman Franjiyeh, because both the Muslim camp and the National Patriotic Forces bloc were demanding his resignation. Although he was still hanging on to power, his constitutional term ran out in September. Elections were due to be held in May and it was painfully clear to anyone who followed Lebanese politics that Franjiyeh would not be reelected. It seemed to us that if we wanted to learn the Christian side's responses to these questions, the person we needed to meet with was Pierre Gemayel, leader of the Maronite party Kataib. His answers would help the Soviet Union determine what stance to take on this very complex situation.

THE COLONEL WHO PILOTED OUR HELICOPTER

To prepare for our meeting, I read all the documents and publications I could get my hands on to familiarize myself with the life of Pierre Gemayel. In his youth, he had been an athlete and had even competed in the 1936 Olympic Games in Berlin. But sports was not the only thing that drew him to Germany: he was also very much interested in the organizational structures and methods used by fascism. That very same year, 1936, saw the creation of the Lebanese Phalange, which became a part of Kataib, which itself was not just a political movement but also a Maronite quasi-military group. The Phalange's close working relationship with the French did not stop it from demanding independence for Lebanon, which led to its being banned. But once Lebanon had gained its independence, the newly legalized Phalange rebuilt its ties with France.

Kataib made considerable gains in parliamentary elections, which meant that Gemayel had been a government minister on more than one occasion. By the time the Civil War began, the Phalange had become the cornerstone of the Lebanese Front, an umbrella body for all of Lebanon's Christian militias. Gemayel insisted on keeping Lebanon's denominational system the way it had been when the Christians were still in the majority, an arrangement that ran counter to the country's Arab makeup. "We are not Arabs, but Phoenicians," he would say. He also favored a close partnership with Western countries and categorically refused to accept the Palestinian presence in Lebanon. These were Gemayel's big picture positions. But were there any tactical moves that could be used to bring stability to the country?

Gemayel was based at Phalange headquarters in Achrafiye in the east of Beirut, behind the city's "Green Line" partition. There was regular gunfire across the line from both sides in the conflict; getting there through the streets of Beirut was simply not possible. I consulted the leaders of the DFLP, who offered to transport me to a Lebanese army base in West Beirut, from which a helicopter could fly me across into East Beirut. Also traveling with me was Vladimir Gukayev, a young member of the Soviet embassy staff who then worked as an interpreter (Gemayel spoke French, a language I unfortunately don't understand) but who later became an excellent diplomat. At the appointed hour on April 17, nobody came to the embassy for us, so we decided to make our own way to the army base. We were very kindly escorted to the base commander, a colonel in the Lebanese army. He had not been given advance warning of our visit, but as soon as he realized that we had made arrangements to meet Gemayel, he said, "I'll fly the helicopter myself," adding, "I'm a Maronite and I don't want the Soviet Union to only have contacts with Muslims." We were joined on the flight by a cardinal from Rome, who also had an appointment with Gemayel. With him was an assistant, who counted his rosary beads and was clearly shocked at the sight of the artillery fire on the ground, which was visible through the helicopter's portholes. We parted company with the cardinal and his companion at the landing site, where a car was waiting for us. Karim Pakradouni, a member of Kataib's politburo, got into the car with us and off we sped through the empty streets; we encountered nothing en route apart from Phalange militia patrols. The walls of the buildings we drove past were plastered with photographs of people who were missing or had been killed.

What follows comes from my notes of a conversation that lasted for many hours. "We don't want to be enemies with the Soviet Union," Gemayel said, "but first and foremost Lebanon has to build friendly relations with the United States, not least because there are two million Lebanese people living there." This part of our discussion led me to draw the following conclusion, which I noted on the spot: that the Phalange wish to avoid a confrontation with the Soviet Union, but their policy is most definitely one of building closer ties with the United States. This means we, the Soviet Union, have little room for maneuver.

Nor, at first glance, did Gemayel's stance toward the Palestinians hold out much more promise: "We cannot sacrifice our sovereignty for the sake of the Palestinians' partisan struggle for their rights." You would expect Gemayel to say this kind of thing, but he underlined his words forcefully, adding: "Even after a peace settlement in Lebanon, Kataib will continue to be opposed to a Palestinian presence in the country. The Phalange does not want to see a return to the situation when Lebanon had one Lebanese government and five Palestinian governments, and one Lebanese army and five Palestinian armies."

All the same, Gemayel signaled that there was a possibility for some leeway in his approach to the Palestinian issue. "We've signed agreements with Arafat on more than one occasion," the Phalange leader said; "and although none of them have yet been complied with, he is closer to us than other Palestinian figures, and I think we could find a common language with him." In response to my questions, Gemayel expanded on the topic of "options for negotiating with Arafat." He told me Kataib's position with regard to the Palestinian movement had recently shifted: "While the Phalangists previously refused to back the 1969 Cairo agreement, which regulates the presence of armed Palestinian groups in Lebanon, they are willing to back it now, but only if the Palestinians will comply with the agreement too." Here, Pakradouni noted that Arafat had established contact with him on his own initiative, in a bid to offer his services as an intermediary in setting up a meeting between Gemayel and Kamal Jumblatt.

The Kataib leader was at pains to stress that he thoroughly approved of Syria's "mission" in Lebanon. The Phalange had initially feared Syrian interference, he said, but Syria had "extended us the hand of friendship." In December 1975, Assad and Gemayel had met in Damascus for talks; in the course of their four-hour meeting, Gemayel said, he realized that: "the Syrian leader is an honest man. Up until then, everybody had given us advice on what we should do, yet the only one who helped us was Syria." For this reason, I paid particular attention to Gemayel's words, noting that he said he would be willing "to disband our militia as long as there is a force capable of defending us."

Pakradouni was confident and at ease, and joined in our discussion, telling me that the Phalange was "in constant contact with Damascus, which allows us to align our positions with the Syrians." In the car, as we were driving back to our waiting helicopter, Pakradouni confided in me about an agreement reached between Syria and Kataib, in which the new, soon-to-be-elected Lebanese president would offer to sign a joint security pact with Syria. This would give the Syrians the required legal basis for keeping their troops in Lebanon. The Phalange leadership, Pakradouni said, did not want President Franjiyeh's signature on the pact; he was already on his way out of the political arena, and his name might compromise it.

The main conclusion that I drew from my visit to Gemayel's headquarters was that there were prospects of a peace settlement in Lebanon, albeit not without grounds for dispute. The Phalange leader was in close contact with Syria and, with help from Damascus, was possibly seeking an accommodation with Arafat. This information would prove helpful in our efforts to bring the Lebanese Civil War to an end. There was ample reason to believe that the USSR had a positive role to play, especially as Gemayel concluded our meeting with these words: "The biggest favor the Soviet Union could do for this unfortunate country is to help us put out the fire. After that, we'll be open to discuss anything."

HOPES FAIL TO MATERIALIZE

The next day, April 18, I sat down with Kamal Jumblatt. It was not the first time I had met him. The head of the Druze community in Lebanon and the founding leader of the Lebanese Progressive Socialist Party was well known in the Soviet Union. In 1972 he had been awarded the International Lenin Prize for "building peace between nations." Although Jumblatt's beliefs were a far cry from communist ideology, he had a good relationship with the Soviet Union—albeit one that had taken a long time to build. In his writings, he was critical not only of Marxism, but also of the Soviet totalitarian system "which had divided the people into classes." As the leader of the Druze, he rejected materialism—and I can attest that his belief in the precedence of spiritual values was not a pose but quite genuine and sincere. He spoke to me about the greatness of Hindu philosophy, which had much in common with the teachings of the Druze. He was highly educated, having studied at university level in England and France as well as in Lebanon. Even his appearance set him apart from the leaders of the various other factions in the Lebanese Civil War: he was tall and lean; his face had the inspired look of a great thinker; he dressed only in civilian clothes; and he carried no weapon whatsoever. Yet this man's quiet, muted voice commanded the allegiance of hundreds of thousands of Lebanon's Druze, who were ready to carry out anything he ordered. By the mid-1970s Jumblatt had become the established leader of the National Patriotic Forces bloc of Muslim and leftist parties. The country's fate was very much in his hands.

After meeting Jumblatt, I realized how unhappy he was with the policy adopted by Syria. He seemed to be thinking out loud when he said: "We have absolutely no trust in Syria. The mood of our people has turned against the Syrians. Iraq and Saudi Arabia are also incensed by Syria's intervention in Lebanon. The Americans have changed tack and are now putting pressure on Damascus and Lebanon's president Franjiyeh. France too is opposed to Syria's intervention. Nor are the Syrians willing to negotiate with us [the NPF] about who will be the next president of Lebanon."

When I asked Jumblatt if he was willing to reconsider his negative response to the idea of replacing the exclusively Syrian troops in Lebanon with a pan-Arab force that would nonetheless be largely made up of Syrian units, he replied: "I stand by my previous insistence that a combination of Lebanese and Palestinian forces should be used to restore order in Lebanon."

At the time of my meeting with Kamal Jumblatt, Syrian troops in Lebanon were still occupying a restricted territory. From what he told me, it was clear that Jumblatt was categorically opposed to the scenario set out by Pakradouni, in which the new Lebanese president would formally ask Syria to deploy its troops to restore order, implicitly inviting Syria to use its military presence to help set up new power structures. It is very hard to keep anything secret in Lebanon; Jumblatt already knew that such an agreement was in place.

Jumblatt also mentioned his recent meeting with Alexander Soldatov, the Soviet ambassador in Lebanon, "which did a lot to change my way of thinking," he said. "I knew that the Americans agreed to the Syrian intervention. But until recently, I believed that the Soviet Union backed it too. Now I've started to doubt that. And the more I doubt it," he told me with his customary directness, "the more interested I am in how the Soviet Union could help us normalize our relations with Syria."

My talks with the Palestinians made it clear to me that not everyone in the Syrian leadership was of the same mind with regard to Lebanon. Nayef Hawatmeh, along with other members of the DFLP leadership, had met Hafez Assad, and believed that the Syrian president "was not particularly pushing for the expansion of Syria's military presence in

Lebanon. At the same time, [Syrian] defense minister Shehabi had a quite different point of view." Hawatmeh had insisted that their post-meeting communiqué should include sharp criticism of the United States. "What? Do you want to drag Syria into a confrontation with the Americans?" Assad asked him. Hawatmeh's reply, he told me, was: "We want to make sure that none of us fall into the American trap."

It was around this time, Hawatmeh told me, that differences between the Syrians and Yasser Arafat emerged. Arafat was in favor of the "Arabization" of the conflict. "That's because of his links with Egypt, Iraq, and Saudi Arabia on Lebanese matters," Hawatmeh said. "In any case, Arafat was opposed to an expansion of Syria's military or political presence in Lebanon."

In the weeks after our meetings with Gemayel, Hawatmeh, Jumblatt, and Abdrabo, the Soviet Union made efforts to bring Assad and Jumblatt together, to reduce the pressure that was building between Damascus and parts of the Palestine Resistance Movement, to ease tensions between Muslims and Christians, and to end the civil war in Lebanon. But events followed their own course. On June 1, 1976, Syria launched a large-scale invasion of Lebanon, and by September Syrian placeman Elias Sarkis had been installed as president. In October, the leaders of Saudi Arabia, Egypt, Syria, Kuwait, Lebanon, and the PLO gathered at a conference in Riyadh, and made a series of decisions. They resolved to return the state of affairs in Lebanon to where it had been before April 1975: to reinstate the agreement between the Lebanese government and the PLO and to create an Arab Deterrent Force (85 percent of which would consist of Syrian troops already in Lebanon) that would be permitted to operate on Lebanese soil as far as the River Litani. No territorial restriction of this kind was actually mentioned in the official conference documentation, but the Arab powers had tacitly conceded that the southern zone of Lebanon, south and east of the Litani, would be under Israel's sway. It did not take long for this to become a reality: with direct backing from Israel, the so-called South Lebanon Army was set up and swiftly assumed control over the territory.

These agreements did not, however, succeed in bringing stability to Lebanon. Based outside Beirut, National Liberal Party leader Camille

Chamoun played a key role in the Christian camp at that time. Conditions were in his favor, so he decided to exploit them to smash the PLO and to wipe Arafat and his followers off the political map. In a bid to prevent this from happening, the Soviet Union approached both Arafat and the Syrian government and attempted to mediate. But it was essential to bring Chamoun into the discussions too, which was made all the more difficult by the fierce fighting that had broken out on the roads leading out of the city. Conditions were so dangerous that high-ranking Soviet diplomats were not permitted to fly their flag. This is how things stood in December 1975 when, as deputy director of Moscow's Institute of World Economy and International Relations, I was given the task of meeting Chamoun. We drove out to meet him in two cars, the second driven by a Soviet intelligence officer named V. P. Zaitsev, who later became a general serving at the highest levels in Afghanistan and Yugoslavia. We seemed to be in luck: all was quiet that day, there was no shooting, and we drove to the front lines with ease. But during the talks Chamoun received a disturbing phone call. His expression changed visibly as he was informed that Phalangists had gunned down dozens of Muslims in the seaport of Beirut, in revenge for the massacre of several of their comrades in the mountains. It was the first clash of a day that would be remembered as Bloody Saturday. As we drove back to the embassy, our escort car came under fire. Zaitsev was lucky; his back was grazed by a bullet that ricocheted off the rear wheel. Robert Martirosyan, his passenger, was seriously wounded.

In March 1977, Kamal Jumblatt himself was assassinated.

SYRIA SWITCHES SIDES

It was in February 1978 that Syrian army units first clashed with pro-Gemayel and pro-Chamoun militias. This was not just a series of chance incidents but signaled the end of Syria's pro-Christian policy in Lebanon. There were several reasons for this. After Jumblatt's assassination, the Muslim side in the Lebanese Civil War had been seriously weakened; the balance of power tipped in favor of the right-wing Christian forces, raising the threat that Lebanon's territory would be permanently divided. Ominously for Syria, the ties between the Maronites and Israel were growing stronger. Nor was Elias Sarkis as unreservedly pro-Damascus as Franjiyeh had been, despite his owing his presidency to the Syrians. Which isn't to say that the Christians were united. The Phalangists' brutal murder of Franjiyeh's son Tony had driven a deep wedge between the two clans. Franjiyeh's had supported Syria's intervention; the Phalangists hadn't.

Sadat's November 1977 visit to Jerusalem had fostered closer ties between Arafat and Syria's President Assad. Differences between the United States and Israel over the Lebanon situation were also emerging—which was no doubt noted in Damascus. All of these developments, to one degree or another, prompted Syria to switch to the side of the National Patriotic Forces bloc.

It would have been logical to expect relations between the United States and Syria to deteriorate once Syria switched sides—and it is quite telling that they did not. America's sympathies were on the side of the right-wing Christians, against whom the Syrians were now fighting; and as if that were not enough, Syria was building bridges to the Palestinian forces, who were anathema to the United States. But Washington was anxious not to jeopardize the planned Israel-Egypt treaty; it even held out some hope that its dealings with Damascus would help dissolve Syrian and Palestinian opposition to it.

Syria's change of course in Lebanon and its baffling relationship with America were discussed at numerous meetings that I took part in when I was in Lebanon and Syria in August 1978, in August 1979, and in March 1981.

In 1978, I met with Lebanese Ba'ath Party leader Assem Kanso—a member of the pan-Arab (Syrian) executive of the Party of Arab Socialist Renaissance and one of Syria's key placemen in Lebanon—and with Zukheir Mohsin, leader of the pro-Damascus Palestinian group al-Saiqa. Both told me that Syria intended to put an end to the right-wing Christian opposition. Damascus wanted to send units from the Lebanese army that had been assembled and trained by Syrian instructors to the Bekaa Valley region and to the south, beyond the Litani River, towards the border with Israel. It was the sort of operation, as Kanso put it, that "would rid the south of the country of the South Lebanon Army while dealing a serious blow to the right-wing Christian forces, isolating them from Israel." Kanso observed that there was "much common ground between the positions taken by the Syrians and the Americans with regard to Lebanon: the United States doesn't want the situation to flare up and has told Chamoun that it doesn't want the situation to flare up; nor does it want to see a clash between Syria and Israel, which could derail Sadat's [peace] mission." Damascus hoped that the fact that the troops "were not actually Syrian troops themselves, but just Lebanese army units trained by the Syrians" would mitigate some of the objections to the incursion. The Syrian government, Kanso said, was counting on the success of this planned operation, "which would put an end to internecine strife in Lebanon." As Kanso was telling me this, the phone rang. As if in confirmation of his words to me, he was told that the U.S. embassy had just promised its support to President Sarkis, should he decide to order Lebanese army units into the south of the country. Kanso let me in on this news there and then, adding: "Assad is hoping the U.S. will restrain Israel [from counterattacking]."

Mohsin was less definite. He too talked of the operation planned by the Syrians but pointed out that "all the same, the Americans have warned the Syrians that they cannot guarantee there'll be no intervention by Israel; and although Assad is willing to pay the price of Israeli air strikes, he fears the prospect of Israeli troops being sent in overland." Mohsin also stressed that the Syrians needed the order from Sarkis to send in the Lebanese army, but right up until that moment he had refused to sanction the operation.

"The Christian right might also go into action," Mohsin added. "Israel has sent them massive supplies of arms. What's holding them back from making a preemptive strike are the differences between Israel and the U.S."

On August 3, 1978, I met with Elias Sarkis. I was picked up at the Soviet embassy in a car driven by an officer from the Deuxième Bureau, the Lebanese Special Forces unit. We raced through the deserted streets of the Muslim part of Beirut at breakneck speed, with a second car carrying bodyguards hot on our tail. The only times we stopped were at roadblocks, but we were waved through without question after the officer presented himself to the armed militia who were part of the Christian forces. Our meeting took place at the presidential palace. What follows is my direct transcript of President Sarkis's words:

When I accepted the presidency, I was guided by the resolutions of the Arab summits in Riyadh and Cairo. In accordance with these resolutions, disarmament was required by both warring factions, including the Palestinians, and we had to establish a regulatory basis for their presence in Lebanon. To this end the Arab Deterrent Force has entered Lebanon, but not the south of the country, which is why they have not been able to carry out their mission. The situation has deteriorated since Sadat's visit to Jerusalem. The Palestinians and the Syrians have found themselves fighting on the same side. The Christians are very much alarmed by this, and their side has launched an anti-Syrian campaign. It has now spilled over into armed skirmishes that have been going on since February. This is a situation beyond my control.

At this point, there was a burst of artillery fire, to which Sarkis responded by saying: "See how I have to work? Even here in the presidential palace?"

His manner, which had been calm and reasonable until then, took a much harsher tone: "Someone wants to impose order by attacking the Christians. But I will not pander to one side being singled out for attack. That is not why the ADF was given its mandate." I was aware that Sarkis was due to receive Syrian foreign minister Abdul Hamil Khaddam, who had just arrived from Damascus, so I asked Sarkis what he expected the meeting to produce. The president shrugged his shoulders. His last words to me were: "Tensions might boil over—I wouldn't rule it out."

The day after my meeting with Elias Sarkis, I called on Camille Chamoun's son Dany in Achrafiye, east Beirut. Again, a car came to pick us up and, accompanied by Yuri Perfiliev from the Soviet embassy, we sped past the museum that marked the limit of the "neutral zone" and drove through still more deserted streets, only this time

they were on the Christian side of the Lebanese capital. We were escorted by Nidal Nadjam, a trusted comrade of Dany's, who pointed
out all the ruined buildings we were passing. Even peaceful areas had
come under artillery fire; the Christian part of Beirut had clearly suffered just as much damage as the Muslim part. Upon our arrival we
met Dany Chamoun, a trim young man who spoke excellent English
and was dressed in jeans and boots, just like a true cowboy. At both
this meeting and our second one, which took place a year later, Dany
told me of Chamoun's efforts to mediate between Israel and Arafat.

To better clarify the situation, it's useful to pause here to focus on
two issues: the situation in the Christian right's camp, and its true
links with Israel. This is what Dany Chamoun told me: "The assassination of Tony Franjiyeh in Ehden two months ago was a heinous
crime. He was my friend and we spent our last weekend together with
our families. But after his assassination, areas where innocent Christian civilians live were subjected to shelling, while Bashir Gemayel
[Pierre Gemayel's son] who orchestrated the murder, along with the
Phalange officers who took part in it, were free to walk the streets of
Achrafiye." I asked Dany about the Chamoun clan's ties with Israel.
"When we were on the verge of being wiped out, we didn't get any
help from the U.S., the Soviet Union, or France," he replied, "only the
Israelis came to our aid. And although it's now been twenty months
since we trained our military staff there, we still have links with them.
When we were on good terms with the Syrians, I mentioned it quite
openly to Assad—he didn't react badly at the time. As for the nature
of Gemayel's links with Israel, that's not my responsibility."

Dany Chamoun emphasized that their "links with Israel were also
dictated by the situation in southern Lebanon. We have no control
over Haddad, the commander of the South Lebanon Army, and neither does the Phalange. He has two Israeli officers at his side at all
times. He is completely in their hands."

As we parted, Dany said: "We very much respect the Soviet
Union's line on the initial deployment of Syrian troops [in Lebanon]."

"But you were the ones who asked them [to intervene]," I said:
"you welcomed them when they fought against your enemies."

"We made a big mistake," Dany replied bitterly.

The Syrian government, meanwhile, was largely focused on forging an alliance between Suleiman Franjiyeh and Rashid Karameh, the prominent Sunni politician and former Lebanese prime minister. A declaration was drawn up, stating that the main aim of the alliance was to safeguard democracy in Lebanon and prevent the country from splitting in two. Syrian foreign minister Abdul Hamil Khaddam brought it to Franjiyeh for his signature on August 8; he would meet with Palestinians upon his return. The declaration stressed the positive role played by Syria, proclaimed that there would be security for all of Lebanon's different faiths, unreservedly condemned any Lebanese forces with links to Israel, and called for the right-wing Christian militiamen to withdraw from west Beirut.

This was how things stood when I traveled via Damascus to northern Lebanon, to Ehden, Zgorta, and Bekaa Safrain, on August 9 and 10, 1978. In Ehden I had a meeting with Franjiyeh, who looked weighed down but not broken by his grief. At his side was Tony Franjiyeh's son, who, by a stroke of good fortune, had been visiting his grandfather when his father was attacked. After I expressed my sincere condolences, Franjiyeh related what had happened. "The Phalangists arrived in a number of cars," he said, his words broken and faltering. "Many of them taxis. They opened fire on Tony, his wife, and his three-year-old daughter, spraying them with bullets. Even after Tony was dead, they disemboweled him."

I keenly felt this grief-stricken father's pain. This vile, sickening act of cold-blooded murder had been the work of Christians. How could they believe in God? The Syrians were often accused of orchestrating and carrying out terrorist acts in Lebanon. They still are, to this day. I cannot be sure that every accusation is unfounded; I have no wish to justify or defend terrorism, no matter who its sponsor may be. But this vicious murder of Tony's family, along with the assassinations of Rashid Karameh and of two Lebanese presidents who in effect owed their position to the regime in Damascus, none of those killings were the work of the Syrians. Those crimes can be clearly attributed to units from the forces of the Christian right.

Yet Franjiyeh believed that Israel's push to make Lebanon absorb the Palestinians was the root cause of most of the troubles. "To do so, they need to divide the country in two. The Muslims are accepting of the Palestinians and are happy to give them shelter," Franjiyeh said, adding: "Unfortunately, there are people in Lebanon who are starting to put that plan into action." I would not rule out the possibility that some of Israel's leaders in the second half of the 1970s did hatch plans to resolve the Palestinian problem by making Palestinians stay on Lebanese soil. But it is hard, and indeed unfair, to blame Lebanon's woes solely on Israel.

On our way to the headquarters of Franjiyeh's military forces, we encountered heavily armed young boys in uniform. From Zgorta, the route took us toward another mountain—the domain of Rashid Karameh. All was peaceful, and for two hours of our night-time journey I saw nothing that gave cause for alarm. Bna Safrain, where Karameh had his headquarters, was a Muslim area, Ehden was a Christian area, yet between them there was no tension, no hostility, and no violent clashes whatsoever. It occurred to me that *this* was how all Lebanese people could live. What also made a difference was that Ramadan was being observed: later that evening, thirty or forty of us sat around a table with Karameh, enjoying a meal under the starry night sky. It put everyone in a peaceful mood. The only reminder that the country was engulfed in civil war was the man guarding the entrance with a machine gun. Karameh, dressed in a brown *burnus* that marked him out from the others, came over and cheerfully greeted me with a kiss.

From our conversation it became clear that Karameh had accepted the proposal that he and Franjiyeh jointly head a body designed to restore peace in Lebanon. "I have no intention of becoming prime minister again," he said; "I think I can be of more use to my people in my present position." He left little doubt that his alliance with Franjiyeh was being imposed from above, either to work alongside Lebanon's constitutional bodies, or even to replace them. I also visited the Palestinian camp Badaoun near the Lebanese port of Tripoli. In my notebook I wrote that it was "a lamentable sight, with members of the various organizations such as Fatah, al-Saiqa, the NFLP, and the DFLP all sitting around with their guns at the ready, waiting to be attacked—not from outside but by each other."

The situation had hardly changed by the time of my next trip to Lebanon, a little more than a year later, in September 1979. Once again I called on President Sarkis, and once again he told me there had been some improvements, but only on the surface; things could still boil over any minute. Southern Lebanon was a time bomb waiting to explode. Major Saad Haddad, who controlled the zone bordering Israel, took his orders from no one but the Israelis. The neighboring zone was under the control of UN troops, assisted by a Lebanese battalion. Citing figures supplied to him by the UN, Sarkis said three hundred Palestinians guerrillas and another two thousand "as yet unarmed" Palestinians had infiltrated this zone. From here they shelled Israeli territory and carried out raids from the sea. Farther lay the "Palestinian triangle," which enclosed this entire area.

After Saudi Arabia and other Arab countries had withdrawn their armed detachments from the Arab Deterrent Force, the Lebanese army had had to be deployed into the east of the country. The only alternative, Sarkis said, was allowing the Phalangist militia to take control of all of Lebanon. But strenuous opposition, not only from the NPF but also from Syria, had prevented the army from moving into the Muslim- and leftist-controlled west. Sarkis's hopes for the future were pinned on action by "pan-Arab" forces (not Syrian, but pan-Arab). I asked him if he thought Israel would then abandon the idea of occupying the south and cease its shelling of Lebanese territory. Sarkis said he thought it would. The reason he sounded so certain might have been because the Americans, with whom Sarkis was in regular contact, had already given him their assurances on that score.

Karim Pakradouni shed further light on the situation, telling me:

The greatest danger is that posed by Bashir Gemayel. He, possibly more than any of the Lebanese Christians, is the one closest to the Israelis. He dreams of getting the Syrians out. How? By provoking confrontation between the Syrians and the Israelis. If the Syrians pull out, Bashir will immediately try to launch an attack on Franjiyeh's territory. His dream is to amalgamate all the Christian lands in Lebanon from north to south, including the "Haddad" zone. A younger generation of Lebanese leaders is leading the way—Amin

Gemayel [Bashir's brother], Dany Chamoun, and Walid Jumblatt.
If they begin to cooperate with each other, that will be the end for
Bashir. But all the same, dialogue needs to begin, with talks be-
tween the Lebanese and the Syrians.

In March 1981, I met President Sarkis once more. His mood was
even more pessimistic than it had been the previous time. I recalled
him telling me in 1979 that he had been counting on a revival in the
fortunes of the Lebanese army, but he admitted that he no longer
clung to any such hopes. He firmly justified the consolidation of the
Christian forces. Now that the Syrian troops had left the areas controlled by the Phalange, their presence was not as onerous. When I
asked him if he could imagine an end to the deadlock (I used his term
for the situation in Lebanon), he replied: only via a comprehensive
peace settlement. With the creation of an independent Palestinian
state, the armed Palestinian militias would move out of Lebanon.
Sarkis abruptly brought our interview to its close. "That's enough
from me," he said. "I'm nearing the end of my term as president, and
I'm going to write my memoirs."

Why do I devote so much detail to this early phase of Lebanon's
civil war? Because it illustrates so graphically the overlapping interests and constantly shifting relations between various groups that
have made the situation in Lebanon so intractable, while foreshad-
owing subsequent events. The creation of the special zone extending
to the River Litani, which was virtually under Israeli control, and the
links that Israel forged with the Christian right paved the way towards Israel's 1982 invasion. While my description of events may
seem too fine-grained, it provides insight into the to-ing and fro-ing
that would characterize Israel's war in Lebanon in 2006.

Throughout the long Lebanese Civil War, the Soviet Union made
great efforts to halt the bloodshed, to prevent the breakup of the
country, and to avert the annihilation of the Palestinian units. At the
same time, the Kremlin worried that events in Lebanon could, on
the one hand, precipitate a full-scale conflict between Israel and Syria,
and on the other inflict serious damage to the Soviet Union's relations
with Syria or the PLO. There was no single faction in Lebanon that

Moscow could rely upon. This includes the Lebanese Communist Party, which, for all its eagerness to prove its significance to its "Soviet comrades," had scant influence over the members of the NPF bloc—let alone over Lebanon as a whole. Nor was the LCP such a reliable ally. Much to Moscow's displeasure, it enjoyed a close partnership with Iraq, from which it received financial support. As Iraqi foreign minister Tariq Aziz mentioned to me in 1981, "The LCP leadership told us that theirs was the only Arab communist party that was independent of the Soviet Union." If the USSR had no strong ally within Lebanon, neither could it depend on Syria. Though the Syrian regime was the Soviet Union's closest partner in the Middle East, as has been seen in this chapter, its activities were sometimes inimical to Soviet interests or desires.

THE 1982 ISRAELI INVASION OF LEBANON

Shortly after his inauguration as U.S. president in 1981, Ronald Reagan described Lebanon as a zone "of interests vital to the U.S."—despite the fact that the events unfolding in that country posed no threat to the political, economic, or military interests of the United States. On the eve of Israel's invasion in June 1982, the United States began to show a particular interest in Lebanon's affairs. One possible deduction is that Washington thought events there could have a serious impact first, on its efforts to safeguard the Israel-Egypt peace treaty—which it had taken so much trouble to broker—as well as on U.S. plans for a string of separate accords at the expense of Lebanon and Jordan. Second, the United States was anxious that events in Lebanon not be allowed to escalate into a full-scale war between Israel and Syria, which could destabilize the Middle East at large. Finally, the United States feared that if Israel's operation against the PLO in Lebanon was successful, it could strengthen the hands of those in the Israeli government who wanted to overthrow King Hussein of Jordan and "solve" the Palestinian problem on the East Bank. The United States staunchly opposed making a sacrifice of Jordan. As for events within Lebanon, the United States could not have failed to realize that a victory on either side, Muslim or Christian, would exacerbate anti-American feelings in the more conservative Arab states, especially the oil-producing ones of the Persian Gulf. For all these reasons, by mid-1982, the U.S. State Department, the U.S. Council for National Security, and the CIA were focusing much of their attention on Lebanon. As Reagan and his advisers saw it, a dramatic show of force and decisiveness in Lebanon would play to a worldwide audience. When Reagan declared that Lebanon occupied "a central position as a gauge of America's real capabilities on a global scale," he was blatantly referring to its confrontation with the Soviet Union.

Israel's priorities in Lebanon were not always in line with those of the United States. The Israeli government's emphasis was on crushing the PLO's armed militants, squeezing the Palestinians out of Lebanon and, coupled with this, the possibility of annexing the West Bank and Gaza. The logic behind Israel's policies was that it was seeking to weaken Syria. It had not ruled out direct military strikes at Syrian forces within Lebanon—and, if necessary, outside it. This divergence of U.S. and Israeli objectives is corroborated by a number of incidents that came to light later, as well as by statements in various memoirs.

On January 18, 1982, a gathering of State Department officials heard Secretary of State Alexander Haig voice his fears for the fate of the Israel-Egypt peace treaty in the wake of Sadat's assassination. On June 13, a week after Israel's invasion of Lebanon, Haig told a TV interviewer: "Camp David is not dead. I dare to hope that the current tragic situation in Lebanon will present fresh opportunities to revive the peace process."

On June 21, 1982, *Time* magazine ran an interview with General Ariel Sharon in which he said: "The harder we strike and the more damage we inflict on the PLO's infrastructure, the more Arabs on the West Bank and in the Gaza Strip will be prepared to hold talks with us and start to co-exist with us."

On August 27, 1982, after a meeting in the United States with Secretary of State George Schultz (who had replaced Haig in July), Sharon announced before a sea of reporters' microphones that "Israel never has agreed and never will agree to a second Palestinian state . . . There is already a Palestinian state in existence. Jordan is a Palestinian state."

In August 1982, testifying before the U.S. Senate Foreign Affairs Committee, the former deputy undersecretary of state and former U.S. ambassador to the UN George W. Ball said: "The invasion of Lebanon has served the purpose of allowing Israel to push ahead unopposed with its assimilation of the occupied territories. During my conversation with General Sharon in Israel, he made it abundantly clear to me that his long-term strategy is one of squeezing the Palestinians out of the West Bank, allowing only enough of them to remain, as Sharon told one of my friends, for work."

And in an article that year for the journal *Kivunim* ("Directions") Oded Yinon, a prominent former official from the Israeli foreign ministry, wrote that: "Israeli policy, both during times of peace and times of war, must serve one objective—the liquidation of Jordan under its current regime," as well as "increased Palestinian migration from the West to the East Bank."

Was Israel's invasion of Lebanon on June 6, 1982, approved in advance by the United States? I do not believe that the United States steered Israel toward the invasion, but there is also good reason to infer that it did not oppose it. In the early days of June 1982, Sharon paid a visit to Washington, where he had a secret meeting with members of the U.S. military's top brass. It is hard to believe that Sharon, being Israel's defense minister, did not let slip a single word about the military operation that would be carried out within a matter of days. There may well have been doubts and objections to the planned invasion on the American side, but there was no outright opposition. As Bill Quandt wrote in the Spring 1984 edition of the *Middle East Journal*, when the head of Israeli intelligence informed Haig of the planned operation, his only response was: "Not before troops are withdrawn from Sinai."

The Israeli government took the decision to invade Lebanon but the United States dissociated itself from the operation only after it had been carried out. Israel faced no real obstacles from the United States, and because it took Washington's support for granted, there were no constraints on its actions in Lebanon. When Haig was dismissed as secretary of state, the U.S. press cited a whole range of reasons, one of them being that he had "gone too far" with the Israelis.

It would be more accurate to say that the Israeli government had gone too far with the White House.

Yet the United States now found itself in a very tricky position. On June 9, Israeli troops surrounded Sidon (Saida), advanced on Damour, fifteen kilometers from Beirut, and clashed with Syrian troops as they tried to cut them off in the Bekaa Valley. That same day, the United States vetoed a UN Security Council resolution calling on Israel to implement a cease-fire within six hours and to pull its troops out from within the internationally recognized borders of Lebanon. All fourteen of the Security Council's other members had voted *for* the resolution.

On June 26, the United States also vetoed a French draft resolution that called for the disengagement of forces in Beirut. Once again, the United States stood alone; every other member of the Security Council had voted for it. By this time, Israeli forces had encircled West Beirut, cut off the section of the Damascus-Beirut highway that crossed Lebanese territory, and began bombing the Lebanese capital. The following day the United States and Israel were totally isolated at the UN General Assembly, where they cast the only votes against a resolution that was adopted with backing from 127 UN member states that called for the immediate withdrawal of Israeli troops from Lebanon.

The siege of Beirut dragged on despite Yasser Arafat's offer to hold talks on evacuating his soldiers from Beirut in order to spare its civilian population from the bombing. France and Egypt called for troop disengagement, which would involve the evacuation of the Palestinian guerrillas and the Israeli army pulling back to within five kilometers of Beirut—moves that would be first steps towards a comprehensive peace settlement. The Israeli government rejected this offer.

The United States was looking for a way out of the difficult position it found itself in. On July 29 its envoy was absent when the UN voted on a resolution calling on Israel to lift the siege of Beirut; on August 4 the United States abstained from voting on a Security Council resolution that threatened to impose sanctions on Israel unless it enacted an immediate cease-fire and pulled its forces back to where they were before August 1. But resolutions did not work. In a letter to the UN secretary-general, Israel said it would not be withdrawing its troops from West Beirut. The Soviet Union then tabled a draft resolution demanding that all necessary measures be taken to implement the decisions taken earlier—above all the call for a cease-fire and for UN observers to be sent to Beirut and the surrounding area. Eleven member states of the Security Council voted in favor, three (Britain, Zaire, and Togo) abstained, and the United States once again used its veto. Even so, on August 10 a plan was finally agreed on to get the Palestinian guerrillas out of Beirut. Once they'd left Beirut, they were forced to leave Lebanon altogether.

The United States's conduct at the UN lost it a lot of respect in the Arab world (which did not go unnoticed in Washington), and dealt a blow to the Middle East peace initiatives that U.S. diplomats had announced with such fanfare at Camp David. And then something happened that forced the United States to take a more active role. In September 1982, under guidance from the Israeli military command, the Phalange carried out an indiscriminate massacre of Palestinians, including women and children, at the refugee camps of Sabra and Shatila. The worldwide outpouring of outrage prompted the United States to step up its search for an Israel-Lebanon peace agreement. Multinational forces consisting of 1,200 U.S. Marines and troops from France and Italy were deployed in Lebanon at the end of December 1982. Secretary of State George Schultz spent two weeks visiting the two countries in turn, hammering out the details of an agreement that would provide for the creation of a security zone in southern Lebanon, which was the price that had to be paid for Israel to withdraw its troops. The agreement was imposed on Lebanon on May 17, 1983.

I met Syria's President Assad in Damascus on June 2, 1983. He spoke forcefully on the subject of the Israel-Lebanon accord, holding back none of his anger:

> This agreement is unacceptable to us, mainly for two reasons: first because of Syria's own security interests, and second because it imposes restrictions on Lebanon's sovereignty and denies it the freedom to take its own decisions—a freedom enjoyed by any sovereign state. Judge for yourself: under the agreement, Lebanon

doesn't have the right to have any antiaircraft weapons on its territory with a range exceeding five kilometers. This means that Israel will have complete control of the skies over Lebanon. On top of this, the agreement will make the south of the country a no-fly zone for Lebanese planes—this is over Lebanon's own territory—unless the Israeli authorities are given advance notice. And there's this humiliating detail that flies in the face of Lebanon's sovereign rights, which is that under the agreement, any country—Arab or not—that doesn't maintain diplomatic relations with Israel has no right to transport any type of armaments through Lebanese territory, Lebanese waters, or Lebanese airspace. Then, for example, there's also the requirement that all decisions concerning southern Lebanon should be taken jointly by Lebanon and Israel.

Assad said the agreement allowed Israeli soldiers to be just 24 kilometers from Damascus, while Syrian soldiers were 250 kilometers from Tel Aviv. The Syrian president summed it up by saying: "It's all too clear why Syria's attitude to the agreement is negative. Syria is in a state of war with Israel."

Even after the agreement was signed, the situation in Lebanon did not stabilize for a long time. Bashir Gemayel, commander of the Lebanese Front, was elected the country's president in August 1982, but he was assassinated before he took office; the new president was his brother, Amin Gemayel. There was a terrorist attack against the U.S. embassy in Beirut, and later a barracks housing U.S. Marines was bombed. Armed militias from the Druze and the Amal movement meanwhile seized control of West Beirut. By mid-February 1984 the multinational forces had left Lebanon. A few weeks later, under pressure from Damascus, President Amin Gemayel declared the Israel-Lebanon agreement null and void.

I do not intend to describe subsequent events in great detail, as they are now common knowledge. I will, however, draw attention to several points:

1. The close ties that were forged between Israel and the forces of the Lebanese Christian right went beyond their collaboration

in the "security zone" where the South Lebanon Army operated; it can be said with some certainty that the actions of the Phalange were coordinated with the Israeli leadership as well.

2. Syria's armed forces became a permanent fixture in Lebanon. Its special forces assumed control of Lebanese state institutions, while Syria's economy became heavily dependent on the illicit trading in contraband that was made possible by its army's presence on Lebanese soil.

3. Events in Lebanon brought the United States and Israel closer together. In spite of the tough-sounding rhetoric America directed at Israel after the massacre in the Palestinian camps of Sabra and Shatila, the two nations forged a working military alliance.

HARIRI'S ASSASSINATION: TENSIONS REACH THEIR PEAK

Once again Syria came to play a leading role in Lebanese affairs. Kamal Jumblatt and Nahib Berri, the then Shiite leader, met Eli Hobeika, commander of the Christian forces, in Damascus to sign an accord that authorized Syrian troops to remain in those areas that were under their control. But President Amin Gemayel refused to ratify the accord and fired Hobeika from his post. The Syrian government responded by urging Muslim ministers in the Lebanese government to boycott the president—a boycott that lasted until Gemayel stepped down in 1988.

After Israel's unilateral withdrawal from the greater part of Lebanese soil, the South Lebanon Army, now under the command of General Antoine Lahoud, continued to control the "security zone" in the south of the country. This was accompanied by change in the alignment of various forces, now that the Palestinian factor had lost so much of its importance in domestic politics. There was internal wrangling in the camps of both the Christian right and the Muslims, where Hizbollah, a party with a powerful military wing, became increasingly prominent. Before long, opposition to the presence of Syrian troops in Lebanon was growing among a variety of faith groups—members of the Christian right, the Druze, the Sunnis, and the Lebanese left. Under pressure from these opposition forces, whose leader was former prime minister Rafik Hariri (who had until recently been seen as a pro-Syrian figure), the UN Security Council passed resolution 1559 in 2004, calling for the withdrawal of Syrian troops from Lebanon.

My final visit to Lebanon and Syria before writing this book was in February 2005, by which time the events described above had long since passed into history. Hariri, a long-standing acquaintance whom I could call a friend, had invited me to his home for an early breakfast. Naturally, our conversation turned to relations between Lebanon and Syria, especially as Hariri knew I was heading to Damascus to meet with Bashar Assad after my meeting with him. Syria's special forces, he told me with indignation, were giving all the orders in Beirut: "You can't even appoint a doctor to head a clinic unless you have permission from the Syrian authorities," he said. He believed it was essential to halt the "frenzied activity" of the Syrian special forces in the Lebanese capital, and then get the Syrians out of Beirut altogether. Hariri totally agreed that the Syrian army units had played a large part in halting the civil war in his country. But now, he insisted, "they should be restricted to the Bekaa Valley."

Hariri asked me to tell the Syrian president that he and his team were willing to "allay the Syrians' concerns" during negotiations. One of the "concerns" he cited was Syria's fear that Lebanon would unilaterally seek to strike a separate peace deal with Israel. "We are even willing," Hariri said, "for our country's constitution to carry the stipulation that Lebanon will only sign a peace deal with Israel if it is done jointly with Syria." Hariri was anxious to be invited to Damascus to meet Assad. "We want to reach a deal," he said, "on how the Syrians are going to comply with the Security Council resolution. I understand their difficulties, and we're willing to discuss the possibility of a step-by-step approach."

As if sensing the threat to the life of this strong, dynamic, yet likeable man, I said to Hariri: "Your home doesn't seem to have much in the way of bodyguards."

"Don't worry," he replied. "I'm well protected."

On reaching Damascus, I told Bashar Assad of my conversation with Hariri. I did not have the impression that Assad harbored any ill feelings toward him. On the contrary, he had agreed that it would be useful to meet him.

But on February 14, a powerful explosive device was detonated underneath Hariri's armored car. He died on the spot. Across Lebanon there was an eruption of large-scale protests against the Syrians, who were widely believed to be behind the assassination of their opponent. Political tensions flared up, and the elections were won by the anti-Syrian movement.

Without full possession of the facts, I do not wish to throw my weight behind any particular theory relating to Hariri's assassination. I will, however, set out my impressions and thoughts. First, it strikes me that Syrian *politicians* cannot have been the ones behind the assassination; they must have realized that the inevitable outpouring of anti-Syrian feeling in Lebanon would compel the international community to step up its demands for Syria to comply with Security Council resolution 1559—which is indeed what happened. Second, Hariri had enough political enemies within Lebanon who would have liked to get rid of him. And third, I do not accept that one man in Damascus—the president—has total control over everything that happens. He does, of course, wield a great deal of power; but I do not believe that any individual groups or institutions would act solely on his orders while undermining him at the same time.

On a visit to Sana'a at the end of 2005, at the height of the U.S.- and French-led anti-Syrian campaign, I met Yemen's president Ali Abdullah Saleh. He had just been on the phone with President Jacques Chirac of France, who had told him that Syrian vice president Abdul Hamil Khaddam had applied for political asylum while he was in Paris, ostensibly for a medical checkup. We couldn't help wondering if the French were grooming Khaddam to take over from Bashar Assad. Either way, it could barely escape anyone's attention that when Khaddam talked to the press, he focused all his criticism on Assad. And yet it was Khaddam who had for decades, as foreign minister, been responsible for Syria's policies and actions in Lebanon.

After Hariri's assassination, Assad flew to Cairo to meet Hosni Mubarak. Their meeting took place behind closed doors, but it later emerged that the Egyptian president had made a number of recommendations to Assad: one was to impose strict controls on the work of the Syrian special forces; another was to exert a constructive influence on the Palestinian groups based in Damascus for the sake of Mahmoud Abbas, president of the Palestinian Authority; a third was to close the border with Iraq. Assad agreed with Mubarak's points, pointing out that nobody's interests had suffered as much as his own in the aftermath of Hariri's assassination.

Rod Larsen, a UN special envoy sent to observe compliance with resolution 1559, also went to the Middle East "on the trail of events" connected with Hariri's assassination. Larsen held meetings in Egypt with President Mubarak and Omar Suleiman, the head of Egyptian intelligence, and with Saudi foreign minister Saud bin Faisal, King Abdullah of Jordan, Mahmoud Abbas, and Amr Moussa, the secretary-general of the Arab League. On his return to New York, Larsen told everyone he spoke to that nobody had accused Assad of personal involvement in the assassination of the Lebanese former prime minister, but that everyone was concerned that the Syrian president had no control over the activities of his country's special forces.

− 13 −

A Return to
a Harder Line

I N THE 1980S, especially after Ronald Reagan's election as president, the United States adopted a harder overall line on the Middle East. Two factors played a role in this change: one was America's abandonment of the strategy of détente; the other was the downfall of the monarchy in Iran.

LIBYA AS A TESTING GROUND FOR U.S. POLICY

Reagan had stamped his ideology on American policy at the beginning of his presidency by refusing to engage in constructive dialogue with the Kremlin and by announcing a "crusade" against the "Evil Empire." It was a crusade that embraced a doctrine of "direct engagement," with the stockpiling of weapons and the "Star Wars" program. The Soviet Union, which had lost three leaders in rapid succession—Brezhnev, Andropov, and Chernenko—during Reagan's first term (1981–1985), had done everything it could to preserve the global balance of power. So when the United States called for an easing of tensions, the Soviet Union was forced to rise to the challenge.

For many years, the Shah of Iran had been a strong and reliable U.S. ally, assiduously guarding its interests in the Middle East. Iran had acted as a proxy policeman (for example, by suppressing the liberation movement in Oman) and as a caretaker (by patrolling oil shipping routes). America had counted on the shah to actively intervene in the event of a coup in any of the pro-American Gulf states and to deploy the Iranian army, supplied as it was with the latest weaponry, in the event of a "situation X" in relations with Moscow. The United States planned—and actually managed to set up—a number of "observation points" on Iranian soil to keep watch on the Soviet Union. With the shah's overthrow, the United States had lost a vital asset.

Fearing a repeat of the "Iran scenario" in other countries in the region, the United States explicitly declared that it was prepared to go the full route to armed intervention in order to preserve the status quo in other friendly Middle East states. There is reason to believe that Libya was chosen as a testing ground for this strategy. On August 23, 1981, in an op-ed piece in the *New York Times*, former undersecretary of state Joseph Sisco declared that Libya and Colonel Gadaffi had been chosen "as a suitable case for treatment and as an opportunity to display the country's new steel." Libya was singled out because it enjoyed minimal support from other Arab countries, radical and traditional regimes alike, at that time. The Reagan administration also reasoned that since the markets were swimming in surplus oil supplies, the oil factor would not be of pivotal significance when calculating a possible backlash. Measures against Libya, both economic and military, were intensified.

Back in 1979, President Jimmy Carter had given in to a vocal campaign against contact with Libya and recalled U.S. diplomats from Tripoli lest they be taken hostage, as had happened in Tehran. Then in 1981 had come the announcement that the Libyan embassy (People's Bureau) in Washington would be closed down altogether. The U.S. State Department "recommended" that American oil companies recall their staffs from Libya. When this recommendation was not heeded, President Reagan himself called on American citizens to leave Libya and announced that U.S. passports would no longer be valid for travel to that country. The economic pressure culminated with a ban on imports of Libyan oil to the United States, introduced in 1982, and an embargo on supplying Libya with high-tech equipment. The military pressure culminated in the air battle over the Gulf of Sidra in August 1981, in which U.S. fighters shot down two Libyan planes.

In its face-off with the United States, Libya was largely on its own; its appeal for support from the OPEC countries, for example, fell on deaf ears.

THE REAGAN PLAN SABOTAGES THE FEZ SUMMIT

As the United States adopted a more hard-line policy toward the Middle East under Reagan, it began to receive promising signals from the Arab camp; this included the Palestinians who, slowly but surely, were abandoning their previously held position that there was no alternative to armed conflict with Israel. Evidence suggests that the Arab states closest to Washington gave it advance notice that after the 1982 blockade of Beirut, a constructive position would be hammered out by Arab heads of state at their second summit in Fez. Labib Terezi, the PLO's envoy to the United Nations, told me that the Fez plan had been known about in UN circles for a couple of weeks before it was adopted; it is highly likely that the White House knew about it too. This is why the "Reagan Plan," published one week before the resolution adopted at the Arab summit in Fez, was not "parallel" to the Fez plan but specifically designed to preempt the Arabs' initiative; it would also show Israel that by overreaching in Lebanon it was damaging America's wider interests in the region.

The Fez meeting envisaged a pullout of Israeli troops from all Arab territories occupied in 1967—Israel would thus keep the extensive lands it had annexed as a result of the first Arab-Israeli War in 1948. It also declared that settlements built by Israel on occupied territory since 1967 should be dismantled, and that compensation should be paid to those Palestinians who did not want to return to their native lands (payments that could have the effect of drastically reducing the numbers of Palestinians wishing to return to lands that now belonged to Israel). The Fez plan also envisaged putting the West Bank and Gaza under UN control for a transitional period of several months' duration; creating an independent Palestinian state with its capital in Jerusalem (meaning *east* Jerusalem, as there was not a word in the plan about detaching Jerusalem from the rest of Israel or giving it special international status); accepting peacekeeping guarantees from the UN Security Council for all countries in the region (for which, read Israel too—there was for the time being only oblique talk of according Israel full recognition); and an undertaking that the Security Council would ensure that these plans were implemented. The Fez plan was not set in stone; rather, it was an agenda, Middle East experts realized, that was open to clarification and modification during the negotiating process.

The "parallel" Reagan plan contained the following proposals: "self-governance" for the Palestinians on the West Bank and in Gaza under a specific form of association with Jordan (in other words, there would *not* be an independent Palestinian state); halting the construction of any new Israeli settlements on these territories, while leaving open the question of what would happen with the existing settlements, of which there were already more than one hundred— under President Lyndon Johnson, only those settlements built before 1967 had been considered legal.

Reagan's apparent strategy in the plan that bore his name was very accurately summed up by one of America's leading commentators, Leslie Gelb. Writing in the *New York Times* on October 31, 1982, Gelb quoted U.S. government officials as saying that Reagan's objective was "to convince Arab moderates and Palestinian leaders that it is 'either now or almost never'—either recognize Israel and give King Hussein of Jordan the green light to negotiate over the West Bank and the Gaza Strip, or face the prospect of de facto incorporation of these territories into Israel."

Israel opposed the Arab plan adopted in Fez. The Begin-Sharon government also opposed the Reagan initiative because it did not explicitly and openly allow for conditions in which Israel could annex the West Bank and Gaza. The fact that the "positive elements" in the Reagan Plan had won the backing of Israel's opposition Labor Party did little to endear it to the Likud government.

There was much comment in the Israeli press about the similarity between the Reagan Plan and the "Allon Plan," which had been adopted as Labor policy on the future of the occupied territories. The Allon Plan envisaged maintaining Israeli military control over the territories by stationing troops within a fifteen kilometer zone along the River Jordan (Israel's military border) and in a series of other outposts, while placing the rest of the West Bank under "administrative control" by Jordan.

In January 1983 I was in the United States and had the opportunity to meet with Assistant Secretary of State Nicholas Veliotes, who was responsible for Middle East matters. When I asked him how he saw the Reagan Plan working, he replied: "There have to be negotiations between Jordan and all interested parties, and when they begin the logic of the plan will become apparent."

"Yes, but within what framework do you propose to hold these negotiations?" I asked. "Will you be asking Jordan to instigate talks whose objective is to give the Palestinians their own government in the West Bank and Gaza, while maintaining the territories under Israeli control—or do you have something else in mind?"

Veliotes, a man who moved in academic circles, did not give me the impression of being a traditional State Department figure. He spoke fluently and the manner in which he touched on various issues was direct, not metaphorical, as he sought to put what he was saying into a firm conceptual framework. And yet this very same Veliotes declined to give a direct answer to my question.

The second question I raised during my meeting with Veliotes also remained unanswered: Was the Reagan Plan a plea by the United States to examine the "eventual fate" of the occupied territories under current circumstances, or was it just a question of talks about the transitional period in the West Bank and Gaza?

I returned from the United States with the firm impression that the Reagan administration was deliberately steering clear of big picture questions like the ones I'd posed to Veliotes; it wanted to avoid having to define the ultimate objective of the peace settlement, even within the interpretation set out in UN resolution 242.

ISRAEL IN AMERICA'S EMBRACE

Not everything was clear-cut in America's relations with Israel. There is a widespread, stereotypical view that Israel uses its U.S.-based lobby so skillfully that it can steer American policy on the Middle East in whatever directions it chooses. This has indeed been the case on more than one occasion, but not at times when it found itself in conflict with the larger interests of the U.S. government or American big business, as often happened during Reagan's time as president.

Nevertheless, on October 18, 1983, Secretary of State George Schultz presented a proposal to the National Security Council that would officially declare Israel to be "America's main partner in the Middle East." A decision was taken to do this by setting out a list of U.S. priorities in the region as approved by President Reagan. And on October 29 that year, Reagan signed Directive 111, the key point of which was the founding of a military alliance with Israel. In one fell swoop, he reinstated the "strategic accord" with Israel of November 30, 1981, which the United States had put on hold because Israel's incursions into Lebanon had exceeded the limits agreed with Washington. Now, however, everything had gone full circle.

But this did not mean Washington was prepared to sacrifice its own interests for the sake of its "military ally." In 1983, the very same year that Directive 111 was signed, U.S. Defense Secretary Caspar Weinberger ordered his staff to devise a plan that would block Israel's development of its Lavi fighter jet. The Israeli project was seen as detrimental to U.S. interests in two respects: on the one hand, it would need to be financed to the tune of billions of dollars—significantly more than the value of U.S.-built aircraft exported to Israel—and U.S. manufacturers of military hardware stood to incur losses if Israel was able to build its own. On the other hand, the Pentagon was afraid that Israeli-built combat aircraft might eventually be sold to China or South Africa. The Lavi project was scrapped, despite vigorous efforts by the Israelis to get the Jewish lobby in the United States to overcome the Americans' resolve. Curiously enough, the execution of this plan to scupper the Israeli project was entrusted to Dov Zakheim, a U.S. defense official with responsibility for the Pentagon's budget who was also known for his close ties to America's Jewish community and to the U.S. military-industrial complex. Zakheim, who had once been a rabbi, was dubbed a "traitor to his family" by Israeli defense minister Moshe Arens for carrying out the task that Weinberger had given him.

Zakheim's dedication earned him a promotion: from 1985 to 1987, he served as U.S. deputy undersecretary for defense, in charge of planning and resources. At the beginning of the 1990s, he became a consultant to the U.S. aerospace company McDonnell Douglas, where part of his responsibility was to oversee the production of the F-15 fighter jet. The company and the Pentagon also put him to work defusing Israeli opposition to the sale of a shipment of F-15s to Saudi Arabia.

It is also worth noting that Zakheim subsequently became one of the neocons who assisted George W. Bush in winning the presidency. He was also put forward for the post of Pentagon comptroller by the team advising Vice President Dick Cheney. In mid-2004 he was involved in resurrecting the "Committee on Contemporary Threats," whose stated mission was the U.S. administration's battle against Islam.

The example of what Zakheim did points to two conclusions: first, that even under Reagan, arguably one of the most pro-Israeli U.S. presidents, the United States prioritized its own interests above all else; and second, that the Jewish lobby in the United States generally worked on the assumption that Israel was best served by not overstepping the line where American and Israeli interests ceased to overlap. This explains the sometimes differing points of view between the American Jewish lobby and the Israeli hawks.

Here is another example. In November 1985, the U.S. naval intelligence analyst Jonathan Pollard was arrested on charges of spying for Israel. "Why are they doing that?" Reagan asked, when told what had happened. "We give them our heart and soul and this is how they repay us." Despite enormous pressure on the government from both Israel and Jewish groups in the United States, an American judge sentenced Pollard to spend the rest of his life in jail.

According to Weinberger, the information Pollard had obtained and passed to Israel was "intended for internal use, and disseminating it outside the United States could deal a serious blow to our country's national security." The United States did, of course, share intelligence with the Israeli special forces but apparently only to a degree that would not give Israel opportunities to act independently and without U.S. control. Any breach of this setup by Israel was punished quite harshly, as the Pollard case shows.

In Israel itself there are (and always have been) right-wing politicians who, although they appreciate the importance of their close ties with the United States, would like to loosen Washington's "embrace" and leave Israel more room to maneuver.

One particular thorn in the side of U.S.–Israeli relations is the problem of Jewish settlements in the occupied territories of the West Bank and the Gaza strip. Although the United States has never really put its foot down, it has constantly let Israel know that it does not support maintaining the settlements. That was the case too during the time of President George Bush Sr. and Secretary of State James Baker who, while remaining allies of Israel, were concerned by the first intifada— the Palestinian popular uprising against Israeli occupation in the West Bank, Gaza, and East Jerusalem—and called on Israeli prime minister Yitzhak Shamir to moderate the "enthusiasm for settlements."

Washington has continued to demand that Israel put the building of new settlements on hold in the West Bank and the Gaza Strip. But this was not the only reason for the problems that have from time to time surfaced in U.S.–Israeli relations. During the Kuwait crisis and then during the Gulf War, Israel persisted in offering its assistance to the American administration. But President George Bush Sr. insisted on forging a U.S.-led coalition that had to include the Arab countries, especially Egypt, Syria, and Saudi Arabia—an arrangement that could be wrecked by bringing Israel in on the act. Moreover, Washington had urged Shamir not to retaliate against Iraq in the event of Israel coming under rocket attack. More than forty Iraqi rockets rained down on Israel, but Shamir did as Bush told him despite the psychological trauma that the rocket attack inflicted on the country.

This was a case when U.S. interests even took precedence over a matter as close to Israel's heart as its own security. In a bid to ease the pressure, the United States did supply Israel with several Patriot antiballistic missile systems, which turned out not to be very effective—

but neither did the Iraqi rockets actually cause much damage, either in terms of deaths or material destruction. Yet it was a big risk.

At the time of these events, I was a member of the Kremlin's "crisis group," and I asked if Iraq could fill its warheads with nuclear fuel (satellite intelligence showed Iraq's nuclear reactors had been sealed off), turning its rockets into nuclear weapons. Soviet defense minister Dmitri Yazov replied that it could. There were also fears that Saddam Hussein might use chemical weapons in his rockets. Fortunately, he did not take that risk.

Shamir and Sharon eventually mobilized the pro-Israel lobby in the United States against Bush. The president rose to the challenge and had the support of Congress when, on September 12, 1991, he delivered an address to the American people criticizing pro-Israeli organizations in the United States. His defiance may not have been the only reason, but Bush was not reelected for a second term in office; in Israel, meanwhile, Shamir lost to Rabin. A number of experts believe Shamir lost because he threw down the gauntlet to the president of the United States, while a significant number of Jews living in America voted against Bush.

Moves toward a peaceful settlement of the Middle East conflict were scaled back under George Bush Sr. after the Madrid conference, only to be reinstated under Bill Clinton, particularly during his second term as president—but to no avail.

— 14 —

THE ARAFAT PHENOMENON

THE SITUATION IN THE Middle East has been increasingly shaped by the Palestinian struggle to gain freedom and the right of self-determination—and for those Palestinians who were forced to leave their homeland, to return from exile. Since 1948, the identity of the Palestinian Arab community has been molded by the various military and political groups that have been organized in the Israeli-occupied territories and among the Palestinian diaspora. All of those groups relied on the support of the Arab states; nonetheless, they bore the stamps of the unique individuals who founded them. Much of the credit for the historical evolution of the Palestinian community goes to a figure who bore the nom de guerre of Abu Ammara, but who was much better known as Yasser Arafat.

ARAFAT THE PERSONALITY

Volumes of books and thousands of articles have been written about Arafat, just as they have about Nasser. Some of the authors knew Arafat personally; others may not have known him themselves but are acknowledged experts in the history of the Arab-Israeli conflict. There are those, however, who single-mindedly strive to paint the late Palestinian leader in an unflattering light, basing their writings on a jumble of facts, rumors, and conjecture. There are those who hail him as a peacemaker, pointing out that he was awarded the Nobel Prize

for signing the 1993 Oslo Accords with Israel, which led to the introduction of Palestinian self-rule in parts of the West Bank and the
Gaza Strip (and to Arafat's famous handshake with Israeli prime minister Yitzhak Rabin on the White House lawn). Others, however, insist that Arafat was never more than a terrorist. I met him many
times, in different places and under differing circumstances—in Damascus and Beirut and Sidon, in Tripoli (Lebanon) and Amman, in
Baghdad, Moscow, Prague, Cairo, and Gaza. I feel that I am well
placed to describe this complex historical figure.

So who was he really, this man who for decades retained uninterrupted leadership of the Palestinian resistance movement? There can
be no doubt that Arafat led the life of an ascetic. This could be seen
in everything from the tiny barracks-like rooms in Beirut and Damascus where he ate, slept, and worked, to his simple diet and his very
appearance—the quasi-military khaki army jacket, the holster with a
pistol at his waist, and the checkered kaffiyeh he always wore on his
head. I am pretty sure he spent next to nothing on himself, despite the
huge sums of money that passed through his hands as they were
transferred from various Arab countries to finance the Palestinian
movement. It wasn't until he was sixty-three years old that he got
married, to a beautiful young Christian woman named Suha Tawil,
who converted to Islam and bore him a daughter. But even when he
had been elected head of the Palestinian Authority, he did not permit
himself the luxury of a family home and hearth; he still lived in a war
zone, his life filled with danger, his wife and daughter kept a safe distance away. It was rumored that Arafat had a close relationship with
his secretary Nadjla Yassin before he got married. This can be believed, but I also know from a source close to Arafat that he ended
their relationship in 1985 after his comrades-in-arms told him that a
romance with his secretary would not help their cause. As Arafat put
it, his only cause was "the Palestinian revolution."

Where Arafat was born remained a mystery to the end of his days.
Asked about it in interviews, he would name various places, but always
in Palestine: Jerusalem, Gaza, and Tsaft. Some claim he was born in
Cairo. One way or another, it cannot be disputed that his father was a
landowner from Gaza and that his mother was from a well-known

Jerusalem family. Arafat's parents moved from Palestine to Egypt, which is where he, the family's sixth child, was registered. This paved the way for his admission to Cairo University in 1948. But after his mother died, Arafat lived with his uncle in Jerusalem for several years.

Arafat never told me about his childhood or adolescence, but I did learn that, before he applied to Cairo University, he had considered attending a university in Texas—an idea that he was forced to abandon when he was denied a U.S. visa. How different would his life have been if he had spent his childhood in Cairo instead of Jerusalem, and had studied engineering at an American university instead of in Cairo? Of course those circumstances might have affected his outlook on life, but I do not think they would have changed his fundamental way of thinking. All his life he remained a Palestinian; a Palestinian nationalist and a patriot. Arafat loved his country and his people, but never to an invidious extreme. When a nationalist compares his land and his people to what he considers to be less worthy countries and peoples, he oversteps the line of patriotism and lapses into outright chauvinism. This was definitely not the case with Arafat. The hatred for Israel that so consumed him in the 1950s and 1960s never turned into a hatred for Jews. The first time I met Arafat, at the Palestinian-occupied positions on the East Bank, not far from the River Jordan, I was struck by his unmistakably Jewish appearance. After we'd chatted for a while, I told him he looked just the same as many Israelis. "There is nothing special about that," Arafat replied, quoting Nasser's words about the genetic ties between Arabs and Jews. "Palestinians and Jews are cousins."

In the 1960s, Nabil Shaat, one of the leading figures of the Palestinian resistance movement, proposed the idea of creating a democratic Palestinian state in which Jews, Muslims, and Christians would all live on an equal footing. Arafat was not opposed to the idea, and Shaat later became a member of Fatah's central committee. But this proposal for a single Jewish-Arab state, which had originally been put forward by the Soviet Union, long before the founding of Israel, had absolutely no chance of ever becoming a reality.

It is impossible, however, to have a clear picture of Arafat's psychological makeup without focusing on the different stages of his life and struggle, and on his various interpretations of the goals of the Palestinian movement. His path, it must be said, was a long and difficult one; one on which he overcame various obstacles, polished up his act, and discarded all notions that were not grounded in real life— and yet he did so while remaining true to a cause to which he devoted himself wholeheartedly.

In 1948 Arafat broke off his studies to fight in the first Arab-Israeli War. After the Arabs were defeated, he remained in Gaza, which was under Egypt's administrative control, until 1950. Then he resumed his studies at Cairo University, where he set up and headed the General Union of Palestine Students (GUPS). He underwent military training, qualified as an officer, and served as a lieutenant in command of a Palestinian battalion unit during the tripartite Anglo-French-Israeli offensive against Egypt in 1956.

The student movement played a big part in the establishment of a Palestinian community in the 1950s, not just in Egypt, but in other Arab countries too. It was not a politically homogenous movement: for example, the executive committee of the GUPS, which Arafat set up in Cairo, had four independent members, one Ba'athist, one member of the Muslim Brotherhood, and one communist. There is reason to believe that Arafat, who headed this multiparty committee, was at that time close to the Muslim Brotherhood himself. To some extent Arafat had been driven in that direction, not just by information that leaked out about Nasser's secret meetings with the Israelis, but because the Egyptian leader forbade Palestinians residing in Egypt or in Egyptian-controlled Gaza from undertaking any anti-Israeli military activities on their own. The only thing that the Palestinians were allowed to do was to discuss the topic of returning to their homeland. Any practical activities, such as setting up military training camps in Gaza, required permission from the Egyptian authorities. In 1954 Arafat was thrown in an Egyptian jail—albeit not for very long—for doing just that.

Finding himself opposed to Nasser in most things, Arafat emigrated to Kuwait, where by now a large Palestinian community was successfully engaged in business. Arafat's move to Kuwait heralded a new stage of activity in his life. In 1958 the Palestinian resistance group Fatah came into being with Arafat as its leader. The group's main objective was the armed struggle against Israel; fedayeen militias made several incursions into Israeli territory. These incursions intensified after Fatah moved its headquarters to Damascus in 1961. In addition to the support he received from the Palestinians living in Kuwait, Arafat sought donations from oil-rich Arab regimes. His efforts were especially successful in Kuwait and Saudi Arabia.

DETACHED FROM ARAB AFFAIRS

In 1961, the rift between Syria and Egypt brought to an end the joint Egyptian-Syrian state, which had lasted just three and a half years. Growing disagreement between the two halves of the merged state had been sparked by the rising influence of the Ba'ath Party in Syria. But the most important dividing line was that drawn between Nasser's Egypt and Saudi Arabia, whose monarch, King Faisal, had called for an international Islamic conference that would include not just the Arab nations, but also Turkey, Iran, and Pakistan. This new alliance was envisioned as a religion-based counterbalance to Nasser's Arab nationalism. To an extent, it was a return to what Nuri al-Said had called for earlier.

A year later, after the coup in Yemen, Egypt found itself in a direct confrontation with Saudi Arabia. The Egyptians had been sending their armed forces to Yemen in support of the republicans. Saudi Arabia, assisted by Britain, meanwhile was increasing its aid to Emir al-Badr. Where did Arafat stand on all this? The fact that Fatah relocated its headquarters from Kuwait to Damascus did *not* mean that the Palestinian movement was necessarily taking sides in the battle that was being played out on so many fronts between the Arabs. Damascus was chosen as a base because it was a lot closer to Israel's borders, not just with Syria, but with Jordan and Lebanon too. Also, out of all the countries bordering Israel, Syria was the most militant.

But Arafat's public detachment from the Arabs' internal battles did not mean that he didn't harbor feelings of sympathy or animosity toward individual Arab states and their leaders. Arafat inwardly supported the Muslim Brotherhood, and not only on ideological grounds;

he was driven by his hostility to Nasser and his closeness to Kuwait and Saudi Arabia, Fatah's principal donors. His antipathy toward Nasser was further inflamed when the Egyptian president permitted UN troops to be deployed on Egyptian soil, along the border with Israel. By then Arafat had abandoned his faith in the idea that the "Palestine issue" could be solved by the Arab states acting against Israel. Instead he embraced the idea that the Palestinians themselves would have to fight to have their sovereign rights restored. This rift is reflected in the founding of the Palestine Liberation Organization in 1964.

I take issue with Palestinian Authority chairman Mahmoud Abbas, who writes in his book *Through Secret Channels: The Road to Oslo*: "Two bodies [the PLO and Fatah] were formed in order to complement each other in the battle for the rights of the Palestinian people." While this did eventually turn out to be true, it was by no means the case when the PLO was first set up. Abbas does, admittedly, accept that the PLO was "the brainchild of the Arab regimes" and that this "was out of step with what the people wanted." But he insists that "in spite of all this, Palestinians saw the PLO as their home."[1] That did eventually come to pass, but only after many years.

The Palestine Liberation Organization was "planned" at Nasser's suggestion at the Arab League summit in Cairo in January 1964. The Arab leaders had convened in connection with Israel's plans to divert a large stretch of the River Jordan to irrigate the Negev Desert. Nasser was clearly trying to avoid a wider confrontation with the Israelis. But Syria and the Palestinians took a different view: the Israeli waterworks came under attack. Israel retaliated by deploying its air force to destroy one of Syria's water systems and by threatening an "all-out war." Having put forward its plan to set up the PLO, Egypt sought to share responsibility for its restraint with a Palestinian *political* group. But the Higher Arab Council, headed by Mufti of Jerusalem Khadj Amin al-Hussein, had to all intents and purposes ceased to exist in 1956; the only influential Palestinian group at the time was Fatah, which was independent and whose stated aim was armed struggle.

The PLO was founded in May 1964 at the Palestinian Congress held at East Jerusalem's Ambassador Hotel. Arafat did not attend the congress; nor had he taken part in the Cairo summit earlier that year.

Abu Jihad attended as an observer, but did not participate in the debates. The first chairman of the PLO was to be Ahmed Shukeiri, a Palestinian serving in the Egyptian diplomatic corps; he was an ineffectual and far from independent figure, which may well be why all the Arab states approved his candidature; it is possible that none of them wanted an independent PLO.

Fatah refused to become part of the PLO; instead it existed and operated in parallel with it. Arafat and Fatah believed at the time that only by taking up arms could they secure any rights for the Palestinian people; they did not even think about how such rights could be secured by political means. Ahmed Shukeiri, meanwhile, did nothing in practical terms while, in a bid to safeguard his reputation, he launched a frenzied radio appeal for the destruction of Israel. There was also some activity—mostly concocted for publicity purposes—by the PLO-founded Palestine Liberation Army. Footage of its soldiers and commanders training to "produce a miracle" on the battlefield was widely screened across the Arab countries. Even so, most ordinary Palestinians clearly preferred Fatah, which had demonstrated its independence from both Nasser and the Arab League and criticized the League for doing nothing to support the Palestinian cause. This kind of parallel development in the Palestinian movement suited the Arab regimes that financed Fatah, the same regimes that were afraid of their own people falling under Nasser's influence.

In Palestinian communities in countries across the Arab world and beyond, Fatah was strengthening its position. This narrowed the gap between it and other Palestinian groups like the Nasserite Arab Nationalist Movement, which would give birth to the Popular Front for the Liberation of Palestine, the pro-Syrian al-Saiqa, and others. At this early stage, Fatah could not be characterized as an anti-Western movement; nor could its leader Yasser Arafat. It wasn't until some years later that Arafat turned against Western regimes for supplying Israel with financing and arms. Indeed, out of all the early Palestinian groups, the only really anti-Western movement was the Arab Nationalist Movement (ANM), whose leader George Khabash advocated toppling pro-Western governments in the Arab nations as a starting point in the battle for Palestinian sovereignty.

The defeat of the Arab states in the 1967 Six-Day War left Arafat more convinced than ever that the Palestinians had to win their struggle all by themselves. Shortly after the war ended, Fatah shifted its base to Jordan. From there it carried out incursions across the River Jordan into the occupied territories, where it clashed with the Israeli army, incurring heavy losses. By December 1967, Shukeiri was forced to step down. Palestinians had long been dissatisfied with his leadership of the PLO and he had lost support in Egypt after the war. In February 1969, at the fifth session of the Palestinian National Council (the PLO's governing body), Arafat was elected chairman of the PLO's executive committee. Fatah became the driving force behind PLO operations, ending the era of "parallelism" between the two movements. The significance of the change for the PLO was underlined by the fact that alongside the Fatah members there were also representatives of other Palestinian military-political factions on its executive committee.

KARAMEH: A TURNING POINT IN
ARAFAT'S RELATIONS WITH NASSER

Fatah's authority as the driving force of the PLO enjoyed an unprecedented boost after it fought the Israeli army at Karameh, on the east bank of the River Jordan. This was the point at which the PLO became a truly Palestinian body.

Israeli defense minister Moshe Dayan had ordered a huge assault on Fatah's fighters. The offensive was targeted on an area near the small town of Karameh, which was close to a camp holding forty thousand Palestinian refugees. It was also close to Shuna, another Palestinian camp, and to the Allenby Bridge (as the Hussein Bridge used to be called) over the River Jordan. The battle commenced on March 21, 1968, with the Israeli army deploying three divisions totaling ten thousand men on the east bank. They also deployed tanks, planes, military helicopters, and heavy artillery that shelled the Palestinian positions from across the river. For several hours, Fatah's forces battled alone, until they were joined by a division of the Jordanian army whose commander "had been unable to get in contact with King Hussein" and so took it upon himself to provide backup for the Palestinians. Having sustained heavy losses—twenty-eight dead, seventy wounded, and several burnt-out tanks—the Israelis retreated. The Palestinian casualties were twice that number, but it was nevertheless a great victory, and looked all the more so in contrast with the crushing defeat that Egypt, Syria, and Jordan had suffered in the Six-Day War. Fatah's ranks had been swollen by volunteers from many countries, including Egypt.

A week after the Battle of Karameh, Nasser invited Arafat to meet him in Cairo. This heralded the beginning of yet another stage in the life of a man whom events had thrust into a leading role in the confrontation with Israel. Arafat was accompanied on his trip to Cairo by Abu Iyad and Farouk Kaddoumi, but the talks that took place were actually between Nasser and Arafat. It was their first face-to-face meeting. The Egyptian president asked Arafat if he thought Israel could be defeated. "Yes," was Arafat's reply. Nasser's response that they also had to think about political means of founding a Palestinian state was met with silence, but Arafat had no hesitation in agreeing to the Egyptian leader's proposal that they fly to Moscow together.

The trip took place in July 1968. Arafat carried a diplomatic passport in the name of Mohsin Amin and was officially counted as a member of the Egyptian delegation, but Nasser introduced him to members of the Soviet leadership in his true capacity. Arafat met with Boris Ponomarev, chief of the Soviet Communist Party's international department, with whom he not only discussed the War of Attrition—which had seen active shelling of Israeli positions across the Suez Canal and of Israeli-occupied Sinai—but also the subject of a peaceful settlement. This may well have been the first time that Arafat gave serious thought to using political means to bolster the armed struggle against Israel.

Nevertheless, Arafat continued to maintain that there was no alternative to armed struggle. He applied this criterion to other Palestinian groups, judging them by whether they took part in the struggle or simply debated the matter. He was not concerned with the Marxist sloganeering of the Popular Front for the Liberation of Palestine or the Democratic Front for the Liberation of Palestine, which had split from the PFLP and was even more vocal about the Marxist orientation of its policies. This kind of "tolerance" helped Fatah—clearly the most powerful Palestinian group at the time—maintain its place at the vanguard of the Palestinian resistance movement. There had also been something of a shift in the outlook of Arafat and his comrades. Here, below, are two quotations from the "common platform" adopted at the seventh session of the Palestinian National Council: "The driving forces of the Palestinian revolution are the Palestinian workers and hard-working masses just as much as anybody else who has a stake in our struggle for national independence." And: "The Palestinian revolution is an inalienable part of the Arab revolution and the worldwide independence movement in its fight against imperialism and international Zionism."

At the end of the 1960s and beginning of the 1970s both Arafat and the Palestinian resistance movement as a whole were still unyielding in their attitude toward the "liquidation of Israel." At least publicly. But if you listened attentively, the mood music seemed to be changing; the idea of setting up a Palestinian state and finding it a place on the map of the Middle East was becoming increasingly audible in the mix.

As I look back through the notebooks in which I recorded my conversations with Arafat all those years ago, I would say that the Abu Ammar who was born with a burning conviction that there was no alternative to taking up arms for the "liberation of all Palestine" gradually—very gradually—evolved into a "warrior-politician." In the early days of course, the politician in Arafat could be glimpsed only through the thick smokescreen of his anti-Israel rhetoric, which, thanks to Israeli actions against local Palestinians, was constantly stoked to an extreme. But in the early 1970s Arafat had started to ponder the possibility that instead of a Palestinian state being created *in place of* Israel, it could initially exist *alongside* it. This sense of "initially" would gradually be abandoned, but not for some years to come.

Two Encounters with Arafat:
Before and After Black September

Arafat's evolution was particularly influenced by events in Jordan. In summer 1970, the tensions between King Hussein and the Palestinian resistance movement escalated sharply. The movement had begun to turn Jordan into a resistance-controlled base for armed operations against Israel, a course primarily embraced by Fatah under Arafat's leadership. Determined not to allow this to happen, King Hussein's government increasingly interfered with the Palestinians' activities, banning them from carrying arms in Amman or setting up ammunition stores in towns and villages. While the Palestinian resistance movement sought to control the situation in Jordan, the state of Jordan was increasingly trying to control them. Yet this does not fully explain the bitterness of a dispute that culminated in Jordan practically taking Israel's side and Syria siding with the Palestinians. In fact, Jordan's government had already been in contact with the Israelis to discuss the fate of the West Bank. Amman envisaged an autonomous Palestinian entity on the West Bank, but only as a part of the Jordanian state. Meanwhile at the August 1970 session of the Palestinian National Council, held in Amman (of all places !), the Palestinians themselves had decided to "use any means to turn the entire Jordan-Palestinian arena into a stronghold for total Palestinian revolution." George Khabash, for example, declared at the time that there was "absolutely no difference between [Israeli defense minister Moshe] Dayan and Hussein."

As the friction intensified, the king imposed a state of emergency and appointed a war cabinet headed by General Daoud. The post of military governor of Jordan, a position with sweeping powers, went to General Madzhali, a man who made no secret of his anti-Palestinian feelings. On September 6, 1970, the Popular Front for the Liberation of Palestine carried out what was in those days an unprecedented terrorist act, hijacking four airliners in the air, forcing them to land at an airfield near Amman and issuing an ultimatum that unless all Palestinians were released from Israeli jails, the aircraft would be blown up along with everyone aboard them. Dayan responded that even if his own daughter were one of the passengers, he would not agree to the PFLP's demands as that would only trigger a chain reaction of endless hostage-taking. After Israel refused to meet the hijackers' demands, the passengers and crews were released and the aircraft destroyed.

My meeting with Arafat came on the eve of 1970's Black September, when the storm clouds were already gathering in the skies over Jordan. We sat for several hours in his tiny room in Damascus, which was furnished only with a small writing table and a narrow camp bed. He eagerly told me that the Palestinians were sure to gain the upper hand in Jordan because a large number of officers in Jordan's royal army were Palestinians and would refuse to take up arms against their brothers. He refused to even entertain the notion that matters were not that simple, that even if the PLO prevailed in Amman, Israel would be sure to intervene. "In that case, the entire Arab world would become a second Vietnam," Arafat replied.

My next meeting with Arafat was also in Damascus, on June 27, 1971. This was after the Palestinians' defeat in Jordan. Iraqi units headquartered in Jordan had not come to the Palestinian's assistance, which Arafat had been counting on; a small number of soldiers and officers from the Jordanian army had gone over to the Palestinians' side, but not an entire division—another thing that Arafat had been counting on. The Palestine Liberation Army, equipped with Syrian armored vehicles, had penetrated Jordanian territory and advanced toward Amman. Israel responded by mobilizing its forces, while the United States sent ships from its Sixth Fleet to the waters between Cyprus and Syria. Despite the cease-fire agreement they had signed, the Palestinian militias were forced to leave Jordan.

While emphasizing that our conversation was of a confidential nature, Arafat told me during our June 27 meeting that "the situation is of course a serious one, but we have had a series of positive developments on the political front since September 1970. We now see more clearly who our enemies are. The UN General Assembly resolution of November 1970, recognizing the rights of Palestinians, should also be added to the list of achievements."

"Are you referring to the creation of a Palestinian state?" I asked. "As far as I know," I added, "the General Assembly resolution did not clarify what rights the Palestinians should have."

"What state are you talking about?" Arafat asked in turn.

"One that could coexist alongside Israel," I replied, spelling it out for him.

"I'll give you a straight answer," Arafat said:

At present we are in no shape to get rid of Israel. Fighting the Israeli regime will be a long process. Given current circumstances, we advocate trying to resolve the situation in favor of the Palestinians, so that our voice is heard, so that our rights are protected. We need a change of tactics. We oppose the November 22 [UN] resolution,[2] but we cannot affect the outcome of the political settlement unless we participate in it. If we don't, we will not be able to stand up for our interests, and the settlement will pass us by. This means our rights are best served if the occupied West Bank is *not* returned to Jordan, and Gaza is *not* returned to Egypt, as things were before 1967; we want to see a Palestinian state on these territories. But it would not be sustainable unless it also covered the east bank of the Jordan. Even Churchill wrote in his memoirs that the east bank was ruled by Palestinian authorities after the First World War.

"Thank you for being so frank," I said. "But now I have to ask you one fairly important question. How will this initiative will be received within the Palestinian movement?"

"That is of no concern to us," Arafat replied. "Where were they when we were fighting in Jordan? We will of course face difficulties but we are not afraid of them."

I went on to ask Arafat how the Arab countries would react. He replied:

The only one that will object will be Iraq. Saudi Arabia might be opposed to it in spirit—and they have got people in our midst whom they could call into action—but we too have 100,000 Palestinians working in Saudi Arabia, some of them in the oil industry. The Saudis realize that we might act too, so they're not likely to do much. When he was in the U.S., King Faisal said the Saudis would accept anything the Palestinians agreed to. Even before that, Faisal did not oppose the blueprint for a "democratic two-nation state in Palestine," which he had once called a renunciation of Islam. Now he'll accept our new blueprint as well. The only one who'll be strongly against us is King Hussein. He might even want to sign a separate peace deal with Israel. We know about the contacts he's been making, with Abba Eban in London, with Moshe Dayan in New York, and with Yigal Allon at the Dead Sea. But Israel doesn't want to negotiate with him; it wants to negotiate with the Palestinians.

Summing up, Arafat said: "The Palestinians see the establishment of a Palestinian state as the way toward a political settlement, not the implementation of UN Security Council resolution 242."

As if to underline his words, Arafat drew me a map of Palestine divided in two. "This will be us," he indicated, "and that will be Israel." I asked him to sign the map, and he did so, without a moment's hesitation. This was back in the summer of 1971; in other words, almost twenty years before Arafat announced for the whole world to hear that it was *not* the aim of the Palestinian movement to ensure the destruction of Israel.

When I reported back to Moscow on our meeting, I stressed several points. It was the dawn of a new phase in the Middle East peace process, one in which the Palestinians were starting to play a part, I wrote in my coded telegram. Arafat had opted for a policy of creating a Palestinian state alongside Israel. His talk of not being able to get rid of the Jewish state *for the time being* should be understood as rhetoric to mask his shift away from his previously declared position. Despite Arafat's insistence that he was not worried about protests from within the Palestinian movement, there was little reason to believe that the resistance could avoid a major split. (I had had talks in Damascus with al-Saiqa leader Zukheir Mohsin and PFLP chief George Khabash, both of whom were extremely hostile to the idea of a Palestinian state. Khabash had gone as far as to call it a "betrayal.") My conversation with Arafat came immediately after he had met with Egypt's President Sadat and Saudi Arabia's King Faisal in Cairo, and there is reason to believe that they approved of the Palestinians' new policy, which also had implications for their future relations with King Hussein of Jordan.

In short, a policy of establishing a Palestinian state in the occupied territories, if openly adopted, would significantly change the nature of the search for a political settlement. The extent to which the United States would be involved in any such change of direction would clearly have to be spelled out. It would be better for the Soviet Union not to keep to the sidelines of the process, especially one that looked so promising in terms of the region's history. Soviet links with Fatah not only might help the Middle East peace process along but could also boost Moscow's influence in the region, including in the planned new state, no matter what form it took.

I was in Syria and Lebanon during the 1973 Yom Kippur War. The war itself, which this time had been started by Egypt and Syria, prompted Arafat and most of his comrades to revisit their previous thinking: that the route to a Palestinian settlement might, after all, lie via military action against Israel by the Arab nations' regular armed forces. The gains made by Egypt and Syria in the initial stages of the war encouraged them. Temporarily, at least, in those exhilarating first hours of fighting, it seemed that myth after myth was being dispelled—that the superpowers had been plotting against the Palestinians, or that the Soviets had supplied the Egyptian and Syrian armies with inferior arms. Now everyone was talking about the SA-6 and SA-7 surface-to-air missiles that had been used to shoot down Israeli planes. Mohamed Oda, whom I met in Beirut on October 13, not long after he arrived from Cairo, put it very vividly: "Compared to 1967, I would say the Israelis are now more like Arabs, and we're more like Jews."

TIME TO EMBRACE POLITICS

The Arabs' ultimate defeat in the 1973 war and the events that followed it convinced Arafat that political means were indeed needed to tackle the Palestinian issue. What drove him to this conclusion was almost certainly King Hussein's stance toward the Palestinians. On October 9, Saleh Raafat, a leading member of the Popular Democratic Front for the Liberation of Palestine, had been dispatched to Amman, where he held a meeting with the king. His task was to raise two questions with

Hussein: would Jordan enter the war? And would the Palestinian re-sistance movement be allowed back into Jordan? This is how the king replied: "The Americans have warned me that the Egyptian and Syrian forces will be wiped out a few days from now. So I will launch military action only if the Golan Heights are liberated and the Egyptians secure their positions on the east bank of the Suez Canal. Yet unless I launch military action, it would be out of the question for the Palestinian re-sistance to be allowed back into Jordan."

I presume that the order to sound out King Hussein had come di-rectly from Arafat himself. In any case, the king's line would have been immediately reported to Arafat, so he could not have failed to realize that the door had been firmly closed on the prospect of mak-ing Jordan a base for armed operations against Israel. Stressing that this was how Arafat felt too, DFLP leader Nayef Hawatmeh told me on October 13 that: "The war means there'll be a relatively reduced part for the resistance to play, so it's all the more important to have a constructive program for the creation of a Palestinian state."

But what kind of state, and how? In theory, the Palestinians had three options: (1) pressing ahead with military force to wrest the oc-cupied West Bank and Gaza Strip from Israeli control, which was im-possible without triggering another wider war with Israel; (2) using political means to reach an agreement to set up the structure of some sort of Palestinian state on the West Bank within Jordanian territory, possibly in the form of a confederation with Jordan; or (3) striving for a fully independent Palestinian state.

The United States came out in favor of the second option, which in all probability was not so much acceptable to the Jordanian govern-ment as imposed on it. Palestinian National Council chairman Khaled Fakhoum, a man close to the Syrian government, told me where the Syrians stood during our October 15 meeting in Damascus, where I had traveled from Beirut. President Assad, he said, thought the only solution for the Palestinians was the liberation of the West Bank; only after that happened could they think about a joint state with Jordan. At the time, Arafat found both parts of this formula unacceptable, which he confirmed to me once again when we met in Sidon on Oc-tober 23 (with me was Soviet diplomat Vasily I. Kolotusha). "We want nothing less than a fully independent state, which we should try to secure using a combination of military and political means," Arafat said. "However, nothing and nobody will force us back under the rule of the Bedouins with their ties to the Americans and the British." He launched into this fighting talk without any prompting, and was obviously very concerned about the reaction from Jordan and Syria to the idea of a Palestinian state. It could be that he was privately counting on support from Cairo. Whatever the case, he said the Palestinians had made a mistake by not being "sufficiently flexible" with regard to the Rogers Plan put forward by U.S. secretary of state William Rogers—translated and agreed to by Nasser—but then on reflection, he added: "As a result we didn't have the Egyptians behind us in September 1970. We would not make that mistake again."

Arafat was less volatile than he had been in the past, less inclined to swing to the left, then to the right; he was also increasingly serious in his approach to political issues. He was becoming a realist. This was in stark contrast with several other Palestinian leaders. As an example, here is a highlight from my conversation with George Khabash, who was clever and struck me as likeable, but who remained a "lefty" to his core. We met in Beirut, where I traveled directly after meeting Arafat in Sidon. Our conversation kicked off with Khabash's assertion that "everything was decided by the working masses in the Palestinian movement, [by] their revolutionary drive."

We had been on friendly terms for many years, so I meant no offense when I interrupted him, saying, "But all the same, there is a difference between revolutionary romanticism and revolutionary realism." I added that while I had great respect for Che Guevara, and at times even admired him, I had to acknowledge that he had not brought revolution to Bolivia.

"Very well," Khabash said. "Then this is how I would define the policy of the Popular Front: we oppose UN resolution 242, we oppose anti-Sovietism, and on the issue of a political settlement we are as yet undecided."

After the 1973 Yom Kippur War, Arafat was given more room for maneuver. In November of that year, the PLO, which was still dominated by Fatah, was recognized by the Arab conference in Algiers as "the sole legitimate representative of the Palestinian people." The PFLP, which rejected outright any political path toward settling the Palestinian problem, had quit the executive committee of the PLO on September 26, 1974.

In Jordan, King Hussein engaged in an initial "tug-of-war" over the PLO: in 1974 he succeeded in having the following stipulation inserted in his communiqué on his talks with Anwar Sadat in Alexandria: "The PLO is the legitimate representative of the Palestinian people, *except* those resident in the Hashemite Kingdom of Jordan." The king was, however, forced to comply with the decisions of the Rabat summit of Arab heads of state in October 1974, after which Jordan "absolved itself of responsibility" for the West Bank. (Because Jordan had no territorial disputes with the Israelis, this cleared the way for it to sign a peace treaty with Israel.)

Once he had officially relinquished control over the West Bank, King Hussein chose to proceed along his own path. During one of our conversations, he told me: "It was my idea to go to war with Israel in 1967 and we lost the West Bank as a result. That taught me a great deal." He stopped short at those words but I finished the sentence for him in my head: "And now I don't want to lose my state or my throne because of the West Bank." So I could understand his position too.

After all that had happened, the main problem for Arafat, Fatah, and the PLO became recognition of UN Security Council resolutions 242 and 338. It was an issue on which the United States and the Soviet Union saw eye-to-eye, the only difference being that the United States and Israel pointed to the PLO's rejection of these resolutions as proof that it was impossible to negotiate with the Palestinians. In his book *Through Secret Channels: The Road to Oslo*,[3] Mahmoud Abbas writes:

> Time went by . . . [and] every time that official Palestinian delegations came to Moscow, Andrei Gromyko would tell them: "You have no other choice but to recognize resolutions 242 and 338. These resolutions are a strong trump card in your hands, one that must be played at the right moment; do not let that moment pass you by. I ask you to let us play that trump card in negotiations with the

Americans, the Europeans and the Israelis. Then perhaps we might manage to find the solution you need." But the Palestinians' response was always the same: "No, we cannot accept these resolutions."[4]

These talks always took place in Moscow and, without exaggerating the effect of the "Soviet factor," they seem to have played a role in changing the PLO's stance on the UN resolutions. The PLO *could* have continued to reject the resolutions (its opposition being based on the fear that accepting them would mean having to recognize Israel, even though the resolutions did not envisage the creation of a Palestinian state but dealt only with the issue of Palestinian refugees) if one of the superpowers had at least been neutral. But when the PLO realized that it was facing the prospect of being isolated in the Arab world, where the vast majority of states had accepted the resolutions, as well as in wider world opinion, and moreover that its continuing failure to recognize the resolutions posed an insurmountable hurdle to developing the contacts the Palestinians had already started to make—initially with representatives of U.S. Jewish groups and then with various Israeli political groups—the PLO came around.

The United States also exercised an influence on the PLO leadership that should not be underestimated. In the mid-1970s the CIA opened a secret channel of communications with the PLO's intelligence wing Jihaz ar-Rasd; contacts were also made via the U.S. embassy in Beirut and Saudi Arabia. Their purpose was to ensure the security of the U.S. embassy in Beirut during the Lebanese Civil War. In 1976, the United States asked the PLO for its help evacuating American citizens from Beirut. After the Palestinians responded, Henry Kissinger sent Arafat a letter expressing his gratitude. The United States and the Palestinians also cooperated covertly during the American hostage crisis in Iran. At the CIA's request, two PLO representatives were sent to Tehran, where they secured the release of women and African-American hostages. All of this took place against the backdrop of President Carter's declaration that the Palestinians had the right to establish a "national homeland," but America's relationship with the PLO was driven by pragmatic concerns, rather than political ones. Bowing to pressure from Israel and the Israeli lobby in the United States, the Carter administration had been forced to ask for the resignation of Andrew Young, its permanent representative to the United Nations, who had "of his own accord" held a meeting with a PLO representative at the UN. Under the circumstances, these other contacts were kept under wraps.

Arafat's evolution was not an easy one; at various stages along the way he was helped by Abu Iyad, Abu Mazen (Mahmoud Abbas), Yasser Abdrabo, Nabil Shaat, Mahmoud Darwish (the well-known Palestinian poet who lived in Israel), Khaled Hassan, Abu Allah, and others. Some would omit Abu Jihad, one of the founders of the Palestinian movement, from this list. In my opinion, they would be wrong. In all my meetings with the Palestinian leaders listed above, different approaches to the search for a settlement could be noted; but it was Abu Jihad who revealed to me, in Beirut on September 5, 1979, that he had authorized his envoy Natsha to meet with Moshe Dayan. According to Natsha's written notes, Dayan had raised several questions, which included, "Do the Palestinians recognize the plan for autonomy within Jordan?" and "Is it possible to discuss a peaceful settlement for Gaza separately from the West Bank?" Natsha did not venture any answers on his own account, as he was a private individual, but he suggested that they could all be addressed during negotiations with the PLO leadership. This was a sea change—Natsha had in effect told Dayan that talks between Israel and the PLO leadership were a possibility, and Abu Jihad did not wish to disown his envoy's comments. It was, as he put it, "the second instance of contact between us and the Israelis." The Americans too, he added, were sounding out further contacts with the PLO. Hal Saunders, for example, had asked Harvard University professor Walid al-Khalidi for a consultation on Palestinian matters. To which al-Khalidi had replied: "I'm an American citizen. If you want [talks], you can have talks with the PLO." I find it hard to believe that the man telling me all this could have possibly had a hostile attitude to the idea of the Palestinian leadership holding talks with Israel with the aim of securing a political settlement of the Palestinian problem.[5]

At the same time, steps were being taken via yet another channel to organize a confidential meeting between the Israelis and the PLO—

with Arafat's knowledge and approval, of course. The Lebanese Christian leader Camille Chamoun had put himself forward as a mediator. First Nabil Nadjam, a leading member of Chamoun's Liberal Democratic Party, and then Chamoun's son Dany told me that a mediation mission had been planned in detail. Weizman had given his approval. The Palestinians were supposed to be represented by Abu Khassan, but he was assassinated just before the meeting. As Nabil Nadjam put it, this complicated matters but did not stop the Chamoun camp's efforts. Dany Chamoun said that the Abu Khassan assassination did not negate the need for secret contacts between Israel and the Palestinians, which he linked to the prospect of Weizman becoming Israel's president. On September 3, 1979, Chamoun and Abu Iyad's aide Mitkhat held yet another discussion about a possible meeting between Israel and the PLO. In return for organizing it, Chamoun wanted armed Palestinian groups to withdraw from southern Lebanon; unarmed Palestinians would be transferred to refugee camps.

Of course, not everybody in the PLO leadership was in favor of secret talks with Israel at that time—as evidenced by the assassination of the would-be negotiator Abu Khassan. But the facts clearly reveal that by 1979, the top leadership of the Palestinian movement no longer categorically rejected the idea of a peaceful settlement with Israel. Even as early as August 1978, the executive committee of the PLO had decided to set up a group in Israeli-occupied territory that would restrict itself to purely legal means of fighting for the Palestinian cause. As Yasser Abdrabo told me: "Just by putting down roots in occupied territory we will be able to hold on to our chances of playing a part in reaching a political settlement."

TENSION WITH SYRIA: A MESSAGE FROM ANDROPOV

I don't want to gloss over Arafat's relations with Syria, which had begun to deteriorate at the end of the 1970s and were strained to the breaking point after the Israeli invasion of Lebanon and the forced expulsion of Palestinians from that country. Many blamed Arafat for the catastrophe. Their reasoning was that he had given up too soon

on the interests of the Palestinian people, before their armed struggle
had forced Israel into a corner, before Israel had given up hope of a
compromise and surrendered. That wasn't the only thing that was
held against Arafat. After the Palestinians lost out in Beirut, went one
rumor, Arafat, having forgotten the events of Black September, met
with King Hussein to discuss a possible confederation. Arafat was
also blamed for his trip to Cairo, which, even after Sadat was killed,
made no shift away from the Camp David accords. It was increasingly thought—especially in the Syrian government and by pro-Syrian
Palestinian groups—that Arafat had shifted to the right, that he had
capitulated.

Moscow was well aware of what was being said about Arafat—
more than one Soviet expert on the Middle East joined the chorus.
But the Kremlin did not follow Damascus's anti-Arafat line. The Soviet Union was all too aware that Syria's key motive was to exert control over the Palestinian movement and use it to strengthen its own
hand in its dealings with the Americans, the aim being to establish
grounds for a settlement with Israel that Syria would find acceptable.

The Kremlin was in a difficult position. On the one hand, Hafez
Assad's Syria had become the mainstay of Soviet policy in the Middle
East since Egypt under Sadat had distanced itself from the Soviet
Union and difficulties had arisen in Moscow's relations with Saddam
Hussein's regime in Iraq. On the other hand, the Kremlin, in its efforts to play an active role in the Middle East peace process, wanted
to see a solution to the crucial problem of the Palestinians and was
therefore anxious to build stronger ties with Fatah, which was indis-
putably the main Palestinian player. It didn't matter how many meetings we held with ideologically more congenial groups, such as the
PFLP and the DFLP. Nothing was as important as forging solid ties
with the Fatah leadership.

Events, meanwhile, did little to further Soviet interests. The Syrians and the Lebanese had urged two prominent Fatah militants, Abu
Musa and Abu Saleh, to stand against Arafat. Abu Musa was widely
known as a military hero in Beirut, which guaranteed him support
from a number of Fatah members, especially from its military faction.
He and his supporters published a pamphlet criticizing the PLO's ex-

ecutive committee and rejecting any compromise with Israel; its mission, it declared, was to liberate all of Palestine. Abu Musa and his followers opposed both the Reagan Plan and the plan set out at the Fez summit; they also opposed PLO cooperation with the more conservative Arab regimes. There were clashes between Palestinian units in the Bekaa Valley, and then in the Lebanese port of Tripoli. As a result, Arafat and four thousand Palestinian militants had to leave Lebanon for Tunisia.

A short while before this happened I was in Beirut, where I had a series of meetings lined up with various Syrian leaders, including President Assad. High on our agenda for those meetings were our efforts to convince the Syrians to drop their hostility toward Fatah and its leader. On June 2, 1983, I arrived at the Syrian president's residence, accompanied by the Soviet ambassador to Damascus, Vladimir Yukhin. During our talks, several points that summed up Syria's position became clear. "A comprehensive Middle East peace settlement," Assad said, "can only be possible if there is parity between the [armed] forces of those taking part in the negotiations. Now that Egypt has abandoned the conflict, the parity has to be between the forces of Syria and Israel." And while he welcomed the idea of a Middle East peace conference cochaired by the United States and the Soviet Union, Assad said it wouldn't be a realistic possibility until there was a clearly defined parity between the opposing forces.

Yukhin and I later asked each other's opinion of our meeting. We realized that by stressing "parity between forces," Assad was trying to get the Soviet Union to step up its supplies of arms to Syria by playing on Moscow's eagerness to see a peace deal. His unyielding opposition to a negotiated peace under the prevailing circumstances also shed light on why there was growing Syrian hostility to those Palestinian groups that felt that they could come to a compromise deal with Israel on their own.

Although it was a lengthy meeting, Assad did not respond in any depth to my remarks about the need to ease the tension in his relations with Arafat. Whether Assad agreed with him or not, I said, Arafat was the recognized leader of the Palestinians. To focus only on his opponents was untenable, while the split in the Palestinian movement seriously weakened the Arab side and was not helping to find a solution to the conflict with Israel.

In a telegram to Moscow on June 1, I wrote that the reality did not correspond to what the Palestinians were being told about Syria's policy of noninterference in their affairs or even its acceptance of Arafat as the leader of the Palestinian resistance. I was told by Abdul Halim Khaddam, the Syrian foreign minister, that Arafat had been "extremely damaged" and that Abu Saleh's group was stronger. During confidential talks, Kafri, head of the foreign ministry's eastern Europe section (and Syria's former ambassador in Moscow), went even further, declaring that "Syrians will only be happy when there's an opportunity to get rid of Arafat." Meanwhile, I pointed out in my telegram, the anti-Arafat tendency was not supported by most Palestinians. The vast majority of Palestinian groups resented interference in their affairs by the Arab states. Syria's opposition only strengthened Arafat's position. I therefore proposed, as a matter of urgency, that a program be aired on Moscow Radio and articles be written in, the Soviet press criticizing the split in the Palestinian movement and voicing support for Arafat as the recognized leader of the PLO.

At about this time, in early June 1983, Yukhin received urgent instructions from Moscow to pass on a verbal message to Arafat from Yuri Andropov, then general secretary of the Soviet Communist Party. It was a very important communication: its tenor was the need to shift away from hostility to the Syrian regime and work out a compromise, as well as to overcome internal discord within Palestinian ranks. It also mentioned Soviet efforts to nudge the Syrians in the same direction. Most important was the fact that Arafat had been sent a communication from the leader of the Soviet Union; this emphasized that while the Kremlin enjoyed a close partnership with Syria, it was not pursuing a policy that could be labeled as anti-Arafat.

But how could the message be delivered? After all, Arafat was not even in Damascus. On June 3, however, it emerged that he *was* at Fatah's outpost in the Syrian capital for a very short time on his way to Romania. Yet because Arafat was in Damascus without prior authorization, ambassador Yukhin could not call on him without jeopardizing his relations with Syrian officialdom. The only place he could carry out his instructions was at the Soviet embassy, but for reasons of his own—political and security-related—Arafat preferred not to go to our embassy. Because I enjoyed friendly relations with him, I was asked to call on him at Fatah's bureau and talk him into coming to the Soviet embassy. I was joined by Rostislav Yushchuk, who was in Damascus at the time, and together we managed to persuade him. We traveled to the embassy in an armored car, accompanied by a jeep armed with machine-guns—that was how strained relations had become between Syria and the Palestinian leader, with Arafat alleging he had proof that the Syrian government was involved in a recent attempt to assassinate him.

At the Soviet embassy, Arafat asked us to convey his gratitude to Andropov for his crucial show of support. He had, he said, no doubts about where the Soviet Union stood on this issue, and assured us that he would not allow relations between the Palestinians and the Syrian government to deteriorate any further, though he pointed out that he was caught "between a rock and hard place": if he didn't fight the Syrian troops near Bekaa who were supporting the insurgents, the mutiny would continue indefinitely. We asked Arafat what practical steps he planned to take to ease relations with the Syrian leadership. He replied that the current crisis had been provoked by the Syrians, that they were the ones who should make concessions to the Palestinians, by ceasing to interfere in their affairs. The PLO leader also stressed that he was exercising restraint already, as demonstrated by the fact that he had not sought to put down the rebellion by force, which would have put him on a collision course with the Syrians. Indeed he still held out hope that President Assad would make the first move toward meeting him and Fatah halfway.

Because Arafat was in a hurry to get to the airfield, there was little time. He insisted that Yushchuk and I go see him in Tripoli (in Lebanon) after he had returned from his trip abroad. "The situation calls for a more detailed conversation," he said.

Arafat's trip to Romania, Algeria, Iraq, Southern Yemen, and Kuwait had been aimed at securing support from these countries' leaders to exert a restraining influence on Syria. As soon as he returned, he sent a message via his Damascus representative expressing a wish "to meet Primakov and Yushchuk as soon as possible" at one of his bases in northern Lebanon. We traveled there via the Syrian city of Homs on June 14, guarded by a group of armed Palestinians. We went through the checkpoints on the Syria-Lebanon border without being stopped; then, from Fatah's base near Tripoli, we were escorted by people sent by Arafat. We had to pass through a series of Palestinian security cordons before we reached his temporary command post in the mountains. It was here, in an olive grove, that our meeting with Arafat took place, lasting more than three hours.

Arafat asked us to convey a verbal message of his own in response to Andropov, offering "heartfelt thanks to the Soviet leadership for its timely reaction to attempts to provoke a split in Palestinian ranks." He said that "thanks to Andropov's message on June 3, and to other steps taken by the Soviet Union, the PLO leadership had been able to sense a fall-off in Syrian activity against the PLO." The Palestinian leader asked us to tell Andropov that he would "do all that was expected of him to restore normality within Palestinian ranks and to ease relations with Damascus, now that Syria could not ignore the opinion of the Soviet Union."

Arafat quoted the Syrian president's brother Rifaat Assad as evidence that the Syrians were "gradually starting to abandon their policy of trying to split the Palestinian movement." Assad had told him that from the very outset, the Syrian government had been given unreliable information suggesting that the rebels enjoyed across-the-board support and could attract most of Fatah to their side. Assad, however, had become convinced that this information bore no resemblance to reality, so he was forming a commission to mediate between the warring Palestinian factions. Neither foreign minister Khaddam nor military counterintelligence chief Ali Duba, both known for their opposition to closer ties between Syria and Arafat, had been invited to sit on the commission.

Arafat outlined his position on the peace process by drawing attention to two points: (1) that the Palestinians' forced exodus from Beirut did not for one moment mean that the PLO was basing its political strategy on the Reagan Plan; and (2) that what the "Jordan scenario" meant for the PLO was, above all else, the creation of a

Palestinian state. Only then could there be a confederation between the east and west banks of the River Jordan. His discussions with King Hussein, Arafat said, had not gone beyond those parameters. Arafat also said that while he remained opposed to the Camp David accords, he planned to engage with the political process so as "not to allow time to act against the interests of the Palestinian people." He was referring to the Israelis' continuing settlement of the West Bank and the Gaza Strip, which could inflict irreversible damage to Palestinian interests.

After we bade Arafat a warm farewell, we set off from Northern Lebanon. Two cars filled with armed Palestinian guards escorted us all the way to our embassy in Damascus, to which we returned safe and sound not long before midnight on June 14.

But there was a postscript to this visit. I asked for an appointment with Syria's President Assad so as to set out my thoughts on the meeting with Arafat, and was invited to see him on June 16. Naturally I did my utmost to highlight what common ground there was between the PLO leader and the Syrians. Assad had by then received the Kremlin's communiqué regarding the situation in Lebanon, which had had its intended effect. Assad's tone was quite different from when we had met twelve days earlier; clearly a thaw was in the offing. He said he "agreed in principle with the Soviet government: Syria had to produce constructive ideas on Lebanon, as well as on the wider Middle East peace process, in consultation with Moscow." As for relations with the PLO, Assad said: "It is in Syria's best interests that it [the PLO] maintain its unity, and at the same time that its progressive elements, above all those in Fatah, play a substantial part in shaping the political direction taken by the Palestinian leadership. Syria is maintaining contacts with all interested parties in the Palestinian movement, including Arafat's followers." Assad promised to weigh up all the pros and cons of a possible meeting with Arafat.

The meetings described here could not, of course, have normalized relations between Fatah and Damascus on their own, but they undoubtedly removed much of the tension; this was, after all, a point at which a wider armed conflict between Syria and the Palestinians could have broken out. Fortunately, that did not occur.

PEACE FOR PALESTINIANS AND
ISRAELIS IN EQUAL MEASURE

Arafat above all deserves credit for overcoming the opposition of those within the PLO and outside it who fiercely opposed UN Security Council resolutions 242 and 338. In 1988, at the 19th session of the Palestinian National Council, these resolutions were recognized. It is also to Arafat's credit that he was able to secure a link between the PNC's recognition of resolutions 242 and 338 and agreement from the United States and Israel to the creation of a Palestinian state on the West Bank and in the Gaza Strip. This linkage was secured amid the intifada—the Palestinian uprising in the occupied territories that broke out on December 7, 1987—and King Hussein's decision to relinquish control of the West Bank. This ultimately led to the PLO being recognized as the representative of the Palestinian people, one which the Israeli government had to deal with, one way or another. At the same time, there was an upsurge in international support for the PLO.

After some hesitation and internal wrangling, Arafat set out his position at a press conference in Geneva on the day after his December 14, 1988, address to the UN General Assembly.[6] The statement he made at that press conference was possibly even more important than his speech the day before, as it responded to those critics who suggested that he had left many questions unanswered during his UN address. The most important parts of Arafat's statement are as follows:

> The creation of our state gives freedom to the Palestinians—it guarantees peace for both Palestinians and Israelis in equal measure . . . Yesterday, in my speech, I spoke of General Assembly resolution 181 as the basis for Palestinian independence. I also stressed that we now recognize resolutions 242 and 338 as the basis for talks with Israel in the framework of an international conference. It was recognition of these three resolutions that was announced at the Palestinian National Council's meeting in Algiers.
>
> My speech made it crystal clear that what we understand by our people's rights is the right to freedom and national indepen-

dence in accordance with resolution 181, and the right of all parties involved in the Middle East conflict to live in peace and security, including the state of Palestine, Israel and other neighboring
states, in accordance with resolutions 242 and 338.

As regards terrorism, yesterday I made it abundantly clear—
and I repeat it, so as to confirm our position—that we wholly and
resolutely reject all forms of terrorism, be it carried out by an individual, a group or the state . . . Everybody must understand that
neither Arafat nor anyone else can halt the intifada. It will come to
an end only when there are concrete, practical steps toward realizing our goals and the creation of a Palestinian state.

"In conclusion," Arafat said, "I hereby declare, in your presence,
and ask you to put my message across: we want peace, we pledge ourselves to keeping peace, we want to live in our own Palestinian state,
and may others live the way we want to."

A number of Western commentators—and not just Western commentators—have deliberately disparaged the role that Arafat played
in the period that followed, especially when writing about the secret
Israeli-Palestinian talks in Oslo, where Mahmoud Abbas played a
leading role; about the difficulties he created along the way to the Declaration of Principles signed in Washington on September 3, 1993;
or about the equally difficult bilateral negotiating process at the
Madrid peace conference. Several commentators concluded that what
progress was being made in terms of political engagement was happening without Arafat's consent; that events had "taken him
hostage." Judging by my own conversations with Arafat, I can utterly
refute such conclusions. In fact, virtually no major decision was taken
by Palestinian representatives in either Oslo or at the official Israeli-
Palestinian talks in Washington without his explicit consent. Arafat
understood better than anyone else that it was essential to reach
agreements with Israel that would be acceptable to the majority of
Palestinians. When he was informed of the outcome of one particular
meeting in Oslo, at which the Israeli officials had been in touch with
their superiors and had agreed to initiate an "interim phase" with
troops being pulled out of the Gaza Strip, he said: "That is not

enough. Jericho should be included too—it should be easier for Israel to do that since there are no Jewish settlements in that area." Arafat instructed his officials to insist on his "Gaza-Jericho" project. In his book *Through Secret Channels: The Road to Oslo*, Mahmoud Abbas describes how difficult it was to overcome the Israelis' opposition to this, and acknowledges that, because it was such a thorny issue in the Declaration of Principles, it was "a litmus test of how sincere the Israelis were in their future plans."[7] His words sounded just as relevant in 2006 and 2007, as politicians in Israel lined up to demand that troops not be pulled out of the West Bank, but only out of Gaza.

Arafat was the one who stood firm. At one point, just before the Declaration of Principles was due to be signed, he even threatened that the Palestinians would not come to the White House if the text of the declaration referred only to the Palestinian delegation and not to the PLO. Copies of the declaration had already been prepared, but with the threat of the signing ceremony being called off, the Israelis and the United States agreed to reprint the last page.

That was typical of Arafat: he had learned to show some political give-and-take but he was well aware of its limits. He knew that if he overstepped those limits he could easily wreck the painstaking process of reaching a settlement with Israel. Arafat understood the balance of power in the Palestinian resistance movement all too well; he had a finely tuned sense of the mood of his people, and he showed great skill in making the case for the deal that the Palestinians wanted.

TRUTH VERSUS SMOKE AND MIRRORS

This isn't to say that Arafat's judgment was infallible. As you would expect from any other political leader, he made his fair share of mistakes and blunders. In a political climate as turbulent as that of the Middle East, this was simply unavoidable.

Arafat came under heavy criticism for supporting Saddam Hussein when the Iraqi leader invaded Kuwait. I recall meeting him in 1991, at the height of the crisis. As a member of our country's Security

Council, I had been dispatched to Baghdad by Soviet president Mikhail Gorbachev to sound out the possibility of Saddam withdrawing his troops and avoiding a war. Because my flight had to make a stop in Amman, I decided to consult with Arafat. He rushed to the Jordanian capital with his entire team. "If there's a war against Iraq, it will spark anger right across the Arab world, and it'll be like a second Vietnam," he said, with a look that caught the eye of all those present. I reminded him of our conversation in Damascus in 1970, and pointed out that his predictions then had not been borne out by events. Arafat sat in silence for a minute, then ordered his plane to be made ready to fly to Baghdad. "I will try to prepare the ground for your mission to succeed," he told me. I should point out that from the moment the meeting began, I felt that I had the support of Abu Iyad and Mahmoud Abbas, who were skeptical, to put it mildly, about the action Saddam had taken.

Despite his public statements, I am certain that Arafat did in fact try to get Saddam to withdraw his troops from Kuwait. It may not be common knowledge but it happens to be the truth. Indeed, by the time I made my second trip to Baghdad, a couple of weeks after the first, politicians close to Saddam were complaining that the Palestinians had not supported Iraq "like they ought to."

What lies behind Arafat's significance as a historic figure? Above all, it is the very fact that he became a historic figure at all: he could not have done so if, at any point, he had openly tried to swim against the tide, ignoring the popular mood of the Palestinian people or of his comrades in Fatah, the movement that had become the heart and soul of the PLO. But there was an evolution in his views, in his approach, which had a huge impact on the evolution of the Palestinian resistance movement itself.

I would put this question to anyone who persists in labeling Arafat an extremist: did anyone ever hear Arafat call for jihad? Did anyone ever see him try to depict the Palestinian cause as a religious struggle? The fact that Fatah is still, for the most part, a military-political movement and not a religious one, can largely be attributed to the influence of Yasser Arafat, its founder and uninterrupted leader for decades. The same can also be said of the PLO.

In 1996, when I was Russia's foreign minister, I visited Gaza, which by then had become the base of the Arafat-led Palestinian Authority. I will never forget the meetings I had with him during that period. He had the air of a man who was on the brink of great things, who had signed on in every way to the new era opened up by the peace treaty with Israel. The deal forged by him and Yitzhak Rabin was not just a tactical move for Arafat—of that I have not the slightest doubt. He spoke with pride of how his period of political exile in Tunisia was behind him now, and of how there was a real prospect of creating a Palestinian state. At the same time, Arafat was never in any doubt as to the difficulties on the path that lay ahead; he told me, with some feeling, that even those arrangements already agreed upon with Israel were proving enormously difficult to put into practice, such as the airport in Gaza or the road linking the Gaza Strip with the West Bank.

I came away from our long conversation with the firm impression that he was willing to make compromises—and not just *willing* to make them, but clear in his mind that compromises had to be made. He did at times make mistakes, thinking that more favorable circumstances just might arise, so it might be worth stringing things out in order to secure a better deal. But who in his position hasn't made such errors?

There is much speculation about what strikes me as Arafat's ill-considered hostility toward the Clinton parameters, which were the first to propose dividing Jerusalem in two and handing over some 95 percent of the occupied territories to the new Palestinian state. What lay behind this hostility? Arafat tried to convince me that the Arab world would not accept a wider peace deal unless it guaranteed the right of all Palestinians to return to their homeland. But I was not won over by his argument. Many politicians believed that while Palestinian refugees should have an incontestable right to return to their native land, that right of return could be distinguished from what happened in practice: some refugees would choose to return; others would opt for compensation, enabling them to set up home permanently in Arab countries. I am sure that Arafat realized this but he was stuck with the position he had stated at the Arab League summit. Or maybe he hoped to be able to reach agreement on a whole range of issues with the Israelis themselves at the summit in Taba (in

Sinai in January 2001), which was due to take place after the unveiling of the Clinton plan. Although they negotiated as much as they could at Taba, no deal was reached on what form the accord would take. There were elections on the horizon in Israel, and Ariel Sharon was installed as its new prime minister.

Arafat could be criticized for his refusal to give ground while Ehud Barak's government was still in power in Israel. But it should not be forgotten that the Israelis were not without blame themselves—they too offered little that was constructive and showed scant willingness to compromise. Nor was it Arafat who broke off the talks. He was not the one who provoked the Israeli-Palestinian clashes triggered by Sharon's grandstanding visit to the Temple Mount, the site of the al-Aqsa Mosque, one of Islam's holiest shrines.

To be sure, the Palestinian side is guilty of carrying out attacks—some of them terrorist attacks—on innocent Israeli civilians. The Israeli government would have us believe that Arafat was behind them, but I strongly disagree. And not just because the late Palestinian leader publicly and unequivocally condemned attacks on civilians, but also because he was a pragmatist and a realist: he realized that terrorist methods would not only fail to bring victory, they also compromised the Palestinian resistance and undermined solidarity with the Palestinians from those who were working toward a just settlement of the Middle East conflict.

Some observers say Arafat intentionally neglected to prevent terrorist attacks in the belief that they would force the Israeli government to compromise. I would rule this out too. Given that hundreds of innocent Palestinian civilians were killed as a result of Israeli "reprisals," it was very, very difficult to break this vicious cycle. Arafat could not have failed to see that there was a lurch to the right and increased mobilization of hard-liners in Israeli society as a result of the suicide bombings. In the end, during his forced confinement in Ramallah, it was no longer in his hands alone, as it had been before, to set the mood of the Palestinian resistance movement.

Arafat was without doubt a remarkable leader. He personified the Palestinian people's struggle, and was an icon to those fighting for a Palestinian state.

It has been widely suggested that Arafat's death was due to poison. If this is true, and if he was poisoned by those who regarded him as an obstacle to a settlement between Israel and the Palestinians, then it was not only a heinous crime but also a terrible miscalculation. Arafat wanted to see a peace settlement and did everything he could for that settlement to lead to the creation of a feasible Palestinian state. He understood that that was the only way to bring about a complete halt to terrorist attacks. Arafat was not the problem. With his undisputed authority, no one was more capable of countering those groups that sought to wreck the Middle East peace process.

When I visited Ramallah, I bowed my head before Yasser Arafat's gravestone. His death has already changed and will further change the political situation in the Palestinian Authority, and will undoubtedly affect both the prospects and the nature of any future settlement with Israel. As I see it, the election of Mahmoud Abbas as head of the Palestinian Authority was the best possible outcome. Nevertheless, he does not have the same authority that Arafat had, and even as I write, he is going through a difficult period as leader. Hamas, a group that does not recognize Israel and that won the most seats in the Palestinian parliament in January 2006, has hardened its stance considerably. Within Fatah, there is a growing drift away from the center-ground, not only between the center and its military wing "the al-Aqsa Martyrs," but also in the balance of political power. A younger generation, rallying around Marwan Barghouti, is acquiring ever greater influence.

It is not only the Palestinians, I believe, who will come to regret that Arafat is no longer with us.

— 15 —

THE SOVIET UNION
AND ISRAEL

RELATIONS BETWEEN THE USSR and Israel have never been straightforward or easy. They have been affected at least as much by global issues—especially the Arab-Israeli conflict and the face-off between the two world superpowers—as by their own ideologies and domestic political concerns. During the second half of the twentieth century, the Soviet Union's relationship with Israel was increasingly shaped by the exigencies of the cold war. The United States supported the Israelis; the Soviet Union supported the Arabs. That said, it would still be inaccurate to describe the Soviet position as simply anti-Israeli, even at times of tension between the two countries. The United States always supported Israel, but it also sought at times to sweep aside Arab regimes fighting for independence who would not agree to American control over their affairs—as was the case with the Palestinian movement. But the Soviet Union never, under any circumstances, associated itself with extremist forces calling for Israel to be wiped off the face of the earth. Indeed, in their dealings with Palestinian and Arab leaders, Soviet officials clearly spoke out against extremist tendencies.

Despite their differing approaches to the Middle East, what the United States and the Soviet Union had in common was a healthy fear of the Arab-Israeli conflict taking on global proportions. More than once they intervened to restrain their client states. This ought to have helped advance the peace process; unfortunately, however, opportunities for a settlement were largely wasted, mainly by the Arabs at first, but later by the Israelis too.

FROM IDEOLOGY TO POLITICS

Soviet policy, especially in the 1950s and 1960s, was, to a greater extent than American policy, determined by ideology. This could be seen not only in the case of the postcolonial Arab regimes discussed earlier but also when it came to Israel. As is generally known, the Soviet Union was the first to recognize the state of Israel and it also helped Israel with arms supplies in the 1948–49 war. Stalin had been counting on the creation of a Middle Eastern state with strong ties to the Soviet Union, one that would become a "socialist island," breaking up the Arabs' feudal hold over the surrounding lands and curtailing Britain's influence in the Middle East. Stalin was aware that the Jewish community in Palestine had for decades been made up of poorer, working-class Jews who had emigrated there, largely from Europe. There had also been a considerable influx of immigrants to Palestine after the Second World War, many of them survivors of the atrocities of the Nazi concentration camps. Some had fought alongside Soviet forces or with the partisan brigades of Belorussia, Ukraine, Yugoslavia, or France. In those days, most of the Jews living in Palestine were very much well disposed toward the Soviet Union. The new Jewish settlements, primarily farming communities (moshavim and kibbutzim), had adopted socialist elements in the way property was owned and the organization of labor. And since the beginning of the 1920s, there had been a relatively strong, healthy Palestine Communist Party. All this had made an impression on Stalin. Moreover, the foundation of the state of Israel came some time before the height of the cold war confrontation between the two major superpowers.

But it was not long before the Zionist ideas at the heart of the foundation of Israel clashed irreconcilably with the Soviet Union's Marxist-Leninist ideology. It was not just a question of a clash between ideologies that were, by their very nature, nationalist and internationalist; we have already discussed how Arab nationalism was also at loggerheads with the socialist ideology of the Soviet Union. But when it came to Zionism, the clash of ideologies was a much fiercer affair. The main objective of Zionism was to bring about mass immigration into Israel of Jews from the countries to which they had been "dispersed," with particular attention focused on the Soviet Union—a socialist society, which was seen as "the most progressive and the fairest" type of society. Stalin might have permitted a small stream of emigration, as an investment in Israel's socialist beginnings, but what the Israeli leadership had set in progress was a mass exodus, which could only be seen as a damaging brain drain. Israel staged a series of political propaganda events to further this end, some of them on Soviet territory. For example, Stalin himself was aware that Golda Meir, then Israel's ambassador to Moscow, was very active among Soviet Jews; her sphere of influence included several high-ranking figures and their family members. The Soviet foreign ministry was irritated by Israel's repeated demands for permission to hold "cultural and educational events" on Soviet territory, events that would involve Soviet Jews. The situation was ripe for exploitation by a number of unscrupulous, power-hungry individuals striving for promotion and sometimes also eager to sweep aside their rivals, whom they accused of being involved in Zionist conspiracies. This gave rise to the Doctors' Plot, an alleged attempt to poison Stalin; a campaign was also launched to combat the so-called cosmopolitans, and restrictions were placed on the number of Jews hired to work for the government apparatus or admitted to higher education and training for state institutions. Matters came to a head in February 1953, when a bomb was detonated outside the Soviet embassy in Tel Aviv, wounding three embassy staff. Although the Israeli government was quick to apologize and vowed to find the perpetrators, the Kremlin announced that it was breaking off diplomatic relations. Within four months of Stalin's death, however, diplomatic relations with Israel had been restored. This came after a crackdown by the new Soviet leadership on the organizers or perpetrators of any blatantly anti-Semitic activity.

BERIA PLAYS THE REHABILITATION CARD

After Stalin's death, the process of exposing past wrongs—not just the Doctors' Plot, but a whole series of other unlawful operations—was taken over by the newly appointed interior minister Lavrenty Beria. At the time, Beria was part of the triumvirate of top Soviet leaders, along with Georgy Malenkov and Nikita Khrushchev, but he wanted to secure sole leadership for himself—a path that Khrushchev would also later follow. Beria was guilty of numerous crimes (as indeed were the others), especially during his time in Georgia; he had also striven to unseat Stalin. Though neither Beria nor his colleagues in the triumvirate had thought to initiate a deliberate process of de-Stalinization (as Khrushchev would do in later years), Beria made a point of reviewing cases that he had not personally had a hand in, but which might cast his rivals in a bad light. The following extracts from what were then top secret archived documents shed much light on the domestic factors that influenced the Soviet Union's attitude toward Israel during Stalin's last years.

No.17/B   TOP SECRET   1 April 1953
From: Lavrenty Beria
To: Georgy Malenkov,
*   Presidium of the Central Committee*
*   [of the Soviet Communist Party]*
Subject: Rehabilitation of persons implicated in the
*   so-called Doctors' Plot*

Comrade Malenkov,
In 1952, the Ministry of State Security took on the case of the so-called undercover terrorist ring of doctors whose goal, allegedly, was to cut short the lives of leading Soviet figures by administering toxic medication to them. As you will be aware, this case generated a great deal of sensation, and the special report by TASS, along with articles in Pravda, Izvestia *and other national newspapers, was published even before the investigation was concluded.*
*   In view of the prime importance of the case, the Soviet Ministry of the Interior decided to conduct a thorough examination of all*

materials under investigation. This has led to the conclusion that the entire case, from start to finish, was a provocation dreamt up by former deputy State Security minister Mikhail Ryumin. In a criminal bid to further his own career, Ryumin, then a senior interrogator with State Security, fabricated the story of an undercover terrorist ring of doctors . . . In June 1951, he used unwritten evidence from Prof Yakov Etinger, who had been arrested, but had already died in prison by that time.

Top State Security officials stopped at nothing, blatantly flouting Soviet laws and the fundamental rights of Soviet citizens in their efforts to portray these innocent people, these leading lights of Soviet medicine, as spies and assassins. Only by using unacceptable methods did the interrogators succeed in forcing the detainees to sign [confessions] that the interrogators had dreamt up and dictated to them—allegedly [confessing] that they had practiced medical sabotage against prominent Soviet state officials, and [confessing] to their non-existent links with foreign spies.

This is how the disgraceful Doctors' Plot was fabricated, provoking, as it did, a storm in our country and beyond its borders, and inflicting serious political damage on the prestige of the Soviet Union.

The instigator Ryumin and a number of other State Security staff who actively used illegal interrogation methods and falsification of evidence have been arrested.

No.20/B TOP SECRET   *2 April 1953*
From: *Lavrenty Beria*
To: *Georgy Malenkov,*
             Presidium of the Central Committee
Subject: *Criminal prosecution of those responsible for the*
             murder of Solomon Mikhoels and Vladimir Golubov

Comrade Malenkov,
During examination of materials from the investigation into the so-called "doctor-saboteurs" arrested by the former Ministry of State Security, it was established that one of the main charges leveled at a

number of leading Soviet medical practitioners of Jewish ethnicity were incriminating links with a well-known public figure—People's Artist of the Soviet Union Solomon Mikhoels. These materials portrayed Mikhoels as the leader of a anti-Soviet ring of Jewish nationalists allegedly acting on orders from the U.S. to carry out operations that could damage the Soviet Union.

Reports of terrorist and espionage activity by arrested doctors Miron Vovsi, Boris Kogan, and A. M. Grinshtein were "based" on the fact that they knew Mikhoels and on Vovsi being related to him. Acquaintance with Mikhoels, it should be noted, was also used by the staff from the former Ministry of State Security who fabricated this case as a way to concoct trumped-up charges of nationalist anti-Soviet activity against [Vyacheslav Molotov's wife] Polina Zhemchuzhina, who was arrested and sentenced to exile by a special tribunal of the Ministry of State Security.

The inquiry showed that Mikhoels had for several years been under constant surveillance by State Security agents: along with his positive and justified comments about certain shortcomings in various parts of the Soviet system, he would at times voice dissatisfaction on particular issues—especially those to do with the situation of Jews in the Soviet Union.

It should be stressed that the State Security authorities had no evidence whatsoever of any concrete anti-Soviet activity being carried out by Mikhoels—let alone espionage, terrorism or any other type of anti-Soviet sabotage.

What must also be pointed out is that the speeches Mikhoels gave as chairman of the Soviet Union's Jewish Anti-Fascist Committee, when he traveled to the United States, Canada, Mexico and Britain in 1943, were patriotic speeches.

During scrutiny of the case against Mikhoels, it has transpired that the former deputy State Security minister Ogolydov and former Belorussian State Security minister Lavrenty Tsanava were behind an illegal operation, ordered by former State Security minister Viktor Abakumov, to have Mikhoels assassinated in Minsk in February 1948. Asked about the circumstances behind this criminal *act, Abakumov testified as follows: "As far as I remember, in 1948 the head of the Soviet government, Josef Vissarionovich Stalin, handed me an urgent assignment—to quickly arrange for Mikhoels to be assassinated by State Security agents—a task that he had entrusted to special agents . . . "*

All accomplices to the murders were arrested, prosecuted and executed.

Diplomatic Relations Break Off a Second Time

During the Six-Day War, Israel ignored Soviet demands for an immediate cease-fire. After the Golan Heights were captured, the USSR severed its diplomatic relations. There are some who believe that this was an excessive reaction on the part of the Soviet Union, especially as it took many years for relations to be restored. During this time the Soviet Union, unlike the United States, had only one foot, as it were, in the Middle East; this made it harder for the Kremlin to influence possible political settlements of the Arab-Israeli conflict. But even if you accept the logic behind this argument, the breaking of diplomatic relations with Israel cannot be separated from the reality of the situation in which the decision was taken.

Israel's victory over Arab countries that had been equipped with Soviet military hardware—and supplied with Soviet military expertise from the advisers in Egypt and Syria—required a decisive response from the Soviet Union. As if that were not enough, two additional factors exacerbated matters further: on the one hand, the United States's unequivocal support for Israel; and on the other, the growing discontent in the Arab world at what was seen as Moscow's "passivity." The Soviet Union had ruled out using military force during the Six-Day War, as this could have led to war with the United States, a scenario that both the United States and the Soviet Union were anxious to avoid. Soviet diplomatic efforts to force Israel to implement a cease-fire and withdraw from the occupied territories had been blocked in the UN Security Council by the United States and its allies, and thus failed to produce the desired effect; nor did they do much to strengthen Soviet positions in the Arab countries. Though the Soviet propaganda machine was set in motion to persuade the world that the Arab countries continued to see the Soviet Union as their "savior," this was only a partial reflection of the truth. I was in Cairo when the news came out that the entire Egyptian air force had been wiped out. As I related elsewhere, I heard lots of people insisting that American planes and pilots had participated in the attacks and cried out in frustration: "So where are the Russian pilots when we need them?"

This was the context in which the decision to break off diplomatic relations with Israel was made—under the circumstances, it was the best course of action possible. Yet it strikes me that the fact that relations were not restored for such a long time was indeed detrimental to the Soviet Union's role in the Arab-Israeli peace process.

In the immediate aftermath of the break there was little motivation for the two countries to seek to reengage. The Soviet position was based entirely on the fact that Israel was a staunch supporter of the Soviet Union's "main adversary," as the United States was known during the cold war. It also mattered a great deal to Moscow that Israel was actively belligerent toward those states that were central to Soviet policy in the Middle East. Israel occupied their territory and essentially ignored UN resolutions calling for it to withdraw. What made matters worse was that because the United States had a policy of pursuing its own Arab-Israeli peace initiatives, the Soviet Union had even less scope than it might have to influence the peace process. The Rogers Plan was a typical example. The renowned American journalist Joseph Alsop, who usually got his information from the State Department, wrote in the *Washington Post* that the U.S. proposals for settling the Middle East conflict had been agreed upon in advance with the Soviet Union. But that was not the case.

Israel all but rejected the plan put forward by U.S. secretary of state William Rogers. But as the leading Israel specialist Irina Zvyagelskaya argues, President Nixon's response was to persuade Golda Meir that the United States would not impose anything on Israel. Instead, on August 19, 1970, a second Rogers Plan was unveiled, which no longer sought a comprehensive peace settlement, but merely an "interim" one. This modified plan was accepted by Egypt, Jordan, and Israel. Two months later, Israel also recognized UN Security Council resolution 242.

This encouraging step might have injected fresh impetus into the peace process, but it coincided with the growing threat of the Soviet Union getting drawn into the Suez conflict. I have already touched on this (see chapter 8) but I will restate what happened: in 1969 Israel's air force started carrying out raids deep into Egyptian territory; in January 1970, Nasser made his trip to Moscow. The Kremlin decided to supply Egypt with antiaircraft defense systems using surface-to-air missiles; Soviet technicians were sent to Egypt to help with the rapid deployment of these systems—along with fighter jets and Soviet pilots.

It was a difficult, contradictory state of affairs. Many suggested that it might be a good idea if the Soviets and the Israelis held secret talks. One of the parties to float that suggestion was the Israeli government itself, some of whose members felt encumbered by the U.S. monopoly on the peace process. One of the ways Washington justified its monopoly was by arguing that Moscow could not be an effective peace mediator so long as it was not talking to Israel. Egypt's President Sadat also made noises in favor of Israeli-Soviet talks.

FROM THE PARTY'S SPECIAL FILE ON SECRET TALKS WITH THE ISRAELIS

When Premier Nikolai Podgorny recalled the TASS "zero file" containing my reports on how changes in Egypt and across the Middle East foretokened bad news for the Soviet Union (see chapter 9), Brezhnev aide Yevgeny Samoteykin made no secret that he was angry with me. Nevertheless he invited me to write a fuller account of the situation, just for Brezhnev's perusal, which is how my report *Questions on the Middle East Crisis*, dated July 28, 1971, came into being. (The following documents and materials come from the archive of the president of the Russian Federation.) "Comrade Primakov's suggestions are quite generalized," Samoteykin wrote in his preface to my report, "but they are nevertheless worthy of attention."

Here are some extracts:

Four years have passed since the beginning of the current Middle East crisis. Several discouraging trends can be discerned:

1. The balance of military power between the Arabs and the Israelis has not seen any radical changes that might work in the Arab countries' favor. It is often said that time is not on Israel's side. From a long-term perspective, this argument is clearly well grounded: especially if we take account of the massive disparities in manpower between the two sides, as well as of developments that will make it possible for the Arab countries to catch up with Israel technologically and economically in the distant future. But if we look at the short or medium term—say fifteen to twenty years from now—we are unlikely to see a level playing field in terms of military capabilities.

2. Contrary to what has been widely believed, the divisive forces now pulling the Arab world apart are stronger than the unifying forces pushing towards Arab unity. The Arabs have not even been united by the need to join forces to fight the common threat posed by Israel.

3. Events have shown that this four-year struggle to eradicate the consequences of Israeli aggression have not, on the whole, led to a surge of revolutionary fervor across the Arab world; indeed, in a number of cases there have been moves in the opposite direction, with the threat of a resurgence of revolutions of nationalist independence.

4. Despite the significant loss of U.S. influence and authority in the Middle East immediately after the Six-Day War, this slide has subsequently been halted; in a number of cases there is reason to believe that the Americans have successfully restored their standing. There is a growing tendency in the Arab countries to see the

U.S. as the country that might play the decisive hand in settling the Middle East conflict.

On all the important issues, the Soviet Union is sufficiently involved with the Middle East that it has the right to expect its allies' governments to conduct themselves in a manner that is sincere, unambiguous and above all not detrimental to our interests.

Along with a more steadfast policy in the Arab states, it would be a good idea if we took some initiatives with regard to Israel and the U.S. The reason Washington still has room to maneuver is that it actively pursues policies in relation to both sides in the Middle East conflict.

When I wrote all this, I did not know about the diplomatic telegram that had been received from Helsinki exactly one month earlier from the Soviet chargé d'affaires, which described a confidential briefing he'd had with Finnish foreign minister Vaino Leskinen on May 28. In it, Leskinen related the details of a conversation he'd had with Golda Meir in an interval between meetings at the Socialist International conference. Meir had asked him to organize a meeting between her and Soviet officials "anytime, any place, at any level—for an exchange of views about the situation in the Middle East."

On June 3, 1971, the Politburo discussed the issue and assigned Yuri Andropov the task of studying it further. On July 23, Konstantin Chernenko, then secretary of the Central Committee, sent the note below to Brezhnev:

Dear Leonid Ilyich,
This short record of his talks with Australian PM Bob Hawke was sent by Comrade Shelepin, who made a point of telephoning me and asking that it be sent to you only.
With my regards,
Konstantin Chernenko

The content of the discussion is presented unedited, with the spelling mistakes unchanged.

TOP SECRET
Only for the two following addressees:
Comrade KIRILENKO (strictly private)
Comrade GROMYKO (strictly private—for immediate delivery)

After his trip to Geneva, Rome and Tel Aviv, R. Fawk, head of the Australian government, was anxious to be invited for talks in the Soviet Union. Given the insistent tone of Fawk's request, I held a meeting with him . . .

Quite unexpectedly, he started talking about the conflict in the Middle East. Fawk said that when he was in Israel, he had met with the prime minister, the deputy prime minister and the foreign minister who, being aware that he was heading for the Soviet Union, had asked him if it would be possible to convey the following to the Soviet government: "The Israeli government is not tied to the borders it acquired in 1967 as a result of the 6-Day War. It is prepared to make concessions and pull back from those borders, and asked him to make this view of the Israeli government known in Soviet government circles . . . The Israeli government is absolutely prepared to reconsider the question of the Holland Heights and to reach a reasonable solution that would be acceptable to both Israel and the Arab states. It is prepared to engage in constructive negotiations and to make concessions. Israel is prepared to pull its troops out of the territory of Senai with the exception of the area around Sharmel Sheikh, which is of great importance to the security of Israel's borders, as the Soviet government should realize.

The Israeli government is prepared to resolve the matter of the Suez Canal and the West Bank, and believes all the conditions are in place for successful negotiations on these issues and that a positive agreement can be reached. However, the Israeli government does not want to see the West Bank occupied by the Jordanian army. The most difficult issue for Israel is that of Jerusalem. We want, they said, to pull out of the overwhelming majority of the occupied territories. That genuinely is the position of the Israeli gov-

ernment, and it asks the Soviet government to have faith in that. The Israeli government asks the Soviet government to use its influence and authority with the governments of the Arab states. The Israeli prime minister and foreign minister also asked Fawk to convey to the Soviet government that "the Israeli government very much wishes to restore diplomatic relations with the Soviet Union."

Fawk, for his part, said: "Currently, the whole world is talking about Nixon's forthcoming trip to Peking." In Fawk's view, the Soviet Union can and must seize the initiative from Nixon and take immediate steps to reestablish contact with Israel. He believes that this would eclipse the matter of what the world thinks of Nixon's trip to Peking and would allow the Soviet Union to seize the initiative and take control of the Middle East peace process. The Soviet Union could gain from this and the U.S. would lose out . . .

Aleksandr Shelepin
22 July 1971

At the same time, we were getting signals from Anwar Sadat. On July 23 a diplomatic telegram from Cairo sent by party secretary Boris Ponomarev relayed the details of a conversation he'd had with the Egyptian president. Sadat had said that it was "not a good thing to have only the U.S., and not the Soviet Union, talking to Israel." He stressed that the way in which we might establish contact with Israel was a matter for the Soviet side.

And so the top secret "Special File" came into being, which recorded the details of the secret talks with the Israeli government that were held on and off between August 1971 and September 1977. In the early stages of these talks, I operated alone; later I was joined by Yuri Kotov, an official from the KGB.

Over time, other unofficial channels of communication were opened too, but it appears that ours was the main conduit. What is interesting is that it shows that even in the absence of diplomatic relations with Israel, the Soviet Union sought all possible means to try to bring about a compromise, a Middle East peace deal that was in the best interest of all parties.

MEETINGS WITH EBAN, MEIR, AND DAYAN

TOP SECRET
'SPECIAL FILE'
Extract from protocol no. 12 of the
Politburo meeting of 5 August 1971
    From: the secretary of the Party Central Committee
    To: Comrades Andropov and Gromyko:
    Re: Soviet Foreign Ministry proposal (on Israel)
    1) To send comrade Primakov to Israel for confidential talks
with Israeli officials.
    2) To approve draft instructions for comrade Primakov's talks
with Israeli leaders.
    3) To approve instructions for the Soviet ambassador in Cairo.

I must point out that the first time I saw all the materials cited here was three decades later when, at my request, they were declassified to assist me with the writing of this book. These matters were so closely held at the time that I didn't learn that I had been entrusted with a mission of such great responsibility until after the decision had been taken. I was still deputy director of the Institute of World Economy and International Relations in Moscow. I happened to be on holiday with my wife at Lake Balaton in Hungary when an official turned up from the Soviet embassy in Budapest and told me: "You've got to fly back to Moscow urgently."

What had happened? The first thought that came into my head was that something terrible had happened with my son, who was not with us. The embassy official, in his dedication to the task in hand, managed to reassure me just a little by saying: "Your wife can stay here on holiday—it's only you that they need."

So I went back to Moscow. As I left the plane, I was met by Vladilen Fyodorov, a colleague who had been involved with the early phase of the "Kurdish saga," of which I have also written in this book (see chapter 17) General Fyodorov was now head of Soviet intelligence's Middle East division; he quickly revealed the reason for my summons to Moscow. What followed were meetings with Yuri An-

dropov, Andrei Gromyko—who underlined the absolutely confidential nature of my trip—and a thorough process of familiarizing myself
with the remit of my mission.

It was decided that the mission would be undertaken with help
from Shalheveth Freier, chairman of the Israeli Atomic Energy Commission, whom I had met at one of the Pugwash Conferences on Science and World Affairs, where he had told me that it would be useful
to arrange contact between the two countries, "albeit at an unofficial
level." Professor Freier, who belonged to one of the Israeli groups that
wanted to see closer ties with the Soviet Union, was a likeable, liberal-
minded man with a frank way of speaking. His position gave him access to the most powerful people in Israel.

Freier was informed that I would like to meet him in Rome. He
rushed there with Hanan Baron, head of the foreign minister's office
and graciously took it upon himself to organize the logistics for my
journey. Armed with a ticket to Cologne, I passed through the transit
hall at Rome airport on August 28, 1971, and boarded an Israeli El-
Al airliner bound for Tel Aviv.

Upon my arrival, they installed me in a flat in a residential block.
I make no secret of the fact that I felt ill at ease: alone, in a strange
country, and thinking, "If anything happens to me, nobody will even
know." At the same time, I realized that it was not in the Israelis' best
interests for anything to happen. I was tired and those thoughts soon
receded; I slept soundly that night. The next day, there was a meeting
with Abba Eban, the Israeli foreign minister. He started off by giving
me a lecture about the creation of Israel and its relations with the
Arab countries. Then he launched into a heated critique of Soviet policy. I decided to interrupt him.

"We could say even more about the shortcomings of *your* policy
but I don't think this exchange of 'niceties' is the purpose of our meeting," I said.

It's worth noting that Eban was reading from a preprepared text
and even suggested that we take minutes of our meeting—which I declined, pointing out that the mission was an unofficial one. He then
tried to make out that Meir's initiative in Finland had actually been a
"proposal for *official* talks." But clearly sensing from my reaction

that Eban was going too far, prime ministerial adviser Simcha Dinitz broke in. He said he had been there when Meir had proposed making contact with us—in whatever shape or form. Dinitz did not stop at that, but also handed Eban a note. Even so, Eban insisted that I clarify whom I represented: "Gromyko, Andropov, or someone else?" he demanded. I patiently replied that, in response to a suggestion of talks made by the Israeli prime minister, the Soviet government had sent me to Israel on an unofficial and confidential mission.

After such an inauspicious beginning, you might have expected the rest of the mission to be a waste of time. But my pessimism was allayed by my subsequent talks, first with Prime Minister Golda Meir, and then with Defense Minister Moshe Dayan—at least my talks with them allowed me to get a better picture of where Israel stood.

Meir was an experienced politician, one able to conceal what she really thought behind a kindly, innocent smile. And what she really thought was far from sentimental. David Ben-Gurion, Israel's first prime minister, once said there was only one real man in his government, and that was Golda Meir. To which I would add that she was at times an overly emotional "man." Born in Kiev in 1898, she lived in the United States from an early age after her family emigrated there. From the age of twenty-three she lived in Palestine, where she was an active member of the Zionist movement.

Restrained and possessed of a military logic, Moshe Dayan was quite different from Meir. He was born in Palestine in 1915, and joined the military group Haganah while still a youth. He got arrested by the British Mandate authorities, but was set free at the height of the Second World War to take part in a British intelligence operation prior to their landing in Syria. It was there that he was wounded: splinters from his shattered binoculars got into his eye and, although he survived, he wore a black eye patch for the rest of his life. After the establishment of Israel, Dayan advanced rapidly through the military ranks to become chief of military staff and defense minister. Despite not being a member of the Likud Party, Menachem Begin invited him to become foreign minister after he won the 1977 elections. Contrary to widespread belief, neither Meir nor Dayan spoke any Russian.

Unlike Eban, Meir tried to bring a sense of goodwill to the talks at first. She had no doubt been briefed about what I had said to the Israeli interpreter (our talks with the Israeli leaders were conducted in Russian and Hebrew) after I had taken my leave of Eban: "It obviously wasn't a good idea to mention the proposal to establish contact." Nor could it have been a coincidence that my meeting with Meir took place at her home in West Jerusalem, and not at the prime minister's official residence. Once she had greeted me, she began our conversation by singing the praises of Moscow (so beautiful!), the Russian language (so rich to listen to!), and the Soviet ambassador Mickel Bodrov (what a sharp intellect he has!), his daughter and son-in-law, a Yemeni Jew (he speaks such good Russian!).

"And now," she said abruptly, "down to business. Israel is keen to improve its relations with the Soviet Union, and we will not be a part of any action directed against the USSR whatsoever. The United States knows perfectly well that it cannot dictate our policy to us." Fine words, but we also knew that Meir, acting on orders from Ben-Gurion, had at one time held talks in Washington about the possibility of Israel joining NATO. I chose not to mention this up front, but asked her what we should therefore make of Dayan's recent statement that the United States was "ignoring the military significance of Israel by refusing to admit it to NATO." Judging by the reference to my conversation with Meir that Dayan made the following day, my comment had clearly hit its mark: "Right away, I want to stress that my statement has been distorted in the Israeli press," he said. "We do not need the USA to protect us, nor do we want fight for U.S. interests and objectives. All we need is arms, which we can get without joining NATO."

Meir too stressed Israel's efforts to safeguard its security. A frown crossed her face when I said: "Security can and should be treated separately from the question of territory, which is of vital importance for the Arabs. I have spent a lot of time in the Arab world and I know they would take to the streets if any Arab government ceased to demand the liberation of territories occupied in 1967."

This prompted an outburst from Meir: "Not even the threat of another war will force Israel to be dictated to by the Arabs, by the

United States, nor by other world powers with regard to restoring things to how they were before June 1967," she said. I pointed out to her that implementation of UN Security Council resolution 242 of November 22, 1967, did not mean restoring things to how they were at all; it would bring Israel recognition from its neighbors, it would give its borders international legal status—indeed, they would be much expanded compared to those within which the state of Israel was created by the UN—and finally it would guarantee Israel's security. But my assurances had absolutely no effect on her.

"Grand-sounding guarantees are not what we need to bring us security," Meir went on, growing increasingly angry. "Where were the UN troops when secretary-general [Dag] Hammerskjold promised they would protect [our] shipping? Our tanks virtually climbed the Golan Heights and we lost a lot of men. Do you think we'll just hand them back? When Nasser started the War of Attrition around Suez, he found out that we published reports of those killed, with their portraits, in the newspapers every morning. He said a nation like ours could not win. He just didn't get it."

I might have not taken seriously these deliberate attempts to convince me of Israel's independence from the United States. After all, our intelligence told us quite a different story. But that was no way to deal with this hard-nosed denial of Israel's need for security guarantees from the UN, the United States, and other world powers. I make no secret of the fact that Moscow had presumed the proposed international security guarantees would make Israel more compliant when it came to withdrawal from the occupied territories (this had also been set out in my briefings). But it soon became clear how problematic it would be to link the two issues; as Dayan told me the day after I had met with Meir: "If the way you frame the issue is to say, 'Pull back to the June 4 line and we'll be willing to discuss any proposals you have to safeguard Israel's security,' then I would be totally against any such solution. There can be a compromise deal with the Arabs, but it must also include territorial issues."

By the end of our exchange, Meir bore little resemblance to a cool, composed politician. "If there's a war, we'll fight that war," she said. "If any aircraft get in our way, we'll shoot them down"—this at a time when there was a real danger of Soviet and Israeli pilots firing on each other in the skies above Egypt. When I asked her: "Could you clarify whose aircraft you intend to shoot down?," she unthinkingly blurted out: "In 1948 [during the first Arab-Israeli War] we shot down five British planes." Meir could tell from my reaction that she had gone too far. Hurriedly, she reiterated the importance of Israel's dialogue with the Soviet Union.

After that meeting, Hanan Baron invited me to lunch, just the two of us, at a Chinese restaurant. I told him bluntly that the decision to send a Soviet representative to Israel for talks with its leaders had been based on indications we had received about Israel's readiness to discuss concrete issues relating to the peace process. Israeli leaders had said things that suggested that there were new aspects to their thinking that might lead to progress. I had yet to see any evidence of that, I said.

In response to that, Baron offered, "Purely as an abstract exercise, a number of ideas for theoretical consideration." Could Egypt, for example, agree to hand over Sharm el-Sheikh to Israel if the Israelis made a statement recognizing it as being part of Egypt's territory? As far as I could see, that was impossible, I replied. He got a similar reply when he asked if I thought Syria would allow permanent Israeli military outposts in the Golan Heights as long as Syria maintained sovereignty over the rest.

Baron got visibly agitated when I mentioned Meir's hints about being prepared to shoot down Soviet military aircraft. "Surely she understands how we would respond to that?" I asked. "Or does she think the Americans would come to your aid and risk a nuclear war?"

"No, of course not," Baron was quick to reply. "Your visit is very important to us. We need to build trust, and that can't be built overnight." He started talking about restoring diplomatic relations between the Soviet Union and Israel, but I did not have the authority to discuss that and told him so explicitly.

My meeting with Moshe Dayan was at the Hilton Hotel in West Jerusalem. We arrived via the underground parking lot and went up in the elevator. Dayan was waiting for us in a room. "I've been ordered to come here to meet you," he said by way of greeting. He smiled when I replied: "I thought you were the one who gave the orders." Dayan was evidently aware of what had been said in my talks with Meir and Baron. He said that Israel was anxious "to avoid any kind of confrontation with Soviet military personnel in Egypt, and the Israeli air force have been given direct orders to that effect." Meanwhile, he said, Israeli aircraft had come under attack by Soviet fighters on the eve of the cease-fire in the Suez Canal zone. "If such attacks continue," he said, "we will either have to leave the canal or defend ourselves in the air. We have no choice but to take the latter option." Did he think, I asked him, that others—the Soviet Union for example—had no choice either? As well as stressing Moscow's efforts to reduce tension and bring about a peace deal in the Middle East, I pointed out to him that our country had a range of obligations that stemmed from our policy of seeking peace in the interests of both Israel and the Arab nations. I also stressed the proximity of the Middle East to our borders, which is why the Soviet Union was particularly sensitive to events in the region and so keen to see a lasting resolution to the conflict. Only a compromise solution could bring about that kind of stability, I said.

Dayan did not dispute that point. Nor did he argue with my judgment that there could not be a military solution. When I said: "Israel is in no fit state to occupy Egypt or Syria or to sustain an occupation, and indeed nobody would allow it to do so," Dayan responded by saying: "We're aware that hostilities with the Arabs will only bring us the same result that we have today—a demarcation line between our forces. But nor will the Arabs achieve anything by resuming hostilities."

Not surprisingly, the issue of a Palestinian state did not go unmentioned. Here too, Dayan was as direct as possible: "We are on Palestinian territory and so is Jordan," he said. "That suits us fine." I felt it necessary to tell him that it was for the Palestinians to resolve the question of a Palestinian state, and that it was unlikely that they would let anyone do it for them.

What I got from our exchanges was a sense that the Israeli government might, at the very most, be interested in a partial withdrawal of troops from Sinai. But this "American idea" drew a hostile response (which they might have been putting on for show) from Meir and especially so from Eban.

The talks I held led me to the conclusion that the Israelis had been banking on keeping the status quo as it had been since the Six-Day War in 1967; they would have liked the situation in the Middle East to remain unchanged long term. Our views, sometimes expressed quite vehemently, were diametrically opposed on almost every issue we discussed. Despite this, I have to say I sensed that there was an effort, particularly by Baron and Freier, to lessen the friction. I recall a dinner at a Hungarian tavern in Tel Aviv, attended by Hanan Baron, his wife, and the prime minister's personal secretary, Lou Kaddar, who clumsily kept butting into the polite conversation. This was much to the annoyance of Mrs. Baron, who clearly did not take kindly to rudeness. Outwardly, however, she had to accord Mrs. Kaddar a certain respect, aware of how important she was.

Freier invited me to a movie theater. I don't remember what film we saw, but I was surprised to see how similar the people in the packed auditorium were to Arabs, not just in their appearance, but in their behavior too—whistling when the film snapped in the projector— it was like being in a cinema in Damascus or Baghdad. I also went to the north of Israel, but declined to visit the occupied territories of the Golan Heights or the West Bank. I was introduced to my guide there as a "scholar from Finland."

I jotted down some brief impressions of my trip in my notebook:

The northern regions. Wherever you look, people are fleeing the shelling. In the kibbutzim, there's little sign of religion. There are no synagogues. The children live separately. There are sports fields and small swimming pools. From four till seven every day, plus Saturday, parents drop off their children. Everyone eats in communal canteens. If guests come, food can be taken home. All means of production are owned by the commune. Many kibbutzim have factories. All decisions are taken by the [commune's] assembly, even a child's admission to university. Members are not forbidden to leave a kibbutz, but the commune keeps their possessions. [There are] émigré settlements. All the houses are different.

Each one has a bomb shelter. Lots of soldiers on the roads, hitch-hiking, trying to get a ride. Military service is compulsory: three years for boys, two years for girls.

Before I returned to Rome, Baron told me that Meir thought our talks had been successful in terms of clarifying where we stood, if only because talks had taken place at all after a gap of four years. Baron suggested that we should hold them on a regular basis.

Back in Moscow, my detailed report on the trip got an encouraging response, and the Soviet ambassador in Cairo was instructed to inform President Sadat that a trip to Israel had been made by a representative of the Soviet Union.

THE VIENNA TALKS ON SOVIET MEDIATION

On September 24, 1971, the Politburo approved another round of talks with Israeli officials, to be held in either Vienna or the Hague. Their purpose was "to consolidate contact with the Israeli government, and to discuss in detail the two sides' positions on the Middle East conflict." Responsibility for the meetings, along with communications between the two sides, was once again entrusted to the KGB.

I was informed that I would be meeting Hanan Baron and the Israeli foreign ministry's director-general, Mordechai Gazit, in Vienna. The Israelis had already arrived when I flew into Vienna on October 7. The talks were held in various small restaurants just outside the city.

The talks were of great importance to the Soviet Union, as they were supposed to build on the plan the Kremlin had set out for a political solution to the Middle East crisis. The first thing the Soviet plan proposed, as a way of immediately taking the heat out of the conflict, was a coordinated withdrawal of Israeli troops from all territories captured in 1967, *at the same time* securing a cessation of hostilities and establishing peace between all the Arab states and Israel. It was envisaged that the troop pullout could be completed in two phases, and that the cessation of hostilities and the peace declaration would come *after* the first phase. There were also a whole range of proposed measures to safeguard the security of the borders of all the countries in the region. It was of particular importance that the fundamentals of the Soviet plan be accepted by the Arab nations: four years earlier they had torpedoed a Latin American draft resolution at an emergency session of the UN General Assembly because they would not, under any circumstances, agree to a cessation of hostilities or declaration of peace with Israel being put in writing. Persistent efforts on the part of the Soviet Union had helped produce a shift in the Arabs' attitude.

Our determination to achieve tangible progress at the Vienna talks was clear to see. In the Politburo-approved briefing for my talks with the Israeli officials, it was emphasized that the Soviet stance was not propaganda-led but had been formulated in the best interests of all sides in the conflict. There was one particular recommendation that "if the Soviet proposals come under detailed scrutiny, [we] should highlight the measures that they include for safeguarding the security of Israel's borders and access to all shipping routes in the region." The Soviet Union truly wanted to play a constructive part as a mediator in the peace process. My assignment was not only to set out our plan, but also to ensure that "the Israeli representative reflected in detail on where his country stood on a range of matters concerning the [occupied] territories, future borders and the posting of UN troops or observers." I had also been instructed to stress our willingness to examine seriously any concrete Israeli proposals, especially if they were constructive ones.

There was an "interim settlement" that we had not ruled out: the opening of the Suez Canal. In fact, my instructions on that subject were that we should examine point by point Sadat's proposals for opening the canal in order to ascertain whether Israel was willing to accept any of the conditions in the Egyptian president's plan. I was also advised to tell the Israelis frankly that they should be more flexible; otherwise Egypt would try even harder to acquire more modern armaments, especially warplanes, where its offensive capacity was less advanced than Israel's. It would be difficult for the Soviet Union to turn down any such requests from Cairo.

However, the Israeli negotiators clearly had no wish to discuss concrete issues, and a chance to make real progress toward a peace settlement was wasted. As Gazit said, the Soviet proposals were based on going through the UN, which did not suit Israel—not even guarantees from the leading world powers were acceptable. Again, we returned to the same old theme, that the only way to safeguard the security of Israel was to hold onto the territories captured in 1967. Whether it had been agreed upon with the United States or not, it seemed that Israel's policy was to completely disregard the situation in hand and to impose its position on the Arab countries, a policy that had been born out of the euphoria of victory in the 1967 war.

Looking to the future, I would say the Soviet plan could have been built on to include what was later set out in the "road map," the plan that at the beginning of the twenty-first century has won international acceptance as the blueprint for peace in the Middle East. The Israeli government had a chance to make decisive steps toward peace with the Arabs back in 1971. I want to stress: the Soviet Union was willing and able to facilitate this peace, not just with Sadat but with the Arabs as a whole.

Both Gazit and Baron also tried to raise topics that had nothing to do with a comprehensive peace settlement, as they themselves pointed out. One example was the possibility of staging the second phase of the Israeli troop withdrawal over longer periods, say of fifteen, ten, or five years, once agreement had been reached on an interim settlement (the "Suez option"). But even this would apply only to Sinai. Another example, yet again, was the scenario mentioned earlier: that of handing Sharm el-Sheikh and Gaza over to Israel "while maintaining the Arab countries' sovereign rights." Or incorporating Israeli contingents into UN troops, should they be deployed. I pointed out to my fellow negotiators that these questions could be considered, but only within the framework of a comprehensive peace settlement, and that even then they should be made a part of the "land for peace" formula. Gazit opposed any such formulation outright; Baron rejected it too, albeit more gently.

The Israelis raised the issue of the nine Israeli prisoners of war being held in Egypt. They had asked for the release of four seriously wounded ones or, at the very least, the Israeli pilot Eyal Ahikar, who had been left paralyzed as the result of bullet wounds. In so doing, they said they were prepared to consider any Egyptian request regarding the more than sixty Egyptian prisoners of war being held in Israel. This Israeli request was set out in detail in Sadat's briefing on the Vienna talks.

A further issue that came to light at the Vienna talks was the Israelis' efforts to derail the Jarring Mission, led by Gunnar Jarring, special envoy of the UN secretary-general, in favor of the "good offices" of the United States.

As in Tel Aviv, questions were raised about the emigration of Jews from the Soviet Union to Israel. At that time there were no longer any direct obstacles to emigration, but a whole range of measures were still in place to discourage it: for example, those who expressed their wish to emigrate could be fired from their jobs or asked to reimburse the Soviet Union for their education. In Israel itself, there was an escalating anti-Soviet campaign, fueled by the fanaticism of the thugs led by the [arch-Zionist] Rabbi Meir Kahane. I told Gazit: "If you were to openly condemn Kahane's provocative tactics, that would be viewed as a welcome move in Moscow."

During our final meeting on October 15, Baron was at pains to stress that his superiors considered these Vienna meetings to be a matter of key importance. Meir, he said, had called him and Gazit in to see her about them twice. The fact that Sadat had traveled to Moscow at the same time that we were meeting, he added, had been duly noted by the Israelis.

THE DIFFICULTIES OF SUSTAINING CONTACT

After my return to Moscow, Yuri Andropov and Andrei Gromyko issued the following memo to the Central Committee of the Soviet Communist Party:

For your consideration:
On November 13 this year, a letter addressed to Yevgeny Primakov was received via our confidential channel of communication with

the Israelis. In the letter, they give the following assessment of the exchange of views that took place in Vienna:

"On our return we presented a full report to the Israeli leaders you met on your visit here [to Israel]. We consider our talks to have been useful. Although there are still differences of opinion, it was nevertheless important to get to know each other's way of thinking. We are confident that it could be of great benefit to have a continuing exchange of views."

The letter was signed by the head of the foreign minister's office Hanan Baron.

In view of the above, it would be a good idea to use the confidential channel to send the Israeli side the following reply, signed by Primakov:

"I have received your letter of November 4. On my return from Vienna, I too presented a report on the talks held there, and our assessment is the same."

Andropov, Gromyko   3 December 1971

The note was marked "for approval," under which were three signatures, those of Mikhail Suslov, Aleksei Kosygin, and Nikolai Podgorny, and a note added by Konstantin Chernenko, saying that Brezhnev had been informed.

At the end of March the Israelis suggested that we begin a fresh round of dialogue. But while their letter said that our talks were of value, it added that they had nothing new to put on the table. Since this offer carried the disclaimer (so as not to raise hopes!) that nothing in the Israeli position had changed, we declined to reply to it.

In September 1972, I attended the 22nd Pugwash Conference in Oxford. Freier was there too—in fact, he told me that the aim of his trip was to meet me and "discuss matters of interest to both sides." He said he had been briefed ahead of the talks by Gazit "and by others in the Israeli leadership."

Freier had always been frank with me and he didn't beat about the bush this time either, telling me that in Israel's view, relations with Moscow would be improved if the Soviet Union recalled its military advisers from Egypt. He also alluded to the remit he had been given, saying that the Israelis were planning to raise the question of restoring diplomatic relations with us. But given the "new set of circumstances," he added, this should be kept separate from the question of Israel's relations with the Arab countries—separate, in other words, from a Middle East peace settlement.

I put it to Freier that Israel was using its talks with us to put pressure on the Americans (who were trying to woo Egypt) as well as to complicate Soviet-Arab relations. I pointed out to him that Moscow still had strong ties to a number of Arab countries—not just Egypt—and in the Palestinian movement, which was why Soviet policy would always play a major role in the continuing developments in the Middle East. Freier did not deny what I had said about Israel's objectives, admitting that "some people in Israel" saw them as related to the meetings we had been holding. But, he said, Meir was not one of them. Freier also said he would report back to Jerusalem on what we had talked about, in detail, via the Israeli embassy in London. Yuri Andropov informed the Party central committee of my meeting with Freier. His note carries the signatures of the three top Soviet leaders who were briefed on it, Suslov, Podgorny, and Kosygin.

Another confidential meeting with the Israelis was held, on an unofficial basis, between March 22 and 26, 1973; once again it took place in Vienna. The Israeli side was again represented by Mordechai Gazit, who had recently become the prime minister's chief of staff, and Hanan Baron, who was no longer director of the Israeli foreign minister's office, having been appointed ambassador to the Netherlands. There were two representatives on the Soviet side too: I was joined in Vienna by Yuri Kotov, one of our top overseas intelligence analysts and a man with an excellent grasp of Middle East affairs. Our meetings took place just outside the Austrian capital in a private two-story villa provided by the Israelis.

From what I was able to gather from the Israelis, their government had already come close to cementing a partial settlement with Egypt that included the reopening of the Suez Canal. Israel was even ready to declare that it would go beyond "interim positions" in its pullout of troops from Sinai. Yet at the same time, it categorically ruled out any kind of timetable for withdrawing its troops from the Arab territories it had occupied since 1967, even from Sinai. The Israelis thought the United States should help put them in direct touch with Sadat, and were counting on holding face-to-face talks with him.

Gazit was obviously trying to show us that the Israelis did not need the Soviet Union's help to pave the way for a partial settlement with Egypt. In fact we knew from our intelligence that the Israelis had promised the United States that they would squeeze the USSR out of playing any broker's role for this "interim" peace deal. But at the final stage, and for a variety of reasons, they evidently did need our approval for their agreement with Egypt to open up the Suez Canal.

When it came to resolving the Palestinian question, the Israeli negotiators felt that an autonomous Palestinian state could exist only within Jordan's borders. They virtually refused to discuss our arguments that the all-too-familiar UN resolutions had granted the Palestinians right of return to their homeland and mandated compensation for those not availing themselves of this right. We told the Israelis that their reluctance to even discuss Palestinian self-determination was all too apparent, stressing the reality that Israel eventually would have to recognize the Palestinians' right to their own state.

I noticed that Gazit, and indeed Baron, did not wish to aggravate matters further and adopted a more conciliatory tone. I also got the impression that, because the Israelis were well aware of their military superiority, they did not expect the Arabs to initiate any hostilities; they assumed they could continue to exploit the disagreements between the Arabs indefinitely, sustaining the existing opposition to a comprehensive peace settlement for as long as they wished. Yet it was only months after our talks that the Yom Kippur War broke out, in October 1973.

A considerable amount of time had passed since our previous talks, as Baron pointed out. When we saw him alone, he told us that the Israeli government had initially thought that fairly regular secret talks might, for the time being, partially compensate for the lack of diplomatic relations between our two countries. Kotov and I pointed out that the reason we had taken so long to respond to the Israelis' offer of a fresh round of talks was their insistence that they had "nothing new to put on the table."

But in fact that was only *one* of the reasons. The other (which we did not, of course, mention) was that contacts with Israel had been impeded by the very terms that we ourselves had set out: that diplomatic relations between Moscow and Israel could be restored only when the causes of their severance were eliminated. That is to say, we wanted Israel to withdraw from the Arab territories it had occupied since 1967 and grant legal rights to the Palestinians, including the creation of their own state. Up to that point, no one in the Soviet leadership had called for these conditions to be changed, so as to avoid being accused of "appeasement" or of "collaboration with the aggressor."

In reality, however, Andropov and Soviet overseas intelligence were in favor of restoring diplomatic relations, while Gromyko was undecided and Brezhnev "had no objections." But there were many who did object. The Andropov-Gromyko memo on our 1973 talks in Vienna, for example, contained a proposal to "inform the Israelis that we might study their request to extend the premises of the consular section of the Dutch embassy[1] in Moscow if Israel raises the issue with the Soviet foreign ministry." But the subsequent Politburo decision of April 18, 1973, stated that its proposals had been "approved but without informing the Israelis that we would study the issue of extending the consular premises. . . ."

Nevertheless, the Politburo decision on the March talks included a proposal to organize another round of talks with the Israelis in Vienna on June 10–15. It suited the Kremlin to keep these talks secret and unofficial, yet because these meetings were turning into a regular occasion, they might have developed into something on an official level anyway. I think that a majority of the Politburo were pushing for just that, although it was obviously not stated openly.

The Israelis, however, began to procrastinate for some reason. We didn't receive letters they claimed to have sent us; then they expressed a willingness to meet with us during Gazit's trip to Europe—thereby rubbing our noses in the fact that the meeting would be nothing but a by-product of his trip. And all the while, the Israeli side still stressed that it had nothing new to put on the table, none of which helped to restore contacts between us.

Meanwhile, the Geneva Middle East peace conference had opened, chaired by Henry Kissinger and Andrei Gromyko. Just before one of the sessions began, Kissinger asked Gromyko if he would be amenable to the two of them holding private meetings with the conference's participants—particularly, with Abba Eban. Gromyko agreed to meet with the Israeli foreign minister. Eban began the meeting by saying that Gromyko's conference speech had been very well received in Israel because it distinctly stated that the Soviet Union continued to recognize Israel's right to exist as an independent sovereign state. Then Eban listened attentively as Gromyko spelled out, in some detail, the ways that Israel's policy of territorial annexation and hostility toward the Arab states was incompatible with its talk of wanting to guarantee its security.

Eban replied that he had in fact been speaking "of the very minimum requirements for security, not of the optimum conditions." But because Israeli elections were imminent, he could not set out what he had in mind specifically, although he had no doubt that Golda Meir would win at the polls.

Our discussion was, to all intents and purposes, pointless. Eban steered it down a well-trodden path: Israel's refusal to end its occupation of the Arab territories seized in 1967. He held out the illusory hope that in time there might just possibly be some shift in its position, but he refused outright to discuss anything concrete. Left alone with Eban, Gromyko raised the issue of the review that Israel was carrying out into restoring its diplomatic relations with the Soviet Union. This, he said, was out of the question at the present time. "When the conference makes progress and reaches agreement on a definitive peace settlement, that's when the time will be ripe to discuss that," Gromyko said, restating the Soviet position.

In the wake of that conversation, there seemed to be no call for secret talks with the Israelis for the foreseeable future.

A NEW ISRAELI GOVERNMENT, A NEW PUSH FOR TALKS

The idea of secret, unofficial talks resurfaced after Golda Meir stepped down in June 1974. Yitzhak Rabin became Israel's new prime minister and Yigal Allon replaced Abba Eban as foreign minister.

A series of fresh developments had dramatically changed the situation in the Middle East. Meir had stepped down as head of government after the publication of the Agranat Commission's report into the causes behind Israel's heavy losses in the early part of the 1973 Yom Kippur War. The war had dealt a profound psychological blow to Israeli society, despite Israel's gains in its closing stages. For the very first time, Israelis had begun to seriously doubt that their country's military superiority over the Arabs would hold out, given the latest Soviet weaponry they were receiving, or that Israel's security was impregnable, based as it was solely on military might.

At the same time a process was underway (as discussed earlier) within the Palestine Liberation Organization, which was beginning to take a softer line toward Israel. A formula had been agreed upon whereby it would stop short of recognizing Israel, although its talk of the creation of a Palestinian state "on territories that had been freed from the occupation" represented progress in that direction. The PLO's international isolation had been broken. For the first time, the Palestinian question was on the agenda of the UN General Assembly not as a purely humanitarian problem (that of refugees) but as an issue of national self-determination. In line with Yasser Arafat's speech, the UN General Assembly adopted a resolution declaring that the Palestinian people had the right to self-rule, national independence, and sovereignty. Such was the backdrop to Israel's accords on the "Jordanian option."

In Moscow, it was felt that an effort should be made to exert influence on Israel over the creation of a Palestinian state, while stressing that Israel's partial solutions with Egypt should be incorporated into the overall context of the Geneva conference. We did not wish to obstruct those agreements; rather we believed that they needed to be tied to an overall peace settlement in the interest of all those directly involved in the Middle East conflict—an issue that had become increasingly urgent, given Sadat's and Kissinger's increasing advocacy of a separate Egypt-Israeli accord.

Caught up in its flirtation with Sadat, the United States' relations with Israel cooled slightly. On becoming president in August 1974, Gerald Ford's emphasis—even more than Nixon's—was on reinforcing America's foothold in Egypt. As a result, there was a moratorium on the signing of any new American arms contracts with Israel from March through June 1975.

Israel acted rashly in a bid to change a situation that was not working out in its favor; hence its refusal to help get the Geneva conference off the ground. The idea that the conference might sit as a permanent body was buried, despite Eban having agreed to just that when he met Gromyko in December 1973. The path it chose instead was to sign the accord with Egypt formulated by Kissinger. At the same time Rabin gave the green light to the building of new Jewish settlements on the West Bank and in the Golan Heights, turning a blind eye to the activities of Gush Emunim, a Zionist group that was building settlements in the occupied territories without government authorization. The "Jordanian option" was something the Israelis tried to produce out of thin air.

Along with the questionable outcome of the 1973 war, these conflicting moves helped fuel a rising polarization in Israeli society. There was no unity in either the ruling Ma'arach coalition nor in the Avoda Party itself, with its escalating battle for the leadership between prime minister Rabin and defense minister Shimon Peres. With all these events and conflicts affecting the situation in the Middle East, the Soviet Politburo decided on March 9, 1975, to organize another round of secret talks with leading Israeli politicians.

BACK TO ISRAEL:
TALKS WITH RABIN, ALLON, AND PERES

From April 4 through April 6, 1975, Yuri Kotov and I held talks with prime minister Yitzhak Rabin, foreign minister Yigal Allon, and defense minister Shimon Peres. All of our meetings took place in their homes: we met with Rabin in a new district of Tel Aviv, with Allon in the Jewish quarter of Jerusalem's Old City, and with Peres at his apartment in the prestigious Tel Aviv area of Ramat Aviv. At the very beginning of the trip, we met with our regular counterpart Mordechai Gazit, at the Hotel Dan.

The two issues we raised with Gazit were probably quite technical in nature. First, Gazit told us that the Israelis were also being "approached" by other people claiming to represent the Soviet leadership, and asked if we had any connection with those efforts. He was evidently referring to Victor Louis, the Moscow correspondent of the London *Evening News*, who was regarded in the West as a KGB agent. Louis had been to Israel and written an article about the possibility of a restoration of diplomatic relations with the Soviet Union. Around this time, Anatoly Dobrynin, the Soviet ambassador in Washington, had been approached by Israeli ambassador Simcha Dinitz, who proposed himself as a conduit to the Israeli government. The Kremlin presumed that the Israelis were testing the reliability and authenticity of our own communication channel: they might have suspected it of being connected to the intelligence services. Dobrynin's instructions from the Soviet Politburo said that "by agreeing to establish contact with the Israeli leadership via Dinitz, we are working on the assumption that it will help bring a just and lasting peace to the Middle East, one that would safeguard the interests of all states, including Israel." As it turned out, the Dobrynin-Dinitz channel was not to be; for now the Kremlin was focusing on resurrecting talks via our own channel. We informed Gazit of this, stressing once more that we had direct access to the Soviet leadership, to whom we reported on the talks, and from whom we received our instructions. We clearly must have passed this "test of our authority," otherwise the meetings we had gone to Israel for would not have even taken place.

The second question was one we raised. A report of the secret contacts between Israel and the Soviet Union had appeared in the Western media. We asked Gazit what he knew about it, expecting him to assure us that his country had strictly abided by our agreement that the talks would be kept confidential, but curious to see how he would react. The source of the leak, Gazit said, "was not Israel, but your adversary," meaning the United States. It was indeed the case that the right-wing American press regarded the presence of Soviet representatives in Israel as an example of "Soviet machinations" in an "area of vital interests to the U.S." Those who opposed détente between the United States and the USSR were well served by this kind of reporting. The Israelis had no doubt informed the U.S. administration of our meetings, and the leak could have come from anyone with access to the information, for example from the CIA. But suspicion could equally fall on the Israeli side too. Dobrynin's reports to Moscow supported that conclusion: most experts, he said, believed that the leaks had been orchestrated by the Israeli government, which had been feeling pressure from Washington, and wanted to show the United States that it was not the only game in town, that Israel had other alternatives in its search for solutions in the Middle East than the ones that Washington was proposing.

Yet our Israeli counterparts didn't say a word about any such alternatives—and that was despite the fact that we had not come empty-handed: the first thing we had been instructed to announce—which we underlined in our talks with all three of the Israeli leaders—was that our meetings were aimed at helping to normalize relations between our two countries. We called for the Geneva conference to be reconvened, saying it could well be the most suitable venue in which to scrutinize every problem, large and small, that related to the peace process—but our call fell on deaf ears. We stressed that no ideas that any party might bring to the conference were taboo, that Moscow was prepared to examine any of them. Nor did the Israelis respond to our proposal for helping the PLO tackle the extremist tendencies of other Palestinian groups in return for its participation in the conference, as soon as it was up and running again. If Israel evinced a more positive attitude toward the creation of a Palestinian state in the West Bank and the Gaza Strip, we told them, then the Soviet Union was ready to play a positive role and use the influence that it had with the PLO.

I think that if the Israeli leaders had been more realistic about the security issues facing their country, these issues would have been the subject of a more in-depth discussion. Especially since we had been authorized to offer the chance of a behind-closed-doors deal under which the Soviet Union would do all it could to prevent anyone from breaching whatever agreement we hammered out. We stressed that the Soviet Union would strive for normalization in the region, that it would do all it could to restrain the Arabs from making any rash moves. But it was important that Israel too should refrain from undertaking any actions that could further aggravate the already incendiary situation.

We also emphasized something we knew all too well: that the conflict could not be settled without the involvement of the United States. We assured the Israelis that we would not seek (nor indeed could we, even if we had wanted to) to break off Israel's relations with the Americans.

What kind of response did we get? Once again, the Israelis said that they could not pull back from the June 4, 1967, line; if they did, they chorused, it would be disastrous for Israel's security. Each one said his piece to back up their argument; each had something critical to say about the policy of the Soviet Union. Worst of all, the Israeli negotiators single-mindedly avoided talking about any concrete issues, even though those were precisely the kind of discussions that would have benefited Israel's own security as well as the overall peace process.

What follows is from my notebook:

Met Rabin on 5 April 1975. He justified Israel's bias toward the U.S. in matters relating to the Middle East peace process by saying Soviet policy was "one-sided." "You represent the Arabs," he told me. "And on that basis, we could hold talks with them without using intermediaries." He must have caught the look of irony on our faces, because he then added: "Believe me, we can do that." By which Rabin clearly meant President Sadat and King Hussein of Jordan, as indicated by what he said next: "We hope that Sadat will not opt for war. He might opt for small-scale hostilities, just as a catalyst for a political solution."

Rabin was upfront about the Palestinian question, saying: "No king reigns forever. There *can* be a Palestinian homeland—on Jordanian territory and in part of the West Bank." Being an army general, he had no qualms about his choice of words: "Peace is what we're aiming for but we also make progress toward peace through war." He was clearly keen to put a lid on any further reports of friction between Israel and the U.S. "Once the energy crisis has subsided," he insisted, "the United States will return to a policy of unconditional support for Israel."

Many years later, in 2004, Bill Clinton's autobiography, *My Life,* was published. At one point, the former U.S. president relates the conversation he had with Rabin over a private lunch after the Israeli-Palestinian peace accord of September 13, 1993, had been signed. I quote directly from Clinton's book:

He explained to me that he had come to realize that the territory Israel had occupied since the 1967 war was no longer necessary to its security and, in fact, was a source of insecurity. He said that the *intifada* that had broken out some years before had shown that occupying territory full of angry people did not make Israel more secure, but made it more vulnerable to attacks from within. Then, in the Gulf War, when Iraq fired Scud missiles into Israel, he realized that the land did not provide a security buffer against attacks with modern weapons from the outside. Finally, he said, if Israel were to hold on to the West Bank permanently, it would have to decide whether to let the Arabs there vote in Israeli elections, as those who lived within the pre-1967 borders did. If the Palestinians got the right to vote, given their higher birth-rate, within a few decades Israel would no longer be a Jewish state. If they were denied the right to vote Israel would no longer be a democracy but an apartheid state.[2]

When I read this, I could scarcely believe my eyes: after all, Kotov and I had been saying all this to Rabin back in 1975, at which time he had harshly rebuffed our arguments. Had it really taken him all of those eighteen bloodstained years to become a realist? Or was it perhaps the case that Rabin and other Israeli leaders automatically rejected anything that came from the Soviet Union? What a waste.

On April 6 we met with Yigal Allon, who impressed us very favorably. "I believe that the Soviet Union is genuinely trying to build peace," he said. "And I believe that until there are talks with Soviet involvement, there will be no progress toward a peace settlement. We do not see it as a choice between either the U.S. or the Soviet Union: we need both them *and* you. But of course in the absence of diplomatic relations with Moscow, the U.S. has the advantage." He smiled and added: "Maybe we were wrong to agree to the Soviet Union cochairing the Geneva Conference when it had relations with only one of the sides in the conflict."

When it came to the Palestinian problem, he basically said the same thing as Rabin, but he phrased it differently: "The Arabs in the West and East Banks are one people; we need to consolidate their relations with each other. We need to find a solution to all the issues, but it is too soon to set out a course of action to solve the Palestinian problem. The Geneva Conference can go ahead without the PLO, even though Israel recognizes resolution 242 and the existence of the Palestinian problem."

Allon's words gave us to believe that he was not counting on any change of regime in Jordan—an issue on which he was apparently at odds with Rabin. "King Hussein," he said, "has not abandoned the West Bank—that's just a tactical move."

Allon also touched on a very specific case, relating to the emigration of Jews from the Soviet Union: "Why don't you make a gesture and release the ones who have been convicted in Leningrad?" he asked, referring to the group that had been arrested after trying to hijack a plane. These were convicted criminals, we replied, adding that we had to distinguish between two issues: allowing emigration and encouraging it. We had no intention of doing the latter.

Our meeting with Peres was unremarkable. First he offered us either vodka or whisky to drink. He poured himself a vodka too and knocked back a glass—actually more than one. Then he started holding forth on "a Marxist analysis of the situation." Peres's brand of "Marxism," however, did nothing to bridge the gap in our views.

At almost every meeting—and the one with Peres was no exception—the Israelis came out with the accusation that the Soviet Union was supplying arms to the Arabs, who had not renounced their objective of "casting Israel into the sea." Moscow, they said, was also providing the Arabs with intelligence on the plans and military strength of Israel's armed forces. At our meeting with Peres, which went on past midnight, the defense minister was particularly antagonistic in the way he raised this issue. This may have been because he was trying to uncork a second bottle of vodka, having not allowed his ministerial aide to do it for him. Either way, Peres was strenuous in his insistence that "Soviet intelligence is working against Israel round-the-clock, and has surrounded it with a network of radar stations that are passing information onto the Arabs." A Soviet warship was on permanent patrol along Israel's maritime border, he went on, conducting electronic surveillance; moreover, he said he knew for a fact that the ship had a crew of specialists fluent in Hebrew who were listening in on Israeli military radio transmissions.

When we cast doubt on these assertions, he interrupted us to say that he could give the order, there and then, for an Israeli military helicopter to fly us to the location of the Soviet ship in the Mediterranean Sea; that it could even land on its deck. We calmly assured him that we had no intention of flying anywhere and advised him *not* to send a helicopter out to intercept a Soviet warship. Peres must have realized that our conversation was about to turn nasty, so he made a joke out of his proposal and changed the subject.

We too tried to take some of the heat out of our exchange, telling Peres that the Soviet Union had always supported Israel's inalienable right to exist as a sovereign independent state. We had never backed calls for Israel to be wiped off the face of the Earth, nor would we allow that to happen, just as we would not allow any solution to be imposed on the Middle East using military force. Yes, we supplied the Arab states with defense equipment, antiaircraft systems, fighter jets and artillery, but we did so in an effort to counterbalance all the arms supplies that Israel received from the United States. There clearly had to be a balance in order to bring compromise to the peace process.

Despite their demonstrated efforts to maintain contact, there must have also been those in the Israeli regime who wanted to cut it off. On April 8, the day after we returned to Vienna from Tel Aviv, the morning edition of the Vienna newspaper *Der Kurier* featured a story about two Soviet representatives visiting Israel for secret talks with the country's leadership. Alongside the article was a cartoon of a man in the uniform of a Soviet colonel holding out an olive branch in one hand, but concealing a missile behind his back in the other. Kotov immediately phoned Gazit for an explanation. Gazit already knew about the article and, in an apologetic tone of voice, said that the Israelis deeply regretted what had happened. He said the government in Tel Aviv suspected that the source of the leak was someone opposed to closer ties between Israel and the Soviet Union, who wanted to scupper our talks. "It's quite possible that this was the doing of an Israeli civil servant who has access to information about your trip to Israel," Gazit said and, on behalf of the Israeli government, he expressed the wish "that this incident will not put an end to the helpful dialogue that has been established between our countries."

Kotov said the Israelis seemed unable to keep our talks confidential, and that it would be up to the Kremlin whether they could continue. The Soviet government did in fact decide to continue its contact with the Israeli leadership.

On our return to Moscow, we gave Yuri Andropov a detailed account of our impressions. Even as we met with him, Andropov called Gromyko and told him it would be of interest to him to hear what we had to say. And so from Andropov, we set off straight away to see Gromyko; he too, like Andropov, wanted to know every detail of our talks with the Israeli leaders.

When we had finished speaking to Andropov, I showed him the *Kurier* cartoon. "Yuri Vladimirovich," I said, "this is a complete falsehood." He agreed that the cartoon did not reflect the nature of our mission at all. "That's not the only thing that's inaccurate about it," I went on. "This cartoon shows a colonel, and Kotov is still only a lieutenant-colonel." We all cracked up laughing—and yet on the other side of the door to Andropov's office, foreign intelligence service deputies Boris Ivanov and Alexey Voskoboy, who had been present at our meeting, were at that very moment discussing whether to give Kotov an early promotion in recognition of his good work. And that was how Yuri Vasilyevich Kotov earned his stripes as a colonel.

BACK TO ISRAEL: A MEETING WITH BEGIN

Both Rabin's government and the one led by Peres after Rabin left office were acutely weakened by (among other things) their reluctance to deal with reality. Ma'arach had lost credibility in the eyes of the voters, and in May 1977 Likud won the elections for the first time in Israel's history. The new government was headed by Menachem Begin; Moshe Dayan, who was a member of a different political party, became his foreign minister.

The Kremlin decided to reengage with the Israelis, thinking it might perhaps have more success discussing the details of the Middle East peace process with their new leaders. Kotov and I flew to Tel Aviv via Vienna and Zurich. The man who met us in Vienna and organized the rest of our trip introduced himself to us as Efraim Palti. Ten years later, as Efraim Halevy (his real name), he would become the director of Mossad. In Tel Aviv, we were met by Eliahu Ben Elissar, head of the prime minister's office. Ben Elissar had led the Likud party's electoral campaign and looked set for political advancement—indeed, he later became chairman of the Knesset foreign affairs and defense committee and, after the Likud party lost power, he led its faction in the Knesset. Before that, he had been Israel's first ambassador to Egypt, and was later ambassador to the United States and to France. The fact that Ben Elissar was our new immediate point of contact was clearly meant to show that Begin's government took its talks with us very seriously.

We met with Begin in the late evening of September 17 at the prime minister's official residence in Jerusalem. This too was clearly intended to show how seriously the new Israeli government took its talks with representatives of the Soviet Union.

Menachem Begin was a complex figure. Born in the Polish city of Brest Litovsk in 1913, he graduated with a degree in law from Warsaw University. Even as a teenager, he was active in the Zionist paramilitary youth group Betar. When the Nazis invaded Poland, he fled to Lithuania, but after Lithuania became part of the Soviet Union in 1940, Begin—who was by then well known as an active member of the Zionist movement—was arrested and incarcerated in a prison camp in Komi, northern Russia. However, when Nazi Germany attacked the Soviet Union, Begin and other Polish citizens were released and drafted into the Polish army led by General Wladyslaw Anders. It was while serving in its ranks that Begin ended up in Transjordan, which at that time was a part of the territory covered by the British Mandate. In May 1942, by which time he had left the Polish army, Begin joined the Zionist militant group Irgun Tzvai Leumi (Etzel) in Palestine. Like its splinter group offshoot Lehi, Etzel was a typical terrorist outfit that employed diversionary tactics. Etzel's emblem was of a hand holding a rifle against the backdrop of a map of Palestine and Transjordan (!), with the motto "Only Thus." In 1944, Menachem Begin became Etzel's leader; two years later, its militants bombed the King David Hotel in Jerusalem. The group also carried out kidnappings: in 1947 Etzel militants seized and executed two British sergeants. In response, the British put what was in those days a high price on Begin's head: $30,000, dead or alive.

After the creation of the state of Israel, the terrorist Begin turned to politics. He headed the right-wing party Herut, which evolved into the main opposition to the ruling left-wing party Mapai. Herut members accused Ben-Gurion of collaborating with the British and later with the Americans. In 1973, Begin became leader of the right-wing Likud, a coalition bloc that had Herut at its core.

Our meeting with Begin took place three months before Sadat's historic visit to Jerusalem, which was followed by the Camp David Accords on September 17, 1978, and the Israel-Egypt Peace Treaty on March 26, 1979. For their efforts, Begin and Sadat were jointly awarded the 1978 Nobel Peace Prize. As I mentioned earlier, the United States had been instrumental in brokering that peace deal, but Begin was not the kind of politician who carried out Washington's bidding. Indeed, Israel's new government had difficulties building relations with the United States; in turn, the U.S. administration was lukewarm to Begin and never trusted him.

Begin was capable of quite unpredictable changes of tack. What distinguished him from many other Israeli leaders was that he was not afraid of making decisions. Paradoxical as it sounds, he had no fear of being attacked from the right, as there was probably nobody further to the right than him in all of Israeli politics.

Begin was the only Israeli leader we met who spoke fluent Russian. When he met us, he broke the ice with some nostalgic reminiscences about the Soviet Union. I should point out that these reminiscences bore not a trace of bitterness over his personal ordeal. On the contrary, he said that "the Russians are the greatest, most noble, most kind-hearted of people, as I'm always telling my young assistants"— and there was nothing put on about the way he said it. He said he had felt that way even when he had been "in confinement" in Komi. Begin, incidentally, wrote a book about his experience called *White Nights: The Story of a Prisoner in Russia*, and even in that book he voices no grudge toward the Soviet Union.

Our differences of opinion on the Middle East peace process became clear to see as the talks ensued: Begin opposed reconvening the Geneva Conference and touched on the issue of emigration of Soviet Jews. At the same time, he repeatedly underlined the Soviet Union's role as one of the main players in the Middle East and on the world stage. Peace, he said, "wasn't built in a day," and only the Soviet Union could exert influence on the Arabs—something the Israelis ought to regard as very valuable, he said. Tellingly, when the conversation turned to U.S. involvement in the peace process, Begin said: "We strongly feel that we can achieve a peace deal by ourselves, with only minimal concessions."

There was a sense that behind these words lay not just hope but a certain confidence that Israel could get Sadat to sign up to a separate peace deal. We went into Begin's study just as Dayan was coming out, fresh from a trip to Morocco, where he had held a secret meeting with Egypt's deputy prime minister. Begin did not let a word of this slip out, but he had of course been influenced by Dayan's report, which led to a breakthrough with Egypt—truly a landmark achievement for Israel.

Absent from our meeting was the combative stance our Israeli counterparts had assumed in the previous rounds of talks. There was also a difference of tone between Begin and his predecessors when he brought up the issue of Jewish emigration from the Soviet Union. Although he raised the specific case of Natan Sharansky,[3] Begin made it clear that he did not want the situation to deteriorate.

We saved the most important matter until the end: we had been tasked with informing Begin that if the Geneva Conference was reconvened, Moscow would be prepared to reinstate diplomatic relations with Israel. It was the first time our side had put forward this kind of blueprint for restoring relations between the two countries. I think the Kremlin had found a way to resolve this thorny issue without loss of face: it would continue to make restored relations conditional on the search for a Middle East peace deal, only this time without demanding that Israel give up the territories it had captured in the 1967 Six-Day War. Although Begin listened to our proposal very carefully, I don't think he appreciated what we were offering. His reply was: "Let Brezhnev go ahead and invite me to Moscow. I guarantee we could reach a deal on all these problems." Nor should this be a secret trip, Begin added, but an official visit by the prime minister of Israel. We tried to convince him that this was impossible absent diplomatic relations between our two countries, but he carried on, insisting: "Tell Brezhnev what my offer is. I'm sure he'll see me, I'm sure we'll come to an agreement on all the issues."

Begin, we reckoned, simply did not realize that the Kremlin had taken a dramatically new step towards restoring its relations with Israel; the fact that it was conditional on the resumption of the Geneva peace conference could not harm Israel in any way. And so as late as 1977, ten years after relations were broken off, still another chance to restore diplomatic relations between the Soviet Union and Israel was squandered. It was an opportunity that could have altered the course of events in the Middle East for the better. It would also have benefited the Soviet Union, by helping to relieve international pressure over the Jewish question. Begin's counterproposal was not even passed on to the Party Central Committee or the Soviet Foreign Ministry.

Overall, we got the sense that the new Israeli regime wanted to demonstrate its good intentions and maintain a dialogue with the Soviet Union, as evidenced by the detail that follows. Even before we set off from Moscow, we knew that, despite its declared opposition to

Israel, the Ethiopian regime of Colonel Haile Mariam Mengistu was receiving regular supplies of arms from Israel via the Kenyan port of Mombasa. Ethiopia was then at war with Somalia, and Mengistu, who swore allegiance to Moscow, had taken great care to conceal his secret dealings with Israel. As we waited to be received by Begin in Jerusalem, we put the question to Ben Elissar directly. He answered us frankly, confirming that Israel was indeed supplying arms to Mengistu. "It is of course a strictly confidential deal," he said. "It would be most unwelcome for Israel if this sensitive transaction became public knowledge: in return for arms supplies, the Ethiopian government has pledged to allow twenty thousand Falashas—Ethiopian citizens who practice Judaism—to leave for Israel. It would also be damaging to Ethiopia if it were found to be in breach of the Arab League's resolutions to boycott Israel. For Israel, though, it's important to repair its relations with Ethiopia so as to split the anti-Israel front that Africa presents."

Our September 1977 trip was to be our last. The secret rounds of talks we had initiated continued right up until December 1991—mainly via the two countries' intelligence services—and were used every so often to settle specific technical and operational matters. By then, however, I was no longer involved in them.

This same period also saw unscheduled meetings between Israeli and Soviet officials in various countries and at the UN, most of them initiated by the Israelis, but none of them carried a lot of political weight.

OFFICIAL MEETINGS:
NETANYAHU AT THE NEGOTIATING TABLE

It was only in the final few months of the Soviet Union's existence that diplomatic relations with Israel were restored. I subsequently visited Israel three times—this time in my official capacity as Russia's foreign minister—in 1996 and 1997.

On April 22, 1996, I had a meeting with prime minister Shimon Peres. It was little different from the unofficial meeting we had had in the early 1970s. "We only need one intermediary and that should be the United States," Peres declared. This was his steely, unyielding response to the proposal I had set out for kick-starting the stalled Middle East peace process. What I had proposed was that all parties to the Arab-Israeli conflict should pledge to honor the agreements already reached under their predecessors so as to shore up the progress made so far. What made this especially important was the prospect of change, with young new leaders poised to take power on both sides who might not feel bound by any prior obligations. I had also proposed that there be movement toward a settlement via all available tracks of the peace process, leaving no stone unturned.

This initiative had been wholeheartedly endorsed by Egypt's president Mubarak, whom I had just met in Cairo; it had also been welcomed by President Assad of Syria when I met him in Damascus. At stake was a document that could be simply be signed in the course of the political working day, without having to convene any special conference. But Peres rejected the idea outright—what's more, the manner in which he did so was quite unacceptable.

On October 31, 1996, on my next trip to the Middle East, I met the new Israeli prime minister, Benjamin Netanyahu, in Tel Aviv. Unlike Peres, Netanyahu said he was keen to see Russia play an active role, pointing out that Russia, alongside the United States, had cochaired the 1991 Madrid peace conference. But life is never that simple: although he won us over with his constructive approach to Russia's role in the peace process, Netanyahu was in fact abandoning all the agreements that the Palestinians had reached with Peres, and before him with Rabin, who had been assassinated by a Jewish terrorist in 1995. I had hoped that signing an agreement to ensure continuity in the peace process would prevent this very outcome, but now it was coming true. I told Netanyahu that Russia would not budge, under any circumstances, from its insistence that there had to be a Palestinian state. After this meeting with Netanyahu, and another one a year later, I backed up what I had said by going to Gaza, where I was the guest of the Palestinian leadership headed by Yasser Arafat. At a press conference there, and at one in Jerusalem, I said that Russia wanted to see Israel comply with the Madrid conference formula of "land in exchange for peace."

Netanyahu nevertheless struck me as a man we could do business with. My first meeting with him came at a time of growing tension along the cease-fire line between Israel and Syria. The Syrians maintained that the Israelis were carrying out military maneuvers on the Golan Heights in preparation for an attack on Syria; the Israelis, meanwhile, thought that the deployment of elite Syrian units in the Golan Heights was a sign that Syria was getting ready to launch its own attack on Israeli positions. A wary Netanyahu asked: "Can I state at a press conference that Russia opposes any violation of the cease-fire in the Golan Heights?" "Of course, you can do that," I replied—and emphasized this point in a subsequent statement to Israeli journalists. He then asked me to tell the Syrians that Israel had no intention of launching hostilities in the Golan Heights and would appreciate receiving similar assurances from Damascus. At Netanyahu's request, I engaged in a round of shuttle diplomacy, flying once more to Damascus, where I told Assad what Netanyahu had said; I then returned to inform Netanyahu that the Syrians had no intention of violating the cease-fire.

Later, I realized why the Israeli prime minister had been worried: the country's military intelligence service had supplied information from its source in Damascus that suggested that the Syrians were preparing to advance into the Golan Heights. Yet Israeli military intelligence had more than once been exposed for the tricks it played in its bids to prove its "outstanding capabilities." Indeed, it soon emerged that its reports from Syria bore no relation to the truth. It was the Russians who reported that the Syrians had no desire to provoke a military confrontation, easing the tensions, and I am pretty sure that this episode confirmed Netanyahu in his feeling that it was important to keep an open channel of communication with us.

This was again in evidence when I was Russian prime minister and played host to Netanyahu in Moscow—a task entrusted to me by President Yeltsin, who had been taken ill. Unlike many of his predecessors, Netanyahu was willing to engage in a frank and open exchange of views, which, I admit, impressed me greatly. On the whole, I get on with Netanyahu much better than most of my counterparts do—and not just those from Arab countries, but from the United

States too. There was, of course, a whole range of basic issues on which his position was diametrically opposed to ours. But contrary to widespread opinion, not least in the United States, Netanyahu was not altogether inflexible. At our talks in Moscow, for example, he stated that he was "not backing down from the Oslo Accords." In reality, this was not quite the full story, but initially he had refused to have anything to do with the accords. It was also possible to discuss the most crucial issues with him—he would not dismiss them out of hand, as many other Israeli leaders had done. A few examples: Netanyahu understood, possibly even better than his predecessors, that it was vital to reach a settlement with Syria. What I am highlighting here is his grasp of the problem, although I disagree with the content he sought to attach to those arrangements. I told him bluntly that Damascus would not agree to surrender its sovereignty over the Golan Heights and that it had Russia's backing on this issue. All the same, Netanyahu heeded my advice that he could not disregard Syria or its foothold in Lebanon; nor could he pull Israeli troops out of southern Lebanon without first discussing it with Syria—be it in secret, obliquely, or out in the open. Destabilization of the situation in Lebanon and stronger opposition to Syria was exactly what many in Israel wanted to see. Netanyahu agreed with me.

"Israel's security is my priority," he insisted. "With that in mind, we are ready to examine the matter of the Golan Heights." But when I asked him if his government would agree to announcing a withdrawal of Israeli troops from the Golan Heights and to recognizing Syria's sovereignty over them, there were a lot of "ifs" and "buts" and he didn't really answer the question.

I would not, of course, idealize Netanyahu; naturally, our approaches to the peace process were very different. But the important thing is that he was a man I could be straight with. We agreed to maintain contact and to continue exchanging views via specially designated appointees who met several times in Europe.

On May 12, 1999, I ceased to be prime minister of Russia. Five days later, on May 17, a snap parliamentary election was held in Israel that led to "Bibi" Netanyahu's ouster and his replacement as prime minister by Ehud Barak. Under Barak the Israeli-Palestinian negotiating process took off, with continued negotiations, including some mediated by the Americans—but they did not produce a breakthrough. Meetings were also held in New York between President Bill Clinton, Barak, and Arafat in early September 2000, but they didn't help either. Those meetings were followed by the second intifada, which was sparked by Ariel Sharon's visit to Temple Mount. And then came the period when Sharon was prime minister.

On May 2, 2002, Moscow and Washington created the Middle East "quartet," consisting of the United States, Russia, the European Union, and the UN. This saw the launch of the "road map to peace," which sets out a three-stage blueprint for bringing about a peace settlement between Israel and the Palestinians. The key thing about the "road map" is not just that it is in stages, but that its ultimate objective is the creation of a Palestinian state. Russia has opposed any attempt to remove this stated objective from the road map and called for an end to armed violence, especially terrorist attacks on peaceful civilians. But by this time, I was no longer directly involved.

Looking back on the evolution of Israel's relations with the Soviet Union, and then with Russia, it is hard to avoid the conclusion that both sides wasted many opportunities to make progress in settling the Middle East conflict—to the detriment of all those who would have benefited from a lasting peace.

THE PHENOMENON THAT
WAS SADDAM HUSSEIN

WHAT GAVE RISE TO the phenomenon that was Saddam Hussein? The answer to that question is key to any analysis of the situation in the Middle East in the final thirty years of the twentieth century and into the early years of the twenty-first. More than anything else, Saddam Hussein's rise was driven by the sheer force of his personality. When Ahmed Hassan al-Bakr's new regime seized power in Baghdad in 1968, hardly anyone could have guessed that the man listed as number five in the seven-member ruling Revolutionary Command Council would have removed his kinsman al-Bakr from power and taken his place within a little more than a decade.

The coup began on the night of July 16/17, 1968, when tanks from a battalion of the presidential guard trained their guns on the presidential palace. General al-Bakr phoned President Abdel Rahman Arif[1] and suggested that he surrender. Arif did so immediately, and was promptly escorted to a Baghdad airfield and flown out of Iraq. The coup had been carried out by a group from the military wing of the Iraqi Ba'ath Party, with the backing of several "independent" officers. The presidential guard, led by Lieutenant-Colonel Ibrahim ad Daud, played a major role. Another key figure was military intelligence chief Abdar Razzaq an Nayif.

Initially, it looked as though Saleh Mahdi Ammash, minister of internal affairs, and several others were far better placed to succeed al-Bakr than Saddam. But while Saddam himself grew closer than anyone to al-Bakr, he was able to get rid of his rivals: some had died, others had left the leadership. He was assertive, driven, brave, and of course (to put it mildly) devoid of sentimentality in the ways that he dealt with his colleagues. Yet before Saddam could become the outsized figure that he was in the eyes of the Iraqi people, the Middle East, and the world, a large part had to be played by both the Soviet Union and the United States. The former enabled him to become the leader of Iraq; the latter helped shape his view of the world, providing the basis of much of his foreign policy.

MOSCOW'S GAMBLE WITH THE EARLY SADDAM

The Kremlin's initial response to the 1968 coup was subdued. Everyone remembered the bloodshed following the first Ba'athist coup that led to the ouster of Abdel Karim Qassem in February 1963. After the Ba'athists seized power in Iraq for a second time, events were closely monitored by the Soviet embassy in Baghdad. Standing in as ambassador at the time was the then minister-counselor Feliks Fedotov, a brilliant and dedicated professional with a sharp, analytical mind. I had been to Baghdad myself, so the two of us spent long hours talking about the situation in Iraq under the new president, al-Bakr.

The coup did not draw much of an overt response from the people of Baghdad; the citizens of Iraq had grown weary of revolution. At the same time, they were waiting nervously to see how the group that had seized power would conduct itself. Many of its members had also been a part of Iraq's first Ba'ath regime, which had unleashed a bloody campaign of repression against the left. It was therefore quite striking that the leaders of this second coup wanted at all costs to avoid comparisons with the predecessor Ba'athist regime. President al-Bakr declared that July 17 was a direct continuation of the July 14, 1958, revolution, rather than a revisiting of any of the subsequent regimes.

Most of what Fedotov and I talked about as the regime took hold was its precipitous and rapidly changing internal balance of power.

By the time we began our discussions, Daud and Nayif had already been fired from the government; all the evidence, and intuition too, suggested that the main rivalry was between two members of the Revolutionary Command Council—Saddam Hussein and Interior Minister Ammash. This was a view shared by the Soviet overseas intelligence *rezident* at the embassy in Baghdad (another bright, experienced, educated figure), who also took part in our comradely discussion.

A number of factors favored Saddam—whom among ourselves we called Che-Pe (abbreviated from the Russian expression "extraordinary incident"), possibly because it was a term that suited his character. Like Ammash, Saddam occupied strong positions in the Ba'ath Party, but Saddam undoubtedly benefited from the approval of the party's general secretary and founder Michel Aflaq. Saddam continued to enjoy Aflaq's unstinting support right up until his death in 1989; Saddam may well have earned it with the brave speech he delivered at the party's sixth pan-Arab congress in Damascus in 1963, in which he denounced Salah al-Saadi, the general secretary of the Iraq division of the party. What struck Fedotov and me was the fact that the Iraqi Ba'athist regional congress removed al-Saadi from office at the recommendation of the pan-Arab one. Even more striking, al-Saadi was fired because of the killing spree Iraq had suffered during his first nine months in power. We therefore associated Saddam's name with a rejection of terror and violence against communists; at the time, we had good reason to do so.

After General Arif overthrew Iraq's first Ba'athist regime, Saddam had gone underground, where he assiduously prepared the party apparatus for a fresh rise to power. Within three months, at Aflaq's recommendation, he was made a member of the Iraqi Ba'ath Party's new five-member leadership. Most importantly, Saddam set up and commanded the party's secret special services wing, whose members were all closely trusted figures.

I was able to build up a picture of Saddam via my personal acquaintance with him, as well as through conversations with his close associate Tariq Aziz, then editor in chief of the party newspaper *Al-Thawra*. Permanent contact with Saddam and Aziz had been established during my mission to Baghdad, the aim of which had been to improve relations and ultimately bring about peace between the Iraqi regime and the Kurds in the north of Iraq (for more on this, see chapter 17). Saddam had been designated to represent the regime in this difficult matter, and thanks largely to Soviet mediation, he enjoyed some success. This undoubtedly brought Saddam closer to the position of leader-in-waiting, and later to becoming president of Iraq, supreme commander, and general secretary of the Iraqi Ba'ath Party.

The Soviet embassy in Baghdad and later the Kremlin undoubtedly took a gamble when it threw its support behind Saddam, but until about 1975 his conduct seemed to vindicate our expectations. In March 1970, an agreement was signed that provided for Kurdish autonomy within the state of Iraq; Saddam also played a positive role in setting up the People's Patriotic Front (or PPF). At his initiative, the Iraqi Communist Party was invited to join the new front, on the condition that it recognized both the "progressive character of the July 17, 1968, revolution" and "the Ba'ath Party's leading role in government, in mass organizations and in the PPF." The Iraqi Communist Party had by this time suffered a de facto split into two halves: the central command headed by Aziz al-Hadj refused to go along with the Ba'ath Party, while the central committee chaired by Aziz Mohammed favored an accommodation with the powers that be. The Soviet Communist Party helped its Iraqi counterpart to prevail over its "hard left," and in July 1973 a "national action" charter setting out the communists' incorporation into the front was signed by al-Bakr, as general secretary of the Ba'ath Party, and by Mohammed, as first secretary of the Iraqi Communist Party. I got the feeling while I was in Iraqi Kurdistan that many of the Kurdistan Democratic Party (KDP) leaders would also have liked to join the front, but those who opposed the idea won the day. With an agreement for Kurdish autonomy already in place, this led to a split within the Kurdish nationalist movement, and several KDP members quit the party.

In 1975, at a meeting in Algiers mediated by President Houari Boumédienne of Algeria, which took place during the March OPEC summit, Saddam signed an accord with the Shah of Iran (Mohammed Reza Pahlavi) on the countries' borders in the area of the

Shatt al-Arab River. The agreement restored the border to the *thalweg*, a line tracing the lowest points of the river valley, a line it had taken Iran many decades to secure. After this came the signing of a pact on borders and neighborly relations between Iraq and Iran. Having built multilateral relations with both countries, the Soviet Union welcomed this normalization. Few could have doubted, however, that Iraq was headed towards a clash of ideologies with the Soviet Union. And the ideology Iraq had chosen was directly associated with Saddam Hussein.

But when I met with Saddam Hussein on January 22, 1973, he expressed great warmth towards the USSR. Our meeting was held at the Republican Palace in Baghdad at 8 p.m. Just four of us were present, the other two being Tariq Aziz and Soviet envoy Viktor Posuvalyuk. In my notebook I wrote the following:

> Right from the start Saddam said he had purposely scheduled the meeting to take place in the evening; that he could choose any time he wished. He had changed since the last time we met. In those three years he had become more serious, more restrained. He alluded to the domestic political situation in Iraq, saying it was "now very hard to overthrow the regime within" [not impossible, just hard]. He also said that the Arab world was undergoing a political shift to the right, especially Egypt. It is worth noting what he said about Sadat: "Nasser never gave him any special prerogatives. He could have become leader after Nasser died if he had carried on with social and economic reform; instead he went down the path of democratization, taking his cue from the fact that the popular masses—not just the bourgeoisie—were unhappy at all the signs of police corruption under Nasser. But after the student arrests and the crackdown on their freedoms, Sadat lost this last trump card too. He started using the slogans of Islam for his own ends but ended up triggering hidden forces that he himself would have trouble controlling."

This is surely a mature analysis that does nothing to corroborate claims that the "early" Saddam was a "primitive" figure. In those days, he was nothing like the figure on the podium saluting military parades with endless bursts of gunfire from a rifle propped against his side—the snapshot of a truly atavistic Saddam that appeared on television screens everywhere in 2003. The "early" Saddam was different, and the Kremlin had good reason to see him as a genuinely promising leader. In that same conversation with me, Saddam was also far from primitive in his explanation of why Iraq was drawn toward a special relationship with the Soviet Union. "It's not a question of giving us additional aid," he said. "Iraq is a rich state. But we need you to help us with the science of building the country. Confidential political consultations are called for."

Iraq had only recently nationalized the Iraq Petroleum Company (IPC), a bold and dangerous move—the IPC was not some second-tier oil company, but its main foreign-owned monopoly. Nationalizing the IPC was just as significant for Iraq as the landmark nationalization of the Suez Canal Company had been for Egypt and its people. Several Western commentators prophesied that Iraq's revolutionary-led regime would meet the same fate as that of Mohammed Mossadegh, who had nationalized Iran's oil industry in 1951, but still found himself unable to break free from its octopus-like embrace. After its nationalization in Iraq in 1972, the IPC—just like the Anglo-Persian Oil Company (APOC) had done in Iran two decades before—threatened court actions against any who dared buy supplies of Iraqi oil that had allegedly been taken from it illegally.

Yet in reality there was no parallel with Iran. With Soviet help, Iraq had already managed to establish a state-run oil extraction industry in northern Rumaylah and had signed contracts to supply Iraqi oil to the Soviet Union, East Germany, Bulgaria, Hungary, Poland, and Czechoslovakia, as well as to France and Italy. Iraq's position was reinforced by backing from Syria, which had simultaneously nationalized all IPC holdings on Syrian territory and had reached an agreement with Iraq on the transportation of Iraqi oil to the Mediterranean. The deal that was signed with the IPC was not limited to compensation for the nationalization. Two of the IPC's subsidiaries, the Mosul Petroleum Company and the Basra Petroleum Company, pledged to pay off a large sum of their debts to Iraq. Under this deal, the first of these two companies was transferred into the hands of the Iraqi state on March 31, 1973, with no compensation whatsoever, while the second upped its payments to the Iraqi government. As one would expect, all of this naturally made the Soviet Union supportive of an Iraqi leadership in which Saddam was playing an increasingly prominent role.

The various economic and military ties between Iraq and the Soviet Union were strengthened by the signing of a friendship and cooperation treaty. And in July 1975, Iraq signed a partnership accord with COMECON (the Council for Mutual Economic Assistance), a bloc of exclusively socialist member states. Nevertheless, Iraq's domestic policy took a rapid turn for the worse in the mid-1970s. There was blatant "Ba'athization" of the army and of the executive branches of power. Conflict with the Kurds flared up too: some 350,000 people from Kurdistan were forcibly resettled and 250 Kurdish villages were burnt to the ground. The army was used to subjugate the Shiites in the south, while along the border with Iran a twenty-five-kilometer–wide "Arab belt" was created and Iraqi Arabs were relocated to populate it. May 1978 saw the unleashing of a virulent anticommunist campaign: almost every member of the Iraqi Communist Party in the People's Patriotic Front was arrested, all the party's publications were banned, and thirty-one communists accused of setting up party cells in the army were executed, having been dubbed "foreign agents" by Saddam. And yet through it all, Saddam continued to justify Iraq's domestic policies in his meetings with Soviet officials. He would claim that the Ba'ath Party was waging a hard battle to forge a popular democratic state, and that its main targets were Kurd and Shiite insurgents acting on the orders of the Shah of Iran, as well as those communists whose objective was to overthrow the Ba'ath regime. Saddam never stopped insisting that the leadership in Baghdad had established and would maintain close relations with those Kurds, Shiites, and communists who had opted to cooperate with the regime.

During his trip to Moscow in April 1975, Saddam invited me to an early morning meeting at the Lenin Hills mansion where he was staying. Soviet premier Aleksei Kosygin was scheduled to arrive at 9:00

a.m. to accompany him to the airport. In an apparent response to remarks made during his meetings in Moscow, Saddam told Kosygin:
"If our Soviet friends are having doubts about our policies, send a
group of observers to Iraq. I'll give them access everywhere they
want, even to the Ba'ath Party wings of the army. Let them see for
themselves, instead of via information from our enemies, that we are
not deviating from our path." In a clear acknowledgment of the personal relationship I'd built with him during our negotiations with the
Kurds, he added: "It would be a good idea if Primakov headed the
group." Kosygin said nothing in reply.

Significantly, the senior Politburo figure hosting Saddam was
Kosygin who, as head of the government, was responsible for economic affairs. By then, the USSR's relationship with Iraq was primarily one of partnership in economic matters and in the field of military
hardware—there were literally thousands of Soviet military and civilian consultants in Iraq. Moscow could not take its military and economic relations with Baghdad for granted, especially as it had started
to lose its foothold in Sadat's Egypt again after a brief period of closer
relations during the 1973 Yom Kippur War. All of these broader
strategic considerations had to be taken into account—it was still the
time of the cold war. Moreover, Saddam knew how to win over his
Soviet partners. He would adopt a thoughtful manner when speaking,
and repeatedly agree with the arguments that were put to him. Of
course top-level talks like these did not get bogged down in direct
criticism of Saddam's activities; unwelcome developments were only
implicitly touched on. All the same, it must be said that he reacted
calmly even to Soviet criticism—although it would have been a different story had one of his Iraqi colleagues tried saying any of the
things that we said to him!

On July 17, 1979, on the anniversary of Iraq's Ba'athist revolution, al-Bakr was relieved of all his official posts and placed under
house arrest. The official story was that he had fallen ill and resigned.
With that Saddam, already the de facto leader of Iraq for a number of
years, became its de jure head of state and party leader. By now, he no
longer had any rivals for power. As soon as al-Bakr had appointed
Saleh Ammash and Hardan al-Tikriti as the country's vice presidents

in 1976, their fates had been sealed. In a matter of months, al-Tikriti and then Ammash too were removed from office. Tikriti was informed of his dismissal when he was on a trip abroad and was offered a post as an ambassador instead. He indignantly refused. Shortly afterwards he was assassinated by an unknown group of people in Kuwait. Ammash accepted the post of ambassador to Finland. By this time, Saddam had total control of the army and the party; and, most importantly, the party intelligence corps and other secret services reported directly to him.

But once he had the situation in hand in Iraq, Saddam began to distance himself from the Soviet Union. The Iran-Iraq War played a particular role in this process. In September 1980, when Saddam launched massive hostilities against Iran, the move came as a complete surprise to the Soviet Union. Literally days before, Saddam had assured Soviet ambassador Anatoly Barkovsky that "there will be no major military operations against Iran in the immediate future." As would be expected, Barkovsky had wasted no time in reporting the blatant lie back to Moscow. This kind of disinformation only fueled the Kremlin's mounting anger; the decision was made to halt Iraq's supply of arms. In an effort to somehow defuse the situation, Tariq Aziz was dispatched to Moscow, where he met with the Soviet Party secretary Boris Ponomarev, who proposed that Iraq should immediately call off the hostilities. I too met with Aziz. When I asked him why Baghdad had made incursions into Iranian territory without informing its ally the Soviet Union, Aziz tried to make out that the war had been started by the Iranians and that Iraq had no other choice but to strike back.

One indication of the Kremlin's anger at what Saddam had done was the fact that the Soviet ambassador in Tehran was instructed to offer military aid to the Iranian prime minister. When Iran turned down the offer, Moscow decided to adopt a position of neutrality. Some time later, after the Iranians had gained the upper hand and—despite incurring massive fatalities—Iranian forces were starting to close in on Baghdad, the Soviet Union resumed supplying arms to Iraq. Although it never said so publicly, Moscow strongly disapproved of the Iraqi invasion of Iran, but not because the attack was unexpected, as the Soviets had indeed considered an invasion to be an imminent possibility. Rather, Iraq's unwillingness to consult the Kremlin was seen as an attempt by Saddam to drag the Soviet Union into his military adventure, on the assumption that Moscow would automatically support whatever he did. The Soviet Union had no intention of doing that.

As soon as Ayatollah Khomeini came to power in Iran, there was a certain amount of brainstorming in Moscow, including a "situational analysis" by a party of experts—not only scholars but hands-on staff from a number of bodies—that I chaired (which won a USSR State Prize for its methodology). This analysis focused on forecasting what changes might come about in the Middle East as a result of the Islamic Revolution in Iran. One of the group's conclusions was that for a variety of reasons (some objective, some not) Iran and Iraq would soon declare war on one another.

In addition to Iran's stated aim of exporting the Islamic Revolution, especially to neighboring countries, there was one quite subjective circumstance to bear in mind. Khomeini hated Saddam, whom he personally blamed for the humiliating end to his many years of exile in Iraq. At the bidding of the Shah of Iran's government, Khomeini had been placed under house arrest. At first agents from Iraq's security service, the Mukhabarat, had surrounded his home in Najaf. Then, in 1978, he had been expelled from the country—literally forced across the border into Kuwait, which also refused to take him in. He was eventually obliged to seek refuge in France.

As for Saddam, we had predicted that he would try to exploit the depletion of the Iranian army after the overthrow of the shah—its ranks had shrunk from 240,000 to 180,000 men, and 250 of its generals had been replaced by the inexperienced Iranian Revolutionary Guard (also known as Islamic Revolutionary Guards Corps)—and seek a change of border with Iran. Saddam was unhappy with the accord he had reached with the shah that modified the course of their border along the Shatt al-Arab River: from 1973 until the signing of this accord, the entire river had been considered Iraqi waters. Saddam had other motives for making war with his neighbor as well—he had set himself the task of forcing Iran to withdraw its troops from Abu

Musa, Greater Tunb, and Lesser Tunb, the three islands in the Straits of Hormuz that Iran had captured in 1971. Another goal was to seize the oil-rich Iranian province of Khuzestan, with its largely Arab population. Victory in the war could help close Iran's border with Iraqi Kurdistan. As events would prove, Saddam could not quash the Kurdish insurgency so long as that border remained open. Baghdad was also worried about the potential mobilization of Iraqi Shiites after the installation of Iran's Shiite Islamic regime. Virtually all of our predictions would come true.

It was around this time that another of Saddam's traits became apparent: his preternatural gift for mimicry, for adapting to circumstances. Keenly aware that Saudi Arabia's Sunni regime was a potential ally in his campaign against Iran, Saddam began playing up his devotion to the faith. Years later, when he was put on trial in Baghdad, he seemed to have always had the Koran in his hand. After the political downfall he had suffered, I can't rule out the possibility that he had sincerely thrown himself into religion. But there had been no sign of such overt religiosity in the "early" Saddam. Of course he paid homage to the customs and rules of his natal Islam, but he never made a point of parading his faith. On the eve of his war against Khomeini's regime, however, it was a different story: Saddam was shown across the Iraqi media paying a visit to the city of Najaf, a holy site for Shiites, and displaying a family tree that all but traced his ancestry back to the Prophet Muhammad. In August 1980, one month before he inaugurated his war against Iran, Saddam made the sacred hajj pilgrimage to Mecca. Across the Arab world, television broadcasts showed him performing the ritual circumambulation of the Kaaba, robed in white and in the company of Crown Prince Fahd, the future king of Saudi Arabia. Ten days before the war broke out, Saddam used an emergency session of the Iraqi parliament to announce that he was tearing up the Algiers accord with Iran, and declared Iraqi and Arab sovereignty over the Shatt al-Arab River.

As events would prove, both Iran and Iraq seriously miscalculated the course and costs of the war. Iraq had counted on an uprising among the Arab population in the Iranian province of Khuzestan;

Iran, meanwhile, had set its hopes on assistance from Iraqi Shiites. Both sides had counted on significant support from the Kurds too: Iran from the Kurds living in northern Iraq, who were in constant conflict with Baghdad; Iraq from Kurds living in Iran who were at loggerheads with Tehran. But none of that was to be. Instead, the war was a long, drawn-out affair with enormous loss of life on both sides. I had not even imagined the scale of the destruction I saw in 1991 when, during the Kuwait crisis, I traveled to Baghdad across Iranian territory adjoining the Iraqi border. On both sides of the road, a no-man's-land stretched for mile after mile, with burnt-out remains of tanks and towns and villages razed to the ground. It was a war where the advantage shifted from one side to the other, and then back again; it finally ended with a peace agreement (in 1988) that gave neither side an advantage.

AMERICA BACKS THE LATER SADDAM

As Saddam Hussein geared up for war against Iran, he knew he would be able to rely on the support of the United States, given the anti-American activities of the new regime in Tehran. Washington, in turn, regarded the war as a God-given chance to settle scores or at least to seriously weaken the post-shah regime in Iran. So the U.S. administration decided to support Iraq—and that meant giving direct backing and aid to Saddam.

Neither Saddam nor Tariq Aziz ever informed the Kremlin of the Iraqi regime's contacts with the U.S. administration, especially when it came to the issue of military supplies. The most information I ever got out of Aziz on this subject was during a lengthy meeting with him in Baghdad on March 28, 1981, when he made this quite abstract, almost cryptic comment: "We have settled the question of sourcing arms for Iraq. But the time has come when we need an answer to another question: will the limited [arms] supplies from the Soviet Union supplement those from our other source or the other way round?" He added: "I should point out that even when you [the Soviet Union] stopped supplying arms, we were not in a critical position." Aziz also used this same meeting to criticize the Kremlin because it no longer regarded Saddam Hussein as the best figure to lead Iraq.

After the outbreak of the Iran-Iraq War, Saddam could clearly be seen to be leaning more and more toward building beneficial relations with the United States—a result that White House policy had been specially geared toward producing. We knew that the United States had begun supplying arms to Iraq on the direct orders of President Ronald Reagan (after he had discussed the matter with Secretary of State George Shultz, Defense Secretary Caspar Weinberger, and the then CIA director, William J. Casey). The CIA regularly supplied the Iraqi leadership with intelligence on Iranian troop movements that it received via long-range reconnaissance aircraft (AWACS) based in Saudi Arabia. The flow of U.S. arms and vital military intelligence to Baghdad continued unabated, even after the Israeli air force destroyed the Osiraq nuclear reactor. In fact, the United States added its voice to the chorus of protest against Israel's audacious air raid. To the uninitiated, it looked as though U.S. intelligence had no information on the planned raid—which was carried out with American F-16 and F-15 fighter aircraft supplied to Israel by the United States—and that therefore the United States was unable to prevent it.

On December 20, 1983, as America continued its flirtation with Iraq, the then U.S. special envoy to the Middle East, Donald Rumsfeld, who would later become defense secretary, met with Saddam in Baghdad, bringing him a personal message from President Reagan. The objective of their lengthy talks, and indeed of Reagan's message, was clearly to restore diplomatic relations between the two countries, which had been broken off by Iraq in 1967. Rumsfeld said the United States and Iraq shared common enemies—Iran and Syria—both of which were backed by the Soviet Union. When foreign minister Tariq Aziz bade farewell to Rumsfeld, he told him, on Saddam's personal instructions, how pleased the Iraqi president had been with their talks. In 1984, the Reagan administration made a point of removing Iraq from its list of terrorist regimes. On June 5, 1984, Saudi fighter jets shot down two Iranian military aircraft with the aid of American AWACS planes. That year also saw the restoration of diplomatic relations between Washington and Baghdad.

The United States could not, of course, support every aspect of Iraq's war against Iran. During a session of the UN Security Council on Iraq's use of chemical weapons, the U.S. representative offered a strongly worded public condemnation of the attack. This caused unconcealed displeasure on the part of the Iraqi regime—and yet very soon afterward, in March 1984, Rumsfeld made another visit to Baghdad. This time Saddam did not receive him, but that did not stop Rumsfeld from accomplishing his "mission of conciliation": he pledged to help Iraq obtain credits from the Export-Import Bank of the United States and to buy dual-purpose equipment in the United States. Shortly after, the Iraqi agriculture ministry (!?) bought a consignment of heavy trucks and Bell helicopters built by the U.S. company Textron.

U.S. companies—as well as politicians—did a lot of business with Iraq in the 1980s. Later, in 1991, a report was submitted by Sam Gejdenson (D-CT), the chairman of the U.S. House Subcommittee of the Foreign Affairs Committee, which said that these companies had helped Saddam move closer to his goal of creating weapons of mass destruction. Even after the war with Iran, Saddam continued to receive indications that the U.S. establishment was well disposed toward him. In April 1990, just months before Iraq launched its invasion of Kuwait, a distinguished delegation of U.S. senators paid a visit to Baghdad. When they met Saddam, they assured him that the Iraqi regime was viewed favorably in Washington's corridors of power.

America's conduct during and after the Iran-Iraq War—right up until the Kuwait crisis in 1990–91—unquestionably had an impact on Saddam's convictions and outlook. But it went further than simply influencing the way Saddam thought and behaved.

A PSYCHOLOGY SHAPED BY U.S. POLICY

It is well known, as I have already mentioned, that Saddam Hussein collaborated with CIA operatives during the assassination attempt on Abdel Karim Qassem. But there is no evidence to confirm that he was actually recruited as an agent. His enemies would have been only too pleased to blacken his name once he had come to be seen as a deplorable hate figure in Washington. And that is not what happened.

Saddam's psychological condition was nevertheless greatly influenced by the United States. I believe this was not just a matter of his intellectually and tactically understanding the importance of the United States as a superpower to be reckoned with. Saddam also clearly based his reasoning on the fact that, while the United States was a superpower that could put him under a certain degree of pressure, it would not sink him outright, because it had a vested interest in the balance of power in the oil-rich Persian Gulf. Still, balances and counterbalances of this sort can be upset by sudden shifts of conflict between the region's countries. By "balancing" Iran with Iraq, the cornerstone of U.S. policy, Iran's post-shah regime was prevented from becoming the region's dominant power. The Iraqi leader reckoned that as long as there was an Islamic regime in Iran that was hostile to America, Washington would not allow Iraq to be seriously weakened. And when the United States gave its full backing to Saddam in his war against Iran, it seemed to confirm the conclusion he had already reached. Because Saddam could associate Iraq only with the power structure that he had imposed upon it himself, he came to believe that the Americans would tolerate his escapades indefinitely, as long as he didn't directly target any U.S. interests. Saddam's faith that the Americans would not wash their hands of him might also have been bolstered by the relationship he had built up with the CIA in his younger days. Whether it did it intentionally or not, the United States did much to make Saddam believe in his lucky star.

The countries of the Persian Gulf also had some influence on Saddam's view of the world. They were all too aware that Iraq could counteract Iran's expansionist ambitions in the region, so they gave Saddam not just moral support, but material aid as well. It was their support in particular that became a sensitive issue during the Iran-Iraq War. Saddam, it must be said, felt he had a right to their unconditional support. But many of them felt taken for granted. During the Iraqi occupation of Kuwait, I had a meeting in Saudi Arabia with the then exiled emir of Kuwait, Jaber al-Sabah. He complained how "unbelievably ungrateful" Saddam had been—Kuwait had not only supplied him with aid during the war but had also allowed him the use of its sea port for deliveries of arms shipments. Another leader who lamented Saddam's "ingratitude" was King Fahd of Saudi Arabia, whom I also met for talks during the Kuwait crisis.

The actual outbreak of this crisis is often dealt with superficially: Saddam, it is said, decided to annex Kuwait, so he invaded it. This is indeed what happened. But without justifying Saddam's actions for a moment, we can acknowledge the underlying oil-related issues that led him to act as he did. Saddam saw his fate as inextricably linked with Iraq's oil resources. He had come to believe that he could not only strengthen his regime but also take on the mantle of pan-Arab leader—an ambition that was jeopardized by the actions of the other Arab oil-producing countries. In an attempt to justify his intervention in Kuwait, Saddam told me quite frankly: "I could not stand by and say nothing when Kuwait had agreed with Saudi Arabia, under pressure from the United States, to sharply reduce world oil prices." After the Iran-Iraq War ended, Saddam asked Saudi Arabia, Kuwait, and Abu Dhabi to provide him with loans and to keep OPEC oil production quotas down so as to maintain higher world petroleum prices. Kuwait responded by saying that since there was no longer any threat from Iran, there was no more need to supply Iraq with financial assistance. At the same time Kuwait and Abu Dhabi increased their oil production quotas, which led to a steep drop in oil prices, from $19 to $11 a barrel. Saddam believed this scenario would drive Iraq into bankruptcy. But if Iraq was joined with Kuwait (whose independence Baghdad had never recognized, even under the monarchy), it would become the region's leading oil producer. World prices would be more dependent on Iraq than on any other country.

Saddam did not believe that the United States was prepared to pay the price of losing its counterweight to Iran—even if Iraqi troops invaded and occupied Kuwait. Before launching his invasion, Saddam met the U.S. ambassador to Iraq, April Glaspie, and asked her how the United States would respond to Iraq's endeavor to settle a territorial dispute with Kuwait. Glaspie replied that this was "an internal matter for the Arabs." What Saddam wanted to know specifically was how the United States would respond, not any other country. Despite the standing agreements between Baghdad and Moscow, Saddam did not even give the Kremlin a hint of his plan for the annexation of Kuwait. That the United States had told him it was taking a "neutral" position could hardly have failed to reinforce his conviction that although the United States might kick up a fuss, it would ultimately be able to stomach even the invasion of Kuwait.

I met with Saddam three times during the Kuwait crisis, and on each occasion I got the sense that he believed that everything would resolve itself in his favor. At first he said that the United States's strongly worded reaction to the invasion was nothing more than bluff, since Washington would be unwilling, under the circumstances, to deploy the full weight of its forces against Iraq. Then, as the bombing raids began, he believed they would go no further than that as the United States "wouldn't want to get involved in a war on the ground." When the Americans did in fact defeat the Iraqi army in Kuwait, Saddam was right to say that President George Bush Sr. would not send U.S. forces—which were at the heart of the anti-Iraq coalition—to attack Baghdad and topple his regime.

Needless to say, Saddam trusted in fate; after all, it had protected him for so many years and had gotten him out of so many sticky situations. However, along with his trust in fate, I think his way of thinking also led him to miscalculate the measures that would be taken against him. Saddam's logic was perhaps underpinned by the recollection of an uncompromising statement that that self-same George Bush Sr. had made at the height of the Iranian army's military advance towards Basra: an Iranian victory, Bush had said, "would utterly destabilize the situation in the Persian Gulf."

Either way, the Americans decided to exercise restraint by limiting their military operation to the Iraq-Kuwait border—which turned out to be the right decision, as the aftermath of George Bush Jr.'s military intervention in 2003 would prove. However, what concerns us here is not the psychological makeup of either American president but that of Saddam Hussein. When I look back at the three meetings I held with Saddam during the Kuwait crisis, it looks increasingly clear to me that every time he came close to a decision that could have prevented a war—or at least land maneuvers by the coalition forces—he would drag his feet. He always seemed to have his hopes pinned on something.

Saddam's Micawber-like hope that something would turn up also seemed to rule his head on the many occasions that he put pressure on the UN Special Commission (UNSCOM) that had been set up to look for signs that Iraq had weapons of mass destruction. In all fairness, it should be pointed out that while Richard Butler was head of UNSCOM—a time when the Iraqis were demanding that it should not be allowed to inspect Saddam's palaces or replace members of its team, and so on—the commission was not impartial and was acting outside its remit. In Scott Ritter's 2005 book, *Iraq Confidential: The Untold Story of the Intelligence Conspiracy to Undermine the UN and Overthrow Saddam Hussein*, the former UNSCOM inspector writes that in 1996–97 the CIA was using the UN's international inspection operation to lay the groundwork for toppling Saddam. Ritter alleges that with the aid of a number of inspectors, the CIA was trying to work out how many men made up Saddam's personal guard, where they were located, and what means they had at their disposal, as well as mapping out the arrangement of rooms inside his presidential palaces. Ritter was not just another writer describing the events; he was deputy head of the very same commission whose activities he describes.

Russia did everything in its power to get Saddam to pull back from the brink, urging him to refrain from issuing ultimatums to UNSCOM, while at the same time making significant changes to how UNSCOM worked and to the members of its team. But without meaning to belittle the influence that Russia had, it has to be said that Saddam continued to believe in his lucky star, in his own foresight, and ultimately in Allah, who would save him from harm. What sustained his belief was not blind hope, but his realpolitik certainty that, given the prevailing sentiment in the Arab world—and indeed the Americans' own interests—the United States had nothing to gain from bringing about his downfall.

This was plain to see in 1997 too, when UNSCOM inspections were suspended after the Iraqis refused to let the American members of its team have access to the installations that were being inspected. Nor did Saddam lose any of his self-belief when the UN Security Council issued a unanimously adopted resolution condemning Iraq; nor did he quail in the face of the United States' visible preparations for war. In fact, he took a harder line, demanding the immediate expulsion of the American inspectors from Iraq. At my recommendation (I was Russia's foreign minister by this time), President Boris Yeltsin sent Saddam a message proposing that the Iraqi leader announce his continued cooperation with the UNSCOM team in its entirety. Yeltsin informed President Bill Clinton of the message he had sent, and asked him to refrain from using military force. Saddam used a trip to Moscow by Tariq Aziz to pass on the message that he would agree to UNSCOM resuming its work, with the Americans as part of its team. Again, however, he made life difficult for the inspectors, and on October 31, 1998, the Iraqi leadership announced that it was calling a complete halt to UNSCOM activity in Iraq. It took enormous efforts on the part of Russia, France, and UN secretary-general Kofi Annan to hold off military action against Iraq; finally, on November 18, Baghdad said it would "resume cooperation with the special commission and allow it to carry out its normal duties," but only after it had imposed a number of conditions. When President Clinton declared that he was not satisfied, Baghdad responded by clarifying that it was not imposing conditions but setting out wishes that did not affect Iraq's "clear and unconditional" decision to restore cooperation with UNSCOM and the International Atomic Energy Agency. But this concession came too late to help; air strikes were launched against Iraq during Operation Desert Fox, on December 16, 1998.

As became clear after the U.S. military intervention in 2003, Saddam knew all too well that UNSCOM would not be able to uncover anything during its inspections, because Iraq did not at that time have any weapons of mass destruction, nor was it making any. Looking back with hindsight on Saddam's dangerous game, it could be concluded that in his bizarre bid to secure the lifting of UN sanctions against Iraq, he deliberately inflamed the situation every step of the way. But once again, he could do so only because he had ruled out the possibility of the Americans' leading an assault on land. As Tariq

Aziz eventually admitted, the Iraqis were not overly fearful of air strikes. Again Saddam fell prey to a belief in his destiny and to his misinformed expectation that there would be a stronger reaction from the Arab countries to the air strikes against Iraq. He was taken in by his entourage's constant acclaim of his "strategic and tactical genius," and by his own faith that the "game" he was playing with UNSCOM would not end as it did with a U.S. operation to topple him from power.

FIASCO AND FINALE

I met with Saddam Hussein three weeks before the launch of the U.S. operation against Iraq in 2003, in which the Americans went the whole way and overthrew his regime. I flew out to Baghdad after a late night conversation with Vladimir Putin, who had entrusted me with the immediate task of verbally conveying a personal message to Saddam from the Russian president. The message called on Saddam to step down voluntarily from the post of president and for the Iraqi parliament to call democratic elections. But because he feared that Saddam's resignation would trigger domestic instability in Iraq, Putin had also instructed me to suggest to Saddam that he could, for example, hold on to his party post. When I arrived in Baghdad, I declined to meet with Tariq Aziz first because I knew he would try to find out the substance of my mission—and President Putin wanted his proposal to be conveyed to the Iraqi leader as dramatically possible. As bold as Putin's proposal was, it gave the Iraqi leader the opportunity to appear to be making the decision on his own initiative. When he entrusted me with this mission, Putin had told me that it might be the last chance to prevent U.S. military action against Iraq—an action that bypassed the UN Security Council and that was taken in defiance of public opinion around the world and despite opposition from most states, including U.S. allies such as Germany, France, and Belgium.

My meeting with Saddam took place one-on-one, as I had requested. The only other person present was the Soviet foreign ministry interpreter who had flown in with me. During the meeting, Saddam wrote down what I said in a notepad, which raised my hopes that he might actually agree to Putin's proposal. Then he asked me if I could repeat everything I had said in the presence of Tariq Aziz and the chairman of the Iraqi parliament, who were in the adjoining room. And so, with them also present, I once more set out the verbal communiqué from the Russian president. In reply, Saddam came out with a stream of accusations against Russia: we were trying to deceive him once again, he said, just as we had during the Gulf War, when we had said that if he agreed to pull his troops out of Kuwait, there would be no ground operation against the Iraqi army. No less heatedly, I told him that he himself had delayed his decision to pull the troops out, right up until the American ultimatum, by which time it was too late. After listening to what I had to say, Saddam said nothing but patted me on the shoulder and went out of the room. As he left, Aziz called after him, loud enough for Saddam to hear: "Ten years from now, we'll see who was right— our beloved president or Primakov."

That was to be my last meeting with Saddam. He had looked at ease and had a certain confidence that he would still be around "ten years from now"—possibly the result of his own mindset, but also thanks to the influence of those in his inner circle. Their influence may well have been very significant: after all, yet another aspect of Saddam's personality was that he did not want to hear unflattering information. Time after time, my meetings with him had convinced me of that. For example, in our first meeting at the height of the Kuwait crisis, he had assured me (and I think he sincerely believed it) that Arab people everywhere welcomed the Iraqi invasion of Kuwait, and that the Palestinians felt that they were poised on the brink of victory. The fact is that because they lived in fear of incurring his displeasure, members of Saddam's inner circle predominantly told him about incidents, developments, and tendencies that highlighted their great leader's "perspicacity, far-sightedness and genius"; they steered clear of apprising him of unwelcome but truthful information. During the Kuwait crisis, Saddam's only opportunity to get a realistic picture of the situation was when he met personally with overseas envoys—

mainly from the Soviet Union—and meetings of that kind were few and far between.

I do not rule out the possibility that, just before the U.S. military intervention in 2003, Saddam was sent "encouraging signals" via someone close to him from the very same U.S. secret services that had backed him earlier. If this were so, it would have been a classic way of operating. A lot of unanswered questions remain that could support this version of events: For example, why was it that the bridges that the U.S. tanks used to advance on Baghdad were not blown up? Why did the Iraqi army suddenly surrender, along with the Republican Guard, which U.S. experts had deemed to be fully capable of fighting? Who gave the order for a cease-fire? And, as it emerged during Saddam's trial, the real facts about his arrest bore absolutely no resemblance to the publicly aired story of his being dug out of a hole in the ground where he had been hiding, with a beard that had grown almost all the way down to his chest. Something about all this was not quite right.

It is telling that even when he had been toppled from power and thrown in jail, Saddam still thought he was "needed by the United States." This is what he told his lawyer, Khalil al-Duleimi, who, quoting Saddam, said he was "the only leader capable of dealing with the growing influence of Iran and the Shiite fundamentalists, and the United States should recognize the 'harsh reality' in the region: Iran was the enemy of the Arabs, of Islam and of the United States, and the only one who could beat Iran was Saddam Hussein."

Al-Duleimi also said his client saw the prosecution's call for the death sentence as an attempt by the Americans to apply pressure—he believed it was in fact a gambit to secure Saddam's help.

Had he really failed to learn any of life's lessons?

SADDAM'S EXECUTION

On December 30, 2006, at 6:05 a.m., Saddam Hussein was hanged. The first part of the charges against him might have provided a legal basis for his death sentence, but for the vast majority of people the execution was still unexpected. The second part of the trial, during which Saddam faced charges of using gas to kill thousands of Kurds, had only just commenced, yet without waiting for a verdict, Saddam was summarily executed. Why such haste? Perhaps the reason will become clear one day, but for now, all we can do is hypothesize and apply logical analysis in search of an explanation.

It would appear that Saddam's conviction—not just for the Shiite killings, but for the gas attacks that led to the mass extermination of the Kurds—was of benefit to the Bush administration, as it could go some way toward assuaging those critics who reacted particularly fiercely to the discovery that there was no link between the U.S. invasion of Iraq and claims that Saddam possessed nuclear weapons. As the U.S. administration sought a way out of its impasse in Iraq, it had no patience with those who predicted the escalation of violence between Iraq's Sunnis and Shiites that would inevitably follow Saddam's death, along with a hardening of the Saudis' anti-Shiite line. Yet what was predicted was what indeed occurred.

By all accounts, even circumstances outside of Iraq did little to favor Saddam's execution: almost all the Americans' European partners spoke out against it, including as close an ally as British prime minister Tony Blair.

Nor could you have chosen a worse day to carry out this rushed execution: the first day of the important Muslim holiday of Eid al-Adha, the eve of the New Year (the Shiites mark theirs one day later, which also had the effect of aggravating tensions between Sunnis and Shiites).

Despite all this, the execution went ahead. It was carried out after the final document calling for an immediate execution had been signed, not by Iraq's Kurdish president Jalal al-Talabani, but by its Shiite prime minister Nuri al-Maliki. Al-Maliki did so shortly after his return from Jordan, where he had met with President George W. Bush. Saddam was then executed without delay.

Unexpected as it was by Saddam himself, the death sentence might have been carried out before the end of his trial in an attempt to stop him from having the final word—something he was undoubtedly gearing up to do. Everything he had said in court thus far had been "procedural"—relating to specific accusations, or directed at the judge. Yet if he had had the final word, he might have said a great deal more. That, perhaps, is what they wanted to avoid, those who turned out to be less naïve than a dictator who believed that he was the one in control of the political game.

— 17 —

THE SAGA OF THE KURDS

I**T WOULD BE WRONG** to suggest that it was only after Iraq's July 1968 revolution that the Soviet Union sought to repair its relations with Baghdad. Abdel Rahman Arif, who replaced his brother Abdel Salam Arif as president, had had no part in the violence against the forces of the left. Taking into account the importance of Iraq in the region, the Soviet Union took steps toward rebuilding its bridges to the Iraqi leadership as early as 1966. A key part of this drive was an effort to improve relations between Baghdad and the Kurdish insurgents who practically controlled the north of Iraq. The USSR had enjoyed friendly relations with the leader of the Kurdish independence movement, Mullah Mustafa Barzani, for quite some time. A peaceful settlement of the conflict was seen as being very much in Moscow's interests.

FIRST ENCOUNTER WITH MUSTAFA BARZANI

Barzani's story is an interesting one. He was a mere toddler when he was first thrown in jail, together with his mother, after his elder brother Sheikh Ahmed Barzani led an uprising against the Turkish authorities in 1905. He was barely an adolescent when he saw action in the struggle of 1914–16. In 1931 he fought alongside his brother to drive the Baghdad government's forces out of the Barzani tribe's territory; it was only with help from the British air force that the Kurds were defeated. Taken prisoner once again, Mullah Mustafa would spend the next eleven years in exile. In 1943 he secretly returned to his home territory and launched the Kurdish struggle afresh. This time, his efforts led to victory and Nuri al-Said, then prime minister of Iraq, accepted the conditions set out by the Kurds. But two years later, with the help of the British, al-Said launched another assault on Barzani's troops.

During the Second World War, the Kurdish Republic of Mahabad was founded in northwestern Iran and Mustafa Barzani became its defense minister. But after Soviet troops withdrew from Iran at the end of the war, the republic fell apart. Barzani and some five hundred soldiers, mainly from the Barzani tribe, crossed the Iranian border into the Soviet Union. Laying down their arms, they dispersed throughout the region. Some of them settled in Azerbaijan, others in Soviet Central Asia, while Barzani lived in the Soviet Union under the surname of Mamedov, where he would remain for the next twelve years. Along with the soldiers from his tribe, he took care not to advertise his presence. Neither he nor any of those who crossed the border with him ever served in the Soviet armed forces; the widespread rumor that Barzani was a general in the Soviet army is nothing but a lie. In fact, these rumors stem from an episode that Barzani subsequently told me about: once, when he was in Moscow, he bought a general's uniform (which you could do in those days) at Voentorg, the military department store, and had his photo taken wearing the uniform—the photo later fell into the hands of British intelligence.

After Stalin died, there were big changes in Barzani's life and in the lives of those closest to him. Here is my transcript of what Barzani told me (although Barzani spoke Russian, his command of the language was, to put it mildly, far from perfect; I've rephrased his words for grammar and clarity): "I went up to the Spassky Gate of the Kremlin and started knocking. An officer came running out—a slim, good-looking fellow with gray eyes—and asked, 'What are knocking for?' I told him that this wasn't Barzani knocking at the gates of the Kremlin, it was the Kurdish revolution." Barzani went on to say that he was received by Georgy Malenkov, Stalin's successor. Following their meeting, he was sent to study at the Higher Party School, while Barzani's fellow tribesmen were admitted to various educational establishments. When the 1958 Iraqi revolution ended victoriously,

Barzani returned to Iraq, where he was made vice president of the Iraqi Republic: it was important to Abdel Karim Qassem, Iraq's new leader, that he maintain unity with the Kurds. However, their relations soon deteriorated and Barzani left for the north of Iraq, for Kurdistan, and a bloody war broke out between Baghdad and the Kurds yet again. Hostilities escalated under the first President Arif, and continued into the early days of his brother's presidency. In July 1966, the second President Arif signed a peace deal with Barzani, and although there were still armed skirmishes, the wider war abated. That was how things stood when *Pravda* reached me via its Cairo bureau and sent me on assignment to northern Iraq.

Barzani was not isolated: there were people he would meet with, including journalists, but they would all travel to the north of Iraq via Iran. I did not wish to sidestep the Iraqi authorities and, given our efforts to build bridges between Barzani and Baghdad, it would have been counterproductive to try to do so. Instead, I went directly to the top. On December 16, 1966, I met with President Arif. I had already received his written answers to questions I had put to him for an interview to be published in *Pravda*; in response to a question about the Kurds, he had said that bringing stability to the north of Iraq was among the most pressing issues he faced. I referred to his statement when I told him that I intended to meet with Barzani. It would not be appropriate for a Soviet correspondent to travel to Iraqi Kurdistan via Iran, I said, since we in Moscow regarded the Kurdish region as an integral part of Iraq. My argument seemed to have the desired effect and Arif agreed in principle, sending me to the Iraqi defense minister to arrange my "handover" to the Kurds. Eventually, when the details of the trip had been sorted out, I set off for the north in an armored personnel carrier, accompanied by two Iraqi officers, a group of soldiers, and Sasha Zotov, a young colleague from the Soviet embassy in Baghdad who acted as our interpreter and who would later become the Soviet ambassador to Syria. I had been briefed at the embassy that one of the officers was the defense minister's brother—but the other one I found out about myself: during a stop at a checkpoint, I was sharing a joke with the interpreter when we noticed that this second officer could not stop himself from laughing too. On the way back, when the lieutenant in question was left alone with us in the vehicle, we pointedly told him in Russian that there was no point in his acting dumb any longer. He answered us in perfect Russian, saying, "OK then, enough fooling around."

We contacted the Kurds via radio, and they let the officers and myself through, but not the personnel carrier. Their caution was more than understandable—we were headed for Barzani's winter base, where no officials from Baghdad had ever been before.

And so we arrived in Kurdistan. At this point I cannot help indulging in a little poetic digression. For this is a magical land of great beauty, inhabited for two-and-a-half thousand years by the proud, freedom-loving people known as the Kurds—or, as they were sometimes called, "the knights of the east." They have much to be proud of, not least the fact that Saladin, he who repelled the Crusaders, was a Kurd (the fact that Nuri al-Said, Iraq's prime minister during much of the British mandate, was also a Kurd gave them less cause for celebration). Then there's the scenery: mountains soaring into the sky and roaring streams that sparkle with the purity of their water. It is a place of bold, contrasting colors, from the white of the snowcapped peaks to the crags of bronze and the dark green moss underfoot. Gigantic boulders lie sprinkled across this carpet of moss as if to stop it from being blown away by the wind. Tree trunks sprout almost parallel to the ground on the mountain slopes—it's a miracle that they stay rooted. Such is Iraqi Kurdistan.

Our vehicle followed a narrow road, which took us out of the confines of the twelve kilometer–long ravine of Gali Ali Beg. Then we came to a three-way fork in the road: to the right lay the route to Rawanduz, to the left the route toward the town of Diyana. Ahead of us was the road to Haj Umran, which ultimately led to the border with Iran. That was the road we took. After we passed through the final Iraqi army checkpoint, there was not a single Iraqi soldier nor Iraqi government official to be seen. We were now in the territory controlled by the Kurdish militias of Mullah Mustafa Barzani.

Heading in our direction was a Willys jeep manned by three armed men: one was Sami Abd al Rahman, a leading member of the Kurdistan Democratic Party (who held a machine gun in his lap); the others were Barzani's assistant and the driver. After we greeted each other, their jeep went ahead, showing us the way. Further on, a train of mules took us along a narrow trail with a sheer cliff face on one side and a precipice on the other. In this terrain, Sami told us, a mere handful of *peshmerga* ("those who face death," as the Kurdish insurgents call themselves) could hold out against entire battalions.

Barzani's two sons, Idris and Massoud, were with him when he greeted me. The seventeen-year-old Massoud Barzani was then in charge of a radio station. I had brought along a couple of Soviet-made Poljot wristwatches to give them as presents, but was somewhat embarrassed to see that they were wearing Rolexes. Nevertheless Mustafa Barzani greeted me with obvious delight, and without further ado, invited me into a small dugout where a wood fire was burning in a stove on wheels. A piece of canvas was stretched overhead to serve as a ceiling; it sagged in places under the weight of the water caught in it, for a heavy rain mixed with snow was falling outside. From time to time, someone would hit these "sacks" of rainwater with a stick and the contents would come pouring down into a well-placed bucket.

Plates had been set out on the carpet that covered the floor of the dugout and we sat cross-legged and ate—including the Iraqi officers. I had managed to warn Barzani via Sami that one of them understood Russian so our discussion was "tailored" accordingly. At one point Barzani said to me: "Baghdad is full of thieves and swindlers, but there's one good, honest man—that's the defense minister." This was, of course, directed at the minister's brother, who was sitting right there.

The real meeting took place in the middle of the night, when two Kurds with machine guns woke me up and led me to another dugout. There, Barzani embraced me, saying, "The Soviet Union is like a father to me." He told me he welcomed the peace deal but had no faith in Baghdad, where extremists had put up stiff opposition, preventing the government from implementing the truce that it had already agreed upon with the Kurds. He added that with the constant expectation of a resumption of hostilities, it was impossible to seriously address such pressing issues as the need to improve living conditions for the Kurdish people. (I saw for myself how rough they were: little houses clinging to mountain slopes, their walls cobbled together out of stones; roofs of clay with holes that constantly had to be plugged to avoid leaks; the lack of electricity; rooms furnished with just a kerosene lamp and mats laid out on the dirt floor.) Meanwhile Baghdad was in no hurry to help, despite its promises to do so.

We had received reliable information that Barzani had made secret trips to see the shah of Iran; nevertheless, I asked him if he had any connections with Tehran. He answered in the affirmative, without a moment of hesitation: "I don't want to hide anything. What else can I do when my only link with the outside world is via the Iranian border?" But perhaps most important for me was Barzani's answer to my next question. "How do you see the future?" I asked. "After all, you must know there are rumors that the Kurds want their homeland to break away from Iraq."

"That is what the enemies of peace in Iraqi territory say about us," he replied. "But even if the Iraqi government asked us to break away, we would not agree to that. We do not want to secede from Iraq. This is our country. But in that country, Kurds should enjoy all the same rights as the Arabs. That is what we are fighting for."

During my meeting with Sami I learned that a few days before we arrived, one of the *peshmerga* had been detained by armed guards and forced into an underground cell (a crude hole dug in the ground). It was a punishment, Sami explained, for "making anti-Arab speeches. There was a note of racism about them. We will not permit anyone to pervert the nature of our cause."

Barzani's son Idris told me that the insurgents' army was mainly made up of Kurds. "But we have a lot of Assyrians in our number, and Armenians too. One member of the ruling body—the Revolutionary National Command—is an Arab; he commands a battalion made up of members of the Iraqi Communist Party—Arabs and Kurds alike—who fled to the north to escape the pogroms in 1963."

THE MISSION CONTINUES

It was decided in Moscow that the *Pravda* correspondent should continue to be sent on further trips to Iraqi Kurdistan. My next trip to northern Iraq took place in 1968, immediately after the change of government in Baghdad. This time I had no Iraqi escort. A car with a Kurdish driver—a *peshmerga*, a soldier from one of Mustafa Barzani's militia units—came directly to my hotel, and from there we set off for the north. En route, everything around me looked quite different than it had at the end of 1966: the sun had softened the stark colors of winter, bathing the mountain slopes in pastel shades of pale green and lemon. The only reminder of winter was the icy waters of a fast-running stream at the bottom of a gorge. Every minute or so our Land Rover crossed from one bank to the other, only slowing down when it had to cross a high bridge. The fact that we had been allowed through the entry to the gorge meant there were no cars coming in the opposite direction, which is why the driver was so unperturbed. He was a tall, slim Kurd with dark, almost indigo-colored hair and eyes that were truly green—and he drove like a daredevil. Across his chest he wore a tightly strapped bandolier with two spare machine-gun magazines.

What did the near future have in store for Iraq-Kurds and Arabs alike? That was the difficult question I took with me on my second trip to the Kurdish region of northern Iraq. The week I spent in Kurdistan was overloaded with impressions. There were meetings with Barzani and his sons, with top KDP members and with many, many regular *peshmerga*. They all agreed that the most important thing was to find a way to solve the issue that had cost so many lives and brought such suffering to Iraqi Arabs and Kurds alike. Barzani himself expressed little hope that Iraq's new leaders would be any more inclined than the previous ones to settle the Kurdish question. He and his entourage were anxious about the situation within the Kurdish movement too. *Peshmerga* units had been caught up in armed clashes, not just with Iraqi army divisions, but also in violent and occasionally large-scale battles with militias loyal to Jalal Talabani— who had split from the KDP—a man who would go on to be the president of Iraq in 2005. Barzani scornfully called these breakaway militias *djash*, Kurdish for "asses." These splits in the Kurdish camp had been cleverly exploited by Baghdad, which often got others to do its dirty work.

In my first two visits to Iraqi Kurdistan, I came as a journalist—mostly what I did was gather facts and impressions. But on my subsequent trips, I began to play the role of an intermediary. Ahead of my third trip, I met with Saddam Hussein in Baghdad. At that time he was the Iraqi regime's designated representative for "doing business" with the Kurds. He did not yet occupy a senior position in the regime—in fact, he believed that resolving the Kurdish question could provide him with a springboard for his own advancement. Not surprisingly, Saddam used his talks with me to highlight how constructive his position was. He explicitly asked me to tell Barzani how much he was willing to do. Under those circumstances, conditions were ripe for the Kurds to push for comprehensive autonomy within Iraq—a thought shared by Feliks Fedotov, the Soviet Union's acting ambassador in Baghdad.

When we met on January 23, 1970, Saddam spoke of needing to have a dialogue with the "brothers" from Barzani's high command in order "to negotiate true guarantees of autonomy for the Kurds." The only problem that could stand in the way of that, he said, was a crisis of confidence. "Neither the Ba'ath Party nor Barzani are entirely to blame for the conflict and enmity of these past years," he said. "But blood has been spilled, and in order to restore trust we need to apply our good intentions to isolate extremist figures or groups on both sides." These assurances made me feel optimistic and positive about Saddam himself, especially as he said he was keen to see me making regular visits to Kurdistan.

From 1966 through 1970 I was probably the only Soviet representative to meet with Barzani on a regular basis. In the summers, he lived in a hut; in the winters, in a dugout. I was joined on some of my trips by Soviet diplomats Viktor Posuvalyuk and Oleg Peresypkin, but the burden of the mission was on me, the *Pravda* correspondent. I did all I could to build bridges between the two sides. In seeking to influence Barzani, I was helped by the aforementioned Sami (real name Muhammad Mahmoud Abdarrahman) and Mahmoud Osman, otherwise known as Dr. Mahmoud, who were both leading figures in the KDP. The latter was a qualified medical doctor who still tended to the sick. He joked that his "sign of the zodiac" was the syringe and the rifle.

A prominent Iraqi public figure who played a very large and positive role in bringing about a peace deal between the two sides was Aziz Sherif, a wise, modest, and charming man who had been awarded the Lenin Prize for peace. After the 1968 coup, he returned from exile and was made a member of the government. I believe he visited Kurdistan at Saddam's suggestion in late 1969. Shortly after, I made yet another trip there myself, just as the fate of a new peace deal was being decided. On the eve of our arrival, talks had been held in Kurdistan with a delegation from Baghdad. Agreement had been reached on a number of issues, chief among them the principle of Kurdish autonomy. But as yet they had failed to find common ground on the issue of Kurds being involved in the Revolutionary Command Council, the highest authority in Iraq. There were also unresolved questions on the future of Kirkuk and the *peshmerga*, and on a timetable for declaring Kurdish autonomy.

The three of us—Barzani, Sherif, and I—had lunch together and shared a bottle of Iranian (yes, Iranian) cognac. Barzani was more open and talkative than ever, and proposed a toast to the people of Russia and the Soviet Union. Speaking candidly, he told us that Soviet recommendations had played a large role in convincing him to enter negotiations with the regime in Baghdad. He cited one of the recommendations as being: "Even the act of agreeing to talks could bolster the position of the Kurds and the KDP."

But after meetings with Dr. Mahmoud, who headed the Kurdish delegation, and with Sherif, who was staying in the same dugout as me, as well as with a number of Kurds whom I already knew well, I realized that it wasn't that simple. Sherif and I agreed that the most important thing for the Kurds right now was not to focus on the questions that remained unresolved but rather to prolong the negotiations and send their own negotiating team to Baghdad. They agreed with us.

Just a few weeks later, a Kurdish delegation arrived in Baghdad. I met them at the Soviet embassy on February 6, 1970. It was unusual to see Idris and Massoud Barzani, Dr. Mahmoud and Sami dressed in suits and ties. On February 14 we met at the embassy once more. In the intervening time, their negotiations had seen progress on a number of issues. It had taken our influence to get both sides to make compromises with each other. On the issue of Kirkuk, for example, the Kurds had agreed that the city would fall under Kurdish autonomous rule, except in matters of oil extraction, which would remain in the hands of the central government.

On March 11, 1970, President al-Bakr went on Baghdad radio and television to read out a statement declaring peace in the north of Iraq on the basis of his government's recognition of the Kurds' right to national autonomy within the framework of the Iraqi state. The Kurds, it was declared, were as fundamental a nationality in Iraq as the Arabs. A Kurd was named vice president; five others became ministers in the government in Baghdad. This was the first time in history that any of this had happened.

The document that came to be known as the "11 March 1970 program" was welcomed rapturously throughout Iraq. Thousands of Kurdish bonfires were lit on the hills around Kirkuk. During a mass celebration of the declaration of peace, the ceremonial podium on Baghdad's at-Takhrir Square was like an island amid a sea of people. On that podium, alongside Iraq's President al-Bakr and Saddam Hussein, stood Mustafa Barzani's sons Idris and Massoud, dressed in their national costume, and Dr. Mahmoud.

Sadly, however, relations with the government in Baghdad began to deteriorate after a while. Once again, the threat of another war began to loom on the horizon.

FAREWELL TO KURDISTAN

It was against this backdrop that I made yet another trip to northern Iraq. Before I departed I met with Saddam Hussein in Baghdad, on January 22, 1973. It was he who urged me to see Barzani, saying that the Kurdish leader would not understand if I failed to see him, after a three-year interval, during my visit to Iraq. "It is in our interest that he doesn't think the Soviet Union has lost interest in him," Saddam told me. "We highly value your influence on him." A plane would be made available to fly me to Kirkuk, and then a helicopter to reach Rawanduz, he added.

I return to my notes: In Rawanduz, the snow was knee-deep. A car met me, and I was driven in stages. The first leg of the relay took me to a *peshmerga* checkpoint. The driver, a Kurd, had come right into the heart of an Iraqi military camp to pick us up, but this did not point to any absence of friction—far from it. At the first Kurdish checkpoint there was a barrier and an armed guard, just like in the days before the peace deal. We arrived at a small settlement. At one house were Idris and Massoud; I sensed that Idris was agitated. This became even more apparent once Barzani arrived. We spoke Russian for several hours, a language Idris did not understand. I was told, in confidence, that Idris had been in contact with the Iranians, so I was not surprised when he told me "there was no sign that Baghdad had any intention of implementing the agreement."

Two developments had especially soured relations between Barzani and Saddam at that time. I was told of the first by Mustafa Barzani himself. A group of sheikhs had come to see him. He had received them in his tent, while the driver of the minibus that had brought them stayed with his vehicle. One of the sheikhs had asked if he could record their conversation on a portable tape recorder (in those days, a "portable" weighed several kilograms). But the tape recorder had been packed with explosives and the driver—a member of Iraqi special forces—used a remote control to detonate it. The bomb went off. Barzani's life was saved only by the fact that one of the *peshmerga* was leaning over him serving coffee; his body had shielded Barzani, and he died in the blast. "Those stupid bodyguards of mine shot all the sheikhs and the driver, so there was no one to interrogate," Barzani said. "But I'm sure Saddam Hussein was behind it."

The second aggravating factor related to Barzani's eldest son, Abeydulla. Back when I first visited him, Barzani had told me he had detained Abeydulla and intended to shoot him because he had "revealed to our enemies the route by which we receive supplies of materials." I said that perhaps Abeydulla had not acted with hostile intent, but by mistake; I don't know if my words had any effect, but Abeydulla was allowed to live. In fact, when he came down with appendicitis, they let him go to Baghdad. Once there, Abeydulla never returned, and all appeals to the Iraqi authorities to send him back remained unanswered.[1]

The Iraqi government was particularly concerned (as was the Kremlin, I must admit) by Barzani's growing ties with the shah's regime in Iran—a relationship that the United States had done much to foster. There was also reliable evidence of trips to Tel Aviv by Barzani emissaries. Israel, in its efforts to exploit the Kurdish problem in Iraq and thereby weaken its potential adversary, had sent money to the Kurdish movement, albeit in relatively small amounts. When I asked Barzani directly about the nature of his relations with the shah of Iran, he replied: "I knocked on one door, asking for bread, and was turned away [a reference to Baghdad]. What am I supposed to do, starve to death? So I knocked on another door. Who's to blame? Me or the one that turned me away?" Nor did Barzani deny receiving arms from Iran, his explanation being that he himself would not initiate a war but he had to be prepared to defend himself.

We sat with Barzani until night fell. When he left, accompanied by a convoy of bodyguards' cars, Dr. Mahmoud and I prepared to retire for the night. As we did so, he asked me directly to try to persuade Barzani to mend his fences with Baghdad. We took a stroll, escorted by two guards with machine guns, our feet sinking in the snow. We then walked back to go to bed. My notes bring the scene back to me vividly: It's cold; the guard is adding fuel to the stove. Each time he throws in a log, he opens a window so we don't suffocate in the fumes. I keep waking up because of the cold, even though I'm sleeping in a thick woolen outfit.

AMERICA AND THE KURDISH FACTOR

In 1975, war once more broke out between the Kurds and the Iraqi government. One year earlier, in 1974, the regime in Baghdad had passed law No. 33 on the creation of an autonomous Kurdish region. The law had had a hostile reception from Barzani, as it came at a time when Kurdish families in the area around Kirkuk were being forcibly resettled and replaced by Iraqi Arabs. But the Kurdish uprising did not in any way equate to a campaign to secede from Iraq. So long as the Kurds regarded themselves as Iraqis there was a chance of reaching an agreement with them. This remained the case during the Iran-Iraq War—even when, in its closing stages, the Kurds were subjected to savage attacks by the Iraqi army, using chemical weapons.

Even when the regime in Baghdad was weakened and incapable of putting up any decisive resistance, the Iraqi Kurds never raised the question of secession—for example, after Iraq's defeat in the Gulf War, or when its most battle worthy forces were deployed in the south to put down the Shiite uprising. This remained the case even after the Kurds established control over the entire Kurdish-populated territory, which included Mosul, Arbil, Suleimaniya, and, for a while, Kirkuk. It should be noted that the question of seceding from Iraq didn't even come up after the UN Security Council's decision in 1991 to impose a security zone north of the 36th parallel, an area from which Iraqi troops were withdrawn entirely. This led to the first elections to the National Council and the formation of a Kurdish government. Even then, there was no campaign to break away from Iraq; only to bring full autonomy to Kurdistan. That was the Kurdish movement's policy, and it was supported by the Soviet Union—and later by the Russian Federation—which was well aware of the dire consequences that might ensue should Iraq ever break up.

The period following 2003's U.S. military operation against Iraq did, however, instill a fairly strong separatist mood in the Kurdish movement. It strikes me that the United States was faced with a dilemma: either it could encourage such sentiment and thereby defeat Iraq for good by breaking it up into its constituent parts or it could do what it indeed aimed to do, which was to preserve Iraqi Kurdistan as part of a wider state, in the hope of being able to rely on the Kurds to fight for U.S. interests. Moreover, if the Americans had encouraged the Kurds to establish an independent state, it could have brought the United States into serious disagreement with its NATO ally Turkey.

All the way back in the second half of the 1960s, there had been discord and then a complete split in the Kurdish nationalist movement over the issue of autonomy or outright independence. On my first visit to Iraqi Kurdistan in 1966, KDP general secretary Habib

Mohammad Karim told me Jalal Talabani (the current president of Iraq) had been expelled from the party, along with a group of people close to him, for "engaging in subversive activities." Talabani disbanded his group after the signing of the "11 March 1970 program" and returned to the KDP.

The Kurdish armed uprising against law No. 33 was crushed by Baghdad; Barzani managed to escape to Iran and then to the United States, where he died in 1979. Talabani, meanwhile, quit the KDP once more.

From the second half of the 1970s onward, there were two rival political forces in Kurdistan: the KDP, now headed by Massoud Barzani, and the Patriotic Union of Kurdistan (PUK), founded by Talabani. There was no rapprochement between the two forces (although you might have expected the Iran-Iraq War to draw them together) right up until the mid-1990s. In fact, fierce clashes between Barzani's KDP militias and those of Talabani's PUK broke out in the early 1980s. Only after the Kurds had suffered heavy defeats at the hands of the Iraqi army did they enter negotiations. In 1992, they divided all the seats in the Kurdish parliament between them equally, and formed a "coalition government." But this did not stop the two factions from fighting.

In 1998 the United States sponsored an accord between Barzani and Talabani, for which the two leaders flew to Washington, but even that did not help matters. It was a blatantly anti-Saddam initiative on the part of the United States, which naturally regarded a strong Kurdistan as an effective counterweight to Baghdad. But in reality there were two de facto governments in Iraqi Kurdistan right up until 2002. It was only at the end of 2002—in other words, shortly before the United States launched its military operation against Iraq—that a single government finally took shape. Despite that government's support for the U.S. operation against Saddam's regime, both Barzani and Talabani issued warnings about the consequences of the American intervention.

In local operations against the Iraqi army, the *peshmerga* fought alongside the Americans. In March 2004 the two main Kurdish factions organized a conference in the town of Salah ed-Din to discuss a

pan-Kurdish peace settlement. The Kurds played a central role in the
United States's efforts to set up a provisional government in Baghdad
and draft a new constitution. Jalal Talabani ended up as president of
Iraq, with the agreement that Massoud Barzani would be the leader
of Iraqi Kurdistan.

Yet none of this points to a resolution of the Kurdish question in
Iraq, nor does it mean that the United States can safely rely on the
"Kurdish factor," especially after it pulls its troops out of the country.
Barzani's forces still control the mountainous part of Iraqi Kurdistan—
the provinces of Arbil and Dohuk—while Talabani's forces dominate in the ravine territory of Suleimaniya. There has not been, in
reality, any merging of armed Kurdish forces. Barzani has some fifteen thousand soldiers under his command, plus twice that number
in tribal militias. Talabani's forces are fewer in number. A united
Democratic Patriotic Union of Kurdistan was set up just before the
Iraqi parliamentary elections in 2005, but this was probably just a
tactical maneuver that enabled the Kurds to get seventy-six seats in
the national legislature. A process of "reverse migration" is underway too: Arab families who were settled in the area near Kirkuk
under the previous regime are either being resettled elsewhere or
leaving of their own accord. No one objected when Kirkuk was
made the capital of Iraqi Kurdistan.

In early 2004 the Kurds gathered 1.7 million signatures calling for
a referendum on Kurdistan's independence, and sent them to the UN.
Meanwhile Iraqi Arabs are increasingly uncomfortable with the out-
size role that the Kurds are playing in the national government. In the
end, it is unlikely that centuries of stalemate in relations within Kurdistan or between the Kurds and Baghdad will be overcome in the
near future.

A Nuclear Shadow Over the Arab-Israeli Conflict

Y THE MIDDLE OF THE first decade of the twenty-first century, Iran's nuclear program had provoked a great deal of attention, mistrust, and alarm. Despite Iran's repeated insistences that its nuclear activities are for peaceful purposes only, the United States and Israel have declared that they would be willing to use force to prevent Tehran from getting its hands on nuclear weapons. There are ample grounds to suspect that Iran has been seeking to do just what it's been accused of—a threat that is only aggravated by the irresponsible pronouncements of its leader. Still, the vast majority of countries object to the use of force against Iran. In this chapter I will look at the Iranian nuclear problem, paying special attention to an issue that usually goes unmentioned in discussions of this sort: the existence of a state in the Middle East that already has nuclear weapons—weapons that were built with overt assistance from several Western states and the silent collusion of others. I am talking, of course, about Israel.

The danger of a nuclear-armed Israel is that it has been, and still is, deeply involved in virtually all of the conflicts that have roiled the Middle East. Furthermore, there is reason to believe that its leadership views its nuclear weapons as tactical assets—not just a means of projecting strength or defensive measures to keep in check those countries that pose a threat to Israel's existence, to be used only in the worst extremities. This was especially clear to see during the 1973 Yom

Kippur War. According to *Time* magazine, thirteen Israeli atom bombs were transported from their desert hiding places to a secret underground tunnel during the war and, in the space of seventy-eight hours, hastily readied for use. To protect their arsenal—and their secret—the Israelis were even willing to shoot down a U.S. surveillance plane. *Time* describes how Israeli fighters were sent to intercept and open fire on a U.S. air force SR-71 Blackbird, which nonetheless evaded them by climbing to an altitude they could not reach, and returned safely to base with its "important data."

The fact that Israel possessed nuclear weapons was not news for the Americans; Russia knew it too. But the fact that a scenario had arisen in which Israel was prepared to use them against Egypt and Syria was earth-shattering. Meanwhile it was difficult, if not impossible, to predict whether Israel would maintain its regional monopoly on the possession of nuclear weapons. The frightening prospect of nuclear proliferation appears to be one of the reasons why a significant sector, if not the overwhelming majority, of Israeli society, was hostile to the manufacture of nuclear arms for so long. Back in the days of David Ben-Gurion's government, six out of seven members of the Israeli Atomic Energy Commission (IAEC) resigned and spoke out publicly when they found out that an atomic energy program that was supposedly dedicated to peaceful purposes had secret military objectives. Not just world opinion but Israeli public opinion forced Ben-Gurion and his successors to keep Israel's nuclear program under wraps from then on.

But by the beginning of the twenty-first century, the situation had changed: there is reason to believe that most Israelis now *do* approve of the fact that their country is a nuclear power. This shift has been brought about by years of deadlock in the Arab-Israeli conflict and by the possibility that Iran might have access to nuclear arms. This shift in public opinion must also have been influenced by a potent psychological factor: the fact that so many terrorist acts have been carried out on Israeli soil.

Even so, no legitimate arguments can be made to support Israel's possession of nuclear arms. After all, the wars it fought against the Arab nations were won with conventional weapons, and the battle against terrorism does not require a nuclear capability. As for those Middle East states that *could* get their hands on nuclear weapons in the future, eventually posing a threat to Israel, only the "official" nuclear powers—the United States, Russia, Britain, France, and China—can deter them, not a nuclear-armed Israel. Indeed, rather than having any serious deterrent effect on potential nuclear powers, Israel's possession of nuclear weapons has demonstrably dragged the region into a nuclear arms race.

WHO HELPED ISRAEL BUILD THE BOMB?

Though the United States and Britain were all too aware of Israel's nuclear ambitions, they did not back its efforts at an official level. France was an exception at first, but only temporarily. On an *unofficial* level, however, the picture was very different.

Immediately after the state of Israel was founded, geologists began to look for uranium on Israeli soil. At the same time, Israel began to develop the technology for producing heavy water. When a small percentage of uranium was discovered to be present in phosphates, a process was devised for extracting it as a by-product of the manufacture of phosphoric acid. An industrial facility to do just that was inaugurated at the beginning of the 1950s in Nahal Soreq, south of Tel Aviv. A group of Israeli scientists were sent abroad—to the United States, the Netherlands, Switzerland, and Britain—to specialize in nuclear research. Between 1955 and 1960, fifty-six Israeli specialists underwent training at the Argonne and Oak Ridge National Laboratories in the United States. When the atom-bomb scientists returned, the department of nuclear physics at the Weizmann Institute in Rehovot took full advantage of their newly acquired expertise.

Israel's nuclear collaboration with France began in 1953. In exchange for data on its technology for producing heavy water and extracting uranium from phosphates, Israel was allowed to familiarize itself with France's nuclear program and take part in atomic tests in the Sahara. Encouraged by preliminary results from this collaboration, and with staunch backing from Moshe Dayan and Shimon Peres, his two closest and most important advisers, Ben-Gurion approved a top-secret decision to "develop an independent Israeli nuclear deterrent."[1] This occurred straight after the withdrawal of Israeli troops from Sinai, which had been occupied during the tripartite invasion of Egypt in 1956. Apart from Dayan and Peres, Ben-Gurion did not inform even the members of his own cabinet of his decision.

Acting on Ben-Gurion's personal orders, Peres held a series of secret talks with French government officials in the autumn of 1957. These led to an agreement at the beginning of October that year, under which France would supply Israel with a heavy water reactor fueled by natural uranium, along with assistance in building a scientific research center. Ground was broken on this top secret construction process shortly afterwards at Dimona, in the Negev Desert.

The Americans too had a hand in Israel's nuclear program. In 1957 and 1958 the conservative counterespionage machine of the CIA, headed by James Jesus Angleton, arranged for a number of nuclear scientists to work in Israel. It is easy to reach the conclusion that the CIA was also engaged in a cover-up operation: the U.S. specialists who visited Dimona on several occasions in the 1960s publicly stated that the reactor would be used only for peaceful purposes.

Along with the Dimona reactor—which had always been intended to produce plutonium—the Americans helped the Israelis to build a small reactor in Nahal Soreq under the U.S. "Atoms for Peace" program. The Nahal Soreq reactor achieved criticality in June 1960. Over the course of the next six years, the United States supplied 50 kilograms of highly enriched uranium to keep it working. It was claimed that Nahal Soreq had no direct military applications, but experts believe its reactor opened up a range of possibilities for experimental scientists and engineers involved in "Israel's nuclear deterrent." A complex of buildings grew up around the reactor housing a scientific center devoted to laboratory-based research, some of it military.

The development of an "Israeli nuclear deterrent" was affected by events in France. When President de Gaulle returned to power, he decided to steer France toward a more balanced Middle East policy, and therefore sought to improve relations with the Arab nations. This necessarily meant changes in France's nuclear collaboration with Israel. At Paris's insistence, Ben-Gurion was forced to publicly acknowledge the existence of the reactor at Dimona and to give assurances that it would not be used to manufacture nuclear weapons. However, his forced statement to the Knesset on December 21, 1960, did not reflect the facts. In January 1961, prime minister Ben-Gurion told the U.S. ambassador that he would not agree to foreign inspections of the Dimona nuclear center. He did, admittedly, tell the ambassador that he was willing to allow the Americans to visit the facility from time to time, but only after speculation about Israel's "nuclear deterrent" had died down in the foreign press. At the time, newspapers from almost every Western country were filled with stories about Israel's quest for nuclear arms.

Work on developing nuclear arms slowed down—but did not stop altogether—after Ben-Gurion was replaced as Israeli prime minister and defense minister by Levi Eshkol. Two powerful figures in Eshkol's cabinet were Yigal Allon and military chief of staff Yitzhak Rabin, both of whom believed that work on nuclear weapons was diverting enormous financial resources that could have been better spent on conventional arms. Their views might have pressured Eshkol (who had previously been finance minister and was well aware of the cost of the Israeli nuclear project) into his decision to allow American inspectors to visit Dimona in exchange for President Lyndon B. Johnson's agreement to supply Israel with a sizeable shipment of conventional weaponry, including Skyhawk attack aircraft and Patton tanks.

However, it was during Eshkol's premiership that West Germany would make its appearance on Israel's "nuclear scene." In 1968 a secret deal was brokered between the two countries, in which Israel supplied West Germany with laser technology for uranium enrichment plus a payment of $3.7 million. In return, Germany sent 200 tons of uranium to Israel. This cargo was delivered in a most peculiar manner: the uranium was loaded onto a freighter, the *Scheersberg*, in containers marked "European Atomic Energy Community." But then, in the middle of the Mediterranean, a group of Mossad agents came aboard and transferred the *Scheersberg*'s cargo to another ship that was bound for Israel.

JOHNSON GAGS THE CIA

Operation Plumbat was carried out after the United States had ceased supplying Israel with enriched uranium, casting doubt on the future of the Israeli nuclear program. America withdrew its assistance after the United States Atomic Energy Commission discovered a discrepancy between the amount of highly enriched uranium the U.S. government had supplied to Numec (Israel's Nuclear Materials and Equipment Corporation) between April 1964 and November 1965 and the goods that the company had delivered to the end-user.[2]

Questions were asked about fissionable materials periodically going missing, but the answers were not so complicated: Numec was officially presented as an agency for technical consultation and training of specialists for Israel in the United States.

In December 1977, Carl Duckett, deputy head of the CIA's science and technology directorate from 1967 through 1976, testified before a closed session of the Nuclear Regulatory Commission. Duckett admitted that Israel had made great strides in its nuclear weapons program during those same months that enriched uranium had gone missing from Numec. According to the CIA's own assessment of Israel's nuclear capability, he said, Israel had possessed usable weapons as early as 1968. CIA director Richard Helms had passed this information onto President Johnson at the time—Johnson asked for it to be kept secret.

Israel's nuclear program continued at full speed under Golda Meir, who took over as prime minister in 1969 after Eshkol's death. The two most passionate supporters of the program, Dayan and Peres, joined her cabinet. Before taking over the premiership after Meir and Dayan stepped down, Rabin had been ambassador in Washington for five years. During those years he clearly belonged to the camp that thought that Israel's independent nuclear doctrine did not help its relations with the United States. However, once Rabin became prime minister he apparently changed his views, because he did nothing to halt the development of Israel's independent nuclear deterrent.

This was amply demonstrated in 1976, when Israeli fighter jets shot down a Libyan passenger airliner that had lost its bearings and—

so it seemed to Israeli ground control services—was heading for the Dimona nuclear reactor. In April of that same year South African prime minister B. J. Vorster paid a visit to Israel, where he signed a military, scientific, and technical partnership agreement, which formed the basis for plans to conduct joint Israeli-South African nuclear tests in the Kalahari desert. One such test, scheduled for the summer of 1977, was scrapped in the face of worldwide protests. But two years later, by which time Menachem Begin had taken over as Israeli prime minister, a nuclear explosion near the South African coast was detected by an American satellite. Despite the best efforts of the U.S. administration to keep it hushed up, the secret was revealed three months later by a former State Department official who had gone to work for ABC television. On February 22, 1980, a correspondent for CBS television news also confirmed that Israel had carried out nuclear tests with the cooperation of the South African government.

The U.S. Congress, of course, had passed the Symington-Glenn Amendment to ban U.S. arms supplies to countries seeking to develop nuclear weapons. Yet those restrictions were never enforced when it came to Israel, even though Israel's nuclear ambitions—and achievements—were common knowledge. In 1974 the CIA confirmed that Israel had indeed produced nuclear weapons. Just one year later, in July 1975, the U.S. Department of Defense announced that it would supply Israel with two hundred surface-to-surface Lance missiles, which were capable of carrying nuclear as well as conventional warheads. Around that same time, Israel took delivery of a large number of F-15 and F-16 warplanes, also capable of carrying nuclear bombs.

TARGETING IRAQ IN A BATTLE FOR MONOPOLY

When Menachem Begin's government swept to power after the Likud party's victory in the 1977 elections, it introduced yet another dimension to Israel's so-called nuclear deterrent: it sought to guarantee that Israel would keep its monopoly on nuclear weapons in the region. Iraq found itself in Israel's gunsights, even after the International

Atomic Energy Agency attested that its atomic reactor, which had been built with French assistance, had not been adapted to produce the raw materials needed to build nuclear weapons.

This is how events unfolded:

- On April 4, 1979, three "tourists" carrying European passports turned up in the French Mediterranean port of Toulon. They were joined two days later by four more "tourists," and the group set off in a pair of small trucks for the nearby town of La Seyne-sur-Mer, home to the CNIM Industries warehouses used to store reactor parts due to be shipped to Iraq. The facilities were later torn apart by an explosion.
- On June 13, 1980, Egyptian nuclear scientist Dr. Yahya al-Meshad was found assassinated in the Meridien Hotel in Paris. He had been regarded as one of the best scientists in the Arab world, and he had worked on the nuclear reactor in Iraq.
- On August 7, 1980, bombs exploded near the headquarters of Italian company SNIA-Techint and at the home of its managing director Mario Fiorelli in Rome. The company had earlier agreed to take part in the building of Iraq's nuclear reactor.
- On July 7, 1981, eight Israeli F-16 warplanes, escorted by six F-16 fighter jets, breached Jordanian and Saudi airspace to fly into Iraq and launch strikes on the nuclear reactor, which had not yet been put into service.

In carrying out this raid Begin had not only flouted international law and the United Nations Charter, he had also managed to put Egypt's President Sadat—his counterpart in the Camp David peace process—in a very difficult position. Sadat had met with Begin just a few days before the so-called Operation Babylon (also known as Operation Opera) was carried out. I am fairly sure that Sadat had not been informed of the planned operation—the risk of failure was too high to allow Begin to be so open about it. But true or not, in the Arab world it was widely believed that Sadat had been fully apprised of this Israeli operation in advance.

But if Sadat was most likely left in the dark, it is not logical to assume that the United States had been similarly benighted. Israel would not have dared to blindside Washington, especially as the raid affected U.S. interests—all the more so by flying through the airspace of two Arab states that were close U.S. allies. Circumstantial evidence supports the contention that Israel had shared its plans with Washington—and that the United States had tacitly acceded to them. By that time the United States had supplied Saudi Arabia with its first consignment of AWACS system aircraft, piloted by U.S. personnel. But for some reason they failed to detect any Israeli planes flying towards the Iraqi capital on that July 7.

There was strong international condemnation of the Israeli raid, some of it from countries friendly to the United States. Washington voiced its condemnation too, and even made a point of canceling a shipment of fighter jets that it was contractually bound to deliver to Israel—although once the dust had settled, the aircraft were delivered anyway.

There were further advances in Israel's nuclear program, and they continue to this day. The Israeli nuclear scientist Mordechai Vanunu, who spent fifteen years in prison in Israel for exposing his country's nuclear secrets to the world, said his sense of alarm "mounted" when he realized "just how many nuclear arms Israel was producing." At the same time, and especially at the turn of the millennium, Israel adopted a hawkish anti-Iraq and anti-Iran policy, urging the United States to take decisive action against both countries that, it was said, were "on the threshold of acquiring nuclear weapons."

In Iraq's case, we now know the true story. The United States circumvented the United Nations to invade and occupy that country, its stated aim being to destroy the Iraqi nuclear arsenal that posed such a terrible threat to the world. Not content with the fact that UNSCOM inspectors had found neither nuclear weapons nor evidence that any were being produced, U.S. leaders said American military specialists would be sure to find them. But after many months of searching for weapons of mass destruction on Iraqi territory, the American weapons inspector David Kay, who headed the Iraq Survey Group, decided to resign. He appears to have done this so that he could come clean to the public. Two days later, in an interview with America's National Public Radio network, he admitted that "My summary view, based on what I've seen, is we're very unlikely to find large stockpiles of weapons. I don't think they exist."

Equally dramatic have been the events related to Iran's supposed nuclear program, which I will deal with in detail in the next section. Some cynics have sought to make political capital out of the Iranian situation by directing accusations at Russia. This trend has a long history. During my visit to Israel as Russia's foreign minister in 1997, I met with Israeli military intelligence's top brass, at their own suggestion. There I was told that Russian organizations were helping Iran to build a nuclear arsenal—they even handed me a list of the guilty parties. But our own investigations showed that the list had been plucked out of thin air: for example, the address of one of the "organizations" belonged to a student dormitory, while of one of the educational establishments that was accused of active collaboration was guilty only of allowing Iranian students to matriculate. As it happens, I was also given the same list—word for word—by top officials from the U.S. State Department.

I wanted to establish once and for all that those accusations were unfounded. By the time I received the U.S. list, I was serving as prime minister, so I asked Russia's Federal Security Service (the FSB) to find out whether it was possible that one of the Russian citizens involved in producing our own nuclear arms could have traveled to Iran in an individual capacity. The answer that came back was a convincing one: no Russians engaged in that kind of work had gone abroad at all. Of course, this did not mean no scientists or engineers had left Russia; but neither we, nor the Americans, nor the Israelis, had any concrete information about any of them being involved in building nuclear weapons in Iran.

SEEKING A WAY OUT OF THE MAZE

In 2004, UN secretary-general Kofi Annan set up the so-called "Wise Men's Group," tasked with producing recommendations for combating a range of threats, including homegrown ones. I was one of the sixteen members that Annan selected. The High-Level Group's report into international security warns: "We are fast approaching a point beyond which the erosion of the nuclear non-proliferation regime could become irreversible and open the floodgates in terms of proliferation." This was a warning of a very real danger, and one of the hotbeds of that danger could well be the Middle East, unless serious efforts were made to find a way out of the stalemate. One very serious obstacle to progress—as serious as Iran's refusal to co-operate with inspections—was Israel's refusal to sign up to the Nuclear Non-Proliferation Treaty or to comply with its obligation to place its nuclear facilities under the control of the International Atomic Energy Agency.

A session of the Wise Men's Group was held in July 2004 on the outskirts of Vienna, where the IAEA is based. On July 17 we were addressed by IAEA director-general Mohammed el-Baradei, with whom I spoke afterward. I was particularly keen to hear his impressions of his recent three-day visit to Israel, where he had met with then prime minister Ariel Sharon.

El-Baradei had not been allowed access to any of Israel's reactors on the grounds that Israel was not a signatory to the Nuclear Non-Proliferation Treaty—nor did it fall under the jurisdiction of the IAEA. He was optimistic, nevertheless, saying that Sharon had agreed in principle to open negotiations on the creation of a Middle East nuclear-free zone as part of the overall peace process in the region. It was, as el-Baradei said, a definite step forward by Israel, which has always insisted that it would not hold negotiations or even exchanges of dialogue about its nuclear weapons until a definitive peace with the Arabs had been achieved. The way they approached the issue had created a vicious circle—after all, it was Israel's possession of nuclear arms, among other things, that had made it so difficult to find a peaceful solution to the Arab-Israeli conflict. Israel's nuclear capability had goaded Arab and other Middle Eastern countries and organizations to seek ways of reducing their "handicap."

"Can we really infer from your meeting with Sharon that there has been a shift in Israel's nuclear policy?" I asked.

"We have at least persuaded Israel's government to promise to work jointly in the future on a plan for a nuclear-free Middle East," the IAEA chief replied.

We shall see what we shall see. Obviously Sharon is no longer in a position to carry out his promise.

The call to create a nuclear-free zone in the Middle East is even more relevant in a climate of escalating international terrorism, in which terrorist acts kill larger and larger numbers of innocent civilians. Of particular concern are efforts by international terrorists to get their hands on nuclear weapons. Most dangerous of all in this regard is the black market in nuclear materials, technology, and expertise. With the Middle East conflict becoming an "incubator" for terrorism, the expansion of this black market across its territory is especially perilous. This ought to encourage all of the states in the region—Israel included—to seek a path to a nuclear-free Middle East.

ISRAEL AND THE IRAN-CONTRA AFFAIR

Like other regions, the Middle East is no place to apply double standards. That ought to be a universal rule. And yet it can be seen throughout history—indeed in relatively recent history—that double standards are very much "in vogue." I refer to the Iran-Contra affair, which involved officials from both the United States and Israel. I have decided to dwell in some detail on this scandal, as it graphically illustrates the difference between what is done in the public eye and what is done behind the scenes in the Middle East.

After the shah's regime was toppled in January 1979, relations between the United States and Iran deteriorated severely. In November that year, staff at the American embassy in Tehran were taken hostage. The United States responded by breaking off diplomatic relations, imposing a trade embargo, and freezing Iranian deposits in U.S. banks. The trade embargo was lifted after the American hostages were released in January 1981, but the ban on selling arms to Iran remained in force.

The U.S. national security adviser at that time was Robert McFarlane, who had pressed for covert operations against Iran. But since

SAVAK, the shah's security service, had been dismantled, the U.S. intelligence community had virtually no reliable contacts in Tehran. Even so, the Americans made a risky attempt to gain influence over the Iranian leadership by secretly providing Iran with arms from the United States. One of the main objectives behind this operation was to secure the release of American citizens who were being held hostage in Lebanon by the militant Islamic group Hizbollah, which had close ties to Iran.

Two staffers at the U.S. National Security Council, Donald Fortier and Howard Teacher, had prepared a draft directive making the case that the United States needed to build bridges with Iran. It subsequently emerged during hearings of the Congressional committee set up to investigate the Iran-Contra affair that their directive had never been submitted to President Reagan for his signature. At the last minute, they'd decided that their scheme was too risky—and too politically explosive—to go through official channels. Then Israel (another one of Iran's ostensible enemies) came forward to offer its services and became the main conduit through which Iran was secretly supplied with illegal arms.

Israel was, of course, pursuing its own objectives, which were primarily—but far from exclusively—commercial. Shimon Peres (who was no longer Israel's prime minister by the time the scandal emerged) had sought to strengthen his country's relations with the United States by demonstrating its indispensability for carrying out covert operations in the Middle East. Israel's other objective, as paradoxical as it sounds, was to build bridges with the Islamic regime in Iran. The Israeli leadership knew that it could never restore the deep-seated and far-reaching ties it had enjoyed with the shah, but that didn't stop it from seeking to establish contact with Iran's new Islamic regime. Why else, from January 1985 onward, would Peres have brought together arms dealers Adolph "Al" Schwimmer and Ya'acov Nimrodi, as well as Israeli foreign ministry director-general David Kimche, for a number of secret meetings? It was during these meetings that a proposal was worked out under which Iran would be supplied with American-built TOW (tube-launched optically tracked wire-to-command-link) antitank missiles and Hawk antiaircraft missiles from Israel's own arsenal. To make up the shortfall left by the missiles supplied to Iran, Israel would be guaranteed additional arms supplies from the United States. I would like to stress that Israeli officials cooked up this scheme on their own initiative.

The plan was put into action without delay: Schwimmer got in touch with the Saudi millionaire Adnan Khashoggi, who was appointed the deal's financier. Manucher Ghorbanifar, a former SAVAK agent, was asked to act as the middle man between Iran and Israel. In May 1985, Peres himself met with Michael Ledeen, a consultant to the U.S. National Security Council, and an NSC deputy director named Lieutenant Colonel Oliver North, who was later indicted and convicted for his part in the arms deal, which contravened a whole range of U.S. laws. According to Ledeen, Peres asked him to tell McFarlane that Israel was prepared to sell arms to Iran so long as the government of the United States did not object. There were no such objections.

On July 13, 1985, McFarlane met with Schwimmer in Washington, after which he recommended to President Reagan that he call a select meeting of the National Security Planning Group, which was only convened to discuss the most sensitive, top secret matters. Its members were Secretary of State George Shultz, Defense Secretary Caspar Weinberger, CIA director William J. Casey, Vice President George Bush Sr., McFarlane, and his deputy Admiral John Poindexter. Several days later, Reagan phoned McFarlane to tell him that he agreed to Israel selling the arms requested by Iran and to Israel being reimbursed accordingly. The U.S. Congress was not informed of any of this.

On August 20, Ledeen met Kimche in London and gave him a secret code with which he could communicate directly with McFarlane, the U.S. national security adviser. Within ten days the first shipment of 100 TOW antitank missiles was delivered to Iran. But instead of ordering Hizbollah to release the hostages, Iran demanded an additional 400 missiles. Israel agreed to the sale. On September 14, 408 more American-made missiles were delivered to the Iranian city of Tebriz. The next day the Reverend Benjamin Weir, who had been taken hostage in Iran, was released. Defense Secretary Weinberger gave the order to reimburse Israel for the missiles it had sent to Iran.

In September and October of 1985, North and Ledeen met with Schwimmer, Nimrodi, and Ghorbanifar in Washington and numerous European cities. Once he had taken stock of the outcome of these meetings, Israel's Kimche put a proposal to McFarlane for a third shipment to be sent from Israel to Iran—this time Hawk antiaircraft missiles. It was at this time that Yitzhak Rabin, then Israel's defense minister, also became involved in the deal—although to be fair, his main concern was making sure that Israel was reimbursed with supplies of U.S. missiles.

The Americans were not completely satisfied with all this, as several hostages still remained in captivity. Most importantly, they had not managed to establish reliable contact with any of Iran's leaders. The U.S. National Security Council decided to take the entire matter into its own hands.

When McFarlane resigned on November 30, he was replaced as Reagan's national security adviser by his deputy, Admiral Poindexter. Not wishing to be sidelined in the operation, on January 2, 1986, the Israelis presented Poindexter with a new idea devised by Amiram Nir, the Israeli prime minister's antiterrorism (!) adviser. The idea was that Israel would hand over twenty Hizbollah militants who had been captured by pro-Israeli Lebanese forces in the south of Lebanon to Iran, along with another 400 TOW antitank missiles. In exchange, Hizbollah would release all of the American hostages in its possession. Unbelievably, the plan did not envisage Hizbollah calling a halt to its shelling of Northern Galilee—apparently the Israeli leadership did not want the deal to be weighed down with conditions. The Americans signed on.

The prisoners were duly handed over. The first shipment of TOW antitank missiles was flown from Eilat to the Iranian city of Bender-Abbas on an Israeli aircraft on February 18, while the second shipment was delivered on February 27. Still none of the hostages were released. The Israeli conduit had not worked. An American delegation was sent to Tehran, headed by McFarlane, who was now acting in the capacity of a "private individual." One member of the delegation, designated by the Israeli prime minister as his representative, was Amiram Nir, who was passed off as an American in Tehran. A trip to London followed, and there were long, drawn-out negotiations in other cities too. Eventually, a Lebanese newspaper published a report on McFarlane's trip to Iran, and a storm of indignation broke out in the United States. Then a different side to the deal started to emerge, one that the Israeli government had also been aware of: money from the sale of missiles to Iran was being illegally diverted to the Contras in Nicaragua (who, like Iran, were under an arms ban).

The revelations began to snowball. In December 1986, Reagan broadcast an address to the nation in which he admitted mistakes had been "allowed to happen" in relation to Iran. Oliver North and John Poindexter resigned their positions and a special commission chaired by Senator John Tower was set up to investigate the methods used and the part played by the National Security Council "in the conduct of foreign policy and national security policy." The Congressional hearings into the Iran-Contra affair lasted nearly three months. In Israel, no investigations were carried out whatsoever. Yet in 1992, two weeks before he stepped down as U.S. president, George Bush Sr. pardoned every American official who was responsible for the fiasco.

– 19 –

THE FUTURE OF
THE MIDDLE EAST

A PESSIMIST, THEY SAY, is just an optimist who is well informed. But I would not wish to be classified as a pessimist, even if I do consider myself to be fairly well informed about the situation in the Middle East.

THE IRAQI TRAP

In a move that ran counter to all common sense, the Americans invaded Iraq in 2003. Before long, all the arguments that they had used to justify their actions collapsed. The American officials—who had vociferously insisted that now, *after* the occupation, U.S. military experts would find definitive proof that Iraq not only had nuclear weapons or was close to having them, but was manufacturing chemical and biological weapons of mass destruction—fell silent, their bluster replaced by a series of terse official statements that conceded that no weapons of mass destruction had been found, while the commission of U.S. military experts that had been set up to find them was quietly disbanded. U.S. politicians had declared for all to hear that Saddam Hussein's regime had established close ties with al-Qaeda. These were not abstract accusations but concrete ones—yet they too had no basis in reality. Though U.S. intelligence agencies had devoted all the means at their disposal to their efforts to confirm "Baghdad's links with international terrorism," no less a figure than CIA director George Tenet would testify before Congress that his agency had been able to find absolutely no links between Iraq and Osama bin Laden and his organization. In other words, it had all been a red herring, another pretext for the U.S. invasion that turned out to be as insubstantial as a soap bubble.

The American invasion actually helped fuel the spread of terrorism. The armed forces the United States sent into Iraq had been drawn away from Afghanistan, al-Qaeda's main stronghold. International terrorism always operates opportunistically, filling in the power vacuums left by instability and conflict, as in Afghanistan, the Balkans, and Chechnya. Now thousands of militant fighters are infiltrating Iraq from the lawless tribal areas between Afghanistan and Pakistan. Having established a foothold in Iraq, al-Qaeda has simultaneously gone on the attack against several Arab and non-Arab regimes: Saudi Arabia, Turkey, and Kuwait. The effectiveness of the global fight against terrorism was also, at least for a while, weakened by the inevitable opposition to the U.S. invasion from a large number of countries, some of them major players on the international scene.

Once the United States could no longer plausibly claim that Saddam Hussein had had secret access to weapons of mass destruction or links to al-Qaeda, it increasingly sought to justify its actions by insisting that it was embarking on a mission to spread democracy—and not just to Iraq but to all of the countries of the Middle East. This was an American model of democracy that had pretty much nothing in common with the historic or religious traditions of the Arab nations, nor even with their present-day socioeconomic situations or ways of thinking. Of course, the Middle East is not cut off from the rest of the world; it has been subject to changes in technology as well as to the influence of the general tide of democracy. None of those things can be denied, but neither do they make a convincing case for trying to dress the Middle East (and other parts of the world too) in a democratic suit cut entirely from American cloth. From the outside looking in, the blunders of the United States's own brand of democracy are all too evident, as is its complete unsuitability for being imposed across the board. One size does not fit all. This is not to single out the United States—the same clearly applies to other countries' democratic models too.

The Wise Men's Group (see chapter 18) convened by Kofi Anan unanimously agreed that it was crucial to act against such destructive developments as were occurring, or alleged to be occurring, in Iraq, such as the mass killings of the civilian population, the accelerated push toward acquiring nuclear weapons, and the prospect of the governing regime opening its territory to international terrorist organizations and sharing its weapons of mass destruction with them. However, the existence of such a "homegrown" threat should not be exposed by any one state, acting unilaterally, but only collectively through the UN Security Council after a thorough and objective vetting of the accusations. First and foremost, the wheat should have been separated from the chaff, where Iraq was concerned. And then the Security Council—not the United States and a handful of its allies—should have formulated a system of measures to neutralize whatever threats were proven to exist.

Instead of a concerted, collective response to a clear and present danger, the world found itself up against a situation where one state accused another of having an antidemocratic regime—but instead of stopping at those accusations, it took upon itself to interfere in that sovereign state's domestic matters, using military force to topple a regime that was not to its liking. It's one thing to weigh up a country's homegrown threat to peace and security, but it is quite a different matter to try to impose this or that type of state or social structure on it, whether it wants it or not. It is well known that the Trotskyites used to think it was not only possible but essential to export the revolution to any and all countries, regardless of whether or not the conditions for fostering the process of revolution were present. Those who imagine that democracy can be exported to any country, regardless of its history, its traditions, its way of thinking, its worldview, and its way of life are carrying on rather like the Trotskyites did in their day.

So how have things turned out in Iraq now that America has exported its democracy there? When U.S. troops invaded, Iraq was a secular state, and while I do not wish in any way to condone Saddam Hussein's regime, with the many errors and crimes it committed, it cannot be accused of failing to establish stability on the religious front. After the U.S. occupation, Iraq became a faith-based state, governed according to the Islamic model. Islam is one of the great world religions; it is followed by a large proportion of the earth's population, and has made a major contribution to world civilization. But in a modern setting, a state built on the basis of faith—be it Islam, Christianity, or Judaism—and with all its branches of power run along theological lines, can hardly be said to be on the road to democracy.

On December 15, 2005, elections were held for Iraq's national parliament. Out of 275 parliamentary seats, the Shiite-dominated United Iraqi Alliance won 128, the Democratic Patriotic Alliance of Kurdistan won 53, the Sunni-dominated Iraqi Accord Front and Iraqi National Dialogue Front won 44 and 11 seats respectively, while the Iraqi National List coalition led by Iyad Allawi, who was prime minister in the interim government, won 25 seats. Nine seats were divided among the remaining parties. Two conclusions could be drawn about the composition of the parliament: (1) Shiites were now in a dominant position, and (2) Iraq was heading in a direction where it would take on the attributes of an Islamic state.

What's more, Iraq had been a fairly cohesive state until the U.S.-led occupation. There had been a long-standing Kurdish problem, with the Kurds in the north of Iraq demanding and winning autonomy, but continuing to wage war because they were not satisfied with the ways that their hard-won autonomy was actually put into practice. In those days, however, the Iraqi Kurds were not fighting to break away from Iraq. After the U.S. occupation, Iraq found itself on the brink of disintegration and the verge of civil war. Shiites and Sunnis were blowing up each others' mosques—they were, after all, fighting on religious grounds—and for the first time in recent years, there were sustained gun battles between Shiite and Sunni forces. It is true that there had been Shiite uprisings before, but they were against the regime; the recent conflict is completely motivated by religion, a very different situation. Literally dozens of people are killed every day. Now many Shiites are demanding autonomy in the south of the country. That would be seriously detrimental to the cause of peace and freedom, and not only for Iraq—it would also weaken those who are campaigning to bring democracy to neighboring Iran.

The Kurdish issue also became the focus of renewed attention. The Kurds supported the United States when it sent its troops into Iraq, but not all Kurds share the same political allegiances. As shown earlier, Jalal Talabani, who became president of Iraq, has a very strained relationship with Massoud Barzani, the leader of the Kurdish autonomous region. Their "separation of functions" is no guarantee against the growing confrontation between the two Kurdish leaders; there is rivalry between them, and Barzani's supporters have always been on bad terms with Talabani's.

Perhaps most important of all, the mood in the north of Iraq is increasingly separatist. No matter how fair and just it may sound, the creation of a Kurdish independent state would mean having to redraw the map, and the Turks have already said that if that were to happen, they would send *their* troops into northern Iraq. Even if the Kurds settle for autonomy, they are demanding that the area around Kirkuk, with its rich oilfields, be transferred to the territory of the Kurdish autonomous region—a continuing source of conflict with Iraq's Arab population.

When planning its operation against Iraq, the United States obviously took it for granted that the Iraqi people would welcome its occupying forces as liberators. Instead, their welcome quickly devolved into armed resistance, which has now become entrenched. Even compared with the hated regime in Baghdad, Iraqis regarded the foreign occupation of their country as the greater evil. The Americans thought the resistance would come to an end with the arrest of Saddam Hussein. That they were so wrong provides still more evidence that opposition to the occupation extends far beyond supporters of the deposed regime. Divided as they are, almost all Iraqis regard the foreign occupation of their country as an utterly unacceptable state of affairs.

All this has happened as a result of U.S. military adventurism in Iraq. Almost exactly three months before the invasion was launched, I spoke with Condoleezza Rice, who was the U.S. national security adviser at that time. "By invading Iraq, you'll be making a historic mistake," I told her. To which she replied: "Don't worry—firstly, there has not yet been any political decision, and secondly, if we do strike, we've thought it all through."

But it hadn't been thought through at all. When the Americans went into Iraq, the democratic model they took with them was basically the model that was introduced to West Germany after the downfall of Hitler's regime in the Second World War. In West Germany, of course, the Nazi Party was banned, as was only right and proper. In Iraq, the two-million-member Ba'ath Party—the only party to contain both Shiites and Sunnis, and Arabs and Kurds—was declared illegal. Eighty to 90 percent of its members were indifferent to its ideology; they had joined it purely for the sake of their careers. A select few from that party who were willing to break with their political pasts could have been chosen to spearhead whatever efforts were required to assure domestic stability. But that was not done. The army and the police were disbanded wholesale and by the time they were re-recruited and redeployed many opportunities had been missed along the way.

White House policy gave the impression that it was based on the assumption that the postwar reconstruction of Iraq would not present any particular difficulties. At first great hopes were pinned on the political exiles who had fled the country under Saddam. They were the ones who would steer the machinery of state and bring stability back to Iraq. The political exiles returned, but because of their constant infighting, not to mention their complete lack of popular support, they have had only an insignificant role in running the country.

When it became clear that the exiles were not making a difference, Washington took note of the fact that the insurgency was at its most intense in the "Sunni triangle." Its next strategy called upon the Iraqi Shiites for assistance in neutralizing the Sunnis. The Shiites, who make up the majority of Iraq's population, had been truly oppressed under Saddam. But there was growing resentment of the foreign occupation among the Shiite population too; resentment that found expression in the armed Shiite insurgency led by Muqtada al-Sadr in Fallujah and Nasiriyah.

Iraq went through the difficult process of adopting a provisional constitution, holding elections to parliament, and then forming interim and permanent governments before a framework for its power structure started to take shape. But it was a power structure built on unstable ground—an agreement of expediency between the Shiites and the Kurds. The Sunni element, accounting for 20 percent of the Iraqi population (not counting the Kurds, who are also largely Sunnis), was all but estranged from power. If Iraq were to be rebuilt as a federal state, the Sunnis, who live mostly in the central parts of the country, would be deprived of their oil wealth, because the main oilfields are located in the north and the south.

What is the best way out of the situation in Iraq? That remains a very tricky question.

First, President Bush decided that he would cut Iraq's "Gordian knot" by boosting the numbers of the occupying forces. And so a "new strategy" was published, under which the "surge" of 22,000 additional American troops were sent to Iraq in order to tighten control over Baghdad and parts of the country that had become strongholds of resistance. Before long it became clear that the surge could not radically change the situation in Iraq. Meanwhile, the deployment of the occupying forces brought about a sharp rise in the number of lives lost among the Americans.

When he ordered the surge, President Bush completely ignored the recommendations of the Iraq Study Group (the special commission cochaired by James Baker, former secretary of state, and Lee Hamilton, former Democratic congressman from Indiana, now president of the Woodrow Wilson International Center for Scholars), which had concluded that it was imperative that the United States announce a timetable for troop reduction and troop withdrawal without delay, as well as open talks with Iran and Syria, two countries that were well placed to help bring about normalization in Iraq. The commission's recommendations had won support from numerous politicians and experts. It is common knowledge that Baker—one of the most dynamic secretaries of state the United States had ever seen—had been the right-hand man of President George Bush Sr. The link-up between Baker and Hamilton therefore symbolized a bipartisan approach by the Democratic and Republican parties. Before he was elected to his second term as president, Bush Jr. had spoken a great deal about his intention of being guided by that approach. And no small part in formulating these recommendations was played by a man whom I regard as one of the finest Middle East experts in the United States, Edward Djerejian, head of the Middle East section of the Baker Foundation.

There is no question that U.S. policy in Iraq has created a no-win situation. It led to the Republicans' loss of control of both Houses of Congress and brought about a marked shift in public opinion against Bush, who languished in approval polls in his final years in office. It also triggered the forced resignation of former defense secretary Donald Rumsfeld, one of the most blatant advocates of unilateral military action, as well as the resignations of other prominent neoconservatives in the government, like Paul Wolfowitz and Richard Perle.

The issue of Iraq became increasingly prominent in the 2008 U.S. presidential election campaign. Critics of President Bush's policies on Iraq—mainly Democrats—understood that they had to stay within clearly defined boundaries that they could not overstep for fear of losing votes. It was off-limits to say anything criticizing the army, or indeed to make any criticism that could be construed as unpatriotic. Even Hillary Clinton, who played the Iraq card to great effect in her campaign rhetoric, felt obliged to acknowledge the "success of U.S. forces *in a number of areas in Iraq*" (author's italics).

But did this half-baked acknowledgment of scattered, unspecified successes reflect the truth about what was going on in that tormented country? Let's deal with the facts. On August 23, 2007, a National Intelligence Estimate of the situation in Iraq was published. The report stated: "Political and security trajectories in Iraq continue to be driven by Shia insecurity about retaining political dominance, widespread Sunni unwillingness to accept a diminished political status, factional rivalries within the sectarian communities resulting in armed conflict, and the actions of extremists such as al-Qaeda in Iraq and elements of the Sadrist Jaysh al-Mahdi [the 'Mahdi Army'] that try to fuel sectarian violence."

Well, it seems credit is due to the authors of the report for being so objective.

Many observers of the events in Iraq tend to reduce them to a conflict between Shiites and Sunnis. But that doesn't begin to do justice to the complexity of the situation. The disunity among Shiites, even among those in the broad Shiite coalition that drives the government's policy agenda, has become more noticeable than ever. Prime Minister Nuri al-Maliki could not say that he had the full and unequivocal support of the Shiites' spiritual leader Ayatollah Ali al-Sistani, let alone of followers of the young Shiite leader Muqtada al-Sadr, who commands the Mahdi Army. There have been outbreaks of fierce fighting between Shiite factions.

There is also a lack of unity among the Sunnis. A considerable number of them are inclined to support the Ba'ath Party, which has been operating underground. It would be a mistake, however, to lump all its members together as unregenerate Saddam Hussein supporters: a new Ba'athist leadership has been gradually taking shape whose main concern is how to govern Iraq after the departure of the occupying forces. They recognize that it is not possible to resurrect the Saddam regime, nor indeed would it suit Iraq's needs to do so. In their resentment of the occupation and of Shiite dominance in government and parliament, some Sunnis have forged links with terrorist groups such as al-Qaeda, which now sees Iraq as just about the most important base for its activities. Things are far from settled with the Kurds too, and the mood in northern Iraq is increasingly separatist. But even if the Kurds can be dissuaded from founding their own independent state, would they be willing to cede Kirkuk and its surrounding territories?

The impasse in Iraq, and its effect on public opinion, played no small part in leading to Barack Obama's election as the new president of the United States. In the run-up to Obama's inauguration, Bush had made a number of concessions to Iraqi officials and signed an agreement with the Baghdad government promising that U.S. troops would leave Iraq no later than the end of 2011. Bush gave the impression of being in a hurry to name a date and wanting to delay the U.S. troop pullout—he had realized that Obama might pull the date forward.

A secure future for Iraq cannot be built until three essential conditions are achieved: (1) the foreign occupation must be ended and all power transferred into the hands of the Iraqis themselves; (2) a model for governing the country that takes account of the interests of Arabs and Kurds, Shiites, and Sunnis must be found; and (3) all of Iraq's partisan forces must abide by a cast-iron commitment that they will not give any kind of support to any groups or organizations whose acts of violence are killing hundreds, even thousands of innocent civilians. Freedom fighters and terrorists are not the same thing; there can be no justification for conflating the two.

The most positive thing that UN secretary-general Kofi Annan's Wise Men's Group achieved was to set out the *causes* of terrorism; but neither that group, which debated the issue exhaustively, nor the session of the UN General Assembly that discussed it in 2005 were able to agree on a definition of "terrorism" itself. This is partly because many countries, largely from Africa and Asia, fear that their pro-independence campaigns, their resistance to foreign occupation, might fall under the rubric of terrorism. At the same time, a number of countries fear that their reprisals for terrorist acts might also be classed as terrorism. What is needed in today's world is a universal understanding of the fact that terrorism is the targeted use of force against and murder of innocent civilians—no matter what its motives are, or whatever goals might be used to justify it.

IRAN: A NUCLEAR CROSSWORD PUZZLE

An important feature of the situation in Iraq is the influence of Iran. Iran has close ties with a number of its Shiite movements and political parties: these include the Supreme Council for the Islamic Revolution in Iraq, led by Abdul Aziz al-Hakim, the Islamic Dawa Party of Ibrahim al-Jaafari, the movement led by Muqtada al-Sadr, and others.

Increasingly, a link may come to be discerned between Iran's influence on events in Iraq and the Iranian nuclear problem, but at this point it is quite clearly a separate issue. It can be assumed that no nation in the world has any vested interest in Iran acquiring nuclear weapons. The prospect of its doing so, along with repeated calls from its leadership to wipe Israel off the map, makes for a particularly volatile combination. If these calls were to go beyond the bounds of propaganda, it is difficult to predict what the consequences would be. Perhaps this is merely a symptom of my optimism, but I feel sure that nobody—including Russia—would allow their message to be made a reality.

If Iran made a nuclear breakthrough, it could quite possibly wreck the nonproliferation treaty, paving the way for numerous other countries to get their hands on nuclear weapons, some of them embroiled in dangerous regional conflicts of their own. This would create a radically different and significantly more dangerous situation in the world, not least because international terrorist organizations would gain easier access to nuclear weapons.

That is as it may be. But what makes the current situation with Iran a particularly difficult one is that: (1) Iran claims that it has not made any political decision to build nuclear weapons and does not intend to build any; it denies that its nuclear program has any purposes other than peaceful ones; (2) Iran is a signatory to the nuclear nonproliferation treaty and is not contravening it in any way; (3) Iran is willing to submit its nuclear projects to inspection by the IAEA; and finally, (4) Iran has no intention of halting any projects that fall within the permitted peaceful uses of nuclear power, including the enrichment of uranium, an activity undertaken by more than sixty other countries.

To date, Iran has demonstrated an independent capability through all stages of this cycle, including uranium enrichment. Experts believe that if the Iranian government decided to press ahead with the production of nuclear weapons, it would have them within two to five years. Obviously that is not a very long time.

Two possible approaches to resolving this difficult problem have emerged.

One approach is to step up the pressure on Iran, even going as far as using force. Russia and China have proposed a second approach— one that has the support of many other countries—which is to seek a political solution. In order to eliminate suspicions that Iran is trying to produce nuclear weapons, Russia offered to build, on Russian territory, a facility for the enrichment of uranium earmarked for civilian use in Iran. Russia also expressed its willingness to supply nuclear fuel for an atomic power station being built with Russian help in Bushir, on condition that Iran would return all the spent fuel. Iran agreed to this. As for uranium enrichment on Russian territory, Iran has neither accepted nor rejected this offer.

One further approach is a collective one. President Vladimir Putin talked of the possibility of establishing uranium enrichment facilities on the soil of the recognized nuclear powers to supply countries that have civilian nuclear programs and have not set themselves the goal of building nuclear weapons. The creation of such a network would allow Iran to make use of it on a shared basis without "losing face." Talks on the introduction of a stricter regime of IAEA inspection could then continue, with recognized experts from that international body setting what would be a reasonable degree of enforcement.

If Iran refused to comply, the approach advocated by the Bush administration—escalating the pressure from the UN Security Council—would begin with the imposition of international economic sanctions. Russia, China, and other countries believe that such sanctions would be counterproductive. If the hope is to motivate more realistically minded figures to seize the upper hand in the Iranian leadership, then it's hard to see how sanctions—which would hit ordinary people hardest—would help tip the balance of power toward them. On the contrary, as the example of Iraq has taught us, Iranian politics would become increasingly radicalized.

But that is not the only concern. Suppose the economic sanctions failed. Then, according to the logic of stepping up the pressure on Iran, it would be necessary to resort to other means of force, even to the extent of military intervention. It can be predicted with some certainty that bombing Iran would lead to increased terrorist activity and possibly destabilize a number of moderate secular regimes, mainly in the Arab states. It would add new fuel to the wave of anti-Americanism that is already sweeping the world, especially in countries with Muslim populations. And if the United States went further still by mounting a ground operation, would it be able to withstand a second knockdown, even worse than the one it experienced in Iraq?

In my view, however, none of this justifies Iran's current intransigence, its blanket rejection of any and all compromise solutions to a problem that is so worrying the international community. It looks as though Iran's policy of noncooperation has much to do with the failed U.S. invasion of Iraq. Thanks to its close ties with Iraq's Shiite community, Iran has gained what might be a decisive influence over developments in Iraq, which can no longer be regarded as a reliable counter-balance to Iran in the Persian Gulf. Holding these trump cards in its hands, Iran wants to negotiate directly with the United States. Although the United States is currently opposed to unilateral talks, surely it understands that such a dialogue, in whatever form it takes, is essential. Might it be worth setting up a negotiating forum made up of the United States, Russia, China, India, the European Union, the UN, and Iran?

Whatever happens, the announcement by new U.S. president Barack Obama that he is willing to open talks with Iran has prompted a worldwide sigh of relief. By the time the reader picks up this book, most of the blanks in Iran's nuclear "crossword puzzle" will have been filled in. I would like to believe that by then we will be able to talk about this nuclear threat in the past tense.

HAMAS LEGALIZED:
A NEW CHAPTER IN THE PALESTINIANS' HISTORY

Hamas's rise to power in January 2006 following its democratic election to a majority position in the parliament of the Palestinian Authority has clearly had a crucial impact on the situation in the region and on the Israeli-Palestinian peace process. So what is Hamas, and why did it come out on top in the elections? In order to understand the situation and make reliable predictions about how it might change in the future, both of these questions need to be answered in a realistic, objective way.

Throughout Israel's occupation of the West Bank and Gaza Strip, and until the creation of the Palestinian Authority in 1994, nongovernmental organizations (NGOs) managed most of the Palestinians' social and economic affairs. The Higher Council on Education, for example, was set up to ensure that local universities came up to recognized standards and that their graduates found jobs. NGOs carried out the corresponding government functions of healthcare and agriculture; they used Islamic taxes (the *zakat*) to redistribute money and goods among the poorest members of society as well. There were four political groups behind these social structures: the Popular Front for the Liberation of Palestine (PFLP), Fatah, Hamas, and the Communist Party.

Because these were all underground groups (Fatah only emerged in 1993 after the Oslo Peace Accords), PFLP members called themselves populists in public, Fatah members called themselves nationalists, Hamas members Islamists, and Communists *narodniks*.

The Israeli occupying authorities did not obstruct their activities, which filled the vacuum left by the absence of government structures. In fact, because Israeli politicians feared that the PFLP and Fatah in particular might be growing in strength, they favored the Islamists initially (who were less militant in those days), contrasting them with the populists and nationalists. According to one plausible account, the Israeli intelligence service Mossad actively encouraged Hamas in its early years. All of that changed, needless to say, after the first intifada in 1987 and especially after the second one began in 2000.

Hamas's victory in the 2006 election was undisputed; it brought them control of the Palestinian Authority. Nevertheless Israel, backed by the United States, said it would have no dealings with Hamas because it is a terrorist organization. Let us recall that two Israeli prime ministers, Menachem Begin and Yitzhak Shamir, had actually been terrorists themselves—the British Mandate authorities had put enormous rewards on both of their heads. Yet when *they* won elections and came to power, nobody questioned their legitimacy.

We can't begin to win the battle against international terrorism until we understand the attitude of ordinary Muslims (whether they sympathize with Islamic extremists or not) toward organizations like Hamas—and the complicated makeup of the organizations themselves. Hamas, which enjoys the support of a significant section of the Palestinian population, has two interweaving strands to its ideology: one Islamic and the other nationalistic. If its first achievement was to create an Islamic state in the region, its main objective now is to end the Israeli occupation. There are grounds to believe that the nationalist strand of its ideological platform will gather strength at the expense of its religious element, now that it has won power.

Further complicating this shifting relationship between nationalism and Islam is the fact that Hamas's military wing was set up after it entered a more active phase in its battle against the Israeli occupation. The militant wing had close ties with Hamas's political leadership, but increasingly acted independently of it. Both Israel and the United States have acknowledged this distinction. In January 1998, when (then in his first incarnation as Israeli prime minister) Benjamin Netanyahu and the late Palestinian leader Yasser Arafat visited Washington D.C., Madeleine Albright, the then U.S. secretary of state, sought to build bridges between them by putting forward a plan for safeguarding security that included a ban on the military wing of Hamas, but not on the organization as a whole. The Israeli army had an unspoken rule that militants from this faction—which did indeed resort to terrorist attacks against innocent civilians—were the only ones it should take out.

Yet Israel's antiterrorist operations took on the form of terrorism themselves in the way they were carried out. One case that caused a sensation was the assassination attempt against Khaled Mashal, one of the leaders of Hamas, on a street in Amman in 1997. Here, an Israeli agent used a silvery object to inject poison into his ear, but the two Israelis who carried out the attack were arrested. King Hussein of Jordan was on the verge of breaking off relations with Israel; he warned that if Mashal died, the two Israeli assailants would be put on trial and hanged. Netanyahu personally traveled to Jordan but the king refused to see him. Then an antidote to the poison was sent from Israel and, in order to hush up the scandal, seventy Palestinians were released from prison, among them Sheikh Ahmed Yassin, founder of the Hamas movement.

From 2001 on, Israel adopted a policy of targeted strikes against Hamas's political leaders as well as its militants, and Yassin was killed in a rocket attack in 2004. Yet even before Yassin's death, Hamas's position had started to change. Just a day before he was killed, Yassin told journalists in Gaza that Hamas would participate in the Palestinian elections and—when the Israelis left Gaza—play a part in its administration. It is telling that Hamas did not even mention its aim of introducing a power structure based on Sharia law once it had won the elections.

Hamas in power has also been quite revealing in itself. The fact that there is widespread corruption and that the PLO has been unable to improve a rapidly deteriorating socioeconomic situation in the West Bank and Gaza—despite substantial injections of cash—may well be attributable to internal factors. But the Israelis' policy of dragging their feet on talks and their failure to comply with their obligations under existing agreements—which has an impact on the Palestinian population, entrenching the view that talks have no chance of success unless they are backed by an armed struggle—are external factors, and militants point to them to justify terrorist attacks on innocent civilians. The Israeli army responds by killing innocent Palestinian civilians in its hunt for Hamas members, all but guaranteeing that a bad situation will only grow worse.

So what next? At the end of April and beginning of May 2006 I traveled to Israel and Jordan. In Israel, I met with Israeli political scientists, businessmen, and Israeli foreign minister Tzipi Livni; in Amman, I held long talks with Palestinian president Mahmoud Abbas and other Palestinian leaders.

It was, of course, a difficult situation—one made worse, as far as I could tell, by the Israelis' intransigence. Livni strenuously insisted that there could be no dealings with Hamas; Israel is clearly seeking to isolate the movement completely. In fact, I would go even further. It seems to me that Israel's plan is to topple Hamas using a combination of tactics: cutting off funds to the Palestinians with a view to making them turn their backs on the movement; using U.S. influence to isolate Hamas in the Arab world; and stirring up in-fighting between armed Palestinian factions.

James Wolfensohn, special envoy of the Middle East Quartet (made up of the United States, Russia, the EU, and the UN), resigned his post to protest a policy that puts an economic stranglehold on people living under the Palestinian Authority. Wolfensohn is a straightforward, honest man whom I had occasion to meet when I was prime minister of Russia and he was president of the World Bank (he was one of a very few foreign admirers of Russia's government, as he himself has said). Commenting on his resignation, he said he failed to see how starving the Palestinians or depriving their kids of school could help Israel to win.

Wolfensohn warned that unless Israel scraps its decision to stop transferring taxes paid by Palestinian workers to the Palestinian Authority as it had done before, and lifts its restrictions on the sale of Palestinian-made goods and on Palestinians' freedom of movement—all this while the United States and other foreign donors are maintaining their financial boycott—there will be certain catastrophe. Gross domestic product in the Palestinian territories would drop by 27 percent in 2006 alone (with GDP having fallen by 30 percent as it was since 2000), while spending on healthcare and education would drop by 60 percent. Because Hamas is on its list of terrorist organizations the United States, meanwhile, has sought to cut off the supply of funds to the Palestinian Authority from Iran, the Arab countries, and others by exerting its control over the world's biggest banks and threatening others with sanctions for channeling funds.

These measures do nothing to strengthen Israel's security—quite the contrary. At the 24th session of InterAction Council (IAC) in Jordan in May 2006, a session in which I took part, a communiqué was issued "recognizing that isolation of Hamas will only lead to further radicalization and risks increasing internal fighting and fragmentation of the Palestinian society." The IAC, an organization that brings together former prime ministers and heads of states' from various countries, was right. When Hamas first came to power, it showed that it was moving, albeit slowly, toward more realistic policies: it announced that it would extend the truce that it had implemented unilaterally, despite Israeli army raids into Gaza that were killing innocent Palestinian civilians. The truce was broken, however, on June 9, 2006, when the Israeli army shelled a beach in Gaza, killing and wounding women and children. Israel said that an artillery shell had accidentally gone off-trajectory and apologized—but that did not pacify Hamas.

Hamas's future is, of course, closely bound up with its agreement to recognize the accords signed between Israel and Fatah in Oslo, and to enter into negotiations between the Israelis and the Palestinians with a view to founding a Palestinian state that exists alongside Israel (and not in its place). Its future is also tied to stopping the war, above all the terrorist attacks against the innocent Israeli civilian population. It must be said, though, that it will not be easy for Hamas to go down that path, especially when the victims of Israeli raids on Gaza include innocent civilians, and not just Hamas militants. However, if the Hamas leadership does not begin the process of recognizing Israel, it will inevitably widen the conflict between itself and Fatah (led by President Mahmoud Abbas) and even between itself and some of its members. There are those in Hamas, as well as in Fatah, who are ready to hold talks on establishing a Palestinian state within the pre-1967 borders, with its capital in East Jerusalem.

It is worth remembering that if Hamas continues to remain intransigent, it will only bolster the position of those in Israel who would reject any settlement of the Middle East conflict that is based on compromise.

I should point out that there is increasing support for the Russian position: seeking a political compromise that takes into account the interests of all sides in the conflict. That is something I learned from being involved in the work of a forum as respected as the InterAction Council. My counterparts there said Russia had done the right thing by inviting Hamas leader Khaled Mashal to Moscow; they agreed that Russia's positive influence on the group could be particularly valuable. But that was not the view of Israeli foreign minister Tzipi Livni. I responded to her criticism by telling her: "Russia, as an independent sovereign state, should be allowed to take any decisions it sees fit that might increase the chances of building peace in the Middle East." Livni, seen as a rising star in the Israeli political firmament, admitted that she had perhaps been too emotional.

As could have been expected, the situation rapidly deteriorated. In summer 2006, after an Israeli was taken hostage on Israel's own soil, Israeli forces launched an operation aimed at wiping out Hamas. Innocent civilians died when Israeli tanks rolled into Gaza. Hostilities were at their peak, with the military wing of Hamas engaged in extremist activity and Israel bent on crushing the government of the Palestinian Authority by force. Government ministers and Palestinian lawmakers were arrested; numerous Hamas figures were either killed or driven underground. Israel also launched punitive raids into the West Bank. Relations between Fatah and Hamas were strained to the breaking point. And when the Palestinians had finally succeeded in forming a coalition government of national unity, Israel kept up its hostility toward Hamas, even though there had been no hardening of Hamas's political doctrine during this time.

At the very end of October 2006, I met with Khaled Mashal and his politburo colleagues in Damascus. Sooner or later, I said, and preferably as soon as possible, they would have to recognize Israel. Mashal replied: "Our proposal is to establish a Palestinian state within the borders that existed until June 5, 1967" (that is, before the Six-Day War).

"You might add 'alongside Israel,'" I said.

"A lot will depend on the progress of negotiations to establish a Palestinian state," Mashal said.

Subsequent events changed the situation inside the Palestinian Authority and had an impact on the entire Arab-Israeli peace process. Once it had swiftly crushed resistance from Fatah, Hamas went on to establish sole control over the Gaza Strip. Palestinian president Mahmoud Abbas disbanded the recently formed government of national unity, made up of the two groups, and formed a new government, this time without Hamas. But in practical terms his authority was limited to the West Bank. Gaza and the West Bank were cut off from each other. It was not just a geographical rift, but a political one too. After the military coup in Gaza, Hamas leaders sought to open negotiations with Abbas, but he refused.

On the whole, the Arab world continued to support Fatah and Abbas, but not without subtle differences in their standpoints that varied from one country to the next. Egypt and Jordan were staunch supporters of Fatah, while Syria, which adhered to an official policy of neutrality, nonetheless had greater sympathy toward Hamas. The same was true of Iran, which, though not an Arab country, played an increasingly large role in Middle East affairs. Meanwhile, Saudi Arabia had a more ambivalent attitude to the Palestinians' internal conflict—an attitude evidently born of its wounded pride (the Saudis had been proud of having mediated between Fatah and Hamas leaders when they reached agreement in Mecca on the formation of a Palestinian coalition government). Increased activity by Egypt and Jordan heralded the advent of a new phase in which Saudi Arabia would now "play second fiddle" in terms of Arab-led mediation in the Middle East.

Given these differences in the positions of various Arab countries, the only way the Arab world as a whole would transfer its backing from Fatah to Hamas would be if Hamas managed to deprive Fatah of its control over the West Bank, which is home to three-fifths of the Palestinian population. This possibility, however, can be ruled out, even though Hamas won the January 2006 elections thanks to the support it had not only in Gaza but in West Bank towns too. Nor will Israel allow control over the West Bank to be transferred to Hamas. In spite of all the unhelpful developments over the years, a series of encouraging steps toward an Arab-Israeli peace settlement can be seen, especially on the Arab side.

But unfortunately, though there are often fleeting glimpses of possibilities that could be developed for the good of all, few of them have even been acknowledged by the principal parties in the conflict. One such possibility came in the form of resolutions taken at the Arab League summit held in Riyadh in March 2007. A number of media outlets, mainly the Israeli press, acted as if nothing radical had been proposed. Back in 2002 at the summit in Beirut, they said, the Arabs had also offered to make peace with Israel in exchange for pulling out of the territories occupied in the 1967 war. I disagree with their interpretation of the new Arab peace initiative: the "land for peace" formula put forward in 2002 by the future King Abdullah, and supported by the Beirut summit, was mainly concerned with what it would take for the Arab world to reach a settlement with Israel. This time around, the Arab League had proposed a platform for negotiations with the aim of finding a solution that would suit both sides, Israel and the Palestinians.

Under the League's new initiative, the establishment of peaceful relations with Israel would be tied not only to its relinquishing the land it occupied in 1967 and allowing a Palestinian state to be created there, but also to a "fair solution" to the fate of Palestinian refugees. The issue of Palestinian refugees is a particularly sore point for the Arabs. As I see it, the "framework formula" reached at the 2007 Arab summit is especially significant because it opens up new opportunities. Many a Palestinian leader has told me that quite a few refugees, if not most of them, would prefer to receive compensation and stay in the Arab countries where they have made new lives. As for those living in refugee camps who have thus far been unable to find a place outside them, many of those people too would prefer to receive substantial compensation that would allow them to purchase their own homes, rather than face the uncertainties and dangers attendant upon a return to their ancestral homes. But for those stubborn, brave, and determined souls who are willing to tough it out, there is also the option of returning to the territory of the Palestinian state. All of these options could be considered at the negotiating table.

It is no accident, I think, that the Arab League's summit resolution was welcomed by Russia as well as by the leaders of many European countries and the European Union, and indeed by UN secretary-general Ban Ki-Moon. U.S. secretary of state Condoleezza Rice did not openly join this chorus of approval for all the all-too-familiar reasons, but the fact that she welcomed the Arab peace initiative was evidenced by her urging Israeli prime minister Ehud Olmert to maintain permanent contact with Palestinian president Mahmoud Abbas and to hold talks with him about the "political horizon."

The case for needing to find a compromise is strengthened by a number of hard facts. For instance, there is no scenario whatsoever under which Israel would annex the Arab lands it occupied in 1967. If it did, Israel would lose its identity as a Jewish state—the very reason why it was created. Israel's leaders used to be vociferous in their calls to expand its borders at the expense of the territory captured in 1967, but such voices are no longer heard. Events have shown that forcing local inhabitants out of those territories is impossible—nobody will accept that. Annexing the territories while they are still inhabited by Palestinians would mean that the Jews would become a minority in Israel in the foreseeable future. While I was still writing this book, Fatah had started to make contact with Hamas, opening up the prospect of normalized relations between the two principal Palestinian factions. But it is a difficult, two-way process.

Meanwhile, the United States has stepped up its involvement in the Middle East peace process, setting itself the task of bringing about a peace settlement. It is not the easiest of tasks. Hillary Clinton, Condoleezza Rice's successor as secretary of state, has spoken out in the strongest terms against the ongoing Israeli practice of expanding Jewish settlements in the occupied territories, rightly calling it a serious obstacle on the road to a settlement of the Arab-Israeli conflict.

But just as on previous occasions, terrorism once again returned to make the most damaging impact on the Middle East peace process. In 2008, citing Israel's continued blockade of the Gaza Strip, Hamas militants began launching rocket attacks on Israeli settlements near the border with Gaza. Eight Israelis died as a result of the 1,500 missiles that were fired. There was, of course, no justification for the shelling of inhabited areas. Israel's response, however, was a massive incursion into Gaza that led to the killing of some 1,500 innocent civilians, many of them children. Across the world there was a wave of public outrage—and even a series of UN Security Council resolutions demanding a cease-fire and pullout of Israeli troops.

Let there be no doubt that after the truce agreed on by both sides in Gaza, the search for a peaceful solution must continue with further contact between the Israelis and the Palestinians. Any prolonged hiatus would be highly undesirable. That said, it is clear that the peace process could evolve only after the outcome of the 2009 Knesset elections in Israel—which will determine who becomes prime minister and chief Israeli negotiator—and when Fatah and Hamas find a way of living alongside each other and working together. There will either be a government of national unity, or Hamas will agree to take part in peace talks, or, without trumpeting it too loudly, it will recognize the right of President Mahmoud Abbas to hold talks with Israel on behalf of all Palestinians.

Russia could play an important role in creating the right conditions for the resumption of talks between Israel and the Palestinians, be it as a member of the Middle East Quartet or independently. What differentiates Russia from the other members of this group is that it enjoys good relations not only with Israel and Fatah, but also with all parties that could exert a strong influence on the circumstances of any negotiations: Iran, Syria, Lebanon, Hamas, Hizbollah, Egypt, Saudi Arabia, and other Arab nations.

While it is important for the Israelis and the Palestinians to resume contact, that is not the only factor in the peace process. It is also imperative to mobilize the quartet. Ultimately, I believe, the quartet should formulate a series of decisions on all issues affecting the Israeli-Palestinian peace process. These should be presented to the conflicting parties as a collective resolution by the United States, Russia, the European Union, and the United Nations—not, I stress, as recommendations but as resolutions. When Israel was founded, was it not the international community that dictated the partition of Palestine, with the creation of the Israeli state and an Arab state on Palestinian territory? People might contradict me, saying that times have changed. I agree, but:

1. Before the Israeli offensive against Gaza, the two sides had moved closer to agreement on a number of difficult issues, or at least they no longer seemed diametrically opposed.
2. It was clear that a constructive part was being played by Arab countries that hold sway over the Palestinians, mainly Egypt, Saudi Arabia, and Jordan; witness the position they set out in the Arab Peace Initiative approved at the Riyadh summit in 2007.
3. There is good reason to believe that President Barack Obama will not drag his feet in helping to move the peace process along, and that he is full of serious intent.
4. A peace deal between Israel and the Palestinians would be greatly helped by normalization of relations between Israel and Syria. Without a peaceful resolution of this kind, the overall situation in the Middle East will inevitably deteriorate and be increasingly affected by the situation in Iran, in an unstable Afghanistan and an Iraq with an uncertain future.

Plans to bring regional stability to the wider Middle East must also take account of a number of pressing issues other than settling the Arab-Israeli conflict. The most pressing of these is the creation of a nuclear-free zone in the Middle East. At the time of writing, this is an issue that had grown to be even more of a threat. If concerns were previously limited to Israel's nuclear arsenal, the situation now has the added complication that Iran is technically capable of producing enriched uranium. I am not one of those who believe that Iran is already developing a nuclear arms program, but this is a fear shared by many people, and not just in the Middle East or the Persian Gulf. Even worse, Israel's nuclear arsenal and the fear that Iran is trying to acquire nuclear weapons are stirring up similar ambitions among several other countries in the region. Israel has come out against the creation of a nuclear-free zone. But might Israel tone down its opposition, especially if the Arab-Israeli peace process moves forward and new circumstances arise?

It would be a good idea if the issue of a nuclear-free zone were covered by a system of collective security in the Middle East. This system could be set out by an accord containing clauses that were legally binding on the countries that signed it; an accord that guaranteed the inviolability of state borders and set limits on levels of conventional weapons and arms verification.

A separate issue that needs to be mentioned is the danger posed by terrorist activity. Events in Iraq have shown that terrorist groups such as al-Qaeda are capable of rushing in to fill the power vacuum, and its fighters have flooded in from the tribal zone of the Afghan-Pakistan border. There is also a sizeable number of local terrorist groups and factions in the Middle East. A collective security accord could set out antiterrorist measures, such as an obligation on all signatory states to not allow this type of group to exist on their territory or an undertaking to cut off their funding from community organizations. It would, of course, be no easy matter to negotiate a path toward such a collective security accord. It is a task that cannot be accomplished any time soon. But starting to move in that direction is something we must do.

LEBANON IN FLAMES ONCE MORE

Events have also taken their course on the Israel-Lebanon border. In 2006 Hizbollah decided to follow the example of Hamas and attacked a military outpost on Israeli territory, killing three Israeli soldiers and taking two others prisoner. It is hard to say who was actually behind this Hizbollah raid. Many observers believe it to have been Iran or Syria, which do in fact have close ties to Hizbollah. But such presumptions are not credible. At that very point in time, all the parties that were mediating with Iran, including Russia and China, had agreed without exception to hand its nuclear dossier to the UN Security Council. Iran hardly stood to gain from opening yet another front at that moment. The theory that Iran was using events in Lebanon to distract attention from its nuclear program was a popular one in Israel and the United States, but such talk is devoid of all logic. On the contrary, the deteriorating situation in Lebanon was actually quite damaging to Iran, inasmuch as it increased fears about its nuclear program.

Syria, meanwhile, had little to gain from making matters worse on the Israeli-Lebanon border, and was all too aware of the inevitable Israeli response. I am pretty sure that Damascus did not want any armed conflict with Israel, especially not on its own soil.

And so internal factors were behind both the Hamas raid, which was essentially terrorist in nature, and similar actions by Hizbollah. Without justifying these actions in the slightest, I believe they can be explained as attempts to use hostages as bargaining tools in exchange for the release of Palestinians (Hamas) and Lebanese (Hizbollah) prisoners from Israeli jails. Mahmoud Abbas had broached the subject of releasing a number of Palestinian prisoners on several occasions during his talks with the Israelis. Many in the Palestinian Authority held that this was one of the conditions of an "interim" compromise. Israel, however, had reneged.

But whatever the cause of the Hizbollah attack, Israel's response to it was a military operation that went way beyond counterterrorism, with Israeli tanks rolling into southern Lebanon, and the Israeli air force bombing Beirut's international airport and bridges. Residential areas of Beirut and other Lebanese towns were also subjected to bombing and shelling from the sea. The Israelis said they were destroying Hizbollah targets, but it was Lebanon's vital infrastructure that was being destroyed, and many women and children were killed. Innocent civilians in southern Lebanon were also subjected to the onslaught on the pretext that it was from there (where, from apartment blocks?) that rockets were being fired into Israeli towns. Equally groundless was Israel's explanation its bombs had "missed their targets"—Israeli pilots never missed their targets when they were precision-bombing vehicles carrying militant leaders.

It was starting to look like the 1982 war, which was so violent— for Israel as well as its adversaries—that the Israelis were forced to halt military operations and ultimately withdraw their troops from Lebanon. Nevertheless, there were important differences between the two conflicts. Back in 1982, Israel had relied on forces inside Lebanon—the Phalange—and the Israelis' objective had been to force armed Palestinian militants out of Lebanon. In 2006, the Israeli objective was to destroy Hizbollah—an armed force *within* Lebanon. Israel's bombing raids against civilian targets in Lebanon were clearly a bid to open up rifts between Lebanese politicians, giving rise to a Lebanese armed faction that would be willing to take up arms against Hizbollah—in other words, to plunge Lebanon into the abyss of civil war once again.

The 2006 war was also different from the 1982 war in that now Hizbollah responded with rocket attacks that not only hit towns right on the Israeli border but also Haifa, thirty kilometers away. Here too, the victims were innocent civilians. In effect, Israel lost the war. Hizbollah not only maintained but actually strengthened its foothold in Lebanon. There was a string of high-level resignations in Israel, beginning with the division commander responsible for the security of the border with Lebanon, followed by the commander-in-chief of the northern military district and then the Israeli army chief of staff Dan Halutz. Not only was Prime Minister Ehud Olmert seriously damaged by the failure of the war, but some of his previous misdemeanors came back to haunt him.

A WORLD DIVIDED ALONG RELIGIOUS LINES

The complex, volatile, and often unpredictable events taking place in and around the Middle East have helped give rise to the theory that the world's great civilizations are fundamentally at odds—but instead of ideology, as in the cold war days, the fault lines are drawn along cultural and religious boundaries. Supporters of this theory, such as the U.S. political scientist Samuel P. Huntington, have gone even further, saying that the world is literally being torn in two.

This supposed polarization is understood to be the result of the emergence of international terrorism, which is allegedly linked directly to the religion of Islam. There is plenty of evidence to show how erroneous it is to conflate the two in this way, but I will not dwell on that in great detail—only ignoramuses or spiteful Islamophobes could equate one of the oldest and most widely practiced religions in the world with terrorism. The reality today is that many terrorist organizations, primarily al-Qaeda, do indeed wrap themselves in the flag of Islam and declare that their overriding goal is to found a single caliphate on the territory of all states with a Muslim population. But does that necessarily lead to terrorism against the West? More often than not, al-Qaeda targets its terrorist attacks at Muslim states, especially those with moderate or secular regimes. The number of terrorist acts carried out by al-Qaeda or its offshoots is greater by far in Saudi Arabia, Egypt, and Turkey than in the countries of Western Europe or the United States.

It is vitally important that the differences between Islamic fundamentalism and Islamic extremism be understood—not just in non-Muslim countries, but in Muslim countries as well. Islamic fundamentalism is the building of mosques, the observance of Islamic rituals, and mutual assistance between fellow believers. But it is only when Islamic fundamentalism uses force to impose Islamic rule over a state or a society that it takes on an aggressive or extremist form. There have been stages throughout history that saw Christian fundamentalism turning into Christian or Catholic extremism: we need only think of the Reformation or the Crusades. Today, it is the symptoms of Islamic extremism that we face.

What is the reason for this? Clearly, it is not because Islam itself is intrinsically extremist. Some blame economics, specifically the widening gulf between the richest nations (the United States, Canada, Australia, New Zealand, and the countries of Europe) and the rest of the world, a large part of which is made up of countries with Muslim populations. But this is not the complete answer. In fact, the leaders of terrorist organizations tend to be émigrés from well-to-do families.

In my view, there are several factors behind the rise of Islamic extremism. The main reason is not the clash of civilizations per se but the current breakdown of dialogue between them. The forces of globalization at work in the world today have affected everyone, including countries with Muslim populations. These countries are in no way beyond the reach of the technology that makes modern international civilization what it is, with its enormous, albeit uneven, influence on all aspects of humankind's development. The problem is that there is more to global civilization than just technology. It is knit together out of myriad cultural, religious, and political undercurrents, from a vast variety of communities that have held on to what makes them distinctive while steadily growing closer together. What holds them together is the dialogue that exists between them. And it is this dialogue that is breaking down in today's world. One sure indicator of this is an unthinking obsession on the part of the United States—the leading economic and military power of Western civilization—with "exporting" its model of democracy to other countries, moreover to ones with Muslim populations. Worse still, its "export" has involved the use of military force.

In 2006 Moscow hosted the first meeting of the Strategic Vision Group, which brought together Russian officials and representatives of the Organization of the Islamic Conference. Entitled "Russia and the Islamic World," it was attended by political and spiritual leaders from practically all the major Muslim nations, and was a great success. Delegates noted the value of being able to exchange views with their Russian counterparts on matters of vital importance in today's world relating to the dialogue between civilizations. The meeting's format was no accident, and several speakers stressed that because Russia is one of the great world powers with influence over world events, it does everything it can to hinder the growth of a tendency that is posing a threat to mankind: the division of the world along religious lines.

Indeed, millions of Muslims live in Russia; unlike in many Western countries, they are not immigrants but form part of the indigenous population. There is perhaps no other state with a Christian majority and a Muslim minority that can serve, in the way Russia does, as an example of peaceful cohabitation, of sharing and adopting each other's cultures and creating a very special kind of community. On top of this, Russia enjoys a unique position as a bridge between Europe and Asia.

It is not so long since the world was divided along ideological lines. Humankind coped with that, but I would say that today's newer rift between religions, between civilizations, is no less a threat. And this too is something that humankind must find the strength to overcome.

AFTERWORD

The Arab world underwent momentous evolution in the second half of the twentieth century. The main forces that drove its development were homegrown, but they were greatly influenced by events in the rest of world, especially the global standoff between the Soviet Union and the United States, and the Arab-Israeli conflict.

Across the Arab world, the colonial powers and the local leaders who had close ties to them were supplanted by nationalist revolutionaries. Some of them were more revolutionary than others; some were more committed to nationalism. But they had a great deal in common as well: all of them broke away from the imperial powers, and in the early days, they all enjoyed a special relationship with the United States, which they did not regard as a colonial power. All of them were committed to Arab Socialism, with its own quite specific interpretation of that ideology; they all fought against a religious, Islamic opposition; they all forged closer ties with the Soviet Union and the Soviet-led bloc of socialist countries, while declining to join that bloc.

The fact that these revolutionary nationalist regimes came into conflict with the United States can be blamed on American policy in the Middle East. The United States's original objective was to draw them into military alliances against the Soviet Union; when that did not work out, America cultivated the more conservative Arab regimes and Israel, hoping to create a counterweight to the nationalist revolutionaries. America's efforts to exert control over the radical Arab regimes necessarily brought it closer to Arab Islamists.

The Soviet Union's hopes that it could gradually "co-opt" the Arab nationalist revolutionaries and sign them up to socialist ideals—as Soviet ideologues interpreted them—turned out to be impracticable for many reasons, both objective and subjective. There was no "socialist phase" in the postcolonial development of the Arab nations. The revolutionary romanticism of the postcolonial era gradually disappeared too. What was left was Arab nationalism, which in effect abandoned revolutionary social reform. What's more, the idea of pan-Arab unity lost out to "country-centered" nationalism. All of this, along with the still-unresolved Arab-Israeli conflict, has fueled the rise of Islamic extremists in the Arab world. The nationalist Arab regimes do not intend to make any concessions to them, but should the Arab-Israeli peace process fail, and if the United States persists with its policy of exporting the American model of democracy to the wider Middle East by force, a scenario might arise under which the Islamists bear down on a number of nationalist Arab regimes. Much will depend on how the Iranian nuclear issue is resolved, on whether circumstances arise that bring stability to Iraq, and on whether the Middle East Quartet, whose role is to mediate in that region, will survive.

For a long time, the Soviet Union and the United States were the main foreign players in the Middle East. For all the differences in their approaches to the situation, what they had in common was a determination to not get directly involved in military action, and to prevent the Arab-Israeli conflict from escalating to global proportions. Since the end of the Soviet Union, Russia has had a reduced role as its successor in the Middle East, but the events of the past few years have shown that Moscow is very much focused on taking a more active part in resolving Middle East issues. There are substantial grounds to believe that its policies might succeed: Russia has traditionally enjoyed untarnished relations with the Arab countries and Iran; it has also greatly improved its relations with Israel, while sticking to its essential policy of seeking a settlement to the Middle East conflict that is based on fairness and compromise. After the end of the cold war Russia ceased to "play" the United States in a "game" that no one could win: it dropped the idea that anything that was in American interests was necessarily harmful to Russian interests and vice versa. Russia's greater involvement in the region has been welcomed by all Middle East nations, including Israel, where the public increasingly sees how detrimental it is to have a one-sided policy of alignment with a single global power—the United States—in a world that is ever more complex and polarized.

I submit these thoughts to the consideration of anyone reading this book. So long as I've opened minds and inspired reflection—regardless of whether everyone agrees with my analysis or not—I will be able to feel that my task has been accomplished.

ABOUT THE TRANSLATOR

Paul Gould graduated with a First in Russian from the University of Birmingham, England. He then lived for four years in Russia, where he became a correspondent for United Press International in Moscow, and later in London. Paul is currently a staff journalist at the *Financial Times* in London.

NOTES

PREFACE

1. Most of the material quoted throughout the book is taken from my notes. Where I have quoted from another author's work, I have tried to give an accurate citation of that source.

2. In this book, Middle East refers to the countries of the Arab world, including the north African states and Israel.

CHAPTER 1

1. Wright to Foreign Office, 24 July 1958, National Archives, London FO 371/123201.

2. The Muslim Brotherhood's fanaticism was at the time channeled into terrorist activities against British cronies. One victim was Prime Minister Mahmoud Nukrashi Pasha. Those involved in the attempt to kill al-Banna, who was behind the prime minister's assassination, were not caught until the Free Officers came to power and found it to their advantage to catch the killer and court-martial him.

3. Gamal Abdel Nasser, *The Philosophy of the Revolution* (Buffalo, NY: Smith, Keynes and Marshall, 1959) np.

CHAPTER 2

1. Ben-Gurion finally quit his post only eight years later, in 1963, when Israel's government set up the "Seven Commission" against the prime minister's wishes. The commission acquitted Lavon, and that was the end of the Lavon affair.

CHAPTER 3

1. The Soviet government produced a proposal of this kind in 1957. Its offer, which it put to the other three powers, was in the form of one of the points in a draft declaration on Middle East policy. The plan would see an embargo on the Soviet Union, the United States, Britain, and France sending arms to the region. But speaking to the Soviet ambassador, Yevgeny Kiselyev, in Cairo on February 10,

1957, Nasser objected to the plan. He said the embargo would entrench Israel's existing supremacy over Egypt in terms of weaponry, especially its air force; on the other hand, "Israel would in any case be able to get the arms it needs from Canada," and the countries of the Baghdad Pact would be able to circumvent the ban—Turkey was about to get armaments, not from the United States, but from NATO member Italy, and then supply them to Iraq. Kiselyev pointed out to Nasser that if Canada did supply arms to Israel—despite the draft declaration appealing to all other nations to stick to its principles—then Cairo was not short of other friends like China or Czechoslovakia that would be able to supply Egypt with arms. The Soviet Union's proposed declaration was rejected by the Western powers.

CHAPTER 4

1. In the 1960s, the Ba'ath Party was reborn as two national parties: Syrian and Iraqi. Despite sharing slogans and aims, the two organizations became hostile to each other.

2. S. K. Aburish, *Nasser: The Last Arab* (New York: Thomas Dunne Books, 2004) 195.

CHAPTER 5

1. Like many other old party members, Ulyanovsky was denounced in 1936, and spent seventeen years in exile. His was possibly the only case of someone rising, post-rehabilitation, to be deputy director of the Institute of Eastern Studies at the USSR Academy of Sciences, and later deputy head of the international department of the Central Committee of the Soviet Communist Party. Both before and after his exile, many considered him to be a man who toed the party line.

2. The Al-Wafd party went no further than calling for "neutralization of the Suez Canal," the writing-off of all state debts, and the revocation of overseas rights enjoyed by foreigners in Egypt.

3. Records of the conversation between Anastas I. Mikoyn and prime minister of the Republic of Iraq, Abdel Kerim Qassem, 14 April, 1960, Foreign Policy Archives of the Russian Federation.

CHAPTER 6

1. Southern Sudan is home to the Nile tribes, and a substantial proportion of the population is Christian. The south has for many years been fighting for its independence.

CHAPTER 7

1. House Subcommittee on the Near East of the Committee on Foreign Affairs, *The Near East Conflict: Hearings*, 91st Cong., 2nd Sess., 1970, 69, 81.

CHAPTER 8

1. Dobrynin's book, *In Confidence: Moscow's Ambassador to Six Cold War Presidents,* covered the period from 1962 to 1986. It was first published in English in 1995 by Crown Publishers, Inc., a division of Random House.

CHAPTER 9

1. House Subcommittee on the Near East of the Committee on Foreign Affairs, *The Near East Conflict: Hearings,* 91st Cong., 2nd Sess., 1970, 61.

2. Ibid., 175.

3. Harold H. Saunders, *Conversations with Harold H. Saunders. U.S. Policy for the Middle East in the 1980s* (Washington: American Enterprise Institute for Public Policy Research, 1982), 10–11.

4. A series of regular symposiums that for many years were held by public figures and business leaders from the Soviet Union and the United States. The participants would report the results of their discussions back to their respective governments.

5. See Mohamed Heikal's book *The Road to Ramadan* (New York: Quadrangle/New York Times Book Co., 1975).

CHAPTER 10

1. See Heikal, *The Road to Ramadan,* 25.

2. General Saad Shazly, *The Crossing of Suez: The October War, 1973* (London: Third World Centre for Research and Publishing, 1980) 30, 31.

3. Henry Kissinger, *Years of Upheaval* (Boston, Toronto: Little, Brown & Company, 1982) 460.

4. Dobrynin, *In Confidence,* np.

5. Kissinger, *Years of Upheaval,* 638, 645.

6. Dobrynin, *In Confidence,* np.

7. Kissinger, *Years of Upheaval,* 747.

8. Matti Golan, *The Secret Conversations of Henry Kissinger* (New York: Quadrangle/New York Times Book Co., 1976) 152.

CHAPTER 11

1. Cyrus Vance, *Hard Choices: Critical Years in American Foreign Policy* (New York: Simon and Schuster,1983) 160.

2. Moshe Dayan, *Breakthrough: A Personal Account of the Egypt-Israel Peace Negotiations* (London: Random House, 1981) 37.

3. Sidney Zion and Uri Dan, "The Untold Story of the Mideast Peace Talks," *New York Times Magazine,* January 21, 1979, np.

4. Dayan, *Breakthrough,* 77,78.

5. Zbigniew Brzezinski, *Power and Principle: Memoirs of the National Security Adviser, 1977–1981* (New York: Farrar, Straus and Giroux, 1983), 235–236.

6. Ezer Weizman, *The Battle for Peace* (Toronto: Bantam, 1981) 190.

7. I have been friends for decades with Mahmoud Abbas (Abu Mazen), who became president of the Palestinian National Authority after the death of Yasser Arafat. He completed postgraduate studies and presented his PhD thesis at Moscow's Institute of Oriental Studies at the time when I was the institute's director.

CHAPTER 12

1. The Maronites belong to the Uniate Eastern Catholic Church. They consider themselves Phoenicians who were forced by persecution to resettle in the mountainous areas of Lebanon, and were originally defined as followers of the Monothelite doctrine of one divine will embodied in Christ. Their community came to be known as Maronites after the Deir Mar Maroun Monastery, which became the center of their religion. (Located in a valley of the River Orontes, near the town of Hama, the monastery was named after the Syrian Saint Maron, who lived at the turn of the fourth and fifth centuries.) In the seventh century, the Maronite Church broke away from the Antioch Patriarchate after the Monothelite teachings were condemned as heresy by the Sixth Ecumenical Council, and so the Maronites started to select their own patriarch. With the arrival of the Crusades in the Middle East in the twelfth century, some of the Maronite leaders and their followers signed up for service with the Frankish vassals of the Crusaders. Despite its initial rejection of the newly arrived priests and their people, the Maronite community leadership agreed to enter into union with Rome and to turn its back on the Monothelite doctrine. While becoming part of the Roman Catholic Church, the Maronite Church preserved its own traditional structures and rituals.

2. The Druze are Arabs who adhere to a Muslim sect that combines the principle of a single God with the belief that God manifests Himself in successive incarnations. The name "Druze" comes from the name of Muslim preacher Muhammed Ibn Ismail ad-Darazi, who lived at the beginning of the eleventh century. The beliefs of the Druze draw on elements of both Christian and Asiatic religions—they believe, for example, that some souls pass from one body to another at the moment of death. The Druze honor both the Koran and the New Testament, but also have their own sacred books. They have historically shown an independence and a fearlessness that made them an enemy to be reckoned with for the Crusaders. They are on the whole a good-natured, welcoming people who have no trouble connecting with people of different religious beliefs. There are about half a million Druze, most of whom live in the mountains of Lebanon in the Jebel-Druze region, and Syria. A small number also live in Israel, where they are allowed to serve in the army and police.

3. O. A. Grinevsky, *Tainy Sovetskoi Diplomatii* (Moscow: Vagrius, 2000) 139, 140.

CHAPTER 14

1. Mahmoud Abbas, *Put v Oslo* (*Through Secret Channels: The Road to Oslo*) (Moscow: In-t izucheniia Izrailia i Blizhnego Vostoka, 1996), np.

2. UN Security Council resolution 242, adopted after the Six-Day War of 1967, called on Israel to withdraw its troops from the territories occupied during that war and guaranteed peaceful coexistence for all states within secure borders. But the Palestinians were unhappy about the resolution because its only reference to them was in their capacity as refugees.

3. Abbas, *Put v Oslo*, np.

4. Ibid., 34.

5. Abu Jihad (Khalil al-Wazir) was assassinated in Tunis in 1988 after a covert operation carried out by the Israelis. The planned operation was opposed by Israeli government members Shimon Peres, former air force commander Ezer Weizman, and former president, education minister Yitzhak Navon. Not without reason, they believed that killing Abu Jihad would only complicate the situation in the West Bank and the Gaza strip, which had seen the first intifada flare up. Despite their opposition, those who favored using force won the day. Traveling on different flights, three Mossad agents arrived in Tunis in the guise of Lebanese tourists and hired two minibuses. On the night of April 15/16, a speedboat dropped thirty members of the marine special forces on a beach near Tunis. The minibuses carrying the saboteurs drove to the outskirts of Sidi Bousaid and up to the house where Abu Jihad's family lived. He and two of his bodyguards came under a hail of bullets; the assassination was captured on film by a woman who was a member of the assassination squad. There was radio contact with the saboteurs from on board a Boeing 707 passenger jet flying over the Mediterranean, some thirty miles out from Tunis.

6. To hear Arafat's address, this session of the UN was moved to Geneva at the request of almost all UN member states (only the United States and Israel voted against this), after the United States refused to grant Arafat a visa to attend the General Assembly in New York.

7. Abbas, *Put v Oslo*, 262.

CHAPTER 15

1. There had been talk of opening an Israeli interests section in Moscow under the same roof as the Dutch embassy.

2. Bill Clinton, *Moya Zhizn (My Life)* (Moscow: Alpina Business Books, 2005) 609, 610.

3. Natan Sharansky had been arrested on political grounds. On his release from jail, he emigrated to Israel, where he became a prominent political figure.

CHAPTER 16

1. He is the brother of former President Abdul Salam Arif, who was killed in a helicopter crash in 1966.

CHAPTER 17

1. When I raised this matter with Iraqi foreign minister Tariq Aziz, he told me: "We suggested to Barzani that he give his word that he would not kill Abeydulla,

and then we would let him free. But Barzani refused." To which I remarked: "You should not bargain with Abeydulla's release. This is his son, after all, and Barzani is a tribal chieftain."

CHAPTER 18

1. Amos Perlmutter, Michael Handel, and Uri Bar-Joseph *Two Minutes over Baghdad* (London: Frank Cass Publishers, 2003), np.

2. David Burnham, "The Case of the Missing Uranium," *Atlantic Monthly* 243, no. 4 (April 1979), 79.

WORKS CITED

Abbas, Mahmoud, *Put v Oslo (Through Secret Channels: The Road to Oslo)* (Moscow: In-t izucheniia Izrailia i Blizhnego Vostoka, 1996).

Aburish, S. K., *Nasser: The Last Arab* (New York: Thomas Dunne Books, 2004).

Begin, Menachim, *White Nights: The Story of a Prisoner in Russia* (New York : Harper and Row, 1979).

Brzezinski, Zbigniew, *Power and Principle: Memoirs of the National Security Adviser, 1977–1981* (New York: Farrar, Straus and Giroux, 1983).

Clinton, Bill, *Moya Zhizn (My Life)* (Moscow: Alpina Business Books, 2005).

Darwish, Adel, *Unholy Babylon: The Secret History of Saddam's War* (New York: St. Martins Press, 1991).

Dayan, Moshe, *Breakthrough: A Personal Account of the Egypt-Israel Peace Negotiations* (London: Random House, 1981).

Dobrynin, Anatoly, *In Confidence: Moscow's Ambassador to Six Cold War Presidents* (New York: Crown Publishers, Inc., 1995).

Golan, Matti, *The Secret Conversations of Henry Kissinger* (New York: Quadrangle/New York Times Book Co., 1976).

Grinevsky, O. A., *Tainy Sovetskoi Diplomatii* (Moscow: Vagrius, 2000).

Heikal, Mohamed, *The Road to Ramadan* (New York: Quadrangle/New York Times Book Co., 1975).

Kissinger, Henry, *White House Years* (Boston: Little, Brown and Co., 1979).

——, *Years of Upheaval* (Boston, Toronto: Little, Brown and Co., 1982).

Nasser, Gamal Abdel, *The Philosophy of the Revolution* (Buffalo, NY: Smith, Keynes and Marshall, 1959).

Perlmutter, Amos, Michael Handel, and Uri Bar-Joseph, *Two Minutes over Baghdad* (London: Frank Cass Publishers, 2003).

Ritter, Scott, *Iraq Confidential: The Untold Story of the Intelligence Conspiracy to Undermine the UN and Overthrow Saddam Hussein* (New York: Nation Books, 2005).

Saunders, Harold H., *Conversations with Harold H. Saunders. U.S. Policy for the Middle East in the 1980s* (Washington, D.C.: American Enterprise Institute for Public Policy Research, 1982).

Shazly, General Saad, *The Crossing of Suez: The October War, 1973* (London: Third World Centre for Research and Publishing, 1980).

Vance, Cyrus, *Hard Choices: Critical Years in American Foreign Policy* (New York: Simon and Schuster, 1983).

Weizman, Ezer, *The Battle for Peace* (Toronto: Bantam, 1981).

INDEX